MICHAEL CURTIS is Professor of Political Science at Rutgers University, and has taught at several other institutions, including Yale University, Cornell University, Oberlin College and the University of Massachusetts. Dr. Curtis has written and edited over fifteen books in the fields of comparative politics, political theory, and Middle East affairs.

Other Avon Books by
Michael Curtis

THE GREAT POLITICAL THEORIES, VOL. 1

THE GREAT POLITICAL THEORIES

VOLUME 2

FROM BURKE, ROUSSEAU AND KANT TO MODERN TIMES

*Edited, with introduction
and commentary, by*
MICHAEL CURTIS
Professor of Political Science
Rutgers University

AVON BOOKS
An Imprint of HarperCollins*Publishers*

AVON BOOKS
An Imprint of HarperCollins*Publishers*
10 East 53rd Street
New York, New York 10022-5299

First Avon Books printing: April 1962

Avon Trademark Reg. U.S. Pat. Off. and in Other Countries, Marca
Registrada, Hecho en U.S.A.
HarperCollins® is a trademark of HarperCollins Publishers Inc.

Printed in the U.S.A.

30 29 28 27 26 25 24

Acknowledgments

Extracts abridged from the book *The Social Contract and Discourses* by
Jean Jacques Rousseau, translated by G. D. H. Cole. Everyman's Library.
Reprinted by permission of E. P. Dutton & Co. Inc.

Extracts taken from a *Sketch for a Historical Picture of the Progress of the
Human Mind* by Antoine Nicolas Marquis de Condorcet, translated by
June Barraclough. Copyright The Noonday Press 1955. Reprinted by per-
mission of The Noonday Press.

Extracts from the writings of Georg W. F. Hegel taken from *The
Philosophy of Right*, edited by T. M. Knox. Reprinted by permission of
The Clarendon Press, Oxford.

Extracts taken from *The Selected Writings of Saint-Simon* by Henri Comte de Saint-Simon, edited and translated by F. M. H. Markham. Reprinted by permission of Basil Blackwell & Mott, Ltd.

Extracts taken from *Force and Freedom* by Jacob Burckhardt. Copyright 1943 by Pantheon Books, Inc. Reprinted by permission of Pantheon Books, Inc.

The selection from *The Education of Henry Adams* by Henry Adams, copyright, 1918, by the Massachusetts Historical Society and copyright, 1946, by Charles F. Adams, is reprinted by permission of and arrangement with Houghton Mifflin Company, the authorized publishers.

Extracts from the writings of Theodor Herzl taken from *The Zionist Idea* by Arthur Hertzberg. Copyright © 1959 by Arthur Herzberg. Reprinted by permission of Doubleday and Company, Inc.

The selections from *Mein Kampf* by Adolph Hitler, translated by Ralph Manheim, copyright 1943 by Houghton Mifflin Company, are reprinted by permission of and arrangement with Houghton Mifflin Company, the authorized publishers.

Extracts from *Beyond Good and Evil*, copyright 1955 by Henry Regnery Company, and *Thus Spoke Zarathustra*, copyright 1957 by Henry Regnery Company, by Friedrich Nietzsche. Gateway Editions. Reprinted by permission of Henry Regnery Company, Chicago, Illinois.

Extracts from the writings of Georges Sorel taken from *Reflections on Violence*, translated by T. E. Hulme and J. Roth. Copyright, © 1950, by The Free Press. Reprinted by permission of The Free Press of Glencoe, a division of The Macmillan Company, The Crowell-Collier Publishing Company.

Extracts from *Human Nature in Politics* by Graham Wallas. Copyright, 1921, F. S. Crofts & Co., Inc. Reprinted by permission of Appleton-Century-Crofts, Inc.

Extracts reprinted from Vilfredo Pareto, *The Mind and Society*, edited by Arthur Livingston, translated by Andrew Bongiorno and Arthur Livingston. (New York: Harcourt, Brace & Co., 1935) Vol. III, secs. 2027, 2031–2035, 2041–2047, 2051–2059; Vol. IV, secs. 2174, 2176–2179, with the permission of The Pareto Fund.

Extracts reprinted by permission from *The Ruling Class* by Gaetano Mosca, translated by Hannah D. Kahn, edited and revised with introduction by Arthur Livingston. Copyright, 1939, by the McGraw-Hill Book Company, Inc.

Extracts from the writings of Robert Michels taken from *Political Parties*, translated by Eden and Cedar Paul. Copyright, 1949, by The Free Press. Reprinted by permission of The Free Press of Glencoe, a division of The Macmillan Company, The Crowell-Collier Publishing Company.

Extracts from the writings of Leon Trotsky taken from *The Revolution Betrayed*, translated by Max Eastman. Copyright 1945 by Pioneer Publishers. Reprinted by permission of Pioneer Publishers.

Extracts from writings of Pope Leo XIII taken from *Papal Thought and the State*, edited by Gerald F. Yates. Copyright, © 1958,

Appleton-Century Crofts, Inc. Reprinted by permission of Appleton-Century-Crofts, Inc.

Extracts from *Mater et Magistra* (Mother and Teacher) by Pope John XXIII. Copyright, © 1961, The New York Times Company. Reprinted by permission of The New York Times.

Extracts reprinted with the permission of Charles Scribner's Sons from *The Rights of Man and Natural Law*, pp. 2–6, 8–9, 11–13, 20–22 and 54, by Jacques Maritain. Copyright 1943, Charles Scribner's Sons.

Extracts reprinted with the permission of Charles Scribner's Sons from *Moral Man and Immoral Society*, pp. xi–xiii, xx, xxii, 8, 9, 19, 20, 40, 41, 44–45, by Reinhold Niebuhr. Copyright 1932 by Charles Scribner's Sons; renewal copyright © 1960 Reinhold Niebuhr.

Extracts reprinted with the permission of Charles Scribner's Sons from *The Children of Light and the Children of Darkness*, pp. xii, xiii, 16–22, 151, by Reinhold Niebuhr. Copyright 1944 by Charles Scribner's Sons.

Extracts from the writings of Max Weber taken from *From Max Weber: Essays in Sociology*, translated and edited by H. H. Gerth and C. Wright Mills. Copyright, © 1946, by Oxford University Press, Inc. Reprinted by permission of Oxford University Press.

Extracts from *The Foundations of Sovereignty* by Harold J. Laski. Reprinted by permission of Harcourt, Brace & World, Inc.

Extracts from *Studies in the Problems of Sovereignty* by Harold J. Laski. Copyright, © 1917, by Yale University Press. Reprinted by permission of Yale University Press.

Extracts from *Capitalism, Socialism, and Democracy* by Joseph A. Schumpeter. Copyright 1942, 1947 by Joseph A. Schumpeter. Reprinted by permission of Harper & Brothers.

Extracts from John Stuart Mill's writings taken from *On Liberty*. Copyright © 1912 by Oxford University Press.

Extracts from Alexander Herzen's writings taken from *From the Other Shore*. Copyright © 1956 by Braziller.

Extracts from Antonio Gramsci's writings taken from *Selections from the Prison Notebooks*, edited and translated by Quintin Hoare and Geoffrey Nowell Smith. Copyright © 1971 by Lawrence and Wishart.

Extracts from Sebastian de Grazia's writings taken from *The Political Community*. Copyright © 1948 by University of Chicago Press.

Extracts from John Rawls' writings taken from *A Theory of Justice*. Copyright © 1971 by Harvard University Press.

To RUTH and MARTIN

TABLE OF CONTENTS

Preface... 13

Section I: Rousseau, Condorcet and Kant............. 15
Section II: Revolution and Counterrevolution 48
Section III: Romanticism and Idealism................. 76
Section IV: Utilitarianism..................................105
Section V: Early Socialism and Positivism...........130
Section VI: Marxism..155
Section VII: Liberalism and Aristocratic
    Conservatism...181
Section VIII: Nationalism 234
Section IX: Social Darwinism, History and
    Neo-idealism...254
Section X: Irrationalism and Psychology 285
Section XI: The Elitists......................................320
Section XII: Anarchism, Democratic Socialism
    and Marxism...348
Section XIII: Theological Thought and Politics....395
Section XIV: Sociology, Psychology and
    Pluralism...422

Selected Bibliography..469
Index...483

THE GREAT POLITICAL THEORIES
2

From Burke, Rousseau and Kant
to Modern Times

PREFACE

⟫⟫-⟫⟫-⟫⟫-⟫⟫-⟫⟫-⟫⟫-⟫⟫-⟫⟫

This is the second volume of a book that addresses itself to the student interested in the study of political ideas.

I have attempted to include in this volume some representatives of most of the major schools of thought from the late eighteenth century to the present day. The period that stretches from the last years of the *Ancien Régime* in France to the desperate energy crisis confronting the world has included political upheaval and industrial change of a kind unprecedented in history, the decline in religious belief and in traditional values, the rise of powerful new ideas, the development of methods of controlling human behavior, the spread of literacy and of mass democracy, the interpenetration of scholastic disciplines and the change in the balance of power in both national and international relations. Not surprisingly, the extraordinary diversity and richness of thought in these centuries almost defy limitation and make the task self-defeating.

Keats asked, in his poem *Lamia,* "Do not all charms fly / At the mere touch of cold philosophy?" I hope the student who reads the political philosophers here will find, as I have, that he is warmed and excited rather than chilled by them.

MICHAEL CURTIS
New Brunswick,
New Jersey

SECTION I

ROUSSEAU, CONDORCET AND KANT

Rousseau

Jean-Jacques Rousseau (1712–1778) is the first great modern political philosopher. He is a watershed in political theory, not only because of his preoccupation with ideas and themes that are of contemporary significance, but also because all modern political thought, in a sense, derives from and has been influenced by him. His philosophy is highly personal, an expression of his own fierce insistence on independence and liberty, but at the same time, paradoxical and complex. His inconsistencies can be fully explained only in the light of his own psychological history and emotional experiences. Rousseau was courageous and sincere, sensual and sensitive. A native of Geneva, he admired the qualities—asceticism, puritanism, insistence on right rules—associated with that city. He dedicated his *Discourse on Inequality* to the citizens of Geneva. When, in 1762, the city disapproved of his *Émile*, he renounced his citizenship and attacked the city council in *Letters from the Mountain*. Deeply moved by injustice, and concerned about any degradation of man, he was intensely individualistic and independent. Though he lived off the patronage of wealthy women for some years, he refused to attend the court when ordered to after the successful production of his operetta. He was a man who loved mankind, but who quarreled with all his friends and was unable to get on with his fellow men. The *philosophes* attacked him during his life, as Voltaire had done in *Le Sentiment des Citoyens,* and after his death as Diderot did in his *Essai sur la Vie de Sénèque le philosophe*.

No one fully escapes the dazzling appeal of Rousseau. "He

said nothing new, but set everything on fire," said Madame de Staël. His emotional style, as well as his ideas, produced a considerable impact both on thought and on social behavior: on the behavior of Marie Antoinette playing at being a shepherdess in her Versailles garden as on the political ideas of Marat and Robespierre. His novels led fashionable women sometimes to dreams of romantic love, sometimes to the need for feeling deeply toward their children. His denunciation of luxury and of artificiality, his opposition to sophistication and his praise of simplicity, his appeal for natural behavior and education, his emphasis on natural impulses, all contributed to this impact. Different and conflicting schools of thought claim Rousseau within their inheritance. He has been seen as an individualist, federalist, democrat, advocate of world peace, romanticist, patriot, prophet of totalitarian democracy, all with some justification. He has contributed to the image of General de Gaulle in France—the contemporary embodiment of the Rousseau legislator—and to current views on politics in the newer nations of the world.

Throughout Rousseau's writings, there are remarkable insights. Some of his writing, on institutional arrangements and educational practice—the *Project of a Constitution for Corsica,* the *Considerations on the Government of Poland,* the educational advice in *Émile,* show both his wisdom and moderation. But, like Plato, he concerned himself with significant issues—the nature of morality, the definition of and the need for liberty, the belief in human integrity, the right kind of life, the correct kind of educational system both for individual and social needs, the return to a natural life, the creation of a stable consensus in society, the reconciliation of individual liberty with the need for the right rules, the manner in which man could participate politically in an effective way.

In the *Social Contract* of 1762, Rousseau made his most influential contributions to theory with his concept of the general will, the real source of legitimate authority. To this he added the need for a legislator to found the political system, a civil religion to bind the community together and an educational system which would create citizens and make them patriotic, both through teaching and games. It is these ideas that have led to the attacks on Rousseau by recent writers as the herald of totalitarian democracy, based on the premise of a sole exclusive truth in politics which necessarily leads to a system of coercion. The most disputed of Rousseau's concepts is the idea that it is just and proper to compel an individual to obey if he thinks he has an interest different from the common interest as expressed in the General Will, which is always right and tends to the public advantage. Coercion is justified by reference to the common good; an individual "may be forced to be free." But it is the Rousseau informed by an underlying spirit of equality, aware of the need for a unified, free community, for an economic system which would introduce approximate equality, for a system of morality which would allow men to possess a sense of purpose and for a political system in which all can act freely and responsibly, who has been a more significant influence on liberal thought.

Condorcet

The Marquis Antoine Nicholas de Condorcet (1743–1794) was the most eloquent of the late eighteenth-century advocates of the ideas of progress, rationalism and liberalism. His *Sketch for a Historical Picture of the Progress of the Human Mind*, written in 1793–4 while he was in hiding for fear of the guillotine, was a plea for emancipation, for social improvement and for better education based on humane, liberal principles. For Condorcet, the acquisition of knowledge had always led to the improvement of man, and history was therefore the story of the progress of the human mind. In all the nine epochs of history there had been a cumulative increase in knowledge, and the growth of truth and science over error and superstition. The ninth period—the era of Descartes and the French Revolution—was notable for political concepts such as reason, equality and rights, as well as for scientific advance. The next period would be one of limitless advance, with both man and his environment improving indefinitely on the basis of social cooperation. The tragic fate of Condorcet himself was sadly to belie his optimistic picture of the future. But his work remains as testament to the belief in universal human progress which the historian J. B. Bury called the animating and controlling idea of Western civilization.

Kant

Immanuel Kant (1724–1804), born of a poor, pious family of Scottish descent, led a quiet professorial life confined almost entirely to his native Königsberg. Though his great work was his criticism of pure reason and his ideas on epistemology, his ethical and political theory is significant. Kant was concerned with the moral law and the autonomy of will. Freedom was seen as autonomy. Laws were those conditions under which the will of one individual could be united with those of others according to a general law of freedom. In obeying the moral law, man was obeying an internal law, the result of his reason; he acted because he was aware that he ought to act. The principle of all morality was self-determination. But man should act on the basis of "the categorical imperative," on the basis of general principles which were intuitively recognized and not self-contradictory, such as the keeping of promises or telling the truth. This implied that a person "act according to that maxim which you can at the same time will to be a universal law." Every action was in accordance with Right, which enabled the freedom of each man's will to exist together with the freedom of all others according to the universal law.

From Rousseau, said Kant, he had learned the idea of the dignity of man. All persons should be treated as ends: "Treat humanity, in your own person, and in the person of everyone else, always as an end as well as a means, never merely as a means." This led Kant to stress the rights of man, equality before the law, the need for correct legal procedures and an educational process that would increase enlightenment. Internationally he pleaded, as did Rousseau, for a system of world peace and for world citizenship. Optimistically, he believed that the gurantee of perpetual peace was given by nature which showed a design to make harmony spring from human discord.

ROUSSEAU
The Social Contract

The Social Compact

"The problem is to find a form of association which will defend and protect with the whole common force the person and goods of each associate, and in which each, while uniting himself with all, may still obey himself alone, and remain as free as before." This is the fundamental problem of which the *Social Contract* provides the solution.

The clauses of this contract . . . properly understood, may be reduced to one—the total alienation of each associate, together with all his rights, to the whole community; for, in the first place, as each gives himself absolutely, the conditions are the same for all; and, this being so, no one has any interest in making them burdensome to others.

Moreover, the alienation being without reserve, the union is as perfect as it can be, and no associate has anything more to demand: for, if the individuals retained certain rights, as there would be no common superior to decide between them and the public, each, being on one point his own judge, would ask to be so on all; the state of nature would thus continue, and the association would necessarily become inoperative or tyrannical.

Finally, each man, in giving himself to all, gives himself to nobody; and as there is no associate over which he does not acquire the same right as he yields others over himself, he gains an equivalent for everything he loses, and an increase of force for the preservation of what he has.

If then we discard from the social compact what is not of its essence, we shall find that it reduces itself to the following terms:

"Each of us puts his person and all his power in common under the supreme direction of the general will, and, in our corporate capacity, we receive each member as an indivisible part of the whole."

At once, in the place of the individual personality of each contracting party, this act of association creates a moral and collective body, composed of as many members as the assembly contains voters, and receiving from this act its unity, its common identity, its life, and its will. This public person, so formed by the union of all other persons, formerly took the name of *city*, and now takes that of *Republic* or *body politic;* it is called by its members *State* when passive, *Sovereign* when active, and *Power* when compared with others like itself. Those who are associated in it take collectively the name of *people*, and severally are called *citizens*, as sharing in the sovereign power, and *subjects*, as being under the laws of the State.

. . . The act of association comprises a mutual undertaking between the public and the individuals, and each individual, in making a contract, as we may say, with himself, is bound in a double capacity; as a member of the Sovereign he is bound to the individuals, and as a member of the State to the Sovereign. But the maxim of civil right, that no one is bound by undertakings made to himself, does not apply in this case; for there is a great difference between incurring an obligation to yourself and incurring one to a whole of which you form a part.

. . . The body politic or the Sovereign, drawing its being wholly from the sanctity of the contract, can never bind itself, even to an outsider, to do anything derogatory to the original act, for instance, to alienate any part of itself, or to submit to another Sovereign. Violation of the act by which it exists would be self-annihilation; and that which is itself nothing can create nothing. . . .

Again, the Sovereign, being formed wholly of the individuals who compose it, neither has nor can have any interest contrary to theirs; and consequently the sovereign power need give no guarantee to its subjects, because it is impossible for the body to wish to hurt all its members. We shall also see later on that it cannot hurt any in particular. The Sovereign, merely by virtue of what it is, is always what it should be.

This, however, is not the case with the relation of the subjects to the Sovereign, which, despite the common interest, would have no security that they would fulfil their undertakings, unless it found means to assure itself of their fidelity.

In fact, each individual, as a man, may have a particular will contrary or dissimilar to the general will which he has as a citizen. His particular interest may speak to him quite differently from the common interest: his absolute and naturally independent existence may make him look upon what he owes to the common cause as a gratuitous contribution, the loss of which will do less harm to others than the payment of it is burdensome to himself; and, regarding the moral person which constitutes the State as a *persona ficta,* because not a man, he may wish to enjoy the rights of citizenship without being ready to fulfil the duties of a subject. The continuance of such an injustice could not but prove the undoing of the body politic.

In order then that the social compact may not be an empty formula, it tacitly includes the undertaking, which alone can give force to the rest, that whoever refuses to obey the general will shall be compelled to do so by the whole body. This means nothing less than that he will be forced to be free; for this is the condition which, by giving each citizen to his country, secures him against all personal dependence; in this lies the key to the working of the political machine; this alone legitimizes civil undertakings, which, without it, would be absurd, tyrannical, and liable to the most frightful abuses.

The passage from the state of nature to the civil state produces a very remarkable change in man, by substituting justice for instinct in his conduct, and giving his actions the morality they had formerly lacked. Then only, when the voice of duty takes the place of physical impulses and right of appetite, does man, who so far had considered only himself, find that he is forced to act on different principles, and to consult his reason before listening to his inclinations. . . .

What man loses by the social contract is his natural liberty and an unlimited right to everything he tries to get and succeeds in getting; what he gains is civil liberty and the proprietorship of all he possesses. If we are to avoid mistakes in weighing one against the other, we must clearly distinguish natural liberty, which is bounded only by the strength of the individual, from civil liberty, which is limited by the general will; and possession, which is merely the effect of force or the right of the first occupier, from property, which can be founded only on a positive title.

We might, over and above all this, add, to what man acquires in the civil state, moral liberty, which alone makes him truly master of himself; for the mere impulse of appetite is slavery, while obedience to a law which we prescribe to ourselves is liberty. . . .

(Extracts from Book I, chapters 6, 7 and 8.)

The General Will

The first and most important deduction from the principles we have so far laid down is that the general will alone can direct the State according to the object for which it was instituted, i.e. the common good: for if the clashing of particular interests made the establishment of societies necessary, the agreement of these very interests made it possible. The common element in these different interests is what forms the social tie; and, were there no point of agreement between them all, no society could exist. It is solely on the basis of this common interest that every society should be governed.

I hold then that Sovereignty, being nothing less than the exercise of the general will, can never be alienated, and that the Sovereign, who is no less than a collective being, cannot be represented except by himself: the power indeed may be transmitted, but not the will.

In reality, if it is not impossible for a particular will to agree on some point with the general will, it is at least impossible for the agreement to be lasting and constant; for the particular will tends, by its very nature, to partiality, while the general will tends to equality. It is even more impossible to have any guarantee of this agreement; for even if it should always exist, it would be the effect not of art, but of chance. The Sovereign may indeed say: "I now will actually what this man wills, or at least what he says he wills"; but it cannot say: "What he wills to-morrow, I too shall will" because it is absurd for the will to bind itself for the future, nor is it incumbent on any will to consent to anything that is not for the good of the being who wills. If then the people promises simply to obey, by that very act it dissolves itself and loses what makes it a people; the moment a master exists, there is no longer a Sovereign, and from that moment the body politic has ceased to exist.

This does not mean that the commands of the rulers cannot pass for general wills, so long as the Sovereign, being free to oppose them, offers no opposition. In such a case, universal silence is taken to imply the consent of the people.

Sovereignty, for the same reason as makes it inalienable, is indivisible; for will either is, or is not, general; it is the will either of the body of the people, or only of a part of it. In the first case, the will, when declared, is an act of Sovereignty and constitutes law: in the second, it is merely a particular will, or act of magistracy—at the most a decree.

. . . whenever Sovereignty seems to be divided, there is an illusion: the rights which are taken as being part of Sovereignty are really all subordinate, and always imply supreme wills of which they only sanction the execution. . . .

It follows from what has gone before that the general will is always right and tends to the public advantage; but it does not follow that the deliberations of the people are always equally correct. Our will is always for our own good, but we do not always see what that is; the people is never corrupted, but it is often deceived, and on such occasions only does it seem to will what is bad.

There is often a great deal of difference between the will of all and the general will; the latter considers only the common interest, while the former takes private interest into account, and is no more than a sum of particular wills: but take away from these same wills the pluses and minuses that cancel one another, and the general will remains as the sum of the differences.

If, when the people, being furnished with adequate information, held its deliberations, the citizens had no communication one with another, the grand total of the small differences would always give the general will, and the decision would always be good. But when factions arise, and partial associations are formed at the expense of the great association, the will of each of these associations becomes general in relation to its members, while it remains particular in relation to the State: it may then be said that there are no longer as many votes as there are men, but only as many as there are associations. The differences become less numerous and give a less general result. Lastly, when one of these associations is so great as to prevail over all the rest, the result is no longer a sum of small differences, but a single difference; in this case there is no longer a general will, and the opinion which prevails is purely particular.

It is therefore essential, if the general will is to be able to express itself, that there should be no partial society within the State, and that each citizen should think only his own thoughts: which was indeed the sublime and unique system established by the great Lycurgus. But if there are partial societies, it is best to have as many as possible and to prevent them from being unequal, as was done by Solon, Numa, and Servius. These precautions are the only ones that can guarantee that the general will shall be always enlightened, and that the people shall in no way deceive itself.

(Extracts from Book II, chapters 1, 2 and 3.)

The Sovereign Power

. . . Each man alienates, I admit, by the social compact, only such part of his powers, goods, and liberty as it is important for the community to control; but it must also be granted that the Sovereign is sole judge of what is important.

Every service a citizen can render the State he ought to render as soon as the Sovereign demands it; but the Sovereign, for its part, cannot impose upon its subjects any fetters that are useless to the community, nor can it even wish to do so; for no more by the law of reason than by the law of nature can anything occur without a cause.

The undertakings which bind us to the social body are obligatory only because they are mutual; and their nature is such that in fulfilling them we cannot work for others without working for ourselves. Why is it that the general will is always in the right, and that all continually will the happiness of each one, unless it is because there is not a man who does not think of "each" as meaning him, and consider himself in voting for all? This proves that equality of rights and the idea of justice which such equality creates originate in the preference each man gives to himself, and accordingly in the very nature of man. It proves that the general will, to be really such, must be general in its object as well as its essence; that it must both come from all and apply to all; and that it loses its natural rectitude when it is directed to some particular and determinate object, because in such a case we are judging of something foreign to us, and have no true principle of equity to guide us. . . .

Thus, just as a particular will cannot stand for the general will, the general will, in turn, changes its nature, when its object is particular, and, as general, cannot pronounce on a man or a fact. . . .

It should be seen from the foregoing that what makes the will general is less the number of voters than the common interest uniting them; for, under this system, each necessarily submits to the conditions he imposes on others.

. . . The social compact sets up among the citizens an equality of such a kind, that they all bind themselves to observe the same conditions and should therefore all enjoy the same rights. Thus, from the very nature of the compact, every act of Sovereignty, i.e. every authentic act of the general will, binds or favours all the citizens equally; so that the Sovereign recognizes only the body of the nation, and draws no distinctions between those of whom it is made up. What, then, strictly speaking, is an act of Sovereignty? It is not a convention between a superior and an inferior, but a convention between the body and each of its members. It is legitimate, because based on the social contract, and equitable, because common to all; useful, because it can have no other object than the general good, and stable, because guaranteed by the public force and the supreme power. . . .

We can see from this that the sovereign power, absolute, sacred, and inviolable as it is, does not and cannot exceed the limits of general conventions, and that every man may dispose at will of such goods and liberty as these conventions leave him; so that the Sovereign never has a right to lay more charges on one subject than on another, because, in that case, the question becomes particular, and ceases to be within its competency. . . .

Instead of a renunciation, they [individuals] have made an advantageous exchange: instead of an uncertain and precarious way of living they have got one that is better and more secure; instead of natural independence they have got liberty, instead of the power to harm others security for themselves, and instead of their strength, which others might overcome, a right which social union makes invincible. Their very life, which they have devoted to the State, is by it constantly protected; and when they risk it in the State's defence, what more are they doing than giving back what they have received from it? . . .

When I say that the object of laws is always general, I mean that law considers subjects *en masse* and actions in the abstract, and never a particular person or action. Thus the law may indeed decree that there shall be privileges, but cannot confer them on anybody by name. It may set up several classes of citizens, and even lay down the qualifications for membership of these classes, but it cannot nominate such and such persons as belonging to them; it may establish a monarchical government and hereditary succession, but it cannot choose a king, or nominate a royal family. In a word, no function which has a particular object belongs to the legislative power.

On this view, we at once see that it can no longer be asked whose business it is to make laws, since they are acts of the general will; nor whether the prince is above the law, since he is a member of the State; nor whether the law can be unjust, since no one is unjust to himself; nor how we can be both free and subject to the laws, since they are but registers of our wills. . . .

Of itself the people wills always the good, but of itself it by no means always sees it. The general will is always in the right, but the judgment which guides it is not always enlightened. It must be got to see objects as they are, and sometimes as they ought to appear to it; it must be shown the good road it is in search of, secured from the seductive influences of individual wills, taught to see times and spaces as a series, and made to weigh the attractions of present and sensible advantages against the danger of distant and hidden evils. The individuals see the good they reject; the public wills the good it does not see. All stand equally in need of guidance. The former must be compelled to bring their wills into conformity with their reason; the latter must be taught to know what it wills. If that is done, public enlightenment leads to the union of understanding and will in the social body: the parts are made to work exactly together, and the whole is raised to its highest power. This makes a legislator necessary.

(Extracts from Book II, chapters 4 and 6.)

The Legislator

In order to discover the rules of society best suited to nations, a superior intelligence beholding all the passions of men without experiencing any of them would be needed. This intelligence would have to be wholly unrelated to our nature, while knowing it through and through; its happiness would have to be independent of us, and yet ready to occupy itself with ours; and lastly, it would have, in the march of time, to look forward to a distant glory, and, working in one century, to be able to enjoy in the next. It would take gods to give men laws. . . .

But if great princes are rare, how much more so are great legislators! The former have only to follow the pattern which the latter have to lay down. The legislator is the engineer who invents the machine, the prince merely the mechanic who sets it up and makes it go. . . .

He who dares to undertake the making of a people's institutions ought to feel himself capable, so to speak, of changing human nature, of transforming each individual, who is by himself a complete and solitary whole, into part of a greater whole from which he in a manner receives his life and being; of altering man's constitution for the purpose of strengthening it; and of substituting a partial and moral existence for the physical and independent existence nature has conferred on us all. He must, in a word, take away from man his own resources and give him instead new ones alien to him, and incapable of being made use of without the help of other men. The more completely these natural resources are annihilated, the greater and the more lasting are those which he acquires, and the more stable and perfect the new institutions; so that if each citizen is nothing and can do nothing without the rest, and the resources acquired by the whole are equal or superior to the aggregate of the resources of all the individuals, it may be said that legislation is at the highest possible point of perfection. . . .

Wise men, if they try to speak their language to the common herd instead of its own, cannot possibly make themselves understood. There are a thousand kinds of ideas which it is impossible to translate into popular language. Conceptions that are too general and objects that are too remote are equally out of its range: each individual, having no taste for any other plan of government than that which suits his particular interest, finds it difficult to realize the advantages he might hope to draw from the continual privations good laws impose. For a young people to be able to relish sound principles of political theory and follow the fundamental rules of statecraft, the effect would have to become the cause; the social spirit, which should be created by these institutions, would have to preside over their very foundation; and men would have to be before law what they should become by means of law. The legislator, therefore, being unable to appeal to either force or reason, must have recourse to an authority of a different order, capable of constraining without violence and persuading without convincing.

This is what has, in all ages, compelled the fathers of nations to have recourse to divine intervention and credit the gods with their own wisdom, in order that the peoples, submitting to the laws of the State as to those of nature, and recognizing the same power in the formation of the city as in that of man, might obey freely, and bear with docility the yoke of the public happiness.

This sublime reason, far above the range of the common herd, is that whose decisions the legislator puts into the mouth of the immortals, in order to constrain by divine authority those whom human prudence could not move. But it is not anybody who can make the gods speak, or get himself believed when he proclaims himself their interpreter. The great soul of the legislator is the only miracle that can prove his mission. . . .

(Extract from Book II, chapter 7.)

Systems of Legislation

If we ask in what precisely consists the greatest good of all, which should be the end of every system of legislation, we shall find it reduce itself to two main objects, liberty and equality—liberty, because all particular dependence means so much force taken from the body of the State, and equality, because liberty cannot exist without it.

I have already defined civil liberty; by equality, we should understand, not that the degrees of power and riches are to be absolutely identical for everybody, but that power shall never be great enough for violence, and shall always be exercised by virtue of rank and law; and that, in respect of riches, no citizen shall ever be wealthy enough to buy another, and none poor enough to be forced to sell himself: which implies, on the part of the great, moderation in goods and position, and, on the side of the common sort, moderation in avarice and covetousness.

Such equality, we are told, is an unpractical ideal that cannot actually exist. But if its abuse is inevitable, does it follow that we should not at least make regulations concerning it? It is precisely because the force of circumstances tends continually to destroy equality that the force of legislation should always tend to its maintenance.

But these general objects of every good legislative system need modifying in every country in accordance with the local situation and the temper of the inhabitants; and these circumstances should determine, in each case, the particular system of institutions which is best, not perhaps in itself, but for the State for which it is destined. . . .

What makes the constitution of a State really solid and lasting is the due observance of what is proper, so that the natural relations are always in agreement with the laws on every point, and law only serves, so to speak, to assure, accompany and rectify them. But if the legislator mistakes his object and adopts a principle other than circumstances naturally direct; if his principle makes for servitude, while they make for liberty, or if it makes for riches, while they make for populousness, or if it makes for peace, while they make for conquest—the laws will insensibly lose their influence, the constitution will alter, and the State will have no rest from trouble till it is either destroyed or changed, and nature has resumed her invincible sway.

If the whole is to be set in order, and the commonwealth put into the best possible shape, there are various relations to be considered. First, there is the action of the complete body upon itself, the relation of the whole to the whole, of the Sovereign to the State; and this relation, as we shall see, is made up of the relations of the intermediate terms.

The laws which regulate this relation bear the name of political laws, and are also called fundamental laws, not without reason if they are wise. For, if there is, in each State, only one good system, the people that is in possession of it should hold fast to this; but if the established order is bad, why should laws that prevent men from being good be regarded as fundamental? Besides, in any case, a people is always in a position to change its laws, however good; for, if it choose to do itself harm, who can have a right to stop it?

The second relation is that of the members one to another, or to the body as a whole; and this relation should be in the first respect as unimportant, and in the second as important, as possible. Each citizen would then be perfectly independent of all the rest, and at the same time very dependent on the city; which is brought about always by the same means, as the strength of the State can alone secure the liberty of its members. From this second relation arise civil laws.

We may consider also a third kind of relation between the individual and the law, a relation of disobedience to its penalty. This gives rise to the setting up of criminal laws, which, at bottom, are less a particular class of law than the sanction behind all the rest.

Along with these three kinds of law goes a fourth, most important of all, which is not graven on tablets of marble or brass, but on the hearts of the citizens. This forms the real constitution of the State, takes on every day new powers, when other laws decay or die out, restores them or takes their place, keeps a people in the ways in which it was meant to go, and insensibly replaces authority by the force of habit. I am speaking of morality, of custom, above all of public opinion; a power unknown to political thinkers, on which none the less success in everything else depends. With this the great legislator concerns himself in secret, though he seems to confine himself to particular regulations; for these are only the arc of the arch, while manners and morals, slower to arise, form in the end its immovable keystone. . . .

It is not good for him who makes the laws to execute them, or for the body of the people to turn its attention away from a general standpoint and devote it to particular objects. Nothing is more dangerous than the influence of private interests in public affairs, and the abuse of the laws by the government is a less evil than the corruption of the legislator, which is the inevitable sequel to a particular standpoint. In such a case, the State being altered in substance, all reformation becomes impossible. A people that would never misuse governmental powers would never misuse independence; a people that would always govern well would not need to be governed.

If we take the term in the strict sense, there never has been a real democracy, and there never will be. It is against the natural order for the many to govern and the few to be governed. It is unimaginable that the people should remain continually assembled to devote their time to public affairs, and it is clear that they cannot set up commissions for that purpose without the form of administration being changed. . . .

Besides, how many conditions that are difficult to unite does such a government presuppose! First, a very small State, where the people can readily be got together and where each citizen can with ease know all the rest; secondly, great simplicity of manners, to prevent business from multiplying and raising thorny problems; next, a large measure of equality in rank and fortune, without which equality of rights and authority cannot long subsist; lastly, little or no luxury—for luxury either comes of riches or makes them necessary; it corrupts at once rich and poor, the rich by possession and the poor by covetousness; it sells the country to softness and vanity, and takes away from the State all its citizens, to make them slaves one to another, and one and all to public opinion.

This is why a famous writer has made virtue the fundamental principle of Republics; for all these conditions could not exist without virtue. . . .

It may be added that there is no government so subject to civil wars and intestine agitations as democratic or popular government, because there is none which has so strong and continual a tendency to change to another form, or which demands more vigilance and courage for its maintenance as it is. . . .

Were there a people of gods, their government would be democratic. So perfect a government is not for men.

(Extracts from Book II, chapters 11 and 12; Book III, chapter 4.)

The Preservation of the State

. . . The body politic, as well as the human body, begins to die as soon as it is born, and carries in itself the causes of its destruction. But both may have a constitution that is more or less robust and suited to preserve them a longer or a shorter time. The constitution of man is the work of nature; that of the State the work of art. It is not in men's power to prolong their own lives; but it is for them to prolong as much as possible the life of the State, by giving it the best possible constitution. The best constituted State will have an end; but it will end later than any other, unless some unforeseen accident brings about its untimely destruction.

The life-principle of the body politic lies in the sovereign authority. The legislative power is the heart of the State; the executive power is its brain, which causes the movement of all the parts. The brain may become paralysed and the individual still live. A man may remain an imbecile and live; but as soon as the heart ceases to perform its functions, the animal is dead.

The State subsists by means not of the laws, but of the legislative power. Yesterday's law is not binding to-day; but silence is taken for tacit consent, and the Sovereign is held to confirm incessantly the laws it does not abrogate as it might. All that it has once declared itself to will it wills always, unless it revokes its declaration.

Why then is so much respect paid to old laws? For this very reason. We must believe that nothing but the excellence of old acts of will can have preserved them so long: if the Sovereign had not recognized them as throughout salutary, it would have revoked them a thousand times. This is why, so far from growing weak, the laws continually gain new strength in any well constituted State; the precedent of antiquity makes them daily more venerable: while wherever the laws grow weak as they become old, this proves that there is no longer a legislative power and that the State is dead.

The Sovereign having no force other than the legislative power, acts only by means of the laws; and the laws being solely the authentic acts of the general will, the Sovereign cannot act save when the people is assembled. The people in assembly, I shall be told, is a mere chimera. It is so to-day, but two thousand years ago it was not so. Has man's nature changed?

The bounds of possibility, in moral matters, are less narrow than we imagine: it is our weaknesses, our vices, and our prejudices that confine them. Base souls have no belief in great men; vile slaves smile in mockery at the name of liberty. . . .

It is not enough for the assembled people to have once fixed the constitution of the State by giving its sanction to a body of law; it is not enough for it to have set up a perpetual government, or provided once for all for the election of magistrates. Besides the extraordinary assemblies unforeseen circumstances may demand, there must be fixed periodical assemblies which cannot be abrogated or prorogued so that on the proper day the people is legitimately called together by law, without need of any formal summoning.

But, apart from these assemblies authorized by their date alone, every assembly of the people not summoned by the magistrates appointed for that purpose, and in accordance with the prescribed forms, should be regarded as unlawful, and all its acts as null and void, because the command to assemble should itself proceed from the law. . . .

As soon as public service ceases to be the chief business of the citizens and they would rather serve with their money than with their persons, the State is not far from its fall. When it is necessary to march out to war, they pay troops and stay at home: when it is necessary to meet in council, they name deputies and stay at home. By reason of idleness and money, they end by having soldiers to enslave their country and representatives to sell it.

It is through the hustle of commerce and the arts, through the greedy self-interest of profit, and through softness and love of amenities that personal services are replaced by money payments. Men surrender a part of their profits in order to have time to increase them at leisure. Make gifts of money, and you will not be long without chains. The word "finance" is a slavish word, unknown in the city-state. In a country that is truly free, the citizens do everything with their own arms and nothing by means of money; so far from paying to be exempted from their duties, they would even pay for the privilege of fulfilling them themselves. I am far from taking the common view: I hold enforced labour to be less opposed to liberty than taxes.

The better the constitution of a State is, the more do public affairs encroach on private in the minds of the citizens. Private affairs are even of much less importance, because the aggregate of the common happiness furnishes a greater proportion of that of each individual, so that there is less for him to seek in particular cares. In a well-ordered city every man flies to the assemblies: under a bad government no one cares to stir a step to get to them, because no one is interested in what happens there because it is foreseen that the general will will not prevail, and lastly because domestic cares are all-absorbing. Good laws lead to the making of better ones; bad ones bring about worse. As soon as any man says of the affairs of the State *What does it matter to me?* the State may be given up for lost.

The lukewarmness of patriotism, the activity of private interests, the vastness of States, conquest, and the abuse of government suggested the method of having deputies or representatives of the people in the national assemblies. These are what, in some countries, men have presumed to call the Third Estate. Thus the individual interest of two orders is put first and second; the public interest occupies only the third place.

Sovereignty, for the same reason as makes it inalienable, cannot be represented; it lies essentially in the general will, and will does not admit of representation: it is either the same, or other; there is no intermediate possibility. The deputies of the people, therefore, are not and cannot be its representatives: they are merely its stewards, and can carry through no definitive acts. Every law the people has not ratified in person is null and void—is, in fact, not a law. The people of England regards itself as free: but it is grossly mistaken: it is free only during the election of members of parliament. As soon as they are elected, slavery overtakes it, and it is nothing. The use it makes of the short moments of liberty it enjoys shows indeed that it deserves to lose them.

The idea of representation is modern; it comes to us from feudal government, from that iniquitous and absurd system which degrades humanity and dishonours the name of man. . . .

There is but one law which, from its nature, needs unani-

mous consent. This is the social compact; for civil association
is the most voluntary of all acts. Every man being born free
and his own master, no one, under any pretext whatsoever,
can make any man subject without his consent. To decide that
the son of a slave is born a slave is to decide that he is not
born a man.

If then there are opponents when the social compact is
made, their opposition does not invalidate the contract, but
merely prevents them from being included in it. They are
foreigners among citizens. When the State is instituted, residence constitutes consent; to dwell within its territory is to
submit to the Sovereign.

Apart from this primitive contract, the vote of the majority
always binds all the rest. This follows from the contract itself.
But it is asked how a man can be both free and forced to
conform to wills that are not his own. How are the opponents
at once free and subject to laws they have not agreed to?

I retort that the question is wrongly put. The citizen gives
his consent to all the laws, including those which are passed in
spite of his opposition, and even those which punish him
when he dares to break any of them. The constant will of all
the members of the State is the general will; by virtue of it
they are citizens and free. When in the popular assembly a
law is proposed, what the people is asked is not exactly
whether it approves or rejects the proposal, but whether it is
in conformity with the general will, which is their will. Each
man, in giving his vote, states his opinion on that point; and
the general will is found by counting votes. When therefore
the opinion that is contrary to my own prevails, this proves
neither more nor less than that I was mistaken, and that what
I thought to be the general will was not so. If my particular
opinion had carried the day I should have achieved the opposite of what was my will; and it is in that case that I should
not have been free.

(Extracts from Book III, chapters 11, 12, 13 and 15; Book
IV, chapter 2.)

The Civil Religion

. . . Now, it matters very much to the community that each
citizen should have a religion. That will make him love his
duty; but the dogmas of that religion concern the State and its
members only so far as they have reference to morality and to
the duties which he who professes them is bound to do to
others. Each man may have, over and above, what opinions
he pleases, without its being the Sovereign's business to take

cognizance of them; for, as the Sovereign has no authority in the other world, whatever the lot of its subjects may be in the life to come, that is not its business, provided they are good citizens in this life.

There is therefore a purely civil profession of faith of which the Sovereign should fix the articles, not exactly as religious dogmas, but as social sentiments without which a man cannot be a good citizen or a faithful subject. While it can compel no one to believe them, it can banish from the State whoever does not believe them—it can banish him, not for impiety, but as an anti-social being, incapable of truly loving the laws and justice, and of sacrificing, at need, his life to his duty. If any one, after publicly recognizing these dogmas, behaves as if he does not believe them, let him be punished by death: he has committed the worst of all crimes, that of lying before the law.

The dogmas of civil religion ought to be few, simple, and exactly worded, without explanation or commentary. The existence of a mighty, intelligent, and beneficent Divinity, possessed of foresight and providence, the life to come, the happiness of the just, the punishment of the wicked, the sanctity of the social contract and the laws: these are its positive dogmas. Its negative dogmas I confine to one, intolerance, which is a part of the cults we have rejected.

Those who distinguish civil from theological intolerance are, to my mind, mistaken. The two forms are inseparable. It is impossible to live at peace with those we regard as damned; to love them would be to hate God who punishes them: we positively must either reclaim or torment them. Wherever theological intolerance is admitted, it must inevitably have some civil effect; and as soon as it has such an effect, the Sovereign is no longer Sovereign even in the temporal sphere: thenceforth priests are the real masters, and kings only their ministers.

Now that there is and can be no longer an exclusive national religion, tolerance should be given to all religions that tolerate others, so long as their dogmas contain nothing contrary to the duties of citizenship. But whoever dares to say "Outside the Church is no salvation," ought to be driven from the State, unless the State is the Church, and the prince the pontiff. Such a dogma is good only in a theocratic government; in any other, it is fatal. The reason for which Henry IV is said to have embraced the Roman religion ought to make every honest man leave it, and still more any prince who knows how to reason. . . .

(Extract from Book IV, chapter 8.)

CONDORCET

Sketch for a Historical Picture of the Progress of the Human Mind

The Future Progress of the Human Mind

If man can, with almost complete assurance, predict phenomena when he knows their laws, and if, even when he does not, he can still, with great expectation of success, forecast the future on the basis of his experience of the past, why, then, should it be regarded as a fantastic undertaking to sketch, with some pretence to truth, the future destiny of man on the basis of his history? The sole foundation for belief in the natural sciences is this idea, that the general laws directing the phenomena of the universe, known or unknown, are necessary and constant. Why should this principle be any less true for the development of the intellectual and moral faculties of man than for the other operations of nature? Since beliefs founded on past experience of like conditions provide the only rule of conduct for the wisest of men, why should the philosopher be forbidden to base his conjectures on these same foundations, so long as he does not attribute to them a certainty superior to that warranted by the number, the constancy, the accuracy of his observations?

Our hopes for the future condition of the human race can be subsumed under three important heads: the abolition of inequality between nations, the progress of equality within each nation, and the true perfection of mankind. Will all nations one day attain that state of civilization which the most enlightened, the freest and the least burdened by prejudices, such as the French and the Anglo-Americans, have attained already? Will the vast gulf that separates these peoples from the slavery of nations under the rule of monarchs, from the barbarism of African tribes, from the ignorance of savages, little by little disappear?

Is there on the face of the earth a nation whose inhabitants have been debarred by nature herself from the enjoyment of freedom and the exercise of reason?

Are those differences which have hitherto been seen in every civilized country in respect of the enlightenment, the resources, and the wealth enjoyed by the different classes into which it is divided, is that inequality between men which was aggravated or perhaps produced by the earliest progress of society, are these part of civilization itself, or are they due to the present imperfections of the social art? Will they necessarily decrease and ultimately make way for a real equality, the final end of the social art, in which even the effects of the natural differences between men will be mitigated and the only kind of inequality to persist will be that which is in the interests of all and which favours the progress of civilization, of education, and of industry, without entailing either poverty, humiliation, or dependence? In other words, will men approach a condition in which everyone will have the knowledge necessary to conduct himself in the ordinary affairs of life, according to the light of his own reason, to preserve his mind free from prejudice, to understand his rights and to exercise them in accordance with his conscience and his creed; in which everyone will become able, through the development of his faculties, to find the means of providing for his needs; and in which at last misery and folly will be the exception, and no longer the habitual lot of a section of society?

Is the human race to better itself, either by discoveries in the sciences and the arts, and so in the means to individual welfare and general prosperity; or by progress in the principles of conduct or practical morality; or by a true perfection of the intellectual, moral, or physical faculties of man, an improvement which may result from a perfection either of the instruments used to heighten the intensity of these faculties and to direct their use or of the natural constitution of man?

In answering these three questions we shall find in the experience of the past, in the observation of the progress that the sciences and civilization have already made, in the analysis of the progress of the human mind and of the development of its faculties, the strongest reasons for believing that nature has set no limit to the realization of our hopes. . . .

The time will therefore come when the sun will shine only on free men who know no other master but their reason; when tyrants and slaves, priests and their stupid or hypocritical instruments will exist only in works of history and on the stage; and when we shall think of them only to pity their victims and their dupes; to maintain ourselves in a state of vigilance by thinking on their excesses; and to learn how to recognize and so to destroy, by force of reason, the first seeds of tyranny and superstition, should they ever dare to reappear amongst us.

In looking at the history of societies we shall have had occasion to observe that there is often a great difference between the rights that the law allows its citizens and the rights that they actually enjoy, and, again, between the equality established by political codes and that which in fact exists amongst individuals: and we shall have noticed that these differences were one of the principal causes of the destruction of freedom in the Ancient republics, of the storms that troubled them, and of the weakness that delivered them over to foreign tyrants.

These differences have three main causes: inequality in wealth; inequality in status between the man whose means of subsistence are hereditary and the man whose means are dependent on the length of his life, or, rather, on that part of his life in which he is capable of work; and, finally, inequality in education.

We therefore need to show that these three sorts of real inequality must constantly diminish without however disappearing altogether: for they are the result of natural and necessary causes which it would be foolish and dangerous to wish to eradicate; and one could not even attempt to bring about the entire disappearance of their effects without introducing even more fecund sources of inequality, without striking more direct and more fatal blows at the rights of man. . . .

With greater equality of education, there will be greater equality in industry and so in wealth; equality in wealth necessarily leads to equality in education: and equality between the nations and equality within a single nation are mutually dependent.

So we might say that a well directed system of education rectifies natural inequality in ability instead of strengthening it, just as good laws remedy natural inequality in the means of subsistence, and just as in societies where laws have brought about this same equality, liberty, though subject to a regular constitution, will be more widespread, more complete than in the total independence of savage life. Then the social art will have fulfilled its aim, that of assuring and extending to all men enjoyment of the common rights to which they are called by nature.

The real advantages that should result from this progress, of which we can entertain a hope that is almost a certainty, can have no other term than that of the absolute perfection of the human race; since, as the various kinds of equality come to work in its favour by producing ampler sources of supply, more extensive education, more complete liberty, so equality will be more real and will embrace everything which is really of importance for the happiness of human beings. . . .

We shall show how favourable to our hopes would be a more universal system of education by giving a greater number of people the elementary knowledge which could awaken their interest in a particular branch of study, and by providing

conditions favourable to their progress in it; and how these
hopes would be further raised, if more men possessed the
means to devote themselves to these studies, for at present
even in the most enlightened countries scarcely one in fifty of
the people who have natural talents, receives the necessary
education to develop them; and how, if this were done, there
would be a proportionate increase in the number of men
destined by their discoveries to extend the boundaries of
science.

We shall show how this equality in education and the
equality which will come about between the different nations
would accelerate the advance of these sciences whose progress
depends on repeated observations over a large area; what benefits would thereby accrue to mineralogy, botany, zoology and
meteorology; and what a vast disproportion holds in all these
sciences between the poverty of existing methods which
have nevertheless led to useful and important new truths, and
the wealth of these methods which man would then be able to
employ.

We shall show how even the sciences in which discovery is
the fruit of solitary meditation would benefit from being studied by a greater number of people, in the matter of those
improvements in detail which do not demand the intellectual
energy of an inventor but suggest themselves to mere reflection....

Just as the mathematical and physical sciences tend to improve the arts that we use to satisfy our simplest needs, is it
not also part of the necessary order of nature that the moral
and political sciences should exercise a similar influence upon
the motives that direct our feelings and our actions?

What are we to expect from the perfection of laws and
public institutions, consequent upon the progress of those sciences, but the reconciliation, the identification of the interests
of each with the interests of all? Has the social art any other
aim save that of destroying their apparent opposition? Will
not a country's constitution and laws accord best with the
rights of reason and nature when the path of virtue is no
longer arduous and when the temptations that lead men from
it are few and feeble?

... the moral goodness of man, the necessary consequence
of his constitution, is capable of indefinite perfection like all
his other faculties, and nature has linked together in an un-
breakable chain truth, happiness and virtue.

Among the causes of the progress of the human mind that
are of the utmost importance to the general happiness, we
must number the complete annihilation of the prejudices that

have brought about an inequality of rights between the sexes, an inequality fatal even to the party in whose favour it works. It is vain for us to look for a justification of this principle in any differences of physical organization, intellect or moral sensibility between men and women. This inequality has its origin solely in an abuse of strength, and all the later sophistical attempts that have been made to excuse it are vain. . . .

Once people are enlightened they will know that they have the right to dispose of their own life and wealth as they choose; they will gradually learn to regard war as the most dreadful of scourges, the most terrible of crimes. The first wars to disappear will be those into which usurpers have forced their subjects in defence of their pretended hereditary rights. . . .

Organizations more intelligently conceived than those projects of eternal peace which have filled the leisure and consoled the hearts of certain philosophers, will hasten the progress of the brotherhood of nations, and wars between countries will rank with assassination as freakish atrocities. . . .

No-one can doubt that, as preventative medicine improves and food and housing become healthier, as a way of life is established that develops our physical powers by exercise without ruining them by excess, as the two most virulent causes of deterioration, misery and excessive wealth, are eliminated, the average length of human life will be increased and a better health and a stronger physical constitution will be ensured. The improvement of medical practice, which will become more efficacious with the progress of reason and of the social order, will mean the end of infectious and hereditary diseases and illnesses brought on by climate, food, or working conditions. It is reasonable to hope that all other diseases may likewise disappear as their distant causes are discovered. Would it be absurd then to suppose that this perfection of the human species might be capable of indefinite progress; that the day will come when death will be due only to extraordinary accidents or to the decay of the vital forces, and that ultimately the average span between birth and decay will have no assignable value? Certainly man will not become immortal, but will not the interval between the first breath that he draws and the time when in the natural course of events, without disease or accident, he expires, increase indefinitely? . . .

How consoling for the philosopher who laments the errors, the crimes, the injustices which still pollute the earth and of which he is often the victim is this view of the human race, emancipated from its shackles, released from the empire of fate and from that of the enemies of its progress, advancing with a firm and sure step along the path of truth, virtue and happiness! It is the contemplation of this prospect that rewards him for all his efforts to assist the progress of reason and the defence of liberty. He dares to regard these strivings as part of the eternal chain of human destiny; and in this persuasion he is filled with the true delight of virtue and the pleasure of having done some lasting good which fate can never destroy by a sinister stroke of revenge, by calling back the reign of slavery and prejudice. Such contemplation is for him an asylum, in which the memory of his persecutors cannot pursue him; there he lives in thought with man restored to his natural rights and dignity, forgets man tormented and corrupted by greed, fear or envy; there he lives with his peers in an Elysium created by reason and graced by the purest pleasures known to the love of mankind.

(Extract from *The Tenth Stage*.)

KANT

Fundamental Principles of the Metaphysic of Morals

Will and Law

The first proposition is: That an action, to have moral worth, must be done from duty.

The second proposition is: That an action done from duty derives its moral worth, *not from the purpose* which is to be attained by it, but from the maxim by which it is determined, and therefore does not depend on the realization of the object of the action, but merely on the *principle of volition* by which the action has taken place, without regard to any object of desire. It is clear from what precedes that the purposes which we may have in view in our actions, or their effects regarded as ends and springs of the will, cannot give to actions any unconditional or moral worth. In what, then, can their worth lie, if it is not to consist in the will and in reference to its expected effect? It cannot lie anywhere but in the *principle of the will* without regard to the ends which can be attained by the action. For the will stands between its *à priori* principle, which is formal, and its *à posteriori* spring, which is material, as between two roads, and as it must be determined by something, it follows that it must be determined by the formal principle of volition when an action is done from duty, in which case every material principle has been withdrawn from it.

The third proposition, which is a consequence of the two preceding, I would express thus: *Duty is the necessity of acting from respect for the law.* I may have *inclination* for an object as the effect of my proposed action, but I cannot have *respect* for it, just for this reason, that it is an effect and not an energy of will. . . . It is only what is connected with my will as a principle, by no means as an effect—what does not subserve my inclination, but overpowers it, or at least in case of choice excludes it from its calculation—in other words, simply the law of itself, which can be an object of respect, and hence a command. Now an action done from duty must wholly exclude the influence of inclination, and with it every object of the will, so that nothing remains which can determine the will except objectively the *law*, and subjectively *pure respect* for this practical law, and consequently the maxim that I should follow this law even to the thwarting of all my inclinations.

Thus the moral worth of an action does not lie in the effect expected from it, nor in any principle of action which requires to borrow its motive from this expected effect. For all these effects—agreeableness of one's condition, and even the promotion of the happiness of others—could have been also brought about by other causes, so that for this there would have been no need of the will of a rational being; whereas it is in this alone that the supreme and unconditional good can be found. The pre-eminent good which we call moral can therefore consist in nothing else than *the conception of law* in itself, *which certainly is only possible in a rational being,* in so far as this conception, and not the expected effect, determines the will. . . .

But what sort of law can that be, the conception of which must determine the will, even without paying any regard to the effect expected from it, in order that this will may be called good absolutely and without qualification? As I have deprived the will of every impulse which could arise to it from obedience to any law, there remains nothing but the universal conformity of its actions to law in general, which alone is to serve the will as a principle, *i. e.* I am never to act otherwise than so *that I could also will that my maxim should become a universal law.* Here now, it is the simple conformity to law in general, without assuming any particular law applicable to certain actions, that serves the will as its principle, and must so serve it, if duty is not to be a vain delusion and a chimerical notion.

. . . it is clear that all moral conceptions have their seat and origin completely *à priori* in the reason, and that, moreover, in the commonest reason just as truly as in that which is in the highest degree speculative; that they cannot be obtained by abstraction from any empirical, and therefore merely contingent knowledge; that it is just this purity of their origin that makes them worthy to serve as our supreme practical principle, and that just in proportion as we add anything empirical, we detract from their genuine influence, and from the absolute value of actions; that it is not only of the greatest necessity, in a purely speculative point of view, but is also of the greatest practical importance to derive these notions and laws from pure reason, to present them pure and unmixed, and even to determine the compass of this practical or pure rational knowledge, *i. e.* to determine the whole faculty of pure practical reason; and, in doing so, we must not make its principles dependent on the particular nature of human reason, though in speculative philosophy this may be permitted, or may even at times be necessary; but since moral laws ought to hold good for every rational creature, we must derive them from the general concept of a rational being. . . .

The Categorical Imperative

. . . Everything in nature works according to laws. Rational beings alone have the faculty of acting according *to the conception* of laws, that is according to principles, *i. e.* have a *will*. Since the deduction of actions from principles requires *reason*, the will is nothing but practical reasons. If reason infallibly determines the will, then the actions of such a being which are recognised as objectively necessary are subjectively necessary also, *i. e.* the will is a faculty to choose *that only* which reason independent on inclination recognises as practically necessary, *i. e.* as good. But if reason of itself does not sufficiently determine the will, if the latter is subject also to subjective conditions (particular impulses) which do not always coincide with the objective conditions; in a word, if the will does not *in itself* completely accord with reason (which is actually the case with men), then the actions which objectively are recognised as necessary are subjectively contingent, and the determination of such a will according to objective laws is *obligation*, that is to say, the relation of the objective laws to a will that is not thoroughly good is conceived as the determination of the will of a rational being by principles of reason, but which the will from its nature does not of necessity follow.

The conception of an objective principle, in so far as it is obligatory for a will, is called a command (of reason), and the formula of the command is called an Imperative.

All imperatives are expressed by the word *ought* [or *shall*], and thereby indicate the relation of an objective law of reason to a will, which from its subjective constitution is not necessarily determined by it (an obligation). They say that something would be good to do or to forbear, but they say it to a will which does not always do a thing because it is conceived to be good to do it. That is practically *good*, however, which determines the will by means of the conceptions of reason, and consequently not from subjective causes, but objectively, that is on principles which are valid for every rational being as such. It is distinguished from the *pleasant*, as that which influences the will only by means of sensation from merely subjective causes, valid only for the sense of this or that one, and not as a principle of reason, which holds for every one.

A perfectly good will would therefore be equally subject to objective laws (viz. laws of good), but could not be conceived as *obliged* thereby to act lawfully, because of itself from its subjective constitution it can only be determined by the conception of good. Therefore no imperatives hold for the Divine will, or in general for a *holy* will; *ought* is here out of place, because the volition is already of itself necessarily in unison with the law. Therefore imperatives are only formulæ to express the relation of objective laws of all volition to the subjective imperfection of the will of this or that rational being, *e.g.* the human will.

Now all *imperatives* command either *hypothetically* or *categorically*. The former represent the practical necessity of a possible action as means to something else that is willed (or at least which one might possibly will). The categorical imperative would be that which represented an action as necessary of itself without reference to another end, *i.e.* as objectively necessary.

Since every practical law represents a possible action as good, and on this account, for a subject who is practically determinable by reason, necessary, all imperatives are formulæ determining an action which is necessary according to the principle of a will good in some respects. If now the action is good only as a means *to something else*, then the imperative is *hypothetical;* if it is conceived as good *in itself* and consequently as being necessarily the principle of a will which of itself conforms to reason, then it is *categorical*.

Thus the imperative declares what action possible by me would be good, and presents the practical rule in relation to a will which does not forthwith perform an action simply because it is good, whether because the subject does not always know that it is good, or because, even if it know this, yet its maxims might be opposed to the objective principles of practical reason.

Accordingly the hypothetical imperative only says that the action is good for some purpose, *possible* or *actual*. In the first case it is a Problematical, in the second an Assertorial practical principle. The categorical imperative which declares an action to be objectively necessary in itself without reference to any purpose, *i.e.* without any other end, is valid as an *Apodictic* (practical) principle.

Whatever is possible only by the power of some rational being may also be conceived as a possible purpose of some will; and therefore the principles of action as regards the means necessary to attain some possible purpose are in fact infinitely numerous. All sciences have a practical part, consisting of problems expressing that some end is possible for us, and of imperatives directing how it may be attained. These may, therefore, be called in general imperatives of Skill. Here there is no question whether the end is rational and good, but only what one must do in order to attain it. The precepts for the physician to make his patient thoroughly healthy, and for a poisoner to ensure certain death, are of equal value in this respect, that each serves to effect its purpose perfectly. Since in early youth it cannot be known what ends are likely to occur to us in the course of life, parents seek to have their children taught a *great many things*, and provide for their *skill* in the use of means for all sorts of arbitrary ends, of none of which can they determine whether it may not perhaps hereafter be an object to their pupil, but which it is at all events *possible* that he might aim at; and this anxiety is so great that they commonly neglect to form and correct their judgment on the value of the things which may be chosen as ends.

There is *one* end, however, which may be assumed to be actually such to all rational beings (so far as imperatives apply to them, viz. as dependent beings), and therefore, one purpose which they not merely *may* have, but which we may with certainty assume that they all actually *have* by a natural necessity, and this is *happiness*. The hypothetical imperative which expresses the practical necessity of an action as means to the advancement of happiness is Assertorial. We are not to present it as necessary for an uncertain and merely possible purpose, but for a purpose which we may presuppose with certainty and *à priori* in every man, because it belongs to his being. Now skill in the choice of means to his own greatest well-being may be called *prudence,* in the narrowest sense. And thus the imperative which refers to the choice of means to one's own happiness, *i.e.* the precept of prudence, is still always *hypothetical;* the action is not commanded absolutely, but only as means to another purpose.

Finally, there is an imperative which commands a certain conduct immediately, without having as its condition any other purpose to be attained by it. This imperative is Categorical. It concerns not the matter of the action, or its intended result, but its form and the principle of which it is itself a result; and what is essentially good in it consists in the mental disposition, let the consequence be what it may. This imperative may be called that of Morality. . . .

When I conceive a hypothetical imperative in general I do not know beforehand what it will contain until I am given the condition. But when I conceive a categorical imperative I know at once what it contains. For as the imperative contains besides the law only the necessity that the maxims shall conform to this law, while the law contains no conditions restricting it, there remains nothing but the general statement that the maxim of the action should conform to a universal law, and it is this conformity alone that the imperative properly represents as necessary.

There is therefore but one categorical imperative, namely this: *Act only on that maxim whereby thou canst at the same time will that it should become a universal law.*

Now if all imperatives of duty can be deduced from this one imperative as from their principle, then, although it should remain undecided whether what is called duty is not merely a vain notion, yet at least we shall be able to show what we understand by it and what this notion means.

Since the universality of the law according to which effects are produced constitutes what is properly called *nature* in the most general sense (as to form), that is the existence of things so far as it is determined by general laws, the imperative of duty may be expressed thus: *Act as if the maxim of thy action were to become by thy will a Universal Law of Nature.* . . .

Man as an End

. . . Now I say: man and generally any rational being *exists* as an end in himself, *not merely as a means* to be arbitrarily used by this or that will, but in all his actions, whether they concern himself or other rational beings, must be always regarded at the same time as an end. All objects of the inclinations have only a conditional worth, for if the inclinations and the wants founded on them did not exist, then their object would be without value. But the inclinations themselves being sources of want, are so far from having an absolute worth for which they should be desired, that on the contrary it must be the universal wish of every rational being to be wholly free from them. Thus the worth of any object which is *to be acquired* by our action is always conditional. Beings whose existence depends not on our will but on nature's, have nevertheless, if they are irrational beings, only a relative value as means, and are therefore called *things;* rational beings, on the contrary, are called *persons,* because their very nature points them out as ends in themselves, that is as something which must not be used merely as means, and so far therefore restricts freedom of action (and is an object of respect). These, therefore, are not merely subjective ends whose existence has a worth *for us* as an effect of our action, but *objective ends,* that is things whose existence is an end in itself: an end moreover for which no other can be substituted, which they should subserve *merely* as means, for otherwise nothing whatever would possess *absolute worth;* but if all worth were conditioned and therefore contingent, then there would be no supreme practical principle of reason whatever.

If then there is a supreme practical principle or, in respect of the human will, a categorical imperative, it must be one which, being drawn from the conception of that which is necessarily an end for every one because it is *an end in itself,* constitutes an *objective* principle of will, and can therefore serve as a universal practical law. The foundation of this principle is: *rational nature exists as an end in itself.* Man necessarily conceives his own existence as being so: so far then this is a *subjective* principle of human actions. But every other rational being regards its existence similarly, just on the same rational principle that holds for me: so that it is at the same time an objective principle, from which as a supreme practical law all laws of the will must be capable of being deduced. Accordingly the practical imperative will be as follows: *So act as to treat humanity, whether in thine own person or in that of any other, in every case as an end withal, never as means only.* . . .

This principle, that humanity and generally every rational nature is *an end in itself,* which is the supreme limiting condition of every man's freedom of action, is not borrowed from experience, firstly because it is universal, applying as it does to all rational beings whatever, and experience is not capable of determining anything about them: secondly, because it does not present humanity as an end to men subjectively . . . but as an objective end which must as a law constitute the supreme limiting condition of all our subjective ends . . . it must spring from pure reason. In fact the objective principle of all practical legislation lies in the *rule* and its form of universality which makes it capable of being a law. . . . But the subjective principle is in the end; . . . the subject of all ends is each rational being in as much as it is an end in itself. The third principle of the will, which is the ultimate condition of its harmony with the universal practical reason is the idea of the will, of every rational being as a universally legislative will. . . . The will is not subject simply to the law, but so subject that it must be regarded as itself giving the law, and, on this ground only, subject to the law.

(Extract from the Second Section.)

SECTION II

REVOLUTION AND COUNTERREVOLUTION

For many, the French Revolution was an act of liberation, transforming human society; for Kant, such a phenomenon in history could never be forgotten. But for others it was the beginning of political change based on popular consent, which would logically end in tyranny. For conservatives, the change must be halted or limited; for reactionaries, the "candle snuffers," as Stendhal called them, the *Ancien Régime* must be re-established. The reactionary, unlike the conservative, wants to get rid of the baby as well as the bath water.

Burke

Edmund Burke (1729–1797) remains the articulate spokesman and intellectual apogee of conservatism, the oracle for all right-wing politicians. His political writings are largely polemical, possessing a force and urgency that has attracted even political opponents like Hazlitt in one age and Laski in another. If he attacked Rousseau for his lack of moderation and balance, Burke's own writings are no model of these qualities. For him, the Encyclopaedists were men of "cold hearts and muddy understandings," who used "vulgar, base, and profane language"; the French revolutionaries, by their "cant and gibberish of hypocrisy," produced a "black and savage atrocity of mind" in the French people.

The speeches Burke made during his thirty-year membership in the House of Commons are among the imperishable orations of that body, though, ironically enough, he was known as the "Dinner Bell." He participated in all the great political battles, the struggle for more favorable treatment of the American colonies, the impeachment of Warren Hastings for his behavior in India, the opposition to electoral reform, the defense and justification of political parties, the right of M.P.'s to exercise independent judgment uncontrolled by their constituents, and, above all, the vitriolic attack on the French Revolution.

In the *Reflections on the Revolution in France* of 1790, the first of his three works on the subject, all Burke's major philosophic ideas appear. He attacked theories advocating the rights of man, absolute liberty, equality, democracy, abstract political principles or change by revolution. He emphasized the complexity of both man and nature, the wisdom embodied in institutions—the state, the church and private property—and in traditions. Prescription, presumption and prejudice were a more valuable basis than reason for the operation of government; society was not a conscious creation of man, for men were born subject to established society. To talk of the isolated individual was meaningless, because the individual was always a being molded by those around him and those who had gone before him. Rationalism was of limited value in understanding political phenomena since it neglected passion, prejudice and habit. Reason could never penetrate the essential mystery of the universe.

Burke was the philosophic conservative, opposed equally to unchanging reaction and to revolutionary change. Revolution was undesirable because it would sweep away the sound principles of political action and discard the guidance of nature. Political institutions were part of an order in which things were kept fast in their place. If change were necessary, "I would make the reparation as nearly as possible in the style of the building." The task of the statesman was to take account of all the relevant circumstances, to act on the basis of prudence (the cardinal virtue), to preserve and to improve. The French Revolution represented a complete break with the past, a complete abandonment of tradition, while the English, American and Indian rebellions had all attempted to recover traditions and privileges of which the citizens had been deprived. The British constitution, monarchical, aristocratic, with a State Church, unwritten and based "on a nice equipoise," was the epitome of political skill. English liberty belonged to the people of England without any reference whatever to any other more general or prior right.

Paine

Burke, the intellectual leader of the opposition to the French Revolution, accurately predicted the terrorism, violence and militancy that were to develop. But his eloquence on the fate of the queen, Marie Antoinette, over whose plight he wept, led to the famous retort of Paine, "He pities the plumage, and forgets the dying bird." Thomas Paine (1737–1809), the gifted journalist whose *Common Sense* had acted as a clarion call to Americans hesitating on the threshold of independence, leapt to the defense of the French Revolution in *The Rights of Man* of 1791, dedicated to an unwilling George Washington.

Against the traditionalism of Burke, Paine argued for the right of a nation to do what it chose to do. "I am contending for the rights of the living and against their being willed away by the manuscript-assumed authority of the dead." Every generation was equal in rights to the generations which preceded it, in the same way that every individual was born equal in rights with his contemporaries—the natural rights which all men have formed the basis of civil rights. Unlike Burke, Paine thought that politics was essentially simple. On the basis of reason, the most formidable weapon against errors of every kind, a set of principles as universal as truth and the existence of man could be set up.

Thus monarchy, the enemy of mankind and the source of misery, would be abolished. Eliminate the ambitions of kings, and peace would result. Sovereignty would be restored to its natural and original place; representative government would replace hereditary monarchy and aristocracy. In Paine there is a hint of the unsophisticated anarchism that was to become more pronounced in Godwin (1756–1836) and in Shelley. Society would be organized so that the natural rights of liberty, property and security would be obtained, and oppression prevented. The need for government would decrease as a society developed in which men had equal political rights.

For his support of the revolution, Paine was rewarded with election to the National Assembly, though he could not speak French. But his opposition to the execution of the king and to extremist policies led to a prison term, during which he narrowly escaped the guillotine.

De Maistre

If Burke is the oracle of conservatism, de Maistre (1753–1821), together with de Bonald (1753–1840), is the fount of modern reaction, the prophet of the counterrevolution. De Maistre attacked, in his powerful and trenchant language, not only the eighteenth-century ideas of reason, benevolence, the belief in goodness, the idea of progress, but also most of the great writers and thinkers of Western civilization. For him, violence was inevitable in the universe: great evils, plagues, famine, war were all part of the divine plan. Men were neither good nor perfectible—they killed each other as did all creatures. He believed not only in original sin, but also in divine right and control of conflict. Rationalism assumed that all could be known, but "the things of which we remain ignorant are more important than the things we have to know."

His view of life and men was misanthropic: he saw authority as imposed from above, absolute and despotic in a society inevitably hierarchical. There could be no human society without government, no government without sovereignty, no sovereignty without infallibility. Neither a social contract nor a written constitution was important, since both implied a creativity and independence man did not possess. Society rested not only on authorities such as the Papacy and the monarchy, but also on the principle of terror. Paradoxically, the despised figure of the executioner was the figure on whom society depended, the instrument of God, who was the source of all sovereignty. De Maistre, with his opposition to logic and reason, his stress on emotion, prejudice and the religious basis of institutions, his attacks on revolutionary concepts or the glorification of man's will, his denunciation of democracy and Protestantism, of science and enlightenment, combined in curious fashion ideas of political absolutism, religious orthodoxy and rule based on terror. Yet de Maistre, and more particularly de Bonald, by their insistence on the need to accumulate information and facts in order to understand social phenomena, were precursors of the sociological method, and were to exert an influence on thinkers as diverse as the positivist Comte and the reactionary Charles Maurras.

BURKE

Reflections on the Revolution in France

The Danger of Abstract Theory

   . . . I love a manly, moral, regulated liberty as well as any gentleman of that society, be he who he will. . . . But I cannot stand forward, and give praise or blame to anything which relates to human actions, and human concerns, on a simple view of the object, as it stands stripped of every relation, in all the nakedness and solitude of metaphysical abstraction. Circumstances (which with some gentlemen pass for nothing) give in reality to every political principle its distinguishing colour and discriminating effect. The circumstances are what render every civil and political scheme beneficial or noxious to mankind. Abstractedly speaking, government, as well as liberty, is good. . . . Is it because liberty in the abstract may be classed amongst the blessings of mankind, that I am seriously to felicitate a mad-man, who has escaped from the protecting restraint and wholesome darkness of his cell, on his restoration to the enjoyment of light and liberty? . . .

When I see the spirit of liberty in action, I see a strong principle at work; and this, for a while, is all I can possibly know of it. The wild *gas*, the fixed air, is plainly broke loose: but we ought to suspend our judgment until the first effervescence is a little subsided, till the liquor is cleared, and until we see something deeper than the agitation of a troubled and frothy surface. . . .

It is far from impossible to reconcile, if we do not suffer ourselves to be entangled in the mazes of metaphysic sophistry, the use both of a fixed rule and an occasional deviation; the sacredness of an hereditary principle of succession in our government, with a power of change in its application in cases of extreme emergency. Even in that extremity, (if we take the measure of our rights by our exercise of them at the Revolution), the change is to be confined to the peccant party only; to the part which produced the necessary deviation; and even then it is to be effected without a decomposition of the whole civil and political mass, for the purpose of originating a new civil order out of the first elements of society.

A state without the means of some change is without the means of its conservation. Without such means it might even risk the loss of that part of the constitution which it wished the most religiously to preserve. The two principles of conservation and correction operated strongly at the two critical periods of the Restoration and Revolution, when England found itself without a king. At both those periods the nation had lost the bond of union in their ancient edifice; they did not, however, dissolve the whole fabric. On the contrary, in both cases they regenerated the deficient part of the old constitution through the parts which were not impaired. They kept these old parts exactly as they were, that the part recovered might be suited to them. . . .

The Conservative Approach

. . . The very idea of the fabrication of a new government is enough to fill us with disgust and horror. We wished at the period of the Revolution, and do now wish, to derive all we possess as an *inheritance from our forefathers*. Upon that body and stock of inheritance we have taken care not to inoculate any scion alien to the nature of the original plant. All the reformations we have hitherto made have proceeded upon the principle of reverence to antiquity; and I hope, nay, I am persuaded, that all those which possibly may be made hereafter, will be carefully formed upon analogical precedent, authority, and example.

. . . from Magna Charta to the Declaration of Right, it has been the uniform policy of our constitution to claim and assert our liberties, as an *entailed inheritance* derived to us from our forefathers, and to be transmitted to our posterity. . . .

By this means our constitution preserves a unity in so great a diversity of its parts. We have an inheritable crown; an inheritable peerage; and a House of Commons and a people inheriting privileges, franchises, and liberties, from a long line of ancestors.

This policy appears to me to be the result of profound reflection; or rather the happy effect of following nature, which is wisdom without reflection, and above it. A spirit of innovation is generally the result of a selfish temper, and confined views. People will not look forward to posterity, who never look backward to their ancestors. Besides, the people of England well know, that the idea of inheritance furnishes a sure principle of conservation, and a sure principle of transmission; without at all excluding a principle of improvement. It leaves acquisition free; but it secures what it acquires. Whatever advantages are obtained by a state proceeding on these maxims, are locked fast as in a sort of family settlement; grasped as in a kind of mortmain for ever. By a constitutional policy, working after the pattern of nature, we receive, we hold, we transmit our government and our privileges, in the same manner in which we enjoy and transmit our property and our lives. The institutions of policy, the goods of fortune, the gifts of providence, are handed down to us, and from us, in the same course and order. Our political system is placed in a just correspondence and symmetry with the order of the world, and with the mode of existence decreed to a permanent body composed of transitory parts; wherein, by the disposition of a stupendous wisdom, moulding together the great mysterious incorporation of the human race, the whole, at one time, is never old, or middle-aged, or young, but, in a condition of unchangeable constancy, moves on through the varied tenor of perpetual decay, fall, renovation, and progression. Thus, by preserving the method of nature in the conduct of the state, in what we improve, we are never wholly new; in what we retain, we are never wholly obsolete. By adhering in this manner and on those principles to our forefathers, we are guided not by the superstition of antiquarians, but by the spirit of philosophic analogy. In this choice of inheritance we have given to our frame of polity the image of a relation in blood; binding up the constitution of our country with our dearest domestic ties; adopting our fundamental laws into the bosom of our family affections; keeping inseparable, and cherishing with the warmth of all their combined and mutually reflected charities, our state, our hearths, our sepulchres, and our altars.

Through the same plan of a conformity to nature in our artificial institutions, and by calling in the aid of her unerring and powerful instincts, to fortify the fallible and feeble contrivances of our reason, we have derived several other, and those no small benefits, from considering our liberties in the light of an inheritance. Always acting as if in the presence of canonized forefathers, the spirit of freedom, leading in itself to misrule and excess, is tempered with an awful gravity. This idea of a liberal descent inspires us with a sense of habitual native dignity, which prevents that upstart insolence almost inevitably adhering to and disgracing those who are the first acquirers of any distinction. By this means our liberty becomes a noble freedom. It carries an imposing and majestic aspect. It has a pedigree and illustrating ancestors. It has its bearings and its ensigns armorial. It has its gallery of portraits; its monumental inscriptions; its records, evidences, and titles. We procure reverence to our civil institutions on the principle upon which nature teaches us to revere individual men; on account of their age, and on account of those from whom they are descended. All your sophisters cannot produce anything better adapted to preserve a rational and manly freedom than the course that we have pursued, who have chosen our nature rather than our speculations, our breasts rather than our inventions, for the great conservatories and magazines of our rights and privileges. . . .

All other nations have begun the fabric of a new government, or the reformation of an old, by establishing originally, or by enforcing with greater exactness, some rites or other of religion. All other people have laid the foundations of civil freedom in severer manners, and a system of a more austere and masculine morality. France, when she let loose the reins of regal authority, doubled the licence of a ferocious dissoluteness in manners, and of an insolent irreligion in opinions and practices; and has extended through all ranks of life, as if she were communicating some privilege, or laying open some secluded benefit, all the unhappy corruptions that usually were the disease of wealth and power. This is one of the new principles of equality in France. . . . She has sanctified the dark, suspicious maxims of tyrannous distrust; and taught kings to tremble at (what will hereafter be called) the delusive plausibilities of moral politicians. . . .

In all societies, consisting of various descriptions of citizens, some description must be uppermost. The levellers therefore only change and pervert the natural order of things; they load the edifice of society, by setting up in the air what the solidity of the structure requires to be on the ground. The association of tailors and carpenters, of which the republic (of Paris, for instance) is composed, cannot be equal to the situation, into which, by the worst of usurpations, an usurpation on the prerogatives of nature, you attempt to force them. . . .

The occupation of a hair-dresser, or of a working tallow-chandler, cannot be a matter of honour to any person—to say nothing of a number of other more servile employments. Such descriptions of men ought not to suffer oppression from the state; but the state suffers oppression, if such as they, either individually or collectively, are permitted to rule. In this you think you are combating prejudice, but you are at war with nature.

The Need for Aristocratic Rule

. . . There is no qualification for government but virtue and wisdom, actual or presumptive. Wherever they are actually found, they have, in whatever state, condition, profession, or trade, the passport of Heaven to human place and honour. Woe to the country which would madly and impiously reject the service of the talents and virtues, civil, military, or religious, that are given to grace and to serve it; and would condemn to obscurity everything formed to diffuse lustre and glory around a state! Woe to that country too, that, passing into the opposite extreme, considers a low education, a mean contracted view of things, a sordid, mercenary occupation, as a preferable title to command! Everything ought to be open; but not indifferently to every man. No rotation; no appointment by lot; no mode of election operating in the spirit of sortition, or rotation, can be generally good in a government conversant in extensive objects. Because they have no tendency, direct or indirect, to select the man with a view to the duty, or to accommodate the one to the other. I do not hesitate to say, that the road to eminence and power, from obscure condition, ought not to be made too easy, nor a thing too much of course. If rare merit be the rarest of all rare things, it ought to pass through some sort of probation. The temple of honour ought to be seated on an eminence. If it be opened through virtue, let it be remembered too, that virtue is never tried but by some difficulty and some struggle.

Nothing is a due and adequate representation of a state, that does not represent its ability, as well as its property. But as ability is a vigorous and active principle, and as property is sluggish, inert, and timid, it never can be safe from the invasion of ability, unless it be, out of all proportion, predominant in the representation. It must be represented too in great masses of accumulation, or it is not rightly protected. The characteristic essence of property, formed out of the combined principles of its acquisition and conservation, is to be *unequal*. The great masses therefore which excite envy, and tempt rapacity, must be put out of the possibility of danger. Then they form a natural rampart about the lesser properties in all their gradations. The same quantity of property, which is by the natural course of things divided among many, has not the same operation. Its defensive power is weakened as it is diffused. In this diffusion each man's portion is less than what, in the eagerness of his desires, he may flatter himself to obtain by dissipating the accumulations of others. The plunder of the few would indeed give but a share inconceivably small in the distribution to the many. But the many are not capable of making this calculation; and those who lead them to rapine never intend this distribution.

The power of perpetuating our property in our families is one of the most valuable and interesting circumstances belonging to it, and that which tends the most to the perpetuation of society itself. It makes our weakness subservient to our virtue; it grafts benevolence even upon avarice. The possessors of family wealth, and of the distinction which attends hereditary possession (as most concerned in it), are the natural securities for this transmission. . . .

It is said, that twenty-four millions ought to prevail over two hundred thousand. True; if the constitution of a kingdom be a problem of arithmetic. This sort of discourse does well enough with the lamp-post for its second: to men who *may* reason calmly, it is ridiculous. The will of the many, and their interest, must very often differ; and great will be the difference when they make an evil choice. A government of five hundred country attorneys and obscure curates is not good for twenty-four million of men, though it were chosen by eight and forty millions; nor is it the better for being guided by a dozen of persons of quality, who have betrayed their trust in order to obtain that power. . . .

The Rights of Men

. . . Far am I from denying in theory, full as far is my heart from withholding in practice (if I were of power to give or to withhold), the *real* rights of men. In denying their false claims of right, I do not mean to injure those which are real, and are such as their pretended rights would totally destroy. If civil society be made for the advantage of man, all the advantages for which it is made become his right. It is an institution of beneficence; and law itself is only beneficence acting by a rule. Men have a right to live by that rule; they have a right to do justice, as between their fellows, whether their fellows are in public function or in ordinary occupation. They have a right to the fruits of their industry; and to the means of making their industry fruitful. They have a right to the acquisitions of their parents; to the nourishment and improvement of their offspring; to instruction in life, and to consolation in death. Whatever each man can separately do, without trespassing upon others, he has a right to do for himself; and he has a right to a fair portion of all which society, with all its combinations of skill and force, can do in his favour. In this partnership all men have equal rights; but not to equal things. . . .

Government is not made in virtue of natural rights, which may and do exist in total independence of it; and exist in much greater clearness, and in a much greater degree of abstract perfection: but their abstract perfection is their practical defect. By having a right to everything they want everything. Government is a contrivance of human wisdom to provide for human *wants*. Men have a right that these wants should be provided for by this wisdom. Among these wants is to be reckoned the want, out of civil society, of a sufficient restraint upon their passions. Society requires not only that the passions of individuals should be subjected, but that even in the mass and body, as well as in the individuals, the inclinations of men should frequently be thwarted, their will controlled, and their passions brought into subjection. . . .

The moment you abate anything from the full rights of men, each to govern himself, and suffer any artificial, positive limitation upon those rights, from that moment the whole organization of government becomes a consideration of convenience. This it is which makes the constitution of a state, and the due distribution of its powers, a matter of the most delicate and complicated skill. It requires a deep knowledge of human nature and human necessities, and of the things which facilitate or obstruct the various ends, which are to be pursued by the mechanism of civil institutions. . . .

The science of constructing a commonwealth, or renovating it, or reforming it, is, like every other experimental science, not to be taught *à priori*. Nor is it a short experience that can instruct us in that practical science. . . . It is with infinite caution that any man ought to venture upon pulling down an edifice, which has answered in any tolerable degree for ages the common purposes of society, or on building it up again, without having models and patterns of approved utility before his eyes. . . .

The nature of man is intricate; the objects of society are of the greatest possible complexity: and therefore no simple disposition or direction of power can be suitable either to man's nature, or to the quality of his affairs. When I hear the simplicity of contrivance aimed at and boasted of in any new political constitutions, I am at no loss to decide that the artificers are grossly ignorant of their trade, or totally negligent of their duty. . . .

The Virtues of the British Constitution

. . . The vanity, restlessness, petulance, and spirit of intrigue, of several petty cabals, who attempt to hide their total want of consequence in bustle and noise, and puffing, and mutual quotation of each other, makes you imagine that our contemptuous neglect of their abilities is a mark of general acquiescence in their opinions. . . . Because half a dozen grasshoppers under a fern make the field ring with their importunate chink, whilst thousands of great cattle, reposed beneath the shadow of the British oak, chew the cud and are silent, pray do not imagine that those who make the noise are the only inhabitants of the field; that, of course, they are many in number; or that, after all, they are other than the little, shrivelled, meagre, hopping, though loud and troublesome, insects of the hour. . . .

Thanks to our sullen resistance to innovation, thanks to the cold sluggishness of our national character, we still bear the stamp of our forefathers. We have not (as I conceive) lost the generosity and dignity of thinking of the fourteenth century; nor as yet have we subtilized ourselves into savages. We are not the converts of Rousseau; we are not the disciples of Voltaire; Helvetius has made no progress amongst us. Atheists are not our preachers; madmen are not our lawgivers. We know that *we* have made no discoveries, and we think that no discoveries are to be made, in morality; nor many in the great principles of government, nor in the ideas of liberty, which were understood long before we were born, altogether as well as they will be after the grave has heaped its mould upon our presumption, and the silent tomb shall have imposed its law on our pert loquacity. In England we have not yet been completely embowelled of our natural entrails; we still feel within us, and we cherish and cultivate, those inbred sentiments which are the faithful guardians, the active monitors of our duty, the true supporters of all liberal and manly morals. We have not been drawn and trussed, in order that we may be filled, like stuffed birds in a museum, with chaff and rags and paltry blurred shreds of paper about the rights of man. We preserve the whole of our feelings still native and entire, unsophisticated by pedantry and infidelity. We have real hearts of flesh and blood beating in our bosom. We fear God; we look up with awe to kings; with affection to parliaments; with duty to magistrates; with reverence to priests; and with respect to nobility. Why? Because such ideas are brought before our minds, it is *natural* to be so affected; because all other feelings are false and spurious, and tend to corrupt our minds, to vitiate our primary morals, to render us unfit for rational liberty; and by teaching us a servile, licentious, and abandoned insolence, to be our low sport for a few holidays, to make us perfectly fit for, and justly deserving of, slavery, through the whole course of our lives.

. . . we are generally men of untaught feeling; that instead of casting away all our old prejudices, we cherish them to a very considerable degree, and, to take more shame to ourselves, we cherish them because they are prejudices; and the longer they have lasted, and the more generally they have prevailed, the more we cherish them. We are afraid to put men to live and trade each on his own private stock of reason; because we suspect that this stock in each man is small, and that the individuals would do better to avail themselves of the general bank and capital of nations and of ages. Many of our men of speculation, instead of exploding general prejudices, employ their sagacity to discover the latent wisdom which prevails in them. If they find what they seek, and they seldom fail, they think it more wise to continue the prejudice, with the reason involved, than to cast away the coat of prejudice, and to leave nothing but the naked reason; because prejudice, with its reason, has a motive to give action to that reason, and an affection which will give it permanence. Prejudice is of ready application in the emergency; it previously engages the mind in a steady course of wisdom and virtue, and does not leave the man hesitating in the moment of decision, sceptical, puzzled, and unresolved. Prejudice renders a man's virtue his habit; and not a series of unconnected acts. Through just prejudice, his duty becomes a part of his nature. . . .

Religion and the State

. . . Religion is the basis of civil society, and the source of all good and of all comfort. In England we are so convinced of this, that there is no rust of superstition, with which the accumulated absurdity of the human mind might have crusted it over in the course of ages, that ninety-nine in a hundred of the people of England would not prefer to impiety. . . .

We know, and it is our pride to know, that man is by his constitution a religious animal; that atheism is against, not only our reason, but our instincts; and that it cannot prevail long. . . .

On these ideas, instead of quarrelling with establishments, as some do, who have made a philosophy and a religion of their hostility to such institutions, we cleave closely to them. We are resolved to keep an established church and established monarchy, an established aristocracy, and an established democracy, each in the degree it exists, and in no greater. . . .

It has been the misfortune (not . . . the glory) of this age, that everything is to be discussed, as if the constitution of our country were to be always a subject rather of altercation, than enjoyment.

. . . our church establishment . . . is the first of our prejudices, not a prejudice destitute of reason, but involving in it profound and extensive wisdom. . . . It is first, and last, and midst in our minds. For, taking ground on that religious system, of which we are now in possession, we continue to act on the early received and uniformly continued sense of mankind. That sense not only, like a wise architect, hath built up the august fabric of states, but like a provident proprietor, to preserve the structure from profanation and ruin, as a sacred temple purged from all the impurities of fraud, and violence, and injustice, and tyranny, hath solemnly and for ever consecrated the commonwealth, and all that officiate in it. This consecration is made, that all who administer in the government of men, in which they stand in the person of God Himself, should have high and worthy notions of their function and destination; that their hope should be full of immortality; that they should not look to the paltry pelf of the moment, nor to the temporary and transient praise of the vulgar, but to a solid, permanent existence, in the permanent part of their nature, and to a permanent fame and glory, in the example they leave as a rich inheritance to the world. . . .

The consecration of the state, by a state religious establishment, is necessary also to operate with a wholesome awe upon free citizens; because, in order to secure their freedom, they must enjoy some determinate portion of power. To them therefore a religion connected with the state, and with their duty towards it, becomes even more necessary than in such societies, where the people, by the terms of their subjection, are confined to private sentiments, and the management of their own family concerns. All persons possessing any portion of power ought to be strongly and awfully impressed with an idea that they act in trust: and that they are to account for their conduct in that trust to the one great Master, Author, and Founder of society. . . .

The Wisdom of the Past

. . . But one of the first and most leading principles on which the commonwealth and the laws are consecrated, is lest the temporary possessors and life-renters in it, unmindful of what they have received from their ancestors, or of what is due to their posterity, should act as if they were the entire masters; that they should not think it among their rights to cut off the entail, or commit waste on the inheritance, by destroying at their pleasure the whole original fabric of their society; hazarding to leave to those who come after them a ruin instead of an habitation—and teaching these successors as little to respect their contrivances, as they had themselves respected the institutions of their forefathers. By this unprincipled facility of changing the state as often, and as much, and in as many ways, as there are floating fancies or fashions, the whole chain and continuity of the commonwealth would be broken. No one generation could link with the other. Men would become little better than the flies of a summer.

And first of all, the science of jurisprudence, the pride of the human intellect, which, with all its defects, redundancies, and errors, is the collected reason of ages, combining the principles of original justice with the infinite variety of human concerns, as a heap of old exploded errors, would be no longer studied. Personal self-sufficiency and arrogance (the certain attendants upon all those who have never experienced a wisdom greater than their own) would usurp the tribunal. Of course no certain laws, establishing invariable grounds of hope and fear, would keep the actions of men in a certain course, or direct them to a certain end. Nothing stable in the modes of holding property, or exercising function, could form a solid ground on which any parent could speculate in the education of his offspring, or in a choice for their future establishment in the world. No principles would be early worked into the habits. . . . Barbarism with regard to science and literature, unskilfulness with regard to arts and manufactures, would infallibly succeed to the want of a steady education and settled principle; and thus the commonwealth itself would, in a few generations, crumble away, be disconnected into the dust and power of individuality, and at length dispersed to all the winds of heaven. . . .

Society is indeed a contract. Subordinate contracts for objects of mere occasional interest may be dissolved at pleasure—but the state ought not to be considered as nothing better than a partnership agreement in a trade of pepper and coffee, calico or tobacco, or some other such low concern, to be taken up for a little temporary interest, and to be dissolved by the fancy of the parties. It is to be looked on with other reverence; because it is not a partnership in things subservient only to the gross animal existence of a temporary and perishable nature. It is a partnership in all science; a partnership in all art; a partnership in every virtue, and in all perfection. As the ends of such a partnership cannot be obtained in many generations, it becomes a partnership not only between those who are living, but between those who are living, those who are dead, and those who are to be born. Each contract of each particular state is but a clause in the great primæval contract of eternal society, linking the lower with the higher natures, connecting the visible and invisible world, according to a fixed compact sanctioned by the inviolable oath which holds all physical and all moral natures, each in their appointed place. . . . It is to the property of the citizen, and not to the demands of the creditor of the state, that the first and original faith of civil society is pledged. The claim of the citizen is prior in time, paramount in title, superior in equity. The fortunes of individuals, whether possessed by acquisition, or by descent, or in virtue of a participation in the goods of some community, were no part of the creditor's security, expressed or implied. They never so much as entered into his head when he made his bargain. He well knew that the public, whether represented by a monarch or by a senate, can pledge nothing but the public estate; and it can have no public estate, except in what it derives from a just and proportioned imposition upon the citizens at large. This was engaged, and nothing else could be engaged, to the public creditor. No man can mortgage his injustice as a pawn for his fidelity. . . .

When the useful parts of an old establishment are kept, and what is superadded is to be fitted to what is retained, a vigorous mind, steady, persevering attention, various powers of comparison and combination, and the resources of an understanding fruitful in expedients, are to be exercised; they are to be exercised in a continued conflict with the combined force of opposite vices, with the obstinacy that rejects all improvement, and the levity that is fatigued and disgusted with everything of which it is in possession. But you may object—"A process of this kind is slow. It is not fit for an assembly, which glories in performing in a few months the work of ages. Such a mode of reforming, possibly, might take up many years." Without question it might; and it ought. It is one of the excellencies of a method in which time is amongst the assistants, that its operation is slow, and in some cases almost imperceptible. If circumspection and caution are a part of wisdom, when we work only upon inanimate matter, surely they become a part of duty too, when the subject of our demolition and construction is not brick and timber, but sentient beings, by the sudden alteration of whose state, condition, and habits, multitudes may be rendered miserable. . . . By a slow but well-sustained progress, the effect of each step is watched; the good or ill success of the first gives light to us in the second; and so, from light to light, we are conducted with safety through the whole series. We see that the parts of the system do not clash. The evils latent in the most promising contrivances are provided for as they arise. One advantage is as little as possible sacrificed to another. We compensate, we reconcile, we balance. We are enabled to unite into a consistent whole the various anomalies and contending principles that are found in the minds and affairs of men. From hence arises, not an excellence in simplicity, but one far superior, an excellence in composition. Where the great interests of mankind are concerned through a long succession of generations, that succession ought to be admitted into some share in the councils which are so deeply to affect them. If justice requires this, the work itself requires the aid of more minds than one age can furnish. It is from this view of things that the best legislators have been often satisfied with the establishment of some sure, solid, and ruling principle in government; a power like that which some of the philosophers have called a plastic nature; and having fixed the principle, they have left it afterwards to its own operation. . . .

Old establishments are tried by their effects. If the people are happy, united, wealthy, and powerful, we presume the rest. We conclude that to be good from whence good is derived. In old establishments various correctives have been found for their aberrations from theory. Indeed they are the results of various necessities and expediences. They are not often constructed after any theory; theories are rather drawn from them. In them we often see the end best obtained, where the means seem not perfectly reconcilable to what we may fancy was the original scheme. The means taught by experience may be better suited to political ends than those contrived in the original project. They again react upon the primitive constitution, and sometimes improve the design itself, from which they seem to have departed. I think all this might be curiously exemplified in the British Constitution. At worst, the errors and deviations of every kind in reckoning are found and computed, and the ship proceeds in her course. This is the case of old establishments; but in a new and merely theoretic system, it is expected that every contrivance shall appear, on the face of it, to answer its ends; specially where the projectors are no way embarrassed with an endeavour to accommodate the new building to an old one, either in the walls or on the foundations. . . .

In what I did, I should follow the example of our ancestors. I would make the reparation as nearly as possible in the style of the building. A politic caution, a guarded circumspection, a moral rather than a complexional timidity, were among the ruling principles of our forefathers in their most decided conduct.

PAINE

The Rights of Man

The Rights of the Living

. . . There never did, there never will, and there never can, exist a Parliament, or any description of men, or any generation of men, in any country, possessed of the right or the power of binding and controuling posterity to the *"end of time,"* or of commanding for ever how the world shall be governed, or who shall govern it; and therefore all such clauses, acts or declarations by which the makers of them attempt to do what they have neither the right nor the power to do, nor the power to execute, are in themselves null and void. Every age and generation must be as free to act for itself *in all cases* as the ages and generations which preceded it. The vanity and presumption of governing beyond the grave is the most ridiculous and insolent of all tyrannies. Man has no property in man; neither has any generation a property in the generations which are to follow. The Parliament or the people of 1688, or of any other period, had no more right to dispose of the people of the present day, or to bind or to controul them *in any shape whatever*, than the Parliament or the people of the present day have to dispose of, bind or controul those who are to live a hundred or a thousand years hence. Every generation is, and must be, competent to all the purposes which its occasions require. It is the living, and not the dead, that are to be accommodated. . . .

I am contending for the rights of the *living*, and against their being willed away, and controuled and contracted for, by the manuscript assumed authority of the dead; and Mr. Burke is contending for the authority of the dead over the rights and freedom of the living. There was a time when Kings disposed of their Crowns by will upon their death-beds, and consigned the people, like beasts of the field, to whatever successor they appointed. This is now so exploded as scarcely to be remembered, and so monstrous as hardly to be believed; but the Parliamentary clauses upon which Mr. Burke builds his political church are of the same nature. . . .

Those who have quitted the world, and those who are not yet arrived at it, are as remote from each other as the utmost stretch of mortal imagination can conceive. What possible obligation, then, can exist between them; what rule or principle can be laid down that of two nonentities, the one out of existence and the other not in, and who never can meet in this world, the one should controul the other to the end of time? . . .

From what, or from whence, does Mr. Burke prove the right of any human power to bind posterity for ever? He has produced his clauses, but he must produce also his proofs that such a right existed, and show how it existed. If it ever existed it must now exist, for whatever appertains to the nature of man cannot be annihilated by man. It is the nature of man to die, and he will continue to die as long as he continues to be born. But Mr. Burke has set up a sort of political Adam, in whom all posterity are bound for ever; he must, therefore, prove that his Adam possessed such a power, or such a right. . . .

It requires but a very small glance of thought to perceive that altho' laws made in one generation often continue in force through succeeding generations, yet that they continue to derive their force from the consent of the living. A law not repealed continues in force, not because it *cannot* be repealed, but because it *is not* repealed; and the non-repealing passes for consent. . . .

Natural Rights

. . . The illuminating and divine principle of the equal rights of man (for it has its origin from the Maker of man) relates, not only to the living individuals, but to generations of men succeeding each other. Every generation is equal in rights to the generations which preceded it, by the same rule that every individual is born equal in rights with his contemporary.

Every history of the creation, and every traditionary account, whether from the lettered or unlettered world, however they may vary in their opinion or belief of certain particulars, all agree in establishing one point, *the unity of man;* by which I mean that men are all of *one degree,* and consequently that all men are born equal, and with equal natural rights. . . .

Man did not enter into society to become *worse* than he was before, not to have fewer rights than he had before, but to have those rights better secured. His natural rights are the foundation of all his civil rights. . . .

Natural rights are those which appertain to man in right of his existence. Of this kind are all the intellectual rights, or rights of the mind, and also all those rights of acting as an individual for his own comfort and happiness, which are not injurious to the natural rights of others. Civil rights are those which appertain to man in right of his being a member of society. Every civil right has for its foundation some natural right pre-existing in the individual, but to the enjoyment of which his individual power is not, in all cases, sufficiently competent. Of this kind are all those which relate to security and protection. . . .

The natural rights which [man] retains [in society] are all those in which the *power* to execute it is as perfect in the individual as the right itself. Among this class, as is before mentioned, are all the intellectual rights, or rights of the mind; consequently religion is one of those rights. The natural rights which are not retained, are all those in which, though the right is perfect in the individual, the power to execute them is defective. . . . He therefore deposits this right in the common stock of society, and takes the arm of society, of which he is a part, in preference and in addition to his own. . . .

From these premises two or three certain conclusions will follow:

First, *That every civil right grows out of a natural right; or, in other words, is a natural right exchanged.*

Secondly, *That civil power properly considered as such is made up of the aggregate of that class of the natural rights of man, which becomes defective in the individual in point of power, and answers not his purpose but when collected to a focus becomes competent to the purpose of every one.*

Thirdly, *That the power produced from the aggregate of natural rights, imperfect in power in the individual, cannot be applied to invade the natural rights which are retained in the individual, and in which the power to execute is as perfect as the right itself.* . . .

Society and Government

. . . Society performs for itself almost everything which is ascribed to Government.

To understand the nature and quantity of Government proper for man, it is necessary to attend to his character. As nature created him for social life, she fitted him for the station she intended. In all cases she made his natural wants greater than his individual powers. No one man is capable, without the aid of society, of supplying his own wants; and those wants, acting upon every individual, impel the whole of them into society, as naturally as gravitation acts to a centre.

But she has gone further. She has not only forced man into society by a diversity of wants which the reciprocal aid of each other can supply, but she has implanted in him a system of social effections, which, though not necessary to his existence, are essential to his happiness. There is no period in life when this love for society ceases to act. It begins and ends with our being.

If we examine with attention the composition and constitution of man, the diversity of his wants and talents in different men for reciprocally accommodating the wants of each other, his propensity to society, and consequently to preserve the advantages resulting from it, we shall easily discover that a great part of what is called Government is mere imposition.

Government is no farther necessary than to supply the few cases to which society and civilisation are not conveniently competent; and instances are not wanting to show, that everything which Government can usefully add thereto, has been performed by the common consent of society, without Government. . . .

So far is it from being true, as has been pretended, that the abolition of any formal Government is the dissolution of society, that it acts by a contrary impulse, and brings the latter the closer together. All that part of its organization which it had committed to its Government, devolves again upon itself, and acts through its medium. When men, as well from natural instinct as from reciprocal benefits, have habituated themselves to social and civilised life, there is always enough of its principles in practice to carry them through any changes they may find necessary or convenient to make in their Government. In short, man is so naturally a creature of society that it is almost impossible to put him out of it.

Formal Government makes but a small part of civilised life; and when even the best that human wisdom can devise is established, it is a thing more in name and idea than in fact. It is to the great and fundamental principles of society and civilisation—to the common usage universally consented to, and mutually and reciprocally maintained—to the unceasing circulation of interest, which, passing through its million channels, invigorates the whole mass of civilised man—it is to these things, infinitely more than to anything which even the best instituted Government can perform, that the safety and prosperity of the individual and of the whole depends.

The more perfect civilisation is, the less occasion has it for Government, because the more it does regulate its own affairs, and govern itself; but so contrary is the practice of old Governments to the reason of the case, that the expences of them increase in the proportion they ought to diminish. It is but few general laws that civilised life requires, and those of such common usefulness, that whether they are enforced by the forms of government or not, the effect will be nearly the same. If we consider what the principles are that first condense men into society, and what the motives that regulate their mutual intercourse afterwards, we shall find, by the time we arrive at what is called Government, that nearly the whole of the business is performed by the natural operation of the parts upon each other.

DE MAISTRE

Considérations sur la France,
Étude sur la Souveraineté, Du Pape;
and *Les Soirées de Saint-Pétersbourg*

The French Revolution

We are attached to the Supreme Being by a supple chain which restrains without enslaving us. What is most admirable in the universal order of things is the action of free men under the divine hand. Freely enslaved, they act at the same time voluntarily and by necessity: they do what they want, but without upsetting general plans. Each person occupies the center of a sphere of activity, whose diameter varies according to the eternal geometrician, who knows how to extend, restrict, stop or direct the will without altering its nature. . . .

If one imagines a watch the springs of which continually vary in strength, weight, dimension, form and position, and which, however, will invariably always show the time, one will get some idea of the action of free men relatively to the plans of the Creator.

In the political and moral world, as in the physical, there is a common order and there are exceptions to that order. Commonly we see a series of effects produced by the same causes, but at certain times we see actions suspended, causes paralysed and new effects produced. The miracle is, in effect, produced by a divine or superhuman cause which suspends or contradicts an ordinary cause. . . . The French Revolution, and all that is happening in Europe at this moment, is as marvellous in its way as the instantaneous fructification of a tree in January, yet men, instead of admiring, look elsewhere or talk nonsense. In the time of revolutions the chain which ties man contracts abruptly, his action diminishes and his means deceive him. . . .

What distinguishes the French Revolution and what makes it a unique event in history is that it is radically bad. No element of good relieves the eye of the observer: it is the highest degree of corruption known; it is pure impurity. In what page of history will one find as many vices acting at one time in the same theatre? What a frightful assemblage of baseness and cruelty! What profound immorality! What forgetting of all modesty. . . . There was a certain inexplicable deliriousness, a blind impetuosity, a scandalous scorn of all that is respectable among men, an atrocity of a new kind that joked about its crimes. Above all, an impudent prostitution of reasoning of all the words made to express the ideas of justice and virtue.

And now, see how crime serves as basis for all this republican scaffolding. The word "citizen" has been substituted for the old forms of politeness. . . . It is from this bloody filth that a durable government will arise? . . . Barbarian ignorance has presided, no doubt, over numerous political régimes: but wise barbarism, systematic atrocity, calculated corruption, and, above all, irreligion have never produced anything. Greenness leads to maturity, rottenness leads to nothing. . . .

The government of republican France is thought strong because it is violent, but force differs from violence as much as from feebleness, and the astonishing manner in which it operates at this time only furnishes the proof that it cannot long endure. The French nation does not want this government: it suffers it, it remains subject, perhaps because it cannot help it, or because it fears something worse. The republic rests only on these two factors, which have nothing real about them. One can say that it rests entirely on two negatives. . . . One feels, in all that the friends of the republic say on the stability of government, not the conviction of reason, but the dream of desire.

(Extracts from *Considérations sur la France,* chapters 1 and 4.)

Absolute Power

Every kind of sovereignty is absolute in nature. . . . However one organizes institutions, there will always be, in the last analysis, an absolute power which can do harm with impunity, which will therefore be despotic, and against which there is no bulwark other than insurrection.

Everywhere where powers are divided, the stuggles among the different powers can be considered as the deliberations of a single sovereign whose reason balances the pros and cons. But as soon as the decision is made, the effect is the same . . . and the will of any sovereign is always invincible.

No matter how one defines and places sovereignty, always it is one, inviolable and absolute. . . . The sovereign cannot be judged, for that would imply another sovereign over it. The law by which anyone is judged will be made by a sovereign or by another; the latter would mean a law made by a sovereign against itself or a sovereign below the sovereign, both of which are inadmissible. It is always necessary to remind men of history which is the first or really the only teacher in politics. To say that man is born for liberty, is to utter nonsense.

History is experimental politics, that it is to say, the only good. As in physics, a hundred volumes of speculative theories disappear before a single experiment, so in political science, no system can be admitted if it is not the more or less probable corollary of well-established facts. If one asks what is the most natural government in the world, history replies, "It is monarchy." . . .

Democracy had a brilliant moment—the glory of Athens—and it paid dearly for it. One would, however, make a bad mistake if, comparing moment with moment, one pretended to establish the superiority of democracy over monarchy. It would mean neglecting the consideration of duration which is a necessary element of this kind of estimate. In general, all democratic governments are only passing meteors, whose brilliance excludes duration.

In reality, all governments are monarchies which differ only that they are for life, temporary, hereditary or elective, individual or collegiate. . . . All government is aristocratic, composed more or less of ruling figures. In democracy, that aristocracy is composed of as many persons as the nature of things allowed. Monarchy, or aristocracy, which is inevitable in all governments, is dominated by a single person who is at the pinnacle of the pyramid, and unquestionably, it forms the most natural government for man. But of all monarchies the most strict, the most despotic, the most intolerable, is the monarchical people.

(Extract from *Étude sur la Souveraineté*.)

The Dangers of Individual Reason

Human reason in individuals is useless, not only for creation, but also for the conservation of all religious or political association, because it only produces disputes. Man, to behave, has no need of problems, but of beliefs. His cradle must be surrounded by dogmas, and when his reason awakes, it is necessary that he find all his opinions made. . . . There is nothing so important for him as prejudice. . . . Prejudice does not mean false ideas, but only . . . opinions adopted before examination. Now this kind of opinion is the greatest need of man, the true elements of his happiness, and the palladium of empires. Without it, there can be neither cult, morals, nor government. It is necessary that there be a religion of the state as there is a politics of the state: or rather, that religious and political dogmas, mixed and blended, together form a rather strong universal or national reason in order to repress the aberrations of individual reason which is . . . the mortal enemy of all associations because it produces only divergent opinions.

All known peoples have been happy and powerful to the degree they have most faithfully obeyed that national reason which is nothing but the annihilation of individual dogmas and the absolute and general reign of national dogmas, of useful prejudices. If each man relies on his individual reason for his religious beliefs, the result will be anarchy of belief or the annihilation of religious sovereignty. Similarly, if each person examines the principles of government, the result will be civil anarchy or the annihilation of political sovereignty. Government is a true religion: it has its dogmas, its mysteries, its ministers. To annihilate it or to submit it to the discussion of all individuals, is the same thing. It sees only by national reason . . . by political faith, which is a symbol. The first need of men is that his budding reason be curbed under this double yoke, that it annihilate itself, that it lose itself in national reason in order to change its individual existence into a communal one.

(Extract from *Étude sur la Souveraineté*.)

Papal Power

Infallibility in the spiritual order and sovereignty in the temporal order are two perfectly synonymous words. Both express that high power which dominates all, from which all others derive, which governs and is not governed, which judges and is not judged.

To say the Church is infallible is not to ask any particular privilege for it. We ask only that it enjoy the common right possessed by all sovereignties, to act as if it were infallible, for all government is absolute. From the moment that it can be resisted on the pretext of error or injustice, it no longer exists. . . . The Church must be governed as all other associations, otherwise there will no longer be aggregation, harmony, unity. This government is therefore, by its nature, infallible, absolute. . . .

The monarchical form once established, infallibility is no more than a necessary consequence of supremacy, or rather, it is the same thing under two different names. . . . It is indeed absolutely the same thing in practice not to be subject to error as not to be able to be accused of it. . . . All judgment, properly so-called, is and must be held as just in all human association, under all imaginable forms of government. Every true statesman will understand me when I say that it is not a question of knowing if the Supreme Pontiff *is*, but that he *must be* infallible. . . .

There is no sovereignty more justifiable in Europe than that of the Sovereign Pontiff. It is like divine law, *justificata in semetipsa*. . . .

How could the Church have been able to control the monarchy if the monarchy itself had not been prepared, softened, sweetened by the Popes? What could each prelate, what could even each particular Church do against its master? Nothing. What was necessary was not a human, physical, material power . . . but a spiritual and moral power which reigned only through opinion: such as was the power of the Popes. No right and pure spirit would refuse to recognize the action of Providence which showed to all Europeans the sovereign Pontiff as the source of European sovereignty. The same authority, acting everywhere, obliterated national differences as much as the thing was possible. . . . Providence had confided to the Popes the education of European sovereignty . . . every action of the Popes against monarchs turned to the profit of sovereignty. Never acting otherwise than as divine delegates, even in struggling against monarchs, they did not cease to warn the subject that he could not act against his masters. Immortal benefactors of the human race, they fought at the same time for the divine character of sovereignty and for the legitimate liberty of men. The people, uninterested in any kind of resistance, could neither become full of pride nor emancipate, and the sovereigns, bowing only to divine power, conserved all their dignity. . . . The kings abdicate the power of judging by themselves, and the people in return, declare kings infallible and inviolable. Such is the fundamental law of European monarchy, and it is the work of the Popes: unheard of marvel, contrary to the nature of natural man, contrary to all historical facts, which no one in ancient times dreamed as being possible. . . . The Christian peoples who have never felt, or never felt enough the hand of the Supreme Pontiff, will never have this monarchy. . . . In order to be admitted to the European banquet, in order to be made worthy of this admirable sceptre which has never been given except to those nations that are prepared, . . . all routes are false except that which has conducted us. . . . All European nations withdrawing from the influence of the Holy Seat will be carried inevitably to servitude or to revolt.

(Extracts from *Du Pape*, Book I, chapter 1; Book II, chapter 6; Book III, chapter 4.)

The Executioner and the Soldier

There is in man, in spite of his immense degradation, an element of love that he bears for his fellow man: compassion is as natural as respiration. By what inconceivable magic is he always ready, at the first sound of the drum, to divest himself of this sacred character, to go off without resistance, often even with a certain cheerfulness . . . to cut to pieces on the battlefield his brother who has never offended him and who on his part similarly advances to make him submit if he can. . . .

One can say, glory explains everything. But first, glory is only for the leaders: secondly, this is to move the difficulty back, because I ask from where precisely comes the extraordinary glory attached to war. I have often had a vision. I imagine that an intelligent person, a stranger to our globe, comes here for some sufficient reason and converses with someone on the order of the world. Among the curious things that one relates to him is that corruption and vice require that man, in certain circumstances, die by the hand of fellow man: that this right of killing without crime is confided, among us, only to the executioner and the soldier. "The one kills the guilty, convicted and condemned, and his executions are happily so rare that one of these ministers of death suffices in a province. As for the soldiers, there are never enough of them. They must kill without limit, and always honest men. Of these two professional killers, the soldier and the executioner, one is very honored and always has been among all the nations of the world; the other is equally generally regarded as infamous. Which of these men would be the one who was honored?"

Certainly the travelling genius would not hesitate a moment: he would bestow all praise on the executioner. . . . He would say, "He is a subtle being . . . he is the cornerstone of society . . . take away the executioner and all order disappears with him. Besides, what greatness of soul, what noble disinterestedness one must suppose in the man who devotes himself to such respectable functions. . . . Public opinion surrounds him with all honor of which he has need, and to which he is entitled. As for the soldier, he is . . . a minister of cruelty and injustice. . . . How many individual injustices, horrors and useless atrocities does he commit?"

How this genius would be wrong! Indeed the soldier and the executioner occupy the two extremes of the social ladder, but in the opposite sense of this beautiful theory. There is no one so noble as the first, no one so abject as the second. . . .

A somber signal is given; an abject minister of justice comes to knock on the door and to notify the executioner that he is needed. He departs; he arrives at a public square, crowded with a mob, cramped and throbbing. He is handed a poisoner, a murderer or a blasphemer; he seizes him and stretches him on a horizontal cross; he raises his arm. There is a horrible silence, and one hears only the cracking of bones and the howls of the victim. The executioner detaches him; he carries him to the wheel. The broken limbs are entwined in the spokes; the head hangs; the hair stands on end and the mouth, open like a furnace, speaks only a few bloody words calling for death. The executioner has finished; his heart beats, but it is for joy. He applauds himself; he says in his heart: "Nobody is better at the wheel than I." He descends, he holds out his blood-stained hand and the Law throws him, from afar, a few pieces of gold which he carries away through a double line of men turning away in horror. He sits down to eat; he gets into bed and he sleeps. . . .

And yet, all grandeur, all power, all subordination, rest on the executioner: he is the horror and the tie of the human association. Take away this incomprehensible agent and at that moment, order will give way to chaos, thrones will fall and society will disappear.

(Extracts from *Les Soirées de Saint-Petersbourg,* 1st and 7th Entretiens.)

SECTION III

ROMANTICISM AND
IDEALISM

Some critics of Rousseau, like Irving Babbitt and
T. E. Hulme, have argued that all romanticism springs from
him, because of his belief in individual uniqueness. Romanticism, essentially, was a revolt, beginning in the early nineteenth century, against both the intellectual current and the
industrial changes of the times. The group labeled romantics
rejected the rationalism they felt was supreme in philosophy
and religion and which provided the base for social and economic behavior. They urged the importance of passion, the
impulses of man, of aesthetic and artistic experience, and of
uniqueness. The writers complained of the mediocrity of contemporary life; as artists, "Brahmins, a higher caste," they
hated the environment they could not dominate.

They attacked the philosophy of individualism and the capitalist system for being antisocial, egoistic and based on false
reason. The romantics looked back to the past; in particular,
they rediscovered the Middle Ages and medieval Christianity,
considering them the pinnacle of inspiration and beauty. It
was Goethe who saw their devotion to the cult of the Middle
Ages, the praise of a universal Christendom and the conversions to Catholicism as forms of escape caused by their inability to find happiness.

Romanticism was a movement not confined to one country.
In Germany the leading figures were Novalis (Friedrich von
Hardenberg 1772–1801). August Wilhelm von Schlegel
(1767–1845) and his brother, Friedrich von Schlegel (1772–
1829), Adam Muller (1779–1829), and, associated with
them, J. G. Herder (1744–1803). In France the outstanding
writer was Chateaubriand; in England the poets Coleridge,
Wordsworth and Southey, and Carlyle.

The German writers pictured nations as individual, separate entities, as personalities with traditions, capable of development. Increasingly, they stressed the greatness of the German national character, its virtues and its spiritual mission to re-create a new order. The state was not, as liberals argued, a negative instrument maintaining equilibrium, but a powerful institution to which devotion was owed. It was Herder who linked romanticism to both nationalism and the idea of a philosophy of history, as Fichte was to link idealism and nationalism. Herder emphasized the importance of national character and the national soul, the result of cultural, educational, environmental and racial factors. He saw the spiritual evolution of mankind as the history of different cultures. Each people (*Volk*) was a collective national personality, animated by a certain spirit and a specific form of humanity. Not surprisingly, he argued that the Germans had contributed more than any other people to European life, and that the cultural unity of Germany was desirable for the sake of all mankind.

The English romantic poets, who had welcomed the French Revolution in their youth, became preoccupied with the need for public order, internal peace and established institutions, and turned to political reaction. Coleridge, the most intelligent and articulate of them, criticized both the developing industrial system and the idea of popular sovereignty. He urged the need for elitist rule through a clerisy (literati), a group of individuals free from economic worries and solicitous for the spiritual improvement of the people.

Carlyle

Thomas Carlyle (1795–1881) like Coleridge, attacked industrialism, feared political Jacobinism and derided utilitarianism. He had equal distaste for the plutocracy and the mass. The first group, the "millocracy concerned only for money" were insensitive to the sufferings of the workers, and substituted the cash nexus for personal relationships; the second was composed mainly of fools "full of beer and nonsense." The rule of all life was inequality. In politics, this meant rule by the most competent, the aristocrats. The embodiment of aristocratic rule was the great man, the hero, the man of wisdom and insight. Normally, he was recognized and welcomed by the masses, but occasionally violence might be necessary to establish his superiority. History was the biography of great men.

Carlyle is the prototype of the antiliberal, opposed to the extension of suffrage and to the participation of the people in political affairs, the advocate of strong governmental powers to avoid the anarchy of economic and political liberalism, the proponent of possible regimentation of the labor force, the racist believer in Teutonic superiority, the anti-Semite and Negro baiter.

German Idealism

Idealism, the philosophy propounded in Germany in the early nineteenth century, has its roots in the Rousseau and Kant conceptions of will, but produced political conclusions coinciding happily with the need for German political unification and rising nationalism. Based on the need for the self-determination of individuals, idealism assumed that the expression of their real will coincided with that of society. Society was seen as organic, not mechanistic, as having grown over a process of time, rather than having resulted from one creative effort, as an inseparable whole rather than a total sum of finite individual entities. Individual self-realization was possible only within society, since individual existence had significance only in society. Self-realization, in effect, meant obedience to authority, because the individual will, the true rational will, was part of and expressed in the will of the state. The unity of interest realized in a community and its real will were expressed by the state in an institutional way. The state had a will, a consciousness and a moral end of its own, on a higher level than that of any individual. Neither internally nor externally was the state limited by moral laws, since it was itself the fount of such laws.

Fichte and Hegel

Idealism attained significant expression with Johann Gottlieb Fichte (1762–1814) and Georg Wilhelm Friedrich Hegel (1770–1831). Fichte started as an individualist interested in the rights of the individual and the sovereignty of the people, and ended as a strong nationalist. His early writing is largely commentary on the individual ego, which posited nature in order to realize itself. The ego looked within to obtain an inner vision and true ideal. It recognized no law "but the one given by oneself to oneself." The moral subject, acting by free will, was the starting point of reality. Man must regain his original status as an independent being, and be capable of acting. But man could not live in isolation—cooperation with others, also recognized as free independent beings, was necessary. The true self, common to all, was incorporated in society: "The universe is myself." Moreover, man had a definite place in the chain of things; the state "must place everyone in a position which is his due."

But Fichte, inspired by the example of French nationalism, increasingly emphasized the nation, of which individuals were echoes, and the state. The state was an artistic creation; it should strengthen itself politically and economically. Against the liberal, free-trade concept, Fichte argued the need for an autarkic state with control over commerce and industry, and closed to foreigners. Citizens must be molded, by education and other means, so that they were excited by "the devouring flame of higher patriotism," and prepared to sacrifice themselves. The individual should set no limit whatever to his sacrifices for the sake of race and nation. The fourteen *Addresses to the German Nation* delivered by Fichte in Berlin during 1807–8 were the first great attempt to educate a people in the desirable principles of nationalism, to restore the self-confidence of a military defeated nation and to insist on the future intellectual and political greatness of Germany.

Hegel, the most significant of the idealists, has had far-reaching intellectual influence, extending to modern existentialism as well as to Marxism. But the difficulty and ambiguity of so much of his writing have produced widely conflicting interpretations and evaluations. For some, he is Germany's most outstanding nineteenth-century philosopher; others, who regard him as the spokesman for Prussian aggression or, like Popper, as "the renaissance of Tribalism," see him as a precursor of twentieth-century Nazism.

For Hegel, ultimate reality was conceived in terms of the spirit or idea, which developed and revealed itself throughout history on the path to absolute knowledge. This development occurred dialectically. Every stage of development was inevitably imperfect; everything was in a condition both of being and becoming. The spirit was embodied in concrete institutions, in peoples and in states. History was a rational process, and reason pervaded all these institutions. The real world was as it ought to be.

History was seen as the contributions of nations to world civilization and as the struggle of different nations for world domination. Some peoples—the Greeks and the Jews—had affected historical development more than others; Prussia was the contemporary example of such a nation. In the same way, great men, propelled "by the cunning of reason," had forwarded the movement of history. Possessed of passionate convictions, capable of action and with insight into the needs of their age, they were the agents of the world spirit, drawing their purpose from a spring that is hidden beneath the surface of things. History was also the scene of conflict, violence and war, a slaughter bench, rather than a theater of happiness.

The universal spirit was embodied in the state. In history, only those peoples who formed a state could come under our notice. While civil society was formed of individuals, all concerned with self-interest and property, the state was a unity, superior both to society and family relationships. The state contained "the essence of self-consciousness"—it was humanity at its present peak. Its highest law was its own welfare. The good of the state had a justification quite apart from the good of the individual. Hegel had argued that the history of the world was the progress of the consciousness of freedom. But freedom, the recognition of necessity, involved acting in accordance with reason, which was expressed in the state. In contrast to the Anglo-Saxon association of liberty and individuality, Hegel associated freedom and rationality. Man, by obeying the state, was acting rationally and freely.

Hegel invented a new subject, the philosophy of history, the method of explaining historical phenomena through a pattern of inevitably progressive developments. If he did not pretend to forecast the future, he was remarkably prescient about developments to come in science and in art. Hegel is the forerunner of all those, from Saint-Simon and Comte to Arnold Toynbee, who claim to have found meaning in the whole historical process, even if it cannot all be understood. The concept of historical inevitability is truly the homage that metaphysics pays to science.

CARLYLE

On Heroes, Hero-worship and the Heroic in History

The Hero and History

. . . Universal History, the history of what man has accomplished in this world, is at bottom the History of the Great Men who have worked here. They were the leaders of men, these great ones; the modellers, patterns, and in a wide sense creators, of whatsoever the general mass of men contrived to do or to attain; all things that we see standing accomplished in the world are properly the outer material result, the practical realisation and embodiment, of Thoughts that dwelt in the Great Men sent into the world: the soul of the whole world's history, it may justly be considered, were the history of these. . . .

We cannot look, however imperfectly, upon a great man, without gaining something by him. He is the living light-fountain, which it is good and pleasant to be near. The light which enlightens, which has enlightened the darkness of the world; and this not as a kindled lamp only, but rather as a natural luminary shining by the gift of Heaven; a flowing light-fountain of native original insight, of manhood and heroic nobleness;—in whose radiance all souls feel that it is well with them.

. . . the perplexed jungle of Paganism sprang, we may say, out of many roots: every admiration, adoration of a star or natural object, was a root or fibre of a root; but Hero-worship is the deepest root of all; the tap-root, from which in a great degree all the rest were nourished and grown.

And now if worship even of a star had some meaning in it, how much more might that of a Hero! Worship of a Hero is transcendent admiration of a Great Man. I say great men are still admirable; I say there is, at bottom, nothing else admirable! No nobler feeling than this of admiration for one higher than himself dwells in the breast of man. It is to this hour, and at all hours, the vivifying influence in man's life. Religion I find stands upon it; not Paganism only, but far higher and truer religions—all religion hitherto known. Hero-worship, heartfelt prostrate admiration, submission, burning, boundless, for a noblest godlike Form of Man—is not that the germ of Christianity itself? The greatest of all Heroes is One—whom we do not name here! Let sacred silence meditate that sacred matter; you will find it the ultimate perfection of a principle extant throughout man's whole history on earth.

Or coming into lower, less *un*speakable provinces, is not all Loyalty akin to religious Faith also? Faith is loyalty to some inspired Teacher, some spiritual Hero. And what therefore is loyalty proper, the life-breath of all society, but an effluence of Hero-worship, submissive admiration for the truly great? Society is founded on Hero-worship. All dignities of rank, on which human association rests, are what we may call a *Hero*-archy (Government of Heroes),—or a Hierarchy, for it is 'sacred' enough withal! The Duke means *Dux*, Leader; King is *Kön-ning, Kan-ning*, Man that *knows* or *cans*. Society everywhere is some representation, not *in*supportably inaccurate, of a graduated Worship of Heroes;—reverence and obedience done to men really great and wise. . . .

I am well aware that in these days Hero-worship, the thing I call Hero-worship, professes to have gone out, and finally ceased. . . . He was the "creature of the Time," they say; the Time called him forth, the Time did everything, he nothing—

but what we the little critic could have done too! This seems
to me but melancholy work. . . .

The great man, with his free force direct out of God's own
hand, is the lightning. His word is the wise healing word
which all can believe in. All blazes round him now, when he
has once struct on it, into fire like his own. . . . In all epochs of
the world's history, we shall find the Great Man to have been
the indispensable saviour of his epoch;—the lightning, without which the fuel never would have burnt. The History of
the World, I said already, was the Biography of Great Men. . . .

In times of unbelief, which soon have to become times of
revolution, much down-rushing, sorrowful decay and ruin is
visible to everybody. For myself in these days, I seem to see in
this indestructibility of Hero-worship the everlasting adamant
lower than which the confused wreck of revolutionary things
cannot fall. . . . It is an eternal corner-stone, from which they
can begin to build themselves up again. That man, in some
sense or other, worships Heroes; that we all of us reverence
and must ever reverence Great Men: this is, to me, the living
rock amid all rushings-down whatsoever;—the one fixed point
in modern revolutionary history, otherwise as if bottomless
and shoreless. . . .

The most significant feature in the history of an epoch is
the manner it has of welcoming a Great Man. Ever, to the
true instincts of men, there is something godlike in him.
Whether they shall take him to be a god, to be a prophet, or
what they shall take him to be, that is ever a grand question;
by their way of answering that, we shall see, as through a
little window, into the very heart of these men's spiritual
condition. For at bottom the Great Man, as he comes from
the hand of nature, is ever the same kind of thing: Odin,
Luther, Johnson, Burns; I hope to make it appear that these
are all originally of one stuff; that only by the world's recep-
tion of them, and the shapes they assume, are they so im-
measurably diverse. . . .

I should say *sincerity*, a deep, great, genuine sincerity, is
the first characteristic of all men in any way heroic. Not the
sincerity that calls itself sincere; ah, no, that is a very poor
matter indeed;—a shallow braggart conscious sincerity; often-
est self-conceit mainly. The Great Man's sincerity is of the
kind he cannot speak of, is not conscious of: nay, I suppose,
he is conscious rather of *in*sincerity; for what man can walk
accurately by the law of truth for one day? No, the Great
Man does not boast himself sincere, far from that; perhaps
does not ask himself if he is so: I would say rather, his

sincerity does not depend on himself; he cannot help being sincere! The great Fact of Existence is great to him. Fly as he will, he cannot get out of the awful presence of this Reality. His mind is so made; he is great by that, first of all. Fearful and wonderful, real as Life, real as death, is this Universe to him. Though all men should forget its truth, and walk in a vain show, he cannot. At all moments the Flame-image glares in upon him; undeniable, there, there!—I wish you to take this as my primary definition of a Great Man. . . .

Such a man is what we call an *original* man: he comes to us at first-hand. A messenger he, sent from the Infinite Unknown with tidings to us. We may call him Poet, Prophet, God;—in one way or other, we all feel that the words he utters are as no other man's words. Direct from the Inner Fact of things;—he lives, and has to live, in daily communion with that. . . .

The Great Man also, to what shall he be bound apprentice? Given your Hero, is he to become Conqueror, King, Philosopher, Poet? It is an inexplicably complex controversial-calculation between the world and him! He will read the world and its laws; the world with its laws will be there to be read. What the world, on *this* matter, shall permit and bid is, as we said, the most important fact about the world.—

Poet and Prophet differ greatly in our loose modern notions of them. In some old languages, again, the titles are synonymous; *Vates* means both Prophet and Poet: and indeed at all times, Prophet and Poet, well understood, have much kindred of meaning. Fundamentally indeed they are still the same; in this most important respect especially, That they have penetrated both of them into the sacred mystery of the Universe; what Goethe calls "the open secret." "Which is the great secret?" asks one.—"The *open* secret,"—open to all, seen by almost none! That divine mystery, which lies everywhere in all Beings, "the Divine Idea of the World, that which lies at the bottom of Appearance," as Fichte styles it; of which all Appearance, from the starry sky to the grass of the field, but especially the Appearance of Man and his work, is but the *vesture*, the embodiment that renders it visible. This divine mystery is in all times and in all places; veritably is. . . .

But now, I say, whoever may forget this divine mystery, the *Vates*, whether Prophet or Poet, has penetrated into it; is a man sent hither to make it more impressively known to us. That always is his message; he is to reveal that to us,—that sacred mystery which he more than others lives ever present with. While others forget it, he knows it;—I might say, he has been driven to know it; without consent asked of *him*, he finds himself living in it, bound to live in it. Once more, here is no Hearsay, but a direct Insight and Belief; this man too could not help being a sincere man! Whosoever may live in the shows of things, it is for him a necessity of nature to live in the very fact of things. A man once more, in earnest with the Universe, though all others were but toying with it. He is a *Vates*, first of all, in virtue of being sincere. So far Poet and Prophet, participators in the "open secret," are one. . . .

The seeing eye! It is this that discloses the inner harmony of things; what Nature meant, what musical idea Nature has wrapped-up in these often rough embodiments. Something she did mean. To the seeing eye that something were discernible. Are they base, miserable things? You can laugh over them, you can weep over them; you can in some way or other genially relate yourself to them;—you can, at lowest, hold your peace about them, turn away your own and others' face from them, till the hour come for practically exterminating and extinguishing them! At bottom, it is the Poet's first gift, as it is all men's, that he have intellect enough. He will be a Poet if he have: a Poet in word; or failing that, perhaps still better, a Poet in act. Whether he write at all; and if so, whether in prose or in verse, will depend on accidents: who knows on what extremely trivial accidents,—perhaps on his having had a singing-master, on his being taught to sing in his boyhood! But the faculty which enables him to discern the inner heart of things, and the harmony that dwells there (for whatsoever exists has a harmony in the heart of it, or it would not hold together and exist), is not the result of habits or accidents, but the gift of Nature herself; the primary outfit for a Heroic Man in what sort soever. . . .

At first view it might seem as if Protestantism were entirely destructive to this that we call Hero-worship, and represent as the basis of all possible good, religious or social, for mankind. One often hears it said that Protestantism introduced a new era, radically different from any the world had ever seen before: the era of "private judgment," as they call it. By this revolt against the Pope, every man became his own Pope; and learnt, among other things, that he must never trust any Pope, or spiritual Hero-captain, any more! Whereby, is not spiritual union, all hierarchy and subordination among men, henceforth an impossibility? So we hear it said.—Now I need not deny that Protestantism was a revolt against spiritual sovereignties, Popes and much else. Nay I will grant that English Puritanism, revolt against earthly sovereignties, was the second act of it; that the enormous French Revolution itself was the third act, whereby all sovereignties earthly and spiritual were, as might seem, abolished or made sure of abolition. Protestantism is the grand root from which our whole subsequent European History branches out. For the spiritual will always body itself forth in the temporal history of men; the spiritual is the beginning of the temporal. And now, sure enough, the cry is everywhere for Liberty and Equality, Independence and so forth: instead of *Kings,* Ballot-boxes and Electoral suffrages; it seems made out that any Hero-sovereign, or loyal obedience of men to a man, in things temporal or things spiritual, has passed away forever from the world. I should despair of the world altogether, if so. One of my deepest convictions is, that it is not so. Without sovereigns, true sovereigns, temporal and spiritual, I see nothing possible but an anarchy: the hatefulest of things. But I find Protestantism, whatever anarchic democracy it may have produced, to be the beginning of new genuine sovereignty and order. I find it to be a revolt against *false* sovereigns; the painful but indispensable first preparative for *true* sovereigns getting place among us! . . .

Hero-worship never dies, nor can die. Loyalty and Sovereignty are everlasting in the world:—and there is this in them, that they are grounded not on garnitures and semblances, but on realities and sincerities. Not by shutting your eyes, your "private judgment"; no, but by opening them, and by having something to see! Luther's message was deposition and abolition to all false Popes and Potentates, but life and strength, though afar off, to new genuine ones.

All this of Liberty and Equality, Electoral suffrages, Independence and so forth, we will take, therefore, to be a temporary phenomenon, by no means a final one. Though likely to last a long time, with sad enough embroilments for us all, we must welcome it, as the penalty of sins that are past, the pledge of inestimable benefits that are coming. . . . In all this wild revolutionary work, from Protestantism downwards, I see the blessedest result preparing itself: not abolition of Hero-worship, but rather what I would call a whole World of Heroes. If Hero mean *sincere man,* why may not every one of us be a Hero? A world all sincere, a believing world: the like has been; the like will again be,—cannot help being. That were the right sort of Worshippers for Heroes: never could the truly Better be so reverenced as where all were True and Good!

(Extracts from Lectures 1, 2, 3 and 4.)

The Modern Hero

Hero-gods, Prophets, Poets, Priests are forms of Heroism that belong to the old ages, make their appearance in the remotest times; some of them have ceased to be possible long since, and cannot any more show themselves in this world. The Hero as *Man of Letters,* again, of which class we are to speak today, is altogether a product of these new ages; and so long as the wondrous art of *Writing,* or of Ready-writing which we call *Printing,* subsists, he may be expected to continue, as one of the main forms of Heroism for all future ages. He is, in various respects, a very singular phenomenon. . . .

Meanwhile, since it is the spiritual always that determines the material, this same Man-of-Letters Hero must be regarded as our most important modern person. He, such as he may be, is the soul of all. What he teaches, the whole world will do and make. The world's manner of dealing with him is the most significant feature of the world's general position. . . .

He is uttering-forth, in such a way as he has, the inspired soul of him; all that a man, in any case, can do. I say *inspired;* for what we call "originality," "sincerity," "genius," the heroic quality we have no good name for, signifies that. The Hero is he who lives in the inward sphere of things, in the True, Divine and Eternal, which exists always, unseen to most, under the Temporary, Trivial: his being is in that; he declares that abroad, by act or speech as it may be, in declaring himself abroad. His life . . . is a piece of the everlasting heart of Nature herself: all men's life is,—but the weak may know not the fact, and are untrue to it, in most times; the strong few are strong, heroic, perennial, because it cannot be hidden from them. . . . I many a time say, the writers of Newspapers, Pamphlets, Poems, Books, these *are* the real working effective Church of a modern country. Nay not only our preaching, but even our worship, is not it too accomplished by means of Printed Books? The noble sentiment which a gifted soul has clothed for us in melodious words, which brings melody into our hearts,—is not this essentially, if we will understand it, of the nature of worship? . . .

Burke said there were Three Estates in Parliament; but, in the Reporters' Gallery yonder, there sat a *Fourth Estate* more important far than they all. It is not a figure of speech, or a witty saying; it is a literal fact,—very momentous to us in these times. Literature is our Parliament too. Printing, which comes necessarily out of Writing, I say often, is equivalent to

Democracy: invent Writing, Democracy is inevitable. Writing brings Printing; brings universal every-day extempore Printing, as we see at present. Whoever can speak, speaking now to the whole nation, becomes a power, a branch of government, with inalienable weight in law-making, in all acts of authority. It matters not what rank he has, what revenues or garnitures: the requisite thing is, that he have a tongue which others will listen to; this and nothing more is requisite. The nation is governed by all that has tongue in the nation: Democracy is virtually *there*. Add only, that whatsoever power exists will have itself, by and by, organised; working secretly under bandages, obscurations, obstructions, it will never rest till it get to work free, unencumbered, visible to all. Democracy virtually extant will insist on becoming palpably extant.

. . . The Commander over men; he to whose will our wills are to be subordinated, and loyally surrender themselves, and find their welfare in doing so, may be reckoned the most important of Great Men. He is practically the summary for us of *all* the various figures of Heroism; Priest, Teacher, whatsoever of earthly or of spiritual dignity we can fancy to reside in a man, embodies itself here, to *command* over us, to furnish us with constant practical teaching, to tell us for the day and hour what we are to do. . . . Find in any country the Ablest Man that exists there; raise *him* to the supreme place, and loyally reverence him: you have a perfect government for that country; no ballot-box, parliamentary eloquence, voting, constitution-building, or other machinery whatsoever can improve it a whit. . . .

This is the history of all rebellions, French Revolutions, social explosions in ancient or modern times. You have put the too *Un*able man at the head of affairs! The too ignoble, unvaliant, fatuous man. You have forgotten that there is any rule, or natural necessity whatever, of putting the Able Man there. . . .

"Hero-worship" becomes a fact inexpressibly precious; the most solacing fact one sees in the world at present. There is an everlasting hope in it for the management of the world. Had all traditions, arrangements, creeds, societies that men ever instituted, sunk away, this would remain. The certainty of Heroes being sent us; our faculty, our necessity, to reverence Heroes when sent: it shines like a polestar through smoke-clouds, dust-clouds, and all manner of down-rushing and conflagration. . . .

Hero-worship exists forever, and everywhere: not Loyalty alone; it extends from divine adoration down to the lowest practical regions of life. "Bending before men," if it is not to be a mere empty grimace, better dispensed with than practised, is Hero-worship,—a recognition that there does dwell in that presence of our brother something divine; that every created man, as Novalis said, is a "revelation in the Flesh." . . . every Great Man, every genuine man, is by the nature of him a son of Order, not of Disorder. It is a tragical position for a true man to work in revolutions. He seems an anarchist; and indeed a painful element of anarchy does encumber him at every step,—him to whose whole soul anarchy is hostile, hateful. His mission is Order.

(Extracts from Lectures 5 and 6.)

FICHTE

The Science of Knowledge

The Ego and Freedom

. . . The act of the reflecting Ego we have characterized as absolutely spontaneous, ideal activity of the Ego. As such it must be posited, that is, as going beyond the limit into the infinite. But to be reflected upon, it can not go into the infinite; hence, in its going beyond the limit, it must nevertheless be limited. There must be a limitation conjointly with the unlimitedness. How?

The activity can not be reflected as activity (the Ego can never become immediately conscious of its activity), but as *substrate*, that is, as product of an absolute activity of the Ego, a product contemplated by the Ego without consciousness of the contemplation. Hence, in so far as the Ego reflects upon the absolute spontaneity of its reflection in the first act, an unlimited product of the activity of the Ego, as such, is posited. This product, posited as product of the Ego, must be placed in relation to the Ego. It can not be related to the contemplating Ego, for this Ego has not yet been posited; it must be related to the Ego which feels itself limited. But this latter Ego is opposed to that Ego which produces through freedom an unlimited; the Ego which feels itself limited is not free, but is under compulsion; and the producing Ego is not compelled, but produces spontaneously.

Thus, indeed, it must be, if relation and synthetical union is to be possible and necessary; and we have only to find the ground of the relation.

This ground must be activity with freedom, or absolute activity. But such an activity can not be predicated of the limited Ego; hence, a union of both seems impossible.

One step more, and we shall find the surprising result, putting an end to all old errors, and reinstating reason for evermore in her eternal rights.

The Ego is to be the relating. Hence, the Ego necessarily, absolutely of itself, and against the outward ground of limitation, proceeds beyond itself, and thus appropriates the product which, through freedom, it makes its own product; ground of relation and the relating link are the same.

Of this act the Ego never becomes conscious, and never can become conscious; its essence consists in absolute spontaneity, and, as soon as you reflect upon it, it ceases to be spontaneity. The Ego is only free in acting; as soon as it reflects upon this act, it ceases to be free, and the act becomes product.

From the impossibility of the consciousness of a free act arises the whole distinction between ideality and reality, between representation and the thing in itself.

Freedom, or, which is the same, the immediate acting of the Ego, is the uniting link of ideality and reality. The Ego *is* free in positing itself as free, in liberating itself; and it posits itself as free, or liberates itself in being free. Determinateness and being are one; acting and product are one; in determining itself to act, the Ego acts; and in acting it determines itself.

The Ego can not posit itself in reflection as free, for this would be a contradiction which could never lead to freedom. But it appropriates something as product of its own free activity, and thus mediately posits itself free.

The Ego is limited in feeling itself, and posits itself in so far as limited. This was our first statement. The Ego is free, and posits itself at least mediately as free, because it posits the limitation as product of its free activity. This was our second statement. Both statements, limitation in feeling and freedom in producing, are utterly opposites. They might be united by showing that the Ego could posit itself in different respects as free and limited. But our statements have distinctly asserted that the Ego is to posit itself as limited, because and in so far as it posits itself free, and *vice versa*. The Ego is to be free and limited in one and the same respect, and this is the contradiction which is to be solved in a third statement. Let us look at the two statements a little closer.

Thesis.

1st. The Ego is to posit itself as limited because and in so far as it posits itself as free; or, the Ego *is* free only in so far as it *acts*. Now, What is acting? What is its distinction from not-acting? All acting, presupposes power. Absolute acting means, a power determining itself solely through and in itself, that is, giving itself a direction. Before, the power had no direction, was latent power, a mere tendency to apply power. The Ego, to posit itself as absolutely acting, must, therefore, in reflection, also be able to posit itself as not-acting. To determine itself as acting presupposes rest.

Again, the power gives itself a direction, that is, an object. Gives itself an object; hence, it must have had the object before; must have received the object passively. Hence, a self-determining to act on the part of the Ego presupposes passivity.

New difficulties everywhere! But from them the clearest light will be thrown upon a subject.

Antithesis.

2d. The Ego is to posit itself as free because and in so far as it posits itself as limited. The Ego posits itself as limited means, it posits a limit to its activity (it does not produce this limit, but posits it as posited by an opposite power, a Non-Ego). Hence, in order to be limited passively, the Ego must previously have acted; its power must have had a direction, and a self-determined direction. All limitation presupposes free activity.

Synthesis.

3d. The Ego is as yet for itself limited, necessitated, in so far as it goes beyond the limitation and posits a Non-Ego which it contemplates without self-consciousness. Now, this Non-Ego is, as we have seen from our higher stand-point, a product of the Ego, and the Ego must reflect upon it as its product. This reflection necessarily occurs through absolute self-activity.

But the Ego, this very same activity, can not, at the same time, produce a Non-Ego and reflect upon it as its production.

Hence, it must interrupt its first activity; and must so interrupt it through absolute spontaneity. Only thus, indeed, is absolute spontaneity possible. For the Ego is to determine itself. But the Ego is in essence nothing but activity. Hence, it must limit one of its acts; and, because it is nothing but activity, it must limit the act by another opposite act.

Again, the Ego is to posit its product, the opposite Non-Ego *as* its product. Through the same act which interrupts the first one it thus posits the Non-Ego, and elevates it to a higher degree of reflection. The lower, first region of reflection is thus broken off; and all we have to do now is to seek the point of union of both forms of reflection. But since the Ego is never immediately conscious of its acting, it can posit the product as its product only through a new reflection by mediation.

Through this new reflection the product must be posited as product of absolute freedom, the distinctive characteristic whereof is, that it might be otherwise, or might be posited otherwise. Contemplation floats between several determinations, and posits amongst all possible determinations only one, whereby the product receives the peculiar character of an *image*.

In so far as the Ego posits this image as product of its activity, it necessarily opposes to it something which is not its product, which is no longer determinable, but perfectly determined, and thus determined through itself, not through the Ego. This is the *real thing* by which the Ego is guided in sketching its image and which must necessarily appear to it in its representation.

(From the Second Part of the Theoretical Part.)

The Dignity of Man

Philosophy teaches us to look for everything in knowledge, in the Ego. Only through it is order and harmony brought into the dead, formless matter. From man alone does regularity proceed and extend around him. . . . His observation marks out for each object of the infinite diversity its proper place, so that no one may crowd out the other, and brings unity into this infinite variety. By his observations are the heavenly bodies kept together, and form but one organized body; by it the suns move in their appointed courses. Through reason there arises the immense gradation from the worm to the seraph; in it is hidden the system of the whole spirit-world; and man expects justly that the law, which he gives it and himself, shall be applicable to it; expects justly the future universal acknowledgment of that law. In reason we have the sure guarantee that from it there will proceed, in infinite development, order and harmony, where at present none yet exists; that the culture of the universe will progress simultaneously with the advancing culture of mankind. All that is still unshaped and orderless will, through man, develop into the most beautiful order, and that which is already harmonious will become ever more harmonious, according to laws not yet developed. Man will extend order into the shapeless mass, and a plan into universal chaos; through him will corruption form a new creation, and death call to another glorious life.

Such is man, if we merely view him as an observing intelligence; how much greater if we think him as a practical, active faculty? Not only does he apply the necessary order to existing things. He gives them also that order which he selected voluntarily, wherever his footsteps led him. Nature awakens wherever his eyes are cast; she prepares herself to receive from him the new, brighter creation. Even his body is the most spiritualized that could be formed from the matter surrounding him. In his atmosphere the air becomes softer, the climate milder, and nature assumes a brighter smile from the expectation to be changed by him into a dwelling-place and a nurse of living beings. Man commands coarse matter to organize itself according to his ideal, and to furnish him the substance which he needs. What was formerly dead and cold arises at his command from the earth into the nourishing corn, the refreshing fruit, and the animating grape, and will arise into other things as soon as he shall command otherwise. In his sphere the animals become ennobled, cast aside under his intelligent eye their primitive wildness, and receive healthier nourishment from the hand of their master, which they repay by willing obedience.

Still more: around man souls become ennobled; the more a man is a man the more deeply and extensively does he influence men; whatsoever carries the stamp of pure humanity will never be misapprehended by mankind; every human mind, every human heart opens to each pure outflow of humanity. Around the nobler man his fellow-beings form a circle, in which he approaches nearest to the centre who has the greatest humanity. Their souls strive and labor to unite with each other to form but one soul in many bodies. All are one reason and one will, and appear as co-laborers in the great, only possible destination of mankind. The higher man draws by force his age upon a higher step of humanity; the age looks back and is astonished at the gap over which it has leaped; the higher man tears with giant arms whatever he can seize from the year-book of the human race.

Break the hut of clay in which he lives! In his being he is independent of all that is outward; he is simply through himself; and even in that hut of clay he is occasionally, in the hours of his exaltation, seized with a knowledge of this his real existence; in those hours, when time and space and every thing that is not himself vanish, when his soul tears itself by force from his body—returning to it afterward voluntarily in order to carry out those designs, which it would like to carry out yet by means of that body. Separate the two last neighboring atoms, which at present surround him, and he will still be;

and he will be, because it will be his will to be. He is eternal through himself, and by his own power.

Oppose, frustrate his plans! You may delay them; but what are thousand and thousand times thousand years in the year-book of mankind?—a light morning dream when we awake. He continues and he continues to act, and that which appears to you as his disappearance is but an extension of his sphere; what you look upon as death is but ripening for a higher life. The colors of his plans, and the outward forms of them may vanish to him, but his plan remains the same, and in every moment of his existence he tears something from the outward into his own circle; and he will continue thus to tear unto himself until he has devoured every thing; until all matter shall bear the impress of his influence, and all spirits shall form one spirit with his spirit.

Such is man; such is every one who can say to himself: I am man. Should he not then carry within him a holy self-reverence, and shudder and tremble at his own majesty? Such is every one who can say to me: I am. Wherever thou mayest live, thou, who carryest but a human face; whether thou plantest sugar-cane under the rod of the overseer, as yet scarcely distinguishable from the brute creation; or whether thou warmest thyself on the shores of the Fireland at the flame, which thou didst not kindle, until it expires, and weepest bitterly because it will not keep burning by itself; or whether thou appearest to me the most miserable and degraded villain, thou art, nevertheless, what I am; for thou canst say to me: I am. Thou art, nevertheless, my comrade and my brother. Ah! at one time surely I also stood on that step of humanity on which thou now standest—for it is a step of humanity, and there is no gap in the development of its members—perhaps without the faculty of clear consciousness, perhaps hurrying over it so quickly that I had not time to become conscious of my condition; but I certainly stood there also at one time—and thou wilt also stand certainly at some time, even though it lasted million and million times million years—for what is time?—upon the same step on which I now stand; and thou wilt surely at some time stand upon a step, where I can influence thee and thou me. Thou also wilt at some time be drawn into my circle, and wilt draw me into thine. Thee also will I recognize at some time as my co-laborer in my great plan. Such is to me, who am I, every one, who is I. Should I not tremble at the majesty in the form of man, and at the divinity which resides in the temple that bears his impress, though perhaps concealed in mysterious darkness?

Earth and heaven and time and space, and all the limits of materiality, vanish in my sight at this thought, and should not the individual vanish? I shall not conduct you back to him.

All individuals are included in the one great unity of pure spirit. Let this be the last word with which I recommend myself to your remembrance, and the remembrance to which I recommend myself to you.

(Extract from *The Dignity of Man*, 1794.)

HEGEL

The Philosophy of Right

The Idea of Freedom

. . . the ethical order is freedom or the absolute will as what is objective, a circle of necessity whose moments are the ethical powers which regulate the life of individuals. To these powers individuals are related as accidents to substance, and it is in individuals that these powers are represented, have the shape of appearance, and become actualized. . . .[1]

The bond of duty can appear as a restriction only on indeterminate subjectivity or abstract freedom, and on the impulses either of the natural will or of the moral will which determines its indeterminate good arbitrarily. The truth is, however, that in duty the individual finds his liberation; first, liberation from dependence on mere natural impulse and from the depression which as a particular subject he cannot escape in his moral reflections on what ought to be and what might be; secondly, liberation from the indeterminate subjectivity which, never reaching reality or the objective determinacy of action, remains self-enclosed and devoid of actuality. In duty the individual acquires his substantive freedom. . . .

The right of individuals to be subjectively destined to freedom is fulfilled when they belong to an actual ethical order, because their conviction of their freedom finds its truth in such an objective order, and it is in an ethical order that they are actually in possession of their own essence or their own inner universality.

[1] Since the laws and institutions of the ethical order make up the concept of freedom, they are the substance or universal essence of individuals, who are thus related to them as accidents only. Whether the individual exists or not is all one to the objective ethical order. It alone is permanent and is the power regulating the life of individuals. Thus the ethical order has been represented by mankind as eternal justice, as gods absolutely existent, in contrast with which the empty business of individuals is only a game of see-saw.

When a father inquired about the best method of educating his son in ethical conduct, a Pythagorean replied: "Make him a citizen of a state with good laws."

The right of individuals to their *particular* satisfaction is also contained in the ethical substantial order, since particularity is the outward appearance of the ethical order—a mode in which that order is existent.

Hence in this identity of the universal will with the particular will, right and duty coalesce, and by being in the ethical order a man has rights in so far as he has duties, and duties in so far as he has rights. In the sphere of abstract right, I have the right and another has the corresponding duty. In the moral sphere, the right of my private judgement and will, as well as of my happiness, has not, but only ought to have, coalesced with duties and become objective.

The ethical substance, as containing independent self-consciousness united with its concept, is the actual mind of a family and a nation.

The concept of this Idea has been only as mind, as something knowing itself and actual, because it is the objectification of itself, the movement running through the form of its moments. It is therefore

(A) ethical mind in its natural or immediate phase—the *Family*. This substantiality loses its unity, passes over into division, and into the phase of relation, i.e. into

(B) *Civil Society*—an association of members as self-subsistent individuals in a universality which, because of their self-subsistence, is only abstract. Their association is brought about by their needs, by the legal system—the means to security of person and property—and by an external organization for attaining their particular and common interests. This external state

(C) is brought back to and welded into unity in the *Constitution of the State* which is the end and actuality of both the substantial universal order and the public life devoted thereto.

(Extracts from Part 3, sections 145, 149, 153–157.)

The State

The state is the actuality of the ethical Idea. . . . The state is absolutely rational inasmuch as it is the actuality of the substantial will which it possesses in the particular self-consciousness once that consciousness has been raised to consciousness of its universality. This substantial unity is an absolute unmoved end in itself, in which freedom comes into its supreme right. On the other hand this final end has supreme right against the individual, whose supreme duty is to be a member of the state.

If the state is confused with civil society, and if its specific end is laid down as the security and protection of property and personal freedom, then the interest of the individuals as such becomes the ultimate end of their association, and it follows that membership of the state is something optional. But the state's relation to the individual is quite different from this. Since the state is mind objectified, it is only as one of its members that the individual himself has objectivity, genuine individuality, and an ethical life. Unification pure and simple is the true content and aim of the individual, and the individual's destiny is the living of a universal life. His further particular satisfaction, activity, and mode of conduct have this substantive and universally valid life as their starting point and their result. . . .

But if we ask what is or has been the historical origin of the state in general, still more if we ask about the origin of any particular state, of its rights and institutions, or again if we inquire whether the state originally arose out of patriarchal conditions or out of fear or trust, or out of Corporations, &c., or finally if we ask in what light the basis of the state's rights has been conceived and consciously established, whether this basis has been supposed to be positive divine right, or contract, custom, &c.—all these questions are no concern of the Idea of the state. We are here dealing exclusively with the philosophic science of the state, and from that point of view all these things are mere appearance and therefore matters for history. So far as the authority of any existing state has anything to do with reasons, these reasons are culled from the forms of the law authoritative within it.

The philosophical treatment of these topics is concerned only with their inward side, with the thought of their concept. The merit of Rousseau's contribution to the search for this concept is that, by adducing the will as the principle of the state, he is adducing a principle which has thought both for its form and its content, a principle indeed which is thinking itself, not a principle, like gregarious instinct, for instance, or divine authority, which has thought as its form only. Unfortunately, however, as Fichte did later, he takes the will only in a determinate form as the individual will, and he regards the universal will not as the absolutely rational element in the will, but only as a "general" will which proceeds out of this individual will as out of a conscious will. The result is that he reduces the union of individuals in the state to a contract and therefore to something based on their arbitrary wills, their opinion, and their capriciously given express consent; and abstract reasoning proceeds to draw the logical inferences which destroy the absolutely divine principle of the state, together with its majesty and absolute authority. For this reason, when these abstract conclusions came into power, they afforded for the first time in human history the prodigious spectacle of the overthrow of the constitution of a great actual state and its complete reconstruction *ab initio* on the basis of pure thought alone, after the destruction of all existing and given material. The will of its re-founders was to give it what they alleged was a purely rational basis, but it was only abstractions that were being used; the Idea was lacking; and the experiment ended in the maximum of frightfulness and terror.

Confronted with the claims made for the individual will, we must remember the fundamental conception that the objective will is rationality implicit or in conception, whether it be recognized or not by individuals, whether their whims be deliberately for it or not. We must remember that its opposite, i.e. knowing and willing, or subjective freedom (the *only* thing contained in the principle of the individual will) comprises only one moment, and therefore a one-sided moment, of the Idea of the rational will, i.e. of the will which is rational solely because what it is implicitly, that it also is explicitly.[2] The Idea of the state

[2] The state in and by itself is the ethical whole, the actualization of freedom; and it is an absolute end of reason that freedom should be actual. The state is mind on earth and consciously realizing itself there. In nature, on the other hand, mind actualizes itself only as its own other, as mind asleep. Only when it is present in consciousness, when it knows itself as a really existent object, is it the state. In considering freedom, the starting-point must be not individuality, the single self-consciousness, but only the essence of self-consciousness; for whether man knows it or not, this essence is externally realized as a self-subsistent power in which single individuals are only moments. The march of God in the world, that is what the state is. The basis of the state is the power of reason actualizing itself as will. In considering the Idea of the state, we must not have our eyes on particular states or on particular institutions. Instead we must consider the Idea, this actual God, by itself. On some principle or other, any state may be shown to be bad, this or that defect may be found in it; and yet, at any rate if one of the mature states of our epoch is in question, it has in it the moments essential to the existence of the state. But since it is easier to find defects than to understand the affirmative, we may readily fall into the mistake of looking at isolated aspects of the state and so forgetting its inward organic life. The state is no ideal work of art; it stands on earth and so in the sphere of caprice, chance, and error, and bad behavior may disfigure it in many respects. But the ugliest of men, or a criminal, or an invalid, or a cripple, is still always a living man. The affirmative, life, subsists despite his defects, and it is this affirmative factor which is our theme here.

(*a*) has immediate actuality and is the individual state as a self-dependent organism—the *Constitution* or *Constitutional Law;*

(*b*) passes over into the relation of one state to other states —*International Law;*

(*c*) is the universal Idea as a genus and as an absolute power over individual states—the mind which gives itself its actuality in the process of *World-History*.[3]

The state is the actuality of concrete freedom. But concrete freedom consists in this, that personal individuality and its particular interests not only achieve their complete development and gain explicit recognition for their right (as they do in the sphere of the family and civil society) but, for one thing, they also pass over of their own accord into the interest of the universal, and, for another thing, they know and will the universal; they even recognize it as their own substantive mind; they take it as their end and aim and are active in its pursuit. The result is that the universal does not prevail or achieve completion except along with particular interests and through the co-operation of particular knowing and willing; and individuals likewise do not live as private persons for their own ends alone, but in the very act of willing these they will the universal in the light of the universal, and their activity is consciously aimed at none but the universal end. The principle of modern states has prodigious strength and depth because it allows the principle of subjectivity to progress to its culmination in the extreme of self-subsistent personal particularity, and yet at the same time brings it back to the substantive unity and so maintains this unity in the principle of subjectivity itself.

In contrast with the spheres of private rights and private welfare (the family and civil society), the state is from one point of view an external necessity and their higher authority; its nature is such that their laws and interests are subordinate to it and dependent on it. On the other hand, however, it is

---

[3] The state in its actuality is essentially an individual state, and beyond that a particular state. Individuality is to be distinguished from particularity. The former is a moment in the very Idea of the state, while the latter belongs to history. States as such are independent of one another, and therefore their relation to one another can only be an external one, so that there must be a third thing standing above them to bind them together. Now this third thing is the mind which gives itself actuality in world-history. The one and only absolute judge, which makes itself authoritative against the particular and at all times, is the absolute mind which manifests itself in the history of the world as the universal and as the genus there operative.

the end immanent within them, and its strength lies in the unity of its own universal end and aim with the particular interest of individuals, in the fact that individuals have duties to the state in proportion as they have rights against it. . . .

Particular interests should in fact not be set aside or completely suppressed; instead, they should be put in correspondence with the universal, and thereby both they and the universal are upheld. The *isolated* individual, so far as his duties are concerned, is in subjection; but as a member of *civil society* he finds in fulfilling his duties to it protection of his person and property, regard for his private welfare, the satisfaction of the depths of his being, the consciousness and feeling of himself as a member of the whole; and, in so far as he completely fulfills his duties by performing tasks and services for the *state*, he is upheld and preserved. Take duty abstractly, and the universal's interest would consist simply in the completion as duties of the tasks and services which it exacts.

. . . it is often reiterated nowadays that religion is the basis of the state, and because those who make this assertion even have the impertinence to suggest that, once it is made, political science has said its last word. No doctrine is more fitted to produce so much confusion, more fitted indeed to exalt confusion itself to be the constitution of the state and the proper form of knowledge. . . .

The essence of the relation between religion and the state can be determined, however, only if we recall the concept of religion. The content of religion is absolute truth, and consequently the religious is the most sublime of all dispositions. As intuition, feeling, representative knowledge, its task is concentrated upon God as the unrestricted principle and cause on which everything hangs. It thus involves the demand that everything else shall be seen in this light and depend on it for corroboration, justification, and verification. It is in being thus related to religion that state, laws, and duties all alike acquire for consciousness their supreme confirmation and their supreme obligatoriness, because even the state, laws, and duties are in their actuality something determinate which passes over into a higher sphere and so into that on which it is grounded. . . . The state is the divine will, in the sense that it is mind present on earth, unfolding itself to be the actual shape and organization of a world. Those who insist on stopping at the form of *religion*, as opposed to the state, are acting like those logicians who think they are right if they continually stop at the essence and refuse to advance beyond that abstraction to existence, or like those moralists . . . who will only good in the abstract and leave it to caprice to decide what is good. . . .

(Extracts from sections 257–261.)

The Monarch

. . . The truth of subjectivity . . . is attained only in a subject, and the truth of personality only in a person; and in a constitution which has become mature as a realization of rationality, each of the three moments of the concept has its explicitly actual and separate formation. Hence this absolutely decisive moment of the whole is not individuality in general, but a single individual, the monarch. . . .

Hence it is the basic moment of personality, abstract at the start in immediate rights, which has matured itself through its various forms of subjectivity, and now—at the stage of absolute rights, of the state, of the completely concrete objectivity of the will—has become the personality of the state, its certainty of itself. This last reabsorbs all particularity into its single self, cuts short the weighing of pros and cons between which it lets itself oscillate perpetually now this way and now that, and by saying "I will" makes its decision and so inaugurates all activity and actuality. . . .

It is only as a person, the monarch, that the personality of the state is actual. Personality expresses the concept as such; but the person enshrines the actuality of the concept, and only when the concept is determined as person is it the Idea or truth. A so-called "artificial person," be it a society, a community, or a family, however inherently concrete it may be, contains personality only abstractly, as one moment of itself. In an "artificial person," personality has not achieved its true mode of existence. The state, however, is precisely this totality in which the moments of the concept have attained the actuality correspondent to their degree of truth. . . .

The conception of the monarch is . . . of all conceptions the hardest for ratiocination, i.e. for the method of reflection employed by the Understanding. This method refuses to move beyond isolated categories and hence here again knows only *raisonnement*, finite points of view, and deductive argumentation. Consequently it exhibits the dignity of the monarch as something deduced, not only in its form, but in its essence. The truth is, however, that to be something not deduced but purely self-originating is precisely the conception of monarchy. Akin, then, to this reasoning is the idea of treating the monarch's right as grounded in the authority of God, since it is in its divinity that its unconditional character is contained.

We are familiar, however, with the misunderstandings connected with this idea, and it is precisely this "divine" element which it is the task of a philosophic treatment to comprehend. . . .

(Extract from section 279.)

War and International Relations

. . . This destiny whereby the rights and interests of individuals are established as a passing phase, is at the same time the positive moment, i.e. the positing of their absolute, not their contingent and unstable, individuality. This relation and the recognition of it is therefore the individual's substantive duty, the duty to maintain this substantive individuality, i.e. the independence and sovereignty of the state, at the risk and the sacrifice of property and life, as well as of opinion and everything else naturally comprised in the compass of life.

An entirely distorted account of the demand for this sacrifice results from regarding the state as a mere civil society and from regarding its final end as only the security of individual life and property. This security cannot possibly be obtained by the sacrifice of what is to be secured—on the contrary.

The ethical moment in war is implied in what has been said in this Paragraph. War is not to be regarded as an absolute evil and as a purely external accident, which itself therefore has some accidental cause, be it injustices, the passions of nations or the holders of power, &c., or in short, something or other which ought not to be. It is to what is by nature accidental that accidents happen, and the fate whereby they happen is thus a necessity. Here as elsewhere, the point of view from which things seem pure accidents vanishes if we look at them in the light of the concept and philosophy, because philosophy knows accident for a show and sees in it its essence, necessity. It is necessary that the finite—property and life—should be definitely established as accidental, because accidentality is the concept of the finite. From one point of view this necessity appears in the form of the power of nature, and everything is mortal and transient. But in the ethical substance, the state, nature is robbed of this power, and the necessity is exalted to be the work of freedom, to be something ethical. The transience of the finite becomes a willed passing away, and the negativity lying at the roots of the finite becomes the substantive individuality proper to the ethical substance.

War is the state of affairs which deals in earnest with the vanity of temporal goods and concerns—a vanity at other times a common theme of edifying sermonizing. This is what makes it the moment in which the ideality of the particular attains its right and is actualized. War has the higher significance that by its agency . . . "the ethical health of peoples is preserved in their indifference to the stabilization of finite institutions; just as the blowing of the winds preserves the sea from the foulness which would be the result of a prolonged calm, so also corruption in nations would be the product of prolonged, let alone 'perpetual,' peace." This, however, is said to be only a philosophic idea, or, to use another common expression, a "justification of Providence," and it is maintained that actual wars require some other justification.

The ideality which is in evidence in war, i.e. in an accidental relation of a state to a foreign state, is the same as the ideality in accordance with which the domestic powers of the state are organic moments in a whole. This fact appears in history in various forms, e.g. successful wars have checked domestic unrest and consolidated the power of the state at home. . . .

Sacrifice on behalf of the individuality of the state is the substantial tie between the state and all its members and so is a universal duty. Since this tie is a *single* aspect of the ideality, as contrasted with the reality, of subsistent particulars, it becomes at the same time a *particular* tie, and those who are in it form a class of their own with the characteristic of courage. . . .

The fundamental proposition of international law (i.e. the universal law which ought to be absolutely valid between states, as distinguished from the particular content of positive treaties) is that treaties, as the ground of obligations between states, ought to be kept. But since the sovereignty of a state is the principle of its relations to others, states are to that extent in a state of nature in relation to each other. Their rights are actualized only in their particular wills and not in a universal will with constitutional powers over them. This universal proviso of international law therefore does not go beyond an ought-to-be, and what really happens is that international relations in accordance with treaty alternate with the severance of these relations. . . .

It is as particular entities that states enter into relations with one another. Hence their relations are on the largest scale a maelstrom of external contingency and the inner particularity of passions, private interests and selfish ends, abilities and virtues, vices, force, and wrong. All these whirl together, and in their vortex the ethical whole itself, the autonomy of the state, is exposed to contingency. The principles of the national minds are wholly restricted on account of their particularity, for it is in this particularity that, as existent individuals, they have their objective actuality and their self-consciousness. Their deeds and destinies in their reciprocal relations to one another are the dialectic of the finitude of these minds, and out of it arises the universal mind, the mind of the world, free from all restriction, producing itself as that which exercises its right—and its right is the highest right of all—over these finite minds in the "history of the world which is the world's court of judgement."

(Extracts from sections 324, 325, 333 and 340.)

World History

The element in which the universal mind exists in art is intuition and imagery, in religion feeling and representative thinking, in philosophy pure freedom of thought. In world history this element is the actuality of mind in its whole compass of internality and externality alike. World history is a court of judgement because in its absolute universality, the particular—i.e. the *Penates,* civil society, and the national minds in their variegated actuality—is present as only ideal, and the movement of mind in this element is the exhibition of that fact.

Further, world history is not the verdict of mere might, i.e. the abstract and non-rational inevitability of a blind destiny. On the contrary, since mind is implicitly and actually reason, and reason is explicit to itself in mind as knowledge, world history is the necessary development, out of the concept of mind's freedom alone, of the moments of reason and so of the self-consciousness and freedom of mind. This development is the interpretation and actualization of the universal mind. . . .

In the course of this work of the world mind, states, nations, and individuals arise animated by their particular determinate principle which has its interpretation and actuality in their constitutions and in the whole range of their life and condition. While their consciousness is limited to these and they are absorbed in their mundane interests, they are all the time the unconscious tools and organs of the world mind at work within them. The shapes which they take pass away, while the absolute mind prepares and works out its transition to its next higher stage.

Justice and virtue, wrongdoing, power and vice, talents and their achievements, passions strong and weak, guilt and innocence, grandeur in individual and national life, autonomy, fortune and misfortune of states and individuals, all these have their specific significance and worth in the field of known actuality; therein they are judged and therein they have their partial, though only partial, justification. World-history, however, is above the point of view from which these things matter. Each of its stages is the presence of a necessary moment in the Idea of the world mind, and that moment attains its absolute right in that stage. The nation whose life embodies this moment secures its good fortune and fame, and its deeds are brought to fruition.

History is mind clothing itself with the form of events or the immediate actuality of nature. The stages of its development are therefore presented as immediate natural principles. These, because they are natural, are a plurality external to one another, and they are present therefore in such a way that each of them is assigned to one nation in the external form of its geographical and anthropological conditions.

The nation to which is ascribed a moment of the Idea in the form of a natural principle is entrusted with giving complete effect to it in the advance of the self-developing self-consciousness of the world mind. This nation is dominant in world history during this one epoch, and it is only once that it can make its hour strike. In contrast with this its absolute right of being the vehicle of this present stage in the world mind's development, the minds of the other nations are without rights, and they, along with those whose hour has struck already, count no longer in world history. . . .

(Extracts from sections 341–342, 344–347.)

SECTION **IV**

UTILITARIANISM

The utilitarians were a group of writers, politicians and administrators of whom Jeremy Bentham (1748–1832), James Mill (1773–1836) and John Stuart Mill (1806–1873) are the leading figures; the major relevant works are Bentham's *An Introduction to the Principles of Morals and Legislation*, James Mill's *An Essay on Government* and J. S. Mill's *Utilitarianism*. They were interested both in the formulation of political rules and a science of politics, and in the practical need for legal and social reform and efficient, centralized, rationally comprehensible political institutions. The theoretical concepts of utilitarianism were simple, if ambiguous. Its practical impact was substantial, for many of the mid-nineteenth-century reforms, in law, tariffs, political representation, municipal government, colonial relationships, poor law, aid to education, were the work of men who regarded themselves as utilitarians. With considerable justification, J. S. Mill called Bentham the father of English innovation, the great subversive, the great critical thinker of his age and country.

Utilitarianism was essentially a British phenomenon, a philosophy based on empirical investigation, hedonism, the association of ideas and a liberal and humane approach to political and economic affairs. Bentham rejected explanation through the "pretended law of nature," which was really only an author's sentiment or opinion. For the utilitarian, the study of politics could be based on simple rules and principles, obtained by empirical inquiry into human nature and the motivations of human behavior. In this way, a scientific politics and ethics could be formulated. The theory was both scientific and moralistic at the same time, a discussion both of what is and what ought to be.

The fundamental principle was that men, acting in their own self-interest, sought pleasure and avoided pain, the two qualities which determined behavior. Pleasure alone was regarded as good; pain was seen as evil. The utility of anything, therefore, depended on its contribution to the first and its avoidance of the latter.

Government, acting according to the principle of utility, sought to increase pleasure and decrease pain, and thus attained the greatest happiness of the greatest number. Its business was to promote the happiness of society by punishing and rewarding actions. Calculation of behavior was based on two premises: the first, that since men always acted according to self-interest, one could deduce how they would act, and the second, that the equal pleasures of individuals were equally good. Government could then use the complicated felicific calculus which measured the various seven factors on which depended the value of the fourteen simple pleasures and the twelve simple pains. By calculating the relative amounts of pleasure and pain produced by any action, the legislator could know whether or not it was beneficial. Yet the ambiguity of the formula, by which either the greatest *amount* of happiness or the greatest *number* of people involved could be stressed, remained.

The theory was one not only of self-interest, but also of egoism and individualism. The community, for Bentham, was a fictitious body, composed of the individual persons who are considered as constituting its members. Yet part of the function of the legislator was to lead men, by a variety of means, to perform actions that resulted in the pleasure of others as well as in their own and that would make their private interest coincide with the general interest. The gentle and kindly Bentham, opposed to all brutality, himself argued that in him, selfishness somehow took the form of benevolence: "The question is not, can they talk, can they reason, but can they suffer."

The utilitarians brought back the concept of sovereignty, largely neglected since Hobbes. Their chief legal theoretician, John Austin, argued that laws are the commands of the sovereign power, which technically was unlimited. The primary interest of Bentham himself was in the reform of the law, so as to obtain efficiency, codification and simplification of procedure. His humaneness was shown by the length of time and the intensity with which he fought for a Panopticon, his model prison, and his code of criminal law by which crimes would be punished in less barbaric and extreme fashion than was customary in his day.

Bentham applied his rationalistic approach and his questioning spirit to all social institutions. Always afraid of "sinister interests"—those entrenched in positions of power—he argued the desirability of annual elections, the secret ballot and recall. Political power ought to be in the hands of a representative assembly that would not be prevented from introducing the necessary reforms. Like the eighteenth-century *philosophes*, Bentham thought that the extension of the educational process and of literacy would reduce not only ignorance but also antisocial tendencies. And like them, he thought there would be an automatic acceptance of those fitted to rule, the competent middle class. For the utilitarians, representative government was the method by which opposing egoisms could be harmonized and chaos avoided.

The functions of government were essentially limited: the maintenance of security and the provision of sustenance, abundance and equality. The economic principles of utilitarianism were essentially those of Adam Smith, argued in *The Wealth of Nations* of 1776, which held that the individual, acting in his own self-interest, unconsciously promoted the good of the whole society. The functions of the state in economic matters should be reduced to a minimum, since individuals ought to be able to act without undue restriction in conditions of free trade and free competition. Smith, by his searching inquiry into the nature of economic behavior, laid the foundation of the science of economics, provided an economic interpretation of history and put forward the labor theory of value, to be adopted by Marx as the basis for his criticism of capitalism.

The first great systematic criticism of utilitarianism came from John Stuart Mill, the son of Bentham's chief disciple, and perhaps the most highly and intensively educated child in recorded history. In his *Autobiography*, J. S. Mill acknowledged the debt he owed to Wordsworth and the romantic poets whom he discovered at twenty during the nervous breakdown that followed his intensive education. They showed him the importance of the intuitive truths that the austerely rationalistic utilitarianism had neglected. Throughout his life, Mill attempted to combine rationalism and romanticism, intellectual culture with "other kinds of cultivation," though the former always dominated his work.

Against the utilitarian thesis, Mill argued that life had more important ends than simply the pursuit of pleasure. Moreover, not all pleasures were equally valuable—the factor ignored in the felicific calculus was quality. That pleasure preferred by the best judges was of a higher kind than others. Simple hedonism was abandoned; for J. S. Mill, the cultivation of feelings and the development of character were equally important. Bentham had never recognized man as a being capable of pursuing spiritual perfection as an end.

Yet Mill is more significant for his discussion of and contribution to liberalism than for his utilitarianism. It is his defense of free speech and of individuality, his attempt to show the importance of a large variety of types of character in society, his fear that public opinion was encroaching on liberty and his belief that limits ought to be set on the legitimate interference of collective opinion with individual independence, that make Mill one of the great nineteenth-century theorists. Dissatisfied with utilitarianism and simple rationalism, John Stuart Mill also became aware of the insufficiency of classical liberalism. His advocacy of state action, compulsory state education and increased social control made him, at the end of his life, call himself a socialist.

ADAM SMITH
The Wealth of Nations

The Division of Labour

This division of labour, from which so many advantages are derived, is not originally the effect of any human wisdom, which foresees and intends that general opulence to which it gives occasion. It is the necessary, though very slow and gradual, consequence of a certain propensity in human nature which has in view no such extensive utility; the propensity to truck, barter, and exchange one thing for another.

Whether this propensity be one of those original principles in human nature, of which no further account can be given; or whether, as seems more probable, it be the necessary consequence of the faculties of reason and speech, it belongs not to our present subject to enquire. It is common to all men, and to be found in no other race of animals, which seem to know neither this nor any other species of contracts. . . . In civilized society [man] stands at all times in need of the cooperation and assistance of great multitudes, while his whole life is scarce sufficient to gain the friendship of a few persons. In almost every other race of animals each individual, when it is grown up to maturity, is entirely independent, and in its natural state has occasion for the assistance of no other living creature. But man has almost constant occasion for the help of his brethren, and it is in vain for him to expect it from their benevolence only. He will be more likely to prevail if he can interest their self-love in his favour, and shew them that it is for their own advantage to do for him what he requires of them. Whoever offers to another a bargain of any kind, proposes to do this. Give me that which I want, and you shall have this which you want, is the meaning of every such offer; and it is in this manner that we obtain from one another the far greater part of those good offices which we stand in need of. It is not from the benevolence of the butcher, the brewer, or the baker, that we expect our dinner, but from their regard to their own interest. We address ourselves, not to their humanity but to their self-love, and never talk to them of our own necessities but of their advantages. Nobody but a beggar chooses to depend chiefly upon the benevolence of his fellow-citizens. Even a beggar does not depend upon it entirely. . . .

As it is by treaty, by barter, and by purchase, that we obtain from one another the greater part of those mutual good offices which we stand in need of, so it is this same trucking disposition which originally gives occasion to the division of labour. In a tribe of hunters or shepherds a particular person makes bows and arrows, for example, with more readiness and dexterity than any other. He frequently exchanges them for cattle or for venison with his companions; and he finds at last that he can in this manner get more cattle and venison, than if he himself went to the field to catch them. From a regard to his own interest, therefore, the making of bows and arrows grows to be his chief business, and he becomes a sort of armourer. Another excels in making the frames and covers of their little huts or moveable houses. He is accustomed to be of use in this way to his neighbours, who reward him in the same manner with cattle and with venison, till at last he finds it his interest to dedicate himself entirely to this employment, and to become a sort of house-carpenter. In the same manner a third becomes a smith or a brazier; a fourth a tanner or dresser of hides or skins, the principal part of the clothing of savages. And thus the certainty of being able to exchange all that surplus part of the produce of his own labour, which is over and above his own consumption, for such parts of the produce of other men's labour as he may have occasion for, encourages every man to apply himself to a particular occupation, and to cultivate and bring to perfection whatever talent or genius he may possess for that particular species of business.

The difference of natural talents in different men is, in reality, much less than we are aware of; and the very different genius which appears to distinguish men of different professions, when grown up to maturity, is not upon many occasions so much the cause, as the effect of the division of labour. The difference between the most dissimilar characters, between a philosopher and a common street porter, for example, seems to arise not so much from nature, as from habit, custom, and education. When they came into the world, and for the first six or eight years of their existence, they were, perhaps, every much alike, and neither their parents nor playfellows could perceive any remarkable difference. About that age, or soon after, they come to be employed in very different occupations. The difference of talents comes then to be taken notice of, and widens by degrees, till at last the vanity of the philosopher is willing to acknowledge scarce any resemblance. But without the disposition to truck, barter, and exchange, every man must have procured to himself every necessary and conveniency of life which he wanted. All must have had the same duties to perform, and the same work to do, and there could have been no such difference of employment as could alone give occasion to any great difference of talents.

As it is this disposition which forms that difference of talents, so remarkable among men of different professions, so it is this same disposition which renders that difference useful. Many tribes of animals acknowledged to be all of the same species, derive from nature a much more remarkable distinction of genius, than what, antecedent to custom and education, appears to take place among men. By nature a philosopher is not in genius and disposition half so different from a street porter, as a mastiff is from a greyhound, or a greyhound from a spaniel, or this last from a shepherd's dog. Those different tribes of animals, however, though all of the same species, are of scarce any use to one another. . . . Each animal is still obliged to support and defend itself, separately and independently, and derives no sort of advantage from that variety of talents with which nature has distinguished its fellows. Among men, on the contrary, the most dissimilar geniuses are of use to one another; the different produces of their respective talents, by the general disposition to truck, barter, and exchange, being brought, as it were, into a common stock, where every man may purchase whatever part of the produce of other men's talents he has occasion for.

(Extract from Book I, chapter 2.)

Private Interest and Public Benefit

The whole of the advantages and disadvantages of the different employments of labour and stock must, in the same neighbourhood, be either perfectly equal or continually tending to equality. If in the same neighbourhood, there was any employment evidently either more or less advantageous than the rest, so many people would crowd into it in the one case, and so many would desert it in the other, that its advantages would soon return to the level of other employments. This at least would be the case in a society where things were left to follow their natural course, where there was perfect liberty, and where every man was perfectly free both to chuse what occupation he thought proper, and to change it as often as he thought proper. Every man's interest would prompt him to seek the advantageous, and to shun the disadvantageous employment. . . .

Whatever . . . we may imagine the real wealth and revenue of a country to consist in, whether in the value of the annual produce of its land and labour, as plain reason seems to dictate; or in the quantity of the precious metals which circulate within it, as vulgar prejudices suppose; in either view of the matter, every prodigal appears to be a public enemy, and every frugal man a public benefactor.

The effects of misconduct are often the same as those of prodigality. Every injudicious and unsuccessful project in agriculture, mines, fisheries, trade, or manufactures, tends in the same manner to diminish the funds destined for the maintenance of productive labour. In every such project, though the capital is consumed by productive hands only, yet, as by the injudicious manner in which they are employed, they do not reproduce the full value of their consumption, there must always be some diminution in what would otherwise have been the productive funds of the society.

It can seldom happen, indeed, that the circumstances of a great nation can be much affected either by the prodigality or misconduct of individuals; the profusion or imprudence of some, being always more than compensated by the frugality and good conduct of others.

With regard to profusion, the principle which prompts to expence, is the passion for present enjoyment; which, though sometimes violent and very difficult to be restrained, is in general only momentary and occasional. But the principle which prompts to save, is the desire of bettering our condition, a desire which, though generally calm and dispassionate, comes with us from the womb, and never leaves us till we go into the grave. In the whole interval which separates those two moments, there is scarce perhaps a single instant in which any man is so perfectly and completely satisfied with his situation, as to be without any wish of alteration or improvement of any kind. An augmentation of fortune is the means by which the greater part of men propose and wish to better their condition. It is the means the most vulgar and the most obvious; and the most likely way of augmenting their fortune, is to save and accumulate some part of what they acquire, either regularly and annually, or upon some extraordinary occasions. Though the principle of expence, therefore, prevails in almost all men upon some occasions, and in some men upon almost all occasions, yet in the greater part of men, taking the whole course of their life at an average, the principle of frugality seems not only to predominate, but to predominate very greatly.

With regard to misconduct, the number of prudent and successful undertakings is every-where much greater than that of injudicious and unsuccessful ones. . . . Bankruptcy is perhaps the greatest and most humiliating calamity which can befal an innocent man. The greater part of men, therefore, is sufficiently careful to avoid it. Some, indeed, do not avoid it; as some do not avoid the gallows.

Great nations are never impoverished by private, though they sometimes are by public prodigality and misconduct. The whole, or almost the whole public revenue, is in most countries employed in maintaining unproductive hands. Such are the people who compose a numerous and splendid court, a great ecclesiastical establishment, great fleets and armies, who in time of peace produce nothing, and in time of war acquire nothing which can compensate the expence of maintaining them, even while the war lasts. Such people, as they themselves produce nothing, are all maintained by the produce of other men's labour. When multiplied, therefore, to an unnecessary number, they may in a particular year consume so great a share of this produce, as not to leave a sufficiency for maintaining the productive labourers, who should reproduce it next year. The next year's produce, therefore, will be less than that of the foregoing, and if the same disorder should continue, that of the third year will be still less than that of the second. Those unproductive hands, who should be maintained by a part only of the spare revenue of the people, may consume so great a share of their whole revenue, and therefore oblige so great a number to encroach upon their capitals, upon the funds destined for the maintenance of productive labour, that all the frugality and good conduct of individuals may not be able to compensate the waste and degradation of produce occasioned by this violent and forced encroachment.

This frugality and good conduct, however, is upon most occasions, it appears from experience, sufficient to compensate, not only the private prodigality and misconduct of individuals, but the public extravagance of government. The uniform, constant, and uninterrupted effort of every man to better his condition, the principle from which public and national, as well as private opulence is originally derived, is frequently powerful enough to maintain the natural progress of things toward improvement, in spite both of the extravagance of government, and of the greatest errors of administration. Like the unknown principle of animal life, it frequently restores health and vigour to the constitution, in spite, not only of the disease, but of the absurd prescriptions of the doctor. . . .

The general industry of the society never can exceed what the capital of the society can employ. As the number of workmen that can be kept in employment by any particular person must bear a certain proportion to his capital, so the number of those that can be continually employed by all the members of a great society, must bear a certain proportion to the whole capital of that society, and never can exceed that proportion. No regulation of commerce can increase the quantity of industry in any society beyond what its capital can maintain. It can only divert a part of it into a direction into which it might not otherwise have gone; and it is by no means certain that this artificial direction is likely to be more advantageous to the society than that into which it would have gone of its own accord.

Every individual is continually exerting himself to find out the most advantageous employment for whatever capital he can command. It is his own advantage, indeed, and not that of the society, which he has in view. But the study of his own advantage naturally, or rather necessarily leads him to prefer that employment which is most advantageous to the society.

First, every individual endeavours to employ his capital as near home as he can, and consequently as much as he can in the support of domestic industry; provided always that he can thereby obtain the ordinary, or not a great deal less than the ordinary profits of stock.

Thus, upon equal or nearly equal profits, every wholesale merchant naturally prefers the home-trade to the foreign trade of consumption, and the foreign trade of consumption to the carrying trade. In the home-trade his capital is never so long out of his sight as it frequently is in the foreign trade of consumption. He can know better the character and situation of the persons whom he trusts, and if he should happen to be deceived, he knows better the laws of the country from which he must seek redress. . . . Home is . . . the center . . . round

which the capitals of the inhabitants of every country are
continually circulating, and towards which they are always
tending, though by particular causes they may sometimes be
driven off and repelled from it towards more distant employments. But a capital employed in the home-trade . . . necessarily puts into motion a greater quantity of domestic industry, and gives revenue and employment to a greater number of
the inhabitants of the country, than an equal capital employed
in the foreign trade of consumption: and one employed in the
foreign trade of consumption has the same advantage over an
equal capital employed in the carrying trade. Upon equal, or
only nearly equal profits, therefore, every individual naturally inclines to employ his capital in the manner in which it
is likely to afford the greatest support to domestic industry,
and to give revenue and employment to the greatest number
of people of his own country.

Secondly, every individual who employs his capital in the
support of domestic industry, necessarily endeavours so to
direct that industry, that its produce may be of the greatest
possible value.

The produce of industry is what it adds to the subject or
materials upon which it is employed. In proportion as the
value of this produce is great or small, so will likewise be the
profits of the employer. But it is only for the sake of profit
that any man employs a capital in the support of industry;
and he will always, therefore, endeavour to employ it in the
support of that industry of which the produce is likely to be
of the greatest value, or to exchange for the greatest quantity
either of money or of other goods.

But the annual revenue of every society is always precisely
equal to the exchangeable value of the whole annual produce
of its industry, or rather is precisely the same thing with that
exchangeable value. As every individual, therefore, endeavours as much as he can both to employ his capital in the
support of domestic industry, and so to direct that industry
that its produce may be of the gratest value; every individual
necessarily labours to render the annual revenue of the society
as great as he can. He generally, indeed, neither intends to
promote the public interest, nor knows how much he is pro-
moting it. By preferring the support of domestic to that of
foreign industry, he intends only his own security; and by
directing that industry in such a manner as its produce may
be of the greatest value, he intends only his own gain, and he
is in this, as in many other cases, led by an invisible hand to
promote an end which was no part of his intention. Nor is it
always the worse for the society that it was no part of it. By

pursuing his own interest he frequently promotes that of the society more effectually than when he really intends to promote it. I have never known much good done by those who affected to trade for the public good. It is an affectation, indeed, not very common among merchants, and very few words need be employed in dissuading them from it.

What is the species of domestic industry which his capital can employ, and of which the produce is likely to be of the greatest value, every individual, it is evident, can, in his local situation, judge much better than any statesman or lawgiver can do for him. The statesman, who should attempt to direct private people in what manner they ought to employ their capitals, would not only load himself with a most unnecessary attention, but assume an authority which could safely be trusted, not only to no single person, but to no council or senate whatever, and which would nowhere be so dangerous as in the hands of a man who had folly and presumption enough to fancy himself fit to exercise it.

To give the monopoly of the home-market to the produce of domestic industry, in any particular art or manufacture, is in some measure to direct private people in what manner they ought to employ their capitals, and must, in almost all cases, be either a useless or a hurtful regulation. If the produce of domestic can be brought there as cheap as that of foreign industry, the regulation is evidently useless. If it cannot, it must generally be hurtful. It is the maxim of every prudent master of a family, never to attempt to make at home what it will cost him more to make than to buy. . . .

What is prudence in the conduct of every private family, can scarce be folly in that of a great kingdom. If a foreign country can supply us with a commodity cheaper than we ourselves can make it, better buy it of them with some part of the produce of our own industry, employed in a way in which we have some advantage. The general industry of the country, being always in proportion to the capital which employs it, will not thereby be diminished . . . but only left to find out the way in which it can be employed with the greatest advantage. It is certainly not employed to the greatest advantage, when it is thus directed towards an object which it can buy cheaper than it can make. . . . The industry of the country, therefore, is thus turned away from a more, to a less advantageous employment, and the exchangeable value of its annual produce, instead of being increased, according to the intention of the lawgiver, must necessarily be diminished by every such regulation.

The improvement and prosperity of Great Britain, which

has been so often ascribed to [the corn] laws, may very easily be accounted for by other causes. That security which the laws in Great Britain give to every man that he shall enjoy the fruits of his own labour, is alone sufficient to make any country flourish, notwithstanding these and twenty other absurd regulations of commerce; and this security was perfected by the revolution, much about the same time that the bounty was established. The natural effort of every individual to better his own condition, when suffered to exert itself with freedom and security, is so powerful a principle, that it is alone, and without any assistance, not only capable of carrying on the society to wealth and prosperity, but of surmounting a hundred impertinent obstructions with which the folly of human laws too often incumbers its operations; though the effect of these obstructions is always more or less either to encroach upon its freedom, or to diminish its security. In Great Britain industry is perfectly secure; and though it is far from being perfectly free, it is as free or freer than in any other part of Europe. . . .

Though the same capital never will maintain the same quantity of productive labour in a distant as in a near employment, yet a distant employment may be as necessary for the welfare of the society as a near one; the goods which the distant employment deals in being necessary, perhaps, for carrying on many of the nearer employments. But if the profits of those who deal in such goods are above their proper level, those goods will be sold dearer than they ought to be, or somewhat above their natural price, and all those engaged in the nearer employments will be more or less oppressed by this high price. Their interest, therefore, in this case requires that some stock should be withdrawn from those nearer employments, and turned towards that distant one, in order to reduce its profits to their proper level, and the price of the goods which it deals in to their natural price. In this extraordinary case, the public interest requires that some stock should be withdrawn from those employments which in ordinary cases are more advantageous, and turned towards one which in ordinary cases is less advantageous to the public: and in this extraordinary case, the natural interests and inclinations of men coincide as exactly with the public interest as in all other ordinary cases, and lead them to withdraw stock from the near, and to turn it towards the distant employment.

It is thus that the private interests and passions of individuals naturally dispose them to turn their stock towards the employments which in ordinary cases are most advantageous to the society. But if from this natural preference they should turn too much of it towards those employments, the fall of profit in them and the rise of it in all others immediately dispose them to alter this faulty distribution. Without any intervention of law, therefore, the private interests and passions of men naturally lead them to divide and distribute the stock of every society, among all the different employments carried on in it, as nearly as possible in the proportion which is most agreeable to the interest of the whole society.

(Extracts from Book I, chapter 10; Book II, chapter 3; Book IV, chapters 2, 5 and 7.)

BENTHAM

An Introduction to the Principles of Morals and Legislation

The Principle of Utility

1. Nature has placed mankind under the governance of two sovereign masters, "pain" and "pleasure." It is for them alone to point out what we ought to do, as well as to determine what we shall do. On the one hand the standard of right and wrong, on the other the chain of causes and effects, are fastened to their throne. They govern us in all we do, in all we say, in all we think: every effort we can make to throw off our subjection, will serve but to demonstrate and confirm it. In words a man may pretend to abjure their empire: but in reality he will remain subject to it all the while. The "principle of utility" recognizes this subjection, and assumes it for the foundation of that system, the object of which is to rear the fabric of felicity by the hands of reason and of law. Systems which attempt to question it, deal in sounds instead of senses, in caprice instead of reason, in darkness instead of light.

But enough of metaphor and declamation: it is not by such means that moral science is to be improved.

2. The principle of utility is the foundation of the present work: it will be proper therefore at the outset to give an explicit and determinate account of what is meant by it. By the principle of utility is meant that principle which approves or disapproves of every action whatsoever, according to the tendency which it appears to have to augment or diminish the happiness of the party whose interest is in question: or, what is the same thing in other words, to promote or to oppose that happiness. I say of every action whatsoever; and therefore not only of every action of a private individual, but of every measure of government.

3. By utility is meant that property in any object, whereby

it tends to produce benefit, advantage, pleasure, good, or happiness, (all this in the present case comes to the same thing) or (what comes again to the same thing) to prevent the happening of mischief, pain, evil, or unhappiness to the party whose interest is considered: if that party be the community in general, then the happiness of the community: if a particular individual, then the happiness of that individual.

4. The interest of the community is one of the most general expressions that can occur in the phraseology of morals: no wonder that the meaning of it is often lost. When it has a meaning, it is this. The community is a fictitious "body," composed of the individual persons who are considered as constituting as it were its "members." The interest of the community then is, what?—the sum of the interests of the several members who compose it.

5. It is in vain to talk of the interest of the community, without understanding what is the interest of the individual. A thing is said to promote the interest, or to be "for" the interest, of an individual, when it tends to add to the sum total of his pleasures: or, what comes to the same thing, to diminish the sum total of his pains.

6. An action then may be said to be conformable to the principle of utility, or, for shortness' sake, to utility, (meaning with respect to the community at large) when the tendency it has to augment the happiness of the community is greater than any it has to diminish it.

7. A measure of government (which is but a particular kind of action, performed by a particular person or persons) may be said to be conformable to or dictated by the principle of utility, when in like manner the tendency which it has to augment the happiness of the community is greater than any it has to diminish it.

8. When an action, or in particular a measure of government, is supposed by a man to be conformable to the principle of utility, it may be convenient, for the purposes of discourse to imagine a kind of law or dictate, called a law or dictate of utility; and to speak of the action in question as being conformable to such law or dictate.

9. A man may be said to be a partizan of the principle of utility, when the approbation or disapprobation he annexes to any action, or to any measure, is determined by and proportioned to the tendency which he conceives it to have to augment or to diminish the happiness of the community: or in other words, to its conformity or unconformity to the laws or dictates of utility.

10. Of an action that is conformable to the principle of utility one may always say either that it is one that ought to be done, or at least that it is not one that ought to be done. One may also say, that it is right it should be done; at least that it is not wrong it should be done: that it is a right action; at least that it is not a wrong action. When thus interpreted, the words "ought," and "right" and "wrong," and others of that stamp, have a meaning; when otherwise, they have none.

(Extract from chapter 1.)

Pleasure and Pain

It has been shown that the happiness of the individuals, of whom a community is composed, that is their pleasures and their security, is the end and the sole end which the legislator ought to have in view: the sole standard, in conformity to which each individual ought, as far as depends upon the legislator, to be "made" to fashion his behavior. But whether it be this or anything else that is to be "done," there is nothing by which a man can ultimately be "made" to do it, but either pain or pleasure. Having taken a general view of these two grand objects (viz., pleasure, and what comes to the same thing, immunity from pain) in the character of "final" causes; it will be necessary to take a view of pleasure and pain itself, in the character of "efficient" causes or means. . . .

I. Pleasures then, and the avoidance of pains, are the "ends" which the legislator has in view: it behoves him therefore to understand their "value." Pleasures and pains are the "instruments" he has to work with: it behoves him therefore to understand their force, which is again, in other words, their value.

II. To a person considered by "himself," the value of a pleasure or pain considered by "itself," will be greater or less, according to the four following circumstances:

    1. Its "intensity."
    2. Its "duration."
    3. Its "certainty" or "uncertainty."
    4. Its "propinquity" or "remoteness."

III. These are the circumstances which are to be considered in estimating a pleasure or a pain considered each of them by itself. But when the value of any pleasure or pain is considered for the purpose of estimating the tendency of any "act" by which it is produced, there are two other circumstances to be taken into account; these are,

5. Its "fecundity," or the chance it has of being followed by sensations of the "same" kind: that is, pleasures, if it be a pleasure: pains, if it be a pain.
6. Its "purity," or the chance it has of "not" being followed by sensations of the "opposite" kind: that is, pains, if it be a pleasure: pleasures, if it be a pain.

These two last, however, are in strictness scarcely to be deemed properties of the pleasure or the pain itself; they are not, therefore, in strictness to be taken into the account of the value of that pleasure or that pain. They are in strictness to be deemed properties only of the act, or other event, by which such pleasure or pain has been produced; and accordingly are only to be taken into the account of the tendency of such act or such event.

IV. To a "number" of persons, with reference to each of whom the value of a pleasure or a pain is considered, it will be greater or less, according to seven circumstances: to wit, the six preceding ones; viz.
1. Its "intensity."
2. Its "duration."
3. Its "certainty" or "uncertainty."
4. Its "propinquity" or "remoteness."
5. Its "fecundity."
6. Its "purity."
And one other; to wit:
7. Its "extent": that is, the number of persons to whom it "extends"; or [in other words] who are affected by it.
(Extracts from chapters 3 and 4.)

JAMES MILL
An Essay on Government

The End of Government

. . . We may allow . . . in general terms that the lot of every human being is determined by his pains and pleasures, and that his happiness corresponds with the degree in which his pleasures are great and his pains are small. Human pains and pleasures are derived from two sources: they are produced either by our fellow men or by causes independent of other men. We may assume it as another principle that the concern of government is with the former of these two sources: that its business is to increase to the utmost the pleasures, and diminish to the utmost the pains, which men derive from one another.

Of the laws of nature on which the condition of man depends, that which is attended with the greatest number of consequences is the necessity of labor for obtaining the means of subsistence as well as the means of the greatest part of our pleasures. This is no doubt the primary cause of government; for if nature had produced spontaneously all the objects which we desire, and in sufficient abundance for the desires of all, there would have been no source of dispute or of injury among men, nor would any man have possessed the means of ever acquiring authority over another.

The results are exceedingly different when nature produces the objects of desire not in sufficient abundance for all. The source of dispute is then exhaustless, and every man has the means of acquiring authority over others in proportion to the quantity of those objects which he is able to possess. In this case the end to be obtained through government as the means is to make that distribution of the scanty materials of happiness which would insure the greatest sum of it in the members of the community taken altogether, preventing every individual or combination or individuals from interfering with that distribution or making any man to have less than his share.

. . . it is obvious that every man who has not all the objects of his desire has inducement to take them from any other man who is weaker than himself: and how is he to be prevented? One mode is sufficiently obvious, and it does not appear that there is any other: the union of a certain number of men to protect one another. The object, it is plain, can best be attained when a great number of men combine and delegate to a small number the power necessary for protecting them all. This is government. . . .

Whenever the powers of government are placed in any hands other than those of the community—whether those of one man, of a few, or of several—those principles of human nature which imply that government is at all necessary imply that those persons will make use of them to defeat the very end for which government exists. . . .

A man is never satisfied with a smaller degree if he can obtain a greater. And as there is no man whatsoever whose acts, in some degree or other, in some way or other, more immediately or more remotely, may not have some influence as means to our ends, there is no man the conformity of whose acts to our will we would not give something to secure.

The demand, therefore, of power over the acts of other men is really boundless. It is boundless in two ways: boundless in the number of persons to whom we would extend it, and boundless in its degree over the actions of each.

It would be nugatory to say, with a view to explain away this important principle, that some human beings may be so remotely connected with our interests as to make the desire of a conformity between our will and their actions evanescent. It is quite enough to assume, that nobody will deny, that our desire of that conformity is unlimited in respect to all those men whose actions can be supposed to have any influence on our pains and pleasures. With respect to the rulers of a community this at least is certain, that they have a desire for the conformity between their will and the actions of every man in the community. And for our present purpose this is as wide a field as we need to embrace.

With respect to the community, then, we deem it an established truth that the rulers, one or a few, desire an exact conformity between their will and the acts of every member of the community. It remains for us to inquire to what description of acts it is the nature of this desire to give existence.

There are two classes of means by which the conformity between the will of one man and the acts of other men may be accomplished. The one is pleasure, the other pain.

With regard to securities of the pleasurable sort for obtaining a conformity between one man's will and the acts of other men, it is evident from experience that when a man possesses a command over the objects of desire he may, by imparting those objects to other men, insure to a great extent conformity between his will and their actions. It follows, and is also matter of experience, that the greater the quantity of the objects of desire which he may thus impart to other men, the greater is the number of men between whose actions and his own will he can insure a conformity. As it has been demonstrated that there is no limit to the number of men whose actions we desire to have conformable to our will, it follows with equal evidence that there is no limit to the command which we desire to possess over the objects which insure this result.

It is, therefore, not true that there is in the mind of a king, or in the minds of an aristocracy, any point of saturation with the objects of desire. The opinion . . . that a king or an aristocracy may be satiated with the objects of desire and, after being satiated, leave to the members of the community the greater part of what belongs to them, is an opinion founded upon a partial and incomplete view of the laws of human nature. . . .

Pleasure appears to be a feeble instrument of obedience in comparison with pain. It is much more easy to despise pleasure than pain. Above all, it is important to consider that in this class of instruments is included the power of taking away life, and with it of taking away not only all the pleasures of reality but, what goes so far beyond them, all the pleasures of hope. . . . He who desires obedience to a high degree of exactness cannot be satisfied with the power of giving pleasure, he must have the power of inflicting pain. . . .

A man desires that the actions of other men shall be instantly and accurately correspondent to his will. He desires that the actions of the greatest possible number shall be so. Terror is the grand instrument. Terror can work only through assurance that evil will follow any want of conformity between the will and the actions willed.

. . . the very principle of human nature upon which the necessity of government is founded—the propensity of one man to possess himself of the objects of desire at the cost of another—leads on, by infallible sequence, where power over a community is attained and nothing checks, not only to that degree of plunder which leaves the members (excepting always the recipients and instruments of the plunder) the bare means of subsistence, but to that degree of cruelty which is necessary to keep in existence the most intense terror. . . .

(Extracts from chapters 1, 2, 4 and 5.)

The Value of a Representative System

. . . we may be told that good government appears to be impossible. The people as a body cannot perform the business of government for themselves. If the powers of government are entrusted to one man or a few men, and a monarchy or governing aristocracy is formed, the results are fatal; and it appears that a combination of the simple forms is impossible.

Notwithstanding the truth of these propositions, it is not yet proved that good government is unattainable. For though the people, who cannot exercise the powers of government themselves, must entrust them to some one individual or set of individuals, and such individuals will infallibly have the strongest motives to make a bad use of them, it is possible that checks may be found sufficient to prevent them. . . . It is sufficiently conformable to the established and fashionable opinions to say that upon the right constitution of checks all goodness of government depends. . . .

In the grand discovery of modern times, the system of representation, the solution of all the difficulties both speculative and practical will perhaps be found. If it cannot, we seem to be forced upon the extraordinary conclusion that good government is impossible. For as there is no individual or combination of individuals, except the community itself, who would not have an interest in bad government if entrusted with its powers, and as the community itself is incapable of exercising those powers and must entrust them to some individual or combination of individuals, the conclusion is obvious: the community itself must check those individuals, else they will follow their interest and produce bad government. . . .

We may begin by laying down two propositions which appear to involve a great portion of the inquiry, and about which it is unlikely that there will be any dispute.

1. The checking body must have a degree of power sufficient for the business of checking.

2. It must have an identity of interest with the community, otherwise it will make a mischievous use of its power. . . .

There can be no doubt that if power is granted to a body of men, called representatives, they, like any other men, will use their power, not for the advantage of the community, but for their own advantage, if they can. The only question is, therefore, how they can be prevented; in other words, how are the interests of the representatives to be identified with those of the community?

Each representative may be considered in two capacities: in his capacity of representative, in which he has the exercise of power over others, and in his capacity of member of the community, in which others have the exercise of power over him.

If things were so arranged that, in his capacity of representative, it would be impossible for him to do himself so much good by misgovernment as he would do himself harm in his capacity of member of the community, the object would be accomplished. . . . But if the power assigned to the representative cannot be diminished in amount, there is only one other way in which it can be diminished, and that is in duration.

This, then, is the instrument: lessening of duration is the instrument by which, if by anything, the object is to be attained. The smaller the period of time during which any man retains his capacity of representative, as compared with the time in which he is simply a member of the community, the more difficult it will be to compensate the sacrifice of the interests of the longer period by the profits of misgovernment during the shorter. . . .

(Extracts from chapters 6 and 7.)

JOHN STUART MILL
Essay on Utilitarianism

The Qualification of Utilitarianism

. . . It is quite compatible with the principle of utility to recognize the fact that some kinds of pleasure are more desirable and more valuable than others. It would be absurd that, while in estimating all other things quality is considered as well as quantity, the estimation of pleasure should be supposed to depend on quantity alone.

If I am asked what I mean by difference of quality in pleasures, or what makes one pleasure more valuable than another, merely as a pleasure, except its being greater in amount, there is but one possible answer. Of two pleasures, if there be one to which all or almost all who have experience of both give a decided preference, irrespective of any feeling of moral obligation to prefer it, that is the more desirable pleasure. If one of the two is, by those who are competently acquainted with both, placed so far above the other that they prefer it, even though knowing it to be attended with a greater amount of discontent, and would not resign it for any quantity of the other pleasure which their nature is capable of, we are justified in ascribing to the preferred enjoyment a superiority in quality so far outweighing quantity as to render it, in comparison, of small account.

Now it is an unquestionable fact that those who are equally acquainted with and equally capable of appreciating and enjoying both do give a most marked preference to the manner of existence which employs their higher faculties. . . . A being of higher faculties requires more to make him happy, is capable probably of more acute suffering, and certainly accessible to it at more points, than one of an inferior type; but in spite of these liabilities, he can never really wish to sink into what he feels to be a lower grade of existence. We may give what explanation we please of this unwillingness; we may attribute it to pride, a name which is given indiscriminately to some of the most and to some of the least estimable feelings of which mankind is capable; we may refer it to the love of liberty and personal independence, an appeal to which was with the Stoics one of the most effective means for the inculcation of it; to the love of power or to the love of excitement, both of which do really enter into and contribute to it; but its most appropriate appellation is a sense of dignity, which all human beings possess in one form or other, and in some, though by no means in exact, proportion to their higher faculties, and which is so essential a part of the happiness of those in whom it is strong that nothing which conflicts with it could be otherwise than momentarily an object of desire to them. Whoever supposes that this preference takes place at a sacrifice of happiness—that the superior being, in anything like equal circumstances, is not happier than the inferior—confounds the two very different ideas of happiness and content. It is indisputable that the being whose capacities of enjoyment are low has the greatest chance of having them fully satisfied; and a highly endowed being will always feel that any happiness which he can look for, as the world is constituted, is imperfect. But he can learn to bear its imperfections, if they are at all bearable; and they will not make him envy the being who is indeed unconscious of the imperfections, but only because he feels not at all the good which those imperfections qualify. It is better to be a human being dissatisfied than a pig satisfied; better to be Socrates dissatisfied than a fool satisfied. And if the fool, or the pig, are of a different opinion, it is because they only know their own side of the question. The other party to the comparison knows both sides. . . .

On a question which is the best worth having of two pleasures, or which of two modes of existence is the most grateful to the feelings, apart from its moral attributes and from its consequences, the judgment of those who are qualified by knowledge of both, or, if they differ, that of the majority among them, must be admitted as final. And there needs be the less hesitation to accept this judgment respecting the quality of pleasures, since there is no other tribunal to be referred to even on the question of quantity. What means are there of determining which is the acutest of two pains, or the intensest of two pleasurable sensations, except the general suffrage of those who are familiar with both? Neither pains nor pleasures are homogeneous, and pain is always heterogeneous with pleasure. What is there to decide whether a particular pleasure is worth purchasing at the cost of a particular pain, except the feelings and judgment of the experienced? When, therefore, those feelings and judgment declare the pleasures derived from the higher faculties to be preferable *in kind,* apart from the question of intensity, to those of which the animal nature, disjoined from the higher faculties, is susceptible, they are entitled on this subject to the same regard.

I have dwelt on this point as being a necessary part of a perfectly just conception of utility or happiness considered as the directive rule of human conduct. But it is by no means an indispensable condition to the acceptance of the utilitarian standard; for that standard is not the agent's own greatest happiness, but the greatest amount of happiness altogether; and if it may possibly be doubted whether a noble character is always the happier for its nobleness, there can be no doubt that it makes other people happier, and that the world in general is immensely a gainer by it. Utilitarianism, therefore, could only attain its end by the general cultivation of noble-ness of character, even if each individual were only benefited by the nobleness of others, and his own, so far as happiness is concerned, were a sheer deduction from the benefit. But the bare enunciation of such an absurdity as this last renders refutation superfluous.

. . . another class of objectors . . . say that happiness, in any form, cannot be the rational purpose of human life and ac-tion; because, in the first place, it is unattainable; and they contemptuously ask, What right hast thou to be happy? . . .

If by happiness be meant a continuity of highly pleasurable excitement, it is evident enough that this is impossible. A state of exalted pleasure lasts only moments or in some cases, and with some intermissions, hours or days, and is the occasional brilliant flash of enjoyment, not its permanent and steady flame. Of this the philosophers who have taught that happi-ness is the end of life were as fully aware as those who taunt them. The happiness which they meant was not a life of rapture, but moments of such, in an existence made up of few and transitory pains, many and various pleasures, with a de-cided predominance of the active over the passive, and having as the foundation of the whole not to expect more from life than it is capable of bestowing. A life thus composed, to those who have been fortunate enough to obtain it, has always appeared worthy of the name of happiness. And such an existence is even now the lot of many during some consider-able portion of their lives. The present wretched education and wretched social arrangements are the only real hindrance to its being attainable by almost all. . . .

When people who are tolerably fortunate in their outward lot do not find in life sufficient enjoyment to make it valuable to them, the cause generally is caring for nobody but them-selves. . . . Next to selfishness, the principal cause which makes life unsatisfactory is want of mental cultivation. A cultivated mind—I do not mean that of a philosopher, but any mind to which the fountains of knowledge have been opened, and which has been taught, in any tolerable degree, to exercise its faculties—finds sources of inexhaustible interest in

all that surrounds it: in the objects of nature, the achievements of art, the imaginations of poetry, the incidents of
history, the ways of mankind, past and present, and their
prospects in the future. It is possible, indeed, to become indifferent to all this, and that too without having exhausted a
thousandth part of it, but only when one has had from the
beginning no moral or human interest in these things and has
sought in them only the gratification of curiosity. . . .

Though it is only in a very imperfect state of the world's
arrangements that anyone can best serve the happiness of
others by the absolute sacrifice of his own, yet, so long as the
world is in that imperfect state, I fully acknowledge that the
readiness to make such a sacrifice is the highest virtue which
can be found in man. I will add that in this condition of the
world, paradoxical as the assertion may be, the conscious
ability to do without happiness gives the best prospect of
realizing such happiness as is attainable. . . .

The utilitarian morality does recognize in human beings the
power of sacrificing their own greatest good for the good of
others. It only refuses to admit that the sacrifice is itself a
good. A sacrifice which does not increase or tend to increase
the sum total of happiness, it considers as wasted. The only
self-renunciation which it applauds is devotion to the happiness, or to some of the means of happiness, of others, either
of mankind collectively or of individuals within the limits
imposed by the collective interests of mankind.

I must again repeat what the assailants of utilitarianism
seldom have the justice to acknowledge, that the happiness
which forms the utilitarian standard of what is right in conduct is not the agent's own happiness but that of all concerned. As between his own happiness and that of others,
utilitarianism requires him to be as strictly impartial as a
disinterested and benevolent spectator. In the golden rule of
Jesus of Nazareth, we read the complete spirit of the ethics of
utility. "To do as you would be done by," and "to love your
neighbor as yourself," constitute the ideal perfection of utilitarian morality. As the means of making the nearest approach
to this ideal, utility would enjoin, first, that laws and social
arrangements should place the happiness or (as, speaking
practically, it may be called) the interest of every individual
as nearly as possible in harmony with the interest of the
whole; and, secondly, that education and opinion, which have
so vast a power over human character, should so use that
power as to establish in the mind of every individual an indissoluble association between his own happiness and the good
of the whole . . . so that not only he may be unable to

conceive the possibility of happiness to himself, consistently with conduct opposed to the general good, but also that a direct impulse to promote the general good may be in every individual one of the habitual motives of action, and the sentiments connected therewith may fill a large and prominent place in every human being's sentient existence. . . .

SECTION V

EARLY SOCIALISM AND POSITIVISM

The vast industrial and social changes of the nineteenth century produced more numerous and complex problems than in any previous period. The new industrialization had brought bitter industrial relationships, cyclical and technological unemployment and the growth of towns, along with the general increase in prosperity. Protest against the anarchy, misery and squalor of the new conditions took many forms—including the purely destructive, as with the Luddites, who smashed machinery; the philanthropic and humanitarian, as with Shaftesbury and Charles Kingsley; the aesthetic, as with John Ruskin; as well as the more revolutionary. The movements of discontent in England and France were varied: the trade union and cooperative organizations, the struggle for factory legislation and the ten-hour day, the fight against the poor law, the Chartist movement, the use of the strike, the proposals for new communal settlements.

In the 1830's the word "socialism" was coined independently in both England and France. The writers referred to, by Marx and others, as "Utopian Socialists," did not form a group or agree on a common analysis, solution or platform. But they were critics of the established social order and industrial system, hostile to the idea of capitalism—the word itself was coined by them—and often also to competition and private property, and all believed that conditions could and ought to be improved. Of these thinkers, Robert Owen in England, and Fourier, Cabet, Proudhon and Saint-Simon in France, were the most important.

These writers have been called utopians and are criticized for propounding overly-simple analyses of the economic system, for denying the reality of class antagonisms, for rejecting all political, and especially all revolutionary action, for their belief in automatic harmony and peace, for their appeals to the feelings and purses of the *bourgeoisie* and for conjuring up fantastic pictures of future society. Yet if the utopians were often naïve or over-optimistic in their proposals, their writings also contained realistic and incisive analyses. Their themes included the importance of the environment and of the economic system in conditioning character and behavior, the labor theory of value, the nature of surplus value and exploitation, the class struggle, the nature of economic crises, the need for communal ownership, the role of the proletariat and the role of credit in the financial system. The Marxists owed more than they pretended to the arguments of the utopians.

Proudhon

One of the earliest victims of Marx's vituperative attacks was Pierre Joseph Proudhon (1809–1865), self-educated editor and pamphleteer, who had a strong influence on the First International, the Paris Commune and the French syndicalist movement. Of peasant origin, and a self-styled "man of the people," Proudhon was the spokesman for the individualism of the small farmer, rather than for the proletariat. He was no builder of systems, but argued for an end to privilege, the abolition of slavery, the equality of rights and the reign of law. Social change should occur peacefully, with the cooperation of the *bourgeoisie*, and without destroying tradition or family solidarity. Proudhon attacked the power of finance capitalism, preceding Keynes in his analysis of the role of the *rentier*, and argued for the institution of credit unions, popular banks and cooperatives. But he was equally opposed to the claim of trade unions to collective bargaining and the right to strike, and to plans of any future uniform society. For him, Marx was "the tapeworm of socialism" whose dictatorship of the masses would in reality lead to general serfdom.

Proudhon was essentially a libertarian, searching for a free society and for those associations through which the "social republic" might be reached and workers take over their natural inheritance. He constantly attacked centralization of government and industry, believing that it should be replaced by federalism, decentralization, regionalism and mutuality, in which power would be derived from natural groups and working units rather than imposed from above. His emphasis on the federal nature of economic and social organizations and his dislike of political activity was to affect not only the French working-class movements, but also the ideas of Bakunin and Herzen, the Russian anarchists.

Positivism

The contemporary economist Hayek has argued that both modern socialism and modern positivism are essentially reactionary and authoritarian movements. Claude Henri Comte de Saint-Simon (1760–1825) is the link between early socialist thought and positivism. His adventurous life included soldiering in the United States, proposals to build a Panama canal, schemes to link Madrid to the sea, overtures to the Dutch and French governments to combine against the British in India, making a fortune by speculation in the French Revolution and then losing it. Then, at thirty-seven, he decided that his task, after a thorough scientific training, was to rescue humanity.

If much of his writing is nonsensical, it also contains penetrating insights. Engels was not alone in calling Saint-Simon "the most encyclopedic mind of his time." His is the first technocratic theory related to the new industrialism. Concerned for the amelioration of the lot of "the most numerous class," his view of society is essentially authoritarian and hierarchical. Though he changed his views on the precise nature of the ruling group in his voluminous writings, Saint-Simon always held that the new social order should be directed by the most competent, the scientists and artists, the bankers and industrialists—those possessing the requisite scientific knowledge and reason rather than those acting on the basis of eighteenth century abstract principles.

For Saint-Simon, social problems must be examined by the method of "positive," or natural, science. But his advocacy of control over social behavior was accompanied by the recognition of the need for a religious force by which the masses could be moved. Scientific positivism was associated with religious revival, the New Christianity.

The Saint-Simonians, the group of disciples who quarreled over his inheritance and redirected his social preoccupation into a kind of erotic mysticism, emphasized the need for order and discipline, efficiency and technological development. They were interested, not in the revolutionary slogans of freedom and equality, but in greater material productivity and control by experts. If was no coincidence that many of the members of the group were to take their place among the leading bankers, industrialists and entrepreneurs in France.

The greatest of his disciples was Auguste Comte (1798–1857), a student of mathematics who had served as Saint-Simon's secretary, but had broken with him in 1824 in a dispute over the authorship of a work Saint-Simon claimed as his own. Between 1830 and 1842, Comte wrote his six volume *Course of Positive Philosophy* and in 1851 his *System of Positive Polity*. In his approach to social phenomena, Comte is really the first sociologist and founder of the discipline.

Positivism disclaimed the value of a search for final causes or for the essential nature of phenomena. Knowledge was obtained by scientific observation and testing. Through this method, laws of science, including laws of social science, could be formulated and order established. Action could be based on accurate prediction, arising from regular laws.

Saint-Simon had proclaimed that history oscillated between organic and critical periods. Comte, attempting to discover the laws governing historical change, formulated a theory of the three stages of history. History and the development of all knowledge had passed through these overlapping stages, during which society was organized differently and actions based on different principles. The first stage, the theological, was founded on the belief in supernatural beings; the second, the metaphysical, based on the power of abstractions and dominated by those who were articulate, was a period of intellectual anarchy and of a variety of dogmas. The third stage, the positivistic, based on science, was about to begin.

Government in the new era would be hierarchical and orderly, exercised by specialists—predominantly bankers and intellectuals. There would be total organization of human life, and dictatorship exercised by those wielding power. But Comte's austere positivism was always colored by emotion. If there was a cult of facts, there was also a cult of humanity. The new religion of humanity was founded on the principle of social love, the brotherhood of man and the power of the positivist priest. Education, sacraments, public worship, festivals and women, would all foster the worship of humanity. Everyone would act from a sense of duty, not from rights. In this way, positivism combined empirical investigation with faith and worship, social science with morality, in its attempt to create the rational order of society.

PROUDHON

What Is Property? (1840) and *The General Idea of the Revolution in the Nineteenth Century, (1851)*

Property Is Theft

If I were asked to answer the following question: "What is slavery?" and I should answer in one word, "It is murder," my meaning would be understood at once. No extended argument would be required to show that the power to take from a man his thought, his will, his personality, is a power of life and death; and that to enslave a man is to kill him. Why, then, to this other question: "What is property?" may I not likewise answer, "It is robbery," without the certainty of being mis-understood; the second proposition being no other than a transformation of the first?

I undertake to discuss the vital principle of our government and our institutions, property: I am in my right. I may be mistaken in the conclusion which shall result from my inves-tigations: I am in my right. I think best to place the last thought of my book first: still am I in my right.

Such an author teaches that property is a civil right, born of occupation and sanctioned by law; another maintains that it is a natural right, originating in labor,—and both of these doctrines, totally opposed as they may seem, are encouraged and applauded. I contend that neither labor, nor occupation, nor law, can create property; that it is an effect without a cause: am I censurable?

But murmurs arise!

"Property is robbery!" That is the war-cry of '93! That is the signal of revolutions!

Reader, calm yourself. I am no agent of discord, no fire-brand of sedition. I anticipate history by a few days; I disclose a truth whose development we may try in vain to arrest; I write the preamble of our future constitution. This proposi-tion which seems to you blasphemous—"property is robbery" —would, if our prejudices allowed us to consider it, be recog-nised as the lightning-rod to shield us from the coming thun-derbolt; but too many interests stand in the way! . . . Alas! philosophy will not change the course of events: destiny will fulfil itself regardless of prophecy. Besides, must not justice be done and our education be finished?

"Property is robbery!" . . . What a revolution in human ideas! "Proprietor" and "robber" have been at all times ex-pressions as contradictory as the beings whom they designate are hostile; all languages have perpetuated this opposition. On what authority, then, do you venture to attack universal con-sent, and give the lie to the human race? Who are you, that you should question the judgment of the nations and the ages? . . .

Disregard, reader, my title and my character, and attend only to my arguments. It is in accordance with universal consent that I undertake to correct universal error; from the "opinion" of the human race I appeal to its "faith." Have the courage to follow me; and, if your will is untrammelled, if your conscience is free, if your mind can unite two propositions and deduce a third therefrom, my ideas will inevitably become yours. In beginning by giving you my last word, it was my purpose to warn you, not to defy you; for I am certain that, if you read me, you will be compelled to assent. The things of which I am to speak are so simple and clear that you will be astonished at not having perceived them before, and you will say: "I have neglected to think." Others offer you the spectacle of genius wrestling Nature's secrets from her, and unfolding before you her sublime messages; you will find here only a series of experiments upon "justice" and "right," a sort of verification of the weights and measures of your conscience. The operations shall be conducted under your very eyes; and you shall weigh the result.

Nevertheless, I build no system. I ask an end to privilege, the abolition of slavery, equality of rights, and the reign of law. Justice, nothing else; that is the alpha and omega of my argument: to others I leave the business of governing the world. . . .

(Extract from *What Is Property?* chapter 1.)

Social Liquidation and Mutualism

The preceding studies, as much upon contemporaneous society as upon the reforms which it suggests, have taught us several things which it is well to recount here summarily.

1. The fall of the monarchy of July and the proclamation of the Republic were the signal for a social revolution.

2. This Revolution, at first not understood, little by little became defined, determined and settled, under the influence of the very same Reaction which was displayed against it, from the first days of the Provisional Government.

3. This Revolution consists in substituting the economic, or industrial, system, for the governmental, feudal and military system, in the same way that the present system was substituted, by a previous revolution, for a theocratic or sacerdotal system.

4. By an industrial system, we understand, not a form of government, in which men devoted to agriculture and industry, promoters, proprietors, workmen, become in their turn a dominant caste, as were formerly the nobility and clergy, but a constitution of society having for its basis the organization

of economic forces, in place of the hierarchy of political powers.

5. And to explain that this organization must result from the nature of things, that there is nothing arbitrary about it, that it finds its law in established practice, we have said that, in order to bring it about, the question was of one thing only: To change the course of things, the tendency of society.

Passing then to the examination of the chief ideas that offer themselves as principles for guidance, and that serve as banners to parties, we have recognized:

6. That the principle of association, invoked by most "Schools," is an essentially sterile principle; that it is neither an industrial force nor an economic law; that it would involve both government and obedience, two words which the Revolution bars.

7. That the political principle revived recently, under the names of "direct legislation," "direct government," etc., is but a false application of the principle of authority, whereof the sphere is in the family, but which cannot legitimately be extended to the city or the nation.

At the same time we have established:

8. That in place of the idea of association, there was a tendency to substitute in the workmen's societies a new idea, reciprocity, in which we have seen both an economic force and a law.

9. That to the idea of government there was opposed, even in the political tradition itself, the idea of "contract," the only moral bond which free and equal beings can accept.

Thus we come to recognize the essential factors of the Revolution.

Its cause: the economic chaos which the Revolution of 1789 left after it.

Its occasion: a progressive, systematic poverty, of which the government finds itself, willy-nilly, the promoter and supporter.

Its organic principle: reciprocity; in law terms, contract.

Its aim: the guaranty of work and wages, and thence the indefinite increase of wealth and of liberty.

Its parties, which we divide into two groups: the Socialist schools, which invoke the principle of Association; and the democratic factions, which are still devoted to the principles of centralization and of the State.

(Extract from *The General Idea of the Revolution in the Nineteenth Century*, Fifth Study.)

The New Order

Beneath the governmental machinery, in the shadow of political institutions, out of the sight of statesmen and priests, society is producing its own organism, slowly and silently; and constructing a new order, the expression of its vitality and autonomy, and the denial of the old politics, as well as of the old religion.

This organization, which is as essential to society as it is incompatible with the present system, has the following principles:

1. The indefinite perfectibility of the individual and of the race;
2. The honorableness of work;
3. The equality of fortunes;
4. The identity of interests;
5. The end of antagonisms;
6. The universality of comfort;
7. The sovereignty of reason;
8. The absolute liberty of the man and of the citizen.

I mention below its principal forms of activity:

a. Division of labor, through which classification of the People by *Industries* replaces classification by "caste";
b. Collective power, the principle of *Workmen's Associations*, in place of "armies";
c. Commerce, the concrete form of *Contract*, which takes the place of "law";
d. Equality in exchange;
e. Competition;
f. Credit, which turns upon *Interests*, as the governmental hierarchy turns upon "Obedience";
g. The equilibrium of values and properties.

The old system, standing on Authority and Faith, was essentially based upon "Divine Right." The principle of the sovereignty of the People, introduced later, did not change its nature; and it is a mistake to-day, in the face of the conclusions of science, to maintain a distinction which does not touch underlying principles, between absolute monarchy and constitutional monarchy, or between the latter and the democratic republic. The sovereignty of the People has been, if I may say so, for a century past, but a skirmishing line for Liberty. It was either an error, or a clever scheme of our fathers to make the sovereign people in the image of the king-man: as the Revolution becomes better understood, this mythology vanishes, all traces of government disappear and follow the principle of government itself to dissolution. . . .

There is no fusion possible between the political and economic systems, between the system of laws and the system of contracts; one or the other must be chosen. . . . while Society maintains in the slightest degree its political form, it cannot become organized according to economic law. How harmonize local initiative with the preponderance of a central authority, or universal suffrage with the hierarchy of officials; the principle that no one owes obedience to a law to which he has not himself consented, with the right of majorities?

If a writer who understood these contradictions should undertake to reconcile them, it would prove him, not a bold thinker, but a wretched charlatan.

This absolute incompatibility of the two systems, so often proved, still does not convince writers who, while admitting the dangers of authority, nevertheless hold to it, as the sole means of maintaining order, and see nothing beside it but empty desolation. Like the sick man in the comedy, who is told that the first thing he must do is to discharge his doctors, if he wants to get well, they persist in asking how can a man get along without a doctor, or a society without a government. They will make the government as republican, as benevolent, as equal as possible; they will set up all possible guarantees against it; they will belittle it, almost attack it, in support of the majesty of the citizens. They tell us: You are the government! You shall govern yourselves, without president, without representatives, without delegates. What have you then to complain about? But to live without government, to abolish all authority, absolutely and unreservedly, to set up pure "anarchy," seems to them ridiculous and inconceivable, a plot against the Republic and against the nation. What will these people who talk of abolishing government put in place of it? they ask.

We have no trouble in answering.

It is industrial organization that we will put in place of government, as we have just shown.

In place of laws, we will put contracts. —No more laws

voted by a majority, nor even unanimously; each citizen, each town, each industrial union, makes its own laws.

In place of political powers, we will put economic forces.

In place of the ancient classes of nobles, burghers, and peasants, or of business men and working men, we will put the general titles and special departments of industry: Agriculture, Manufacture, Commerce, &c.

In place of public force, we will put collective force.

In place of standing armies, we will put industrial associations.

In place of police, we will put identity of interests.

In place of political centralization, we will put economic centralization.

Do you see now how there can be order without functionaries, a profound and wholly intellectual unity?

You, who cannot conceive of unity without a whole apparatus of legislators, prosecutors, attorneys-general, custom house officers, policemen, you have never known what real unity is! What you call unity and centralization is nothing but perpetual chaos, serving as a basis for endless tyranny; it is the advancing of the chaotic condition of social forces as an argument for despotism—a despotism which is really the cause of the chaos.

Well, in our turn, let us ask, what need have we of government when we have made an agreement? Does not the National Bank, with its various branches, achieve centralization and unity? Does not the agreement among farm laborers for compensation, marketing, and reimbursement for farm properties create unity? From another point of view, do not the industrial associations for carrying on the large-scale industries bring about unity? And the constitution of value, that contract of contracts, as we have called it, is not that the most perfect and indissoluble unity? . . .

Never ask again then what we will put in place of government, nor what will become of society without government, for I assure you that in the future it will be easier to conceive of society without government, than of society with government.

Society, just now, is like the butterfly just out of the cocoon, which shakes its gilded wings in the sunlight before taking flight. Tell it to crawl back into the silken covering, to shun the flowers and to hide itself from the light!

But a revolution is not made with formulas. Prejudice must be attacked at the foundation, overthrown, hurled into dust, its injurious effects explained, its ridiculous and odious nature shown forth. Mankind believes only in its own tests, happy if these tests do not addle its brains and drain its blood. Let us try then by clear criticism to make the test of government so conclusive, that the absurdity of the institution will strike all minds, and Anarchy, dreaded as a scourge, will be accepted as a benefit.

(Extract from *The General Idea of the Revolution in the Nineteenth Century,* Seventh Study.)

SAINT-SIMON

The Organizer (1819),
On Social Organization (1825)
and *The New Christianity* (1825)

The Unjust Society

Suppose that France suddenly lost fifty of her best physicists, chemists, physiologists, mathematicians, poets, painters, sculptors, musicians, writers; fifty of her best mechanical engineers, civil and military engineers, artillery experts, architects, doctors, surgeons, apothecaries, seamen, clockmakers; fifty of her best bankers, two hundred of her best business men, two hundred of her best farmers, fifty of her best ironmasters, arms manufacturers, tanners, dyers, miners, clothmakers, cotton manufacturers, silk-makers, linen-makers, manufacturers of hardware, of pottery and china, or crystal and glass, ship chandlers, carriers, printers, engravers, goldsmiths, and other metal-workers; her fifty best masons, carpenters, joiners, farriers, locksmiths, cutlers, smelters, and a hundred other persons of various unspecified occupations, eminent in the sciences, fine arts, and professions; making in all the three thousand leading scientists, artists, and artisans of France.

These men are the Frenchmen who are the most essential producers, those who make the most important products, those who direct the enterprises most useful to the nation, those who contribute to its achievements in the sciences, fine arts and professions. They are in the most real sense the flower of French society; they are, above all Frenchmen, the most useful to their country, contribute most to its glory, increasing its civilization and prosperity. The nation would become a lifeless corpse as soon as it lost them. It would immediately fall into a position of inferiority compared with the nations which it now rivals, and would continue to be inferior until this loss has been replaced, until it had grown another head. It would require at least a generation for

France to repair this misfortune; for men who are distinguished in work of positive ability are exceptions, and nature is not prodigal of exceptions, particularly in this species.

Let us pass on to another assumption. Suppose that France preserves all the men of genius that she possesses in the sciences, fine arts and professions, but has the misfortune to lose in the same day Monsieur the King's brother, Monseigneur le duc d'Angoulême [and other aristocrats]. . . . Suppose that France loses at the same time all the great officers of the royal household, all the ministers (with or without portfolio), all the councillors of state, all the chief magistrates, marshals, cardinals, archbishops, bishops, vicars-general, and canons, all the prefects and sub-prefects, all the civil servants, and judges, and, in addition, ten thousand of the richest proprietors who live in the style of nobles.

This mischance would certainly distress the French, because they are kind-hearted, and could not see with indifference the sudden disappearance of such a large number of their compatriots. But this loss of thirty-thousand individuals, considered to be the most important in the State, would only grieve them for purely sentimental reasons and would result in no political evil for the State. . . .

The prosperity of France can only exist through the effects of the progress of the sciences, fine arts and professions. The Princes, the great household officials, the Bishops, Marshals of France, prefects and idle landowners contribute nothing directly to the progress of the sciences, fine arts and professions. Far from contributing they only hinder, since they strive to prolong the supremacy existing to this day of conjectural ideas over positive science. They inevitably harm the prosperity of the nation by depriving, as they do, the scientists, artists, and artisans of the high esteem to which they are properly entitled. They are harmful because they expend their wealth in a way which is of no direct use to the sciences, fine arts, and professions: they are harmful because they are a charge on the national taxation, to the amount of three or four hundred millions under the heading of appointments, pensions, gift, compensations, for the upkeep of their activities which are useless to the nation.

These suppositions underline the most important fact of present politics: they provide a point of view from which we can see this fact in a flash in all its extent; they show clearly, though indirectly, that our social organization is seriously defective: that men still allow themselves to be governed by violence and ruse, and that the human race (politically speaking) is still sunk in immorality.

The scientists, artists, and artisans, the only men whose work is of positive utility to society, and cost it practically nothing, are kept down by the princes and other rulers who are simply more or less incapable bureaucrats. Those who control honours and other national awards owe, in general, the supremacy they enjoy, to the accident of birth, to flattery, intrigue and other dubious methods. . . .

These suppositions show that society is a world which is upside down. . . .

Ignorance, superstition, idleness and costly dissipation are the privilege of the leaders of society, and men of ability, hard-working and thrifty, are employed only as inferiors and instruments.

To sum up, in every sphere men of greater ability are subject to the control of men who are incapable. From the point of view of morality, the most immoral men have the responsibility of leading the citizens towards virtue; from the point of view of distributive justice, the most guilty men are appointed to punish minor delinquents.

(Extract from *The Organizer*.)

Who Should Rule?

. . . The men who brought about the Revolution, the men who directed it, and the men who, since 1789 and up to the present day, have guided the nation, have committed a great political mistake. They have all sought to improve the governmental machine, whereas they should have subordinated it and put administration in the first place.

They should have begun by asking a question the solution of which is simple and obvious. They should have asked who, in the present state of morals and enlightenment, are the men most fitted to manage the affairs of the nation. They would have been forced to recognize the fact that the scientists, artists and industrialists, and the heads of industrial concerns are the men who possess the most eminent, varied, and most positively useful ability, for the guidance of men's minds at the present time. They would have recognized the fact that the work of the scientists, artists, and industrialists is that which, in discovery and application, contributes most to national prosperity.

They would have reached the conclusion that the scientists, artists and leaders of industrial enterprises are the men who should be entrusted with administrative power, that is to say, with the responsibility for managing the national interests;

and that the functions of government should be limited to maintaining public order. . . .

The community has often been compared to a pyramid. I admit that the nation should be composed as a pyramid; I am profoundly convinced that the national pyramid should be crowned by the monarchy, but I assert that from the base of the pyramid to its summit the layers should be composed of more and more precious materials. If we consider the present pyramid, it appears that the base is made of granite, that up to a certain height the layers are composed of valuable materials, but that the upper part, supporting a magnificent diamond, is composed of nothing but plaster and gilt.

The base of the present national pyramid consists of workers in their routine occupations; the first layers above this base are the leaders of industrial enterprises, the scientists who improve the methods of manufacture and widen their application, the artists who give the stamp of good taste to all their products. The upper layers, which I assert to be composed of nothing but plaster, which is easily recognizable despite the gilding, are the courtiers, the mass of nobles whether of ancient or recent creation, the idle rich, the governing class from the prime minister to the humblest clerk. The monarchy is the magnificent diamond which crowns the pyramid.

(Extract from *On Social Organization*.)

The New Christianity

New Christianity will be composed of groups similar to those which to-day comprise the various heretic bodies in Europe and America.

New Christianity, like the heretical bodies, will have its morality, form of worship and dogma; it will have its clergy, and its hierarchy. But, despite this similarity, New Christianity will be purged of all the heresies which exist to-day. Moral doctrine will be considered by the new Christians as the most important thing; the form of worship and dogma will be regarded only as secondary features for the purpose of fixing the attention of the faithful of all classes on morality.

In New Christianity all morality will be derived directly from the principle that 'Men should treat each other as brothers.' This principle, which belongs to primitive Christianity, will undergo a transfiguration by which it will be proclaimed as the aim of all religious activity. This principle, regenerated, will be proclaimed as follows: religion should guide the community towards the great aim of improving as quickly as possible the condition of the poorest class.

The founders of New Christianity and leaders of the new Church, should be those men who are most capable of contributing by their efforts to the improvement of the well-being of the poorest class. The functions of the clergy will be confined to teaching the New Christian doctrine. The leaders of the Church should apply themselves unremittingly to the perfecting of this doctrine.

. . . all so-called Christian religions of the present time are nothing but heresies—that is to say, that they do not aim directly at the quickest possible improvement of the well-being of the poorest class, which is the sole aim of Christianity. . . .

I say that Catholics are heretics, and I will prove it. I will prove that the rebirth of Christianity will wipe out the Inquisition, and rid the community of the Jesuits and their Machiavellian doctrines. True Christianity commands all men to act towards each other as brothers. Jesus Christ promised eternal life to those who contributed the most to the improvement of the condition of the poorest class in the moral and physical sense.

Therefore the heads of the Christian Church should be chosen from the men who are the most capable of directing the undertakings aimed at increasing the welfare of the most numerous class; and the clergy should be concerned primarily with teaching to the faithful the conduct they should follow in order to promote the well-being of the majority of the population. . . .

The more society progresses morally and physically, the more subdivision of intellectual and manual labour takes place; in the course of their daily work, men's minds are occupied with things of more and more specialized interest, as the arts, science, and industry progress. The result is that, the more society progresses, the more necessary it is that the form of worship should be improved; for the purpose of the form of worship is to remind men when they assemble periodically on the day of rest, of the interests common to all members of society, of the common interests of the human race. . . .

There are two main ways of calling men's attention to ideas of this sort and giving them a strong impulse; fear must be roused in them by the contemplation of the terrible evils in store for them if they depart from the rules laid down for them, and they must be attracted by the delights which will follow their efforts along the paths put before them. In both cases, the most effective results will be produced by combining all the resources offered by the arts.

The preacher, who naturally uses eloquence, the first of the arts, should make his audience tremble by depicting the mis-

erable state of the man who, in this life, deserves the condemnation of the people; he should show God striking down
with His arm the men whose feelings are not dominated by
love of his fellow men. Alternatively, he should stimulate in
his audience powerful and generous feelings by persuading
them that the happiness which comes from the esteem of
one's fellow men is greater than any other form of happiness.
The poets should help the work of the preachers; they
should provide short poems to be recited in unison, so that all
the faithful may become teachers of one another. The musicians should enrich the religious poems by their harmonies,
and give them a musical character penetrating to the depths of
the soul. Painters and sculptors working in the temple should
remind Christians of acts which are outstandingly Christian.
Architects should build temples so that the preachers, poets,
and musicians, the painters and sculptors can sway the faithful, at will, by feelings of terror or feelings of joy and hope.

These are obviously the lines along which a form of worship should be developed, and the means of making it most
socially useful. . . .

The Protestants will obviously make the objection that,
while Catholics have plenty of singing and their shrines are
decorated with the finest works of painting and sculpture, the
sermons of the reformed clergy have a much more beneficial
effect on their congregations than all the sermons of the
Catholic priests (whose principal object is always to make the
Roman Catholics give as much money as possible for the
maintenance of the church and the clergy), and that there it is
impossible to deny that the Protestant form of worship is
superior to the Catholic.

To this I reply: the object of my work is not to find out
which of the two forms of religion is the less heretical. I have
undertaken to show that they are both heretical, in different
degrees; that is to say, that neither of them is the Christian
religion. I have tried to show that Christianity has been abandoned since the fifteenth century; I have tried to restore and
revitalize it. My aim is to purify this religion (eminently
philanthropic in character) of all superstitions or useless beliefs and practices.

New Christianity is called upon to achieve the triumph of
the principles of universal morality in the struggle which is
going on with the forces aiming at the individual instead of
public interests. This rejuvenated religion is called upon to
organize all peoples in a state of perpetual peace, by allying
them all against the nation which tries to gain its own advantage at the expense of the good of the whole human race,

mobilizing them against any government so anti-Christian as to sacrifice national interests to the private interest of the rulers. It is called upon to link together the scientists, artists, and industrialists, and to make them the managing directors of the human race, as well as of the particular interests of each individual people. It is called upon to put the arts, experimental sciences and industry in the front rank of sacred studies, whereas the Catholics have put them among the profane branches of study.

Finally, New Christianity is called upon to pronounce anathema upon theology, and to condemn as unholy any doctrine trying to teach men that there is any other way of obtaining eternal life, except that of working with all their might for the improvement of the conditions of life of their fellow men.

. . . great harm was done to the community by the neglect in which, since the fifteenth century, the study of universal principles and universal interests had been left. This neglect gave rise to the egoism which became dominant in all classes and individuals. This sentiment, dominating all classes and individuals, made it easier for Caesarism to recover much of the political force which it had lost before the fifteenth century. It is to this egoism that we must attribute the political malady of our own age, a malady which afflicts all the workers who serve the community; which allows kings to waste a great proportion of the wages of the poor on their personal expenses, and those of their courtiers and soldiers; which allows monarchy and hereditary aristocracy to usurp much of the esteem which should go to the scientists, artists, and industrialists, in virtue of their direct positive services to the community.

. . . a creed for New Christians . . . is the only social doctrine appropriate for Europe in its present state of enlightenment and civilization. . . . by adopting this doctrine the huge difficulties arising, since the fifteenth century, from the encroachment of material power on the spiritual sphere can be most easily and peacefully resolved, and these encroachments stopped, by reorganizing the spiritual authority on a new basis, giving it the necessary strength to restrain the unlimited claims of the temporal power.

. . . the adoption of New Christianity, by co-ordinating the study of general ideas with that of the specialized sciences, will promote the progress of civilization infinitely more than any other measure.

. . . We are certainly superior to our ancestors in the particular, applied sciences. It is only since the fifteenth century, and chiefly since the beginning of the last century, that we have made considerable progress in mathematics, physics, chemistry and physiology. But there is a science much more important for the community than physical and mathematical science—the science on which society is founded, namely ethics, the development of which has been completely different from that of the physical and mathematical sciences. It is more than eighteen centuries since its fundamental principle has been produced, and since then none of the researches of the men of the greatest genius has been able to discover a principle superior in universality or precision to that formulated by the Founder of Christianity. I will go further and say that when society has lost sight of this principle, and ceased to use it as a guide to its conduct, it has promptly relapsed under the despotism of Caesar, and the rule of brute force, which this principle of Christianity had subordinated to the rule of reason. . . .

(Extract from *The New Christianity*.)

COMTE

A General View of Positivism

Order and Progress

. . . all the characteristics of Positivism are summed up in its motto, *Order and Progress,* a motto which has a philosophical as well as political bearing, and which I shall always feel glad to have put forward.

Positivism is the only school which has given a definite significance to these two conceptions, whether regarded from their scientific or their social aspect. With regard to Progress, the assertion will hardly be disputed, no definition of it but the Positive ever having yet been given. In the case of Order, it is less apparent but . . . it is no less profoundly true. All previous philosophies had regarded Order as stationary, a conception which rendered it wholly inapplicable to modern politics. But Positivism, by rejecting the absolute, and yet not introducing the arbitrary, represents Order in a totally new light, and adapts it to our progressive civilization. It places it on the firmest possible foundation, that is, on the doctrine of the invariability of the laws of nature, which defends it against all danger from subjective chimeras. The Positivist regards artificial Order in Social phenomena, as in all others, as resting necessarily upon the Order of nature, in other words, upon the whole series of natural laws.

But Order has to be reconciled with Progress: and here

Positivism is still more obviously without a rival. Necessary as the reconciliation is, no other system has even attempted it. But the facility with which we are now enabled, by the encyclopaedic scale, to pass from the simplest mathematical phenomena to the most complicated phenomena of political life, leads at once to a solution of the problem. Viewed scientifically, it is an instance of that necessary correlation of existence and movement, which we find indicated in the inorganic world, and which becomes still more distinct in Biology. Finding it in all the lower sciences, we are prepared for its appearance in a still more definite shape in Sociology. . . . In Sociology the correlation assumes this form: Order is the condition of all Progress; Progress is always the object of Order. Or, to penetrate the question still more deeply, Progress may be regarded simply as the development of Order; for the order of nature necessarily contains within itself the germ of all possible progress. . . . Every social innovation has its roots in the past; and the rudest phases of savage life show the primitive trace of all subsequent improvement.

Progress then is in its essence identical with Order, and may be looked upon as Order made manifest. . . .

. . . the one great object of life, personal and social, is to become more perfect in every way; in our external condition first, but also, and more especially, in our own nature. The first kind of Progress we share in common with the higher animals; all of which make some efforts to improve their material position. It is of course the least elevated stage of progress; but being the easiest, it is the point from which we start towards the higher stages. A nation that has made no efforts to improve itself materially, will take but little interest in moral or mental improvement. This is the only ground on which enlightened men can feel much pleasure in the material progress of our own time. It stirs up influences that tend to the nobler kinds of Progress; influences which would meet with even greater opposition than they do, were not the temptations presented to the coarser natures by material prosperity so irresistible. Owing to the mental and moral anarchy in which we live, systematic efforts to gain the higher degrees of Progress are as yet impossible; and this explains, though it does not justify, the exaggerated importance attributed nowadays to material improvements. . . .

Progress in the higher sense includes improvements of three sorts; that is to say, it may be Physical, Intellectual, or Moral progress; the difficulty of each class being in proportion to its value and the extent of its sphere. Physical progress, which again might be divided on the same principle, seems under some of its aspects almost the same thing as material. But regarded as a whole it is far more important and far more difficult: its influence on the well-being of Man is also much greater. We gain more, for instance, by the smallest addition to length of life, or by any increased security for health, than by the most elaborate improvements in our modes of travelling by land or water, in which birds will probably always have a great advantage over us. . . .

Intellectual and Moral progress . . . is the only kind really distinctive of our race. . . . To strengthen the intellectual powers, whether for art or for science, whether it be the powers of observation or those of induction and deduction, is, when circumstances allow of their being made available for social purposes, of greater and more extensive importance, than all physical, and, *a fortiori* than all material improvements. . . . moral progress has even more to do with our well-being than intellectual progress. The moral faculties are more modifiable, although the effort required to modify them is greater. If the benevolence or courage of the human race were increased, it would bring more real happiness than any addition to our intellectual powers. Therefore to the question, What is the true object of human life, whether looked at collectively or individually? the simplest and most precise answer would be, the perfection of our moral nature; since it has a more immediate and certain influence on our well-being than perfection of any other kind. . . . Keeping then to the question of moral perfection, we find two qualities standing above the rest in practical importance, namely, Sympathy and Energy. Both these qualities are included in the word *Heart*, which in all European languages has a different meaning for the two sexes. Both will be developed by Positivism, more directly, more continuously, and with greater result, than under any former system. The whole tendency of Positivism is to encourage sympathy; since it subordinates every thought, desire, and action to social feeling. Energy is also presupposed, and at the same time fostered, by the system. For it removes a heavy weight of superstition, it reveals the true dignity of man, and it supplies an unceasing motive for individual and collective action. The very acceptance of Positivism demands some vigour of character; it implies the braving of spiritual terrors, which were once enough to intimidate the firmest minds . . .

I have now explained the principal purpose of Positive Philosophy, namely, spiritual reorganization; and I have shown how that purpose is involved in the Positivist motto, Order and Progress. Positivism, then, realizes the highest aspirations of mediaeval Catholicism, and at the same time fulfils the conditions, the absence of which caused the failure of the Convention. It combines the opposite merits of the Catholic and the Revolutionary spirit, and by so doing supersedes them both. Theology and Metaphysics may now disappear without danger, because the service which each of them rendered is now harmonized with that of the other, and will be performed more perfectly. The principle on which this result depends is the separation of spiritual from temporal power. . . .

. . . any immediate attempt to reorganize political administration would only be the signal for fresh attempts at reaction, attempts which now can have no other result than anarchy. It is true that Positivism has just supplied us with a philosophical basis for political reconstruction. But its principles are still so new and undeveloped, and besides are understood by so few, that they cannot exercise much influence at present on political life. Ultimately, and by slow degrees, they will mould the institutions of the future; but meanwhile they must work their way freely into men's minds and hearts, and for this at least one generation will be necessary. Spiritual organization is the only point where an immediate beginning can be made; difficult as it is, its possibility is at last as certain as its urgency. When sufficient progress has been made with it, it will cause a gradual regeneration of political institutions. But any attempt to modify these too rapidly would only result in fresh disturbances. Such disturbances, it is true, will never be as dangerous as they were formerly, because the anarchy of opinion is so profound that it is far more difficult for men to agree in any fixed principles of action. The absolute doctrines of the last century which inspired such intense conviction, can never regain their strength, because, when brought to the crucial test of experience as well as of discussion, their uselessness for constructive purposes and their subversive tendency became evident to every one. They have been weakened, too, by theological concessions which their supporters, in order to carry on the government at all, were obliged to make. Consequently the policy with which they are at present connected is one which oscillates between reaction and anarchy, or rather which is at once despotic and destructive, from the necessity of controlling a society which has become almost as diverse to metaphysical as to theological rule. . . . Quiet at home depends now, like peace abroad, simply on the absence of disturbing forces; a most insecure basis, since it is itself a symptom of the extent to which the disorganizing movement has proceeded. . . . As long as there is such an utter want of harmony in feeling as well as in opinion, there can be no real security against war or internal disorder. . . .

For no one now has any real belief in the organic value of the received metaphysical doctrines. They would never have been revived but for the need of having some sort of political formula to work with, in default of any real social convictions. But the revival is only apparent, and it contrasts most strikingly with the utter absence of systematic principles in most active minds. There is no real danger of repeating the error of the first revolutionists and of attempting to construct with negative doctrines. We have only to consider the vast development of industry, of esthetic culture, and of scientific study, to free ourselves from all anxiety on this head. Such things are incompatible with any regard for the metaphysical teaching of ideologists or psychologists. Nor is there much to fear in the natural enthusiasm which is carrying us back to the first days of the Revolution. It will only revive the old republican spirit, and make us forget the long period of retrogression and stagnation which have elapsed since the first great outbreak; for this is the point on which the attention of posterity will be finally concentrated. But while satisfying these very legitimate feelings, the people will soon find that the only aspect of this great crisis which we have to imitate is the wise insight of the Convention during the first part of its administration, in perceiving that its policy could only be provisional, and that definite reconstruction must be reserved for better times. We may fairly hope that the next formal attempt to set up a constitution according to some abstract ideal, will convince the French nation, and ultimately the whole West, of the utter futility of such schemes. . . .

The same conditions which require our policy to be provisional while the spiritual interregnum lasts, point also to the mode in which this provisional policy should be carried out. Had the revolutionary government of the Convention continued till the end of the war, it would probably have been prolonged up to the present time. But in one most important respect a modification would have been necessary. During the struggle for independence what was wanted was a vigorous dictatorship, combining spiritual with temporal powers: a dictatorship even stronger than the old monarchy, and only distinguished from despotism by its ardour in the cause of progress. Without complete concentration of political power, the republic could never have been saved. But with peace the necessity for such concentration was at an end. The only motive for still continuing the provisional system was the absence of social convictions. But this would also be a motive for giving perfect liberty of speech and discussion, which till then had been impossible or dangerous. For liberty was a necessary condition for elaborating and diffusing a new system of universal principles, as the only sure basis for the future regeneration of society.

This hypothetical view of changes which might have taken place in the Conventional government, may be applied to the existing condition of affairs. It is the policy best adapted for the republican government which is now arising in all the security of a settled peace, and yet amidst the most entire anarchy of opinion. . . .

Meantime there is nothing irrevocable in the republic itself, except the moral principle involved in it, the absolute and permanent preponderance of Social Feeling; in other words, the concentration of all the powers of Man upon the common welfare.

That spirit of devotion to the public welfare, which is the noblest feature of republicanism, is strongly opposed to any immediate attempts at political finality, as being incompatible with conscientious endeavours to find a real solution of social problems. . . . Positivism now offers itself for practical application to the question of social progress, which has become again the prominent question, and will ever remain so. Unfavourable as the present political temper would have been to the rise of Positivism, it is not at all so to its diffusion; always supposing its teachers to be men of sufficient dignity to avoid the snare of political ambition into which thinkers are now so apt to fall. By explaining, as it alone can explain, the futility and danger of the various Utopian schemes which are now competing with each other for the reorganization of society, Positivism will soon be able to divert public attention from these political chimeras, to the question of a total reformation of principles and of life. . . .

Thus Republicanism is, on the whole, favourable to this great principle of Positivism, the separation of temporal from spiritual power, notwithstanding the temptations offered to men who wish to carry their theories into the immediate application. . . .

(Extracts from chapter 2.)

The Religion of Humanity

Love, then, is our principle; Order our basis; and Progress our end. Such is the essential character of the system of life which Positivism offers for the definite acceptance of society; a system which regulates the whole course of our private and public existence, by bringing Feeling, Reason, and Activity into permanent harmony. . . . Life in all its actions and thoughts is brought under the control and inspiring charm of Social Sympathy.

By the supremacy of the Heart, the Intellect, so far from being crushed, is elevated; for all its powers are consecrated to the service of the social instincts, with the purpose of strengthening their influence and directing their employment. By accepting its subordination to Feeling, Reason adds to its own authority. To it we look for the revelation of the laws of nature, of the established Order which dictates the inevitable conditions of human life. The objective basis thus discovered for human effort reacts most beneficially on our moral nature. Forced as we are to accept it, it controls the fickleness to which our affections are liable, and acts as a direct stimulus to social sympathy. . . .

And whilst Reason is admitted to its due share of influence on human life, Imagination is also strengthened and called into constant exercise. Henceforth it will assume its proper function, the idealization of truth. For the objective basis of our conceptions scientific investigation is necessary. But this basis once obtained, the constitution of our mind is far better adapted to esthetic than to scientific study, provided always that imagination never disregard the truths of science, and degenerate into extravagance. Subject to this condition, Positivism gives every encouragement to esthetic studies, being, as they are, so closely related to its guiding principle and to its practical aim, to Love namely, and to Progress. Art will enter largely into the social life of the Future, and will be regarded as the most pleasurable and most salutary exercise of our intellectual powers, because it leads them in the most direct manner to the culture and improvement of our moral nature. . . .

All essential phases in the evolution of society answer to corresponding phases in the growth of the individual, whether it has proceeded spontaneously or under systematic guidance, supposing always that his development be complete. But it is not enough to prove the close connexion which exists between all modes and degrees of human regeneration. We have yet to find a central point round which all will naturally meet. In this point consists the unity of Positivism as a system of life. . . . There should be a central point in the system towards which Feeling, Reason, and Activity alike converge. The proof that Positivism possesses such a central point will remove the last obstacles to its complete acceptance, as the guide of private or of public life.

Such a centre we find in the great conception of Humanity towards which every aspect of Positivism naturally converges. By it the conception of God will be entirely superseded, and a synthesis be formed, more complete and permanent than that provisionally established by the old religions. Through it the new doctrine becomes at once accessible to men's hearts in its full extent and application. From their heart it will penetrate their minds. . . .

This central point of Positivism is even more moral than intellectual in character: it represents the principle of Love upon which the whole system rests. It is the peculiar characteristic of the Great Being who is here set forth, to be compounded of separable elements. Its existence depends therefore entirely upon mutual Love knitting together its various parts. The calculations of self-interest can never be substituted as a combining influence for the sympathetic instincts.

Yet the belief in Humanity, while stimulating Sympathy, at the same time enlarges the scope and vigour of the Intellect. For it requires high powers of generalization to conceive clearly of this vast organism, as the result of spontaneous co-operation, abstraction made of all partial antagonisms. Reason, then, has its part in this central dogma as well as Love. It enlarges and completes our conception of the Supreme Being by revealing to us the external and internal conditions of its existence.

Lastly, our active powers are stimulated by it no less than our feelings and our reason. For since Humanity is so far more complex than any other organism, it will react more strongly and more continuously on its environment, submitting to its influence and so modifying it. Hence results Progress which is simply the development of Order, under the influence of Love. . . .

Positivists then may, more truly than theological believers of whatever creed, regard life as a continuous and earnest act of worship; worship which will elevate and purify our feelings, enlarge and enlighten our thoughts, ennoble and invigorate our actions. It supplies a direct solution, so far as a solution is possible, of the great problem of the Middle Ages, the subordination of Politics to Morals. For this follows at once from the consecration now given to the principle that social sympathy should preponderate over self-love.

Thus Positivism becomes, in the true sense of the word, a Religion; the only religion which is real and complete; destined therefore to replace all imperfect and provisional systems resting on the primitive basis of theology. . . .

(Extracts from chapter 6.)

SECTION VI

MARXISM

The greatest of Socialist theoreticians and the most influential single political writer in the contemporary world is Karl Marx (1818–1883). Marx, descended from a line of rabbis but baptized as a Protestant at six, became a political journalist and editor before being exiled, first temporarily, and then permanently, from Germany. After short stays in Paris and Brussels, where he was connected with the Communist League for whom he and Friedrich Engels (1820–1895) wrote the *Communist Manifesto*, Marx settled in London from 1849 until his death. Leading a life of poverty alleviated from time to time by generous contributions from his intimate colleague, Engels, Marx continually read and wrote in the British Museum, acted as correspondent for the New York *Tribune* and a Viennese newspaper and helped to found and then destroy the First International. In 1867, the fruits of his laborious research appeared in the first volume of *Capital*, the other volumes being published posthumously from his voluminous manuscripts.

It was primarily to distinguish themselves from the utopians that Marx and Engels called their political philosophy "scientific socialism." It claimed to be scientific in its study of historical causes and events, and in its analysis of inevitable trends. But there is no systematic formulation in any coherent way by Marx of his own ideas; this has been a task performed, with varying success, by the epigoni, each of whom has emphasized particular aspects of the inheritance for personal or tactical reasons. Dispute over the inheritance has slain its tens of thousands. Marx claimed he was making a scientific study of the economic and social order and of its historical development. If he ended his research, as indeed he had begun, by calling for a revolution the inevitability of which he foresaw, this was due, not to a sentimental belief that the existing order was intolerable, but to a conviction that the laws of historical development led to revolution.

Marx early became critical of Hegelian idealism by which he had been strongly influenced as a student of philosophy, and boasted that he had found Hegel upside down and turned him right-side up. The fundamental concept of Marx was his analysis of history, what he called the "materialist conception of history," understood through the dialectical method. Though Marx, and more particularly, Engels, towards the end of their lives were to qualify and lessen the rigidity and the possible determinism of the formula, the startling belief was that the mode of production of the material means of life conditioned, in general, the social, political and intellectual processes of life, and the relationships among men. Social being determined consciousness, and not the reverse, as idealism argued. The economic substructure—the forces of production and the relations of production—gave rise to the superstructure. What exactly was included in the "superstructure" and whether any part of it could maintain an independent existence and exercise an influence in the substructure was continually altered in the Marxist writings.

History was propelled by the struggles between classes related to each other in different processes of production. Marx's philosophy of history embraced five different sets of relationship—primitive communism, slavery, feudalism, capitalism and communism. But since it would be utopian to postulate any vision of the future communist society, and since Marx was essentially uninterested in the first three stages, he was preoccupied with analysis of the capitalist system. And since Marx's empirical research was obtained from British sources, his theory is grounded in factual details of British industrialism. Marx praised capitalism for its tremendous industrial advances, but also analyzed its periodic crises, indicating the increasing part played by industry in the economic system, and the tendency to industrial concentration. Based on the concepts of the labor theory of value and of surplus value, his economic theory argued the inevitability of the fall in the rate of profit, the increasing tendency to accumulate capital and the growing monopolization of industry. The dynamics of the industrial process led inevitably to periodic economic crises, each successive one increasing in intensity, the exploitation and socialization of labor, the polarization of classes, the growing misery of the workers, the sharpening antagonism between the classes, until the contradictions inherent in capitalism between the forces of produc-

tion and the relations of production would produce revolution
by the proletariat, the next class to acquire political power.
Political power and the apparatus of coercion, which in the
past were exercised by and in behalf of those who owned the
forces of production, would gradually wither away. The political function, the coercive domination of one class over others,
would be replaced by the economic task, the administration of
things.

But many of Marx's predictions about the course of history
have not been fulfilled. The condition of the working class in
the industrial countries has grown steadily better, not worse;
class struggles have been reduced rather than intensified; the
middle class and other classes between the capitalists and the
proletariat have not been eliminated; state power has not
withered away in communist countries, but has increased in
scope and intensity; the supposed international solidarity of
the working class has retreated before bellicose nationalism.
Perhaps the greatest irony is that the social revolutions that
have occurred have been, not in the most highly industrialized
countries when "the conditions were ripe," as the theory predicted, but in the less developed or undeveloped countries.
The ultimate paradox is reached when a "proletarian revolution" has taken place in a country lacking a proletariat.
Moreover, the theory hardly takes account of the complexity
of contemporary politics; nothing in Marxism coherently or
effectively explains fascist or totalitarian systems in any meaningful way.

The widespread appeal of Marxism is due less to the inci-
siveness of its historical and philosophical analysis than to the
vigor with which the analysis is argued, the assurance of
certainty and of ultimate victory that it provides, the deceptive
ease by which political and economic phenomena can be
characterized and the ultimate ends of communist society, in
which injustice and oppression are to be ended. Marx was a
formidable social scientist whose influence has been felt in
many academic disciplines.

But he was also a revolutionary and a prophet in the old
Hebraic tradition. Understanding of phenomena was not
enough in itself; the task was to change the world. Freedom
was the recognition of necessity, but it was also concerned
with revolutionary action. Marx's analysis of the wretched
working conditions and poverty in mid-nineteenth century
Europe rested on a tacit humanitarianism. His early theories
of alienation, influenced by Hegel and Feuerbach, were concerned with the elimination of the power of social and religious institutions so that man could be emancipated from

their control. His analysis of the principle of the division of labor, the basis of the economic system which became an "objective power" to which man must submit, showed Marx's belief that there must be opportunity for the development of individual faculties and versatility in a society in which the free development of each was the condition for the free development of all. The realm of freedom lay beyond the sphere of proper material production. Embedded deep in Marx were moral impulses as humanitarian and passionate as any to be found in the utopians.

MARX

The Communist Manifesto

The Fundamental Proposition of Marxism
(From the Preface by Friedrich Engels to the English Edition of 1888)

. . . The Manifesto being our joint production, I consider myself bound to state that the fundamental proposition, which forms its nucleus, belongs to Marx. That proposition is that in every historical epoch the prevailing mode of economic production and exchange and the social organization necessarily following from it form the basis upon which is built up, and from which alone can be explained, the political and intellectual history of that epoch; that consequently the whole history of mankind (since the dissolution of primitive tribal society, holding land in common ownership) has been a history of class struggles, contests between exploiting and exploited, ruling and oppressed classes; that the history of these class struggles forms a series of evolutions in which, nowadays, a stage has been reached where the exploited and oppressed class—the proletariat—cannot attain its emancipation from the sway of the exploiting and ruling class—the bourgeoisie—without, at the same time, and once and for all emancipating society at large from all exploitation, oppression, class distinctions, and class struggles.

This proposition, which, in my opinion, is destined to do for history what Darwin's theory has done for biology, we both of us, had been gradually approaching for some years before 1845.

The Theory of Class Struggles in History

The history of all hitherto existing society is the history of class struggles.

Free man and slave, patrician and plebeian, lord and serf, guild master and journeyman, in a word, oppressor and oppressed, stood in constant opposition to one another, carried on an uninterrupted, now hidden, now open fight, a fight that each time ended either in a revolutionary reconstitution of society at large or in the common ruin of the contending classes.

In the earlier epochs of history we find almost everywhere a complicated arrangement of society into various orders, a manifold gradation of social rank. In ancient Rome we have patricians, knights, plebeians, slaves; in the Middle Ages, feudal lords, vassals, guild masters, journeymen, apprentices, serfs; in almost all of these classes, again, subordinate gradations.

The modern bourgeois society that has sprouted from the ruins of feudal society has not done away with class antagonisms. It has but established new classes, new conditions of oppression, new forms of struggle in place of the old ones.

Our epoch, the epoch of the bourgeoisie, possesses, however, this distinctive feature: it has simplified the class antagonisms. Society as a whole is more and more splitting up into two great hostile camps, into two great classes directly facing each other: bourgeoisie and proletariat.

From the serfs of the Middle Ages sprang the chartered burghers of the earliest towns. From these burgesses the first elements of the bourgeoisie were developed.

The discovery of America, the rounding of the Cape opened up fresh ground for the rising bourgeoisie. The East Indian and Chinese markets, the colonization of America, trade with the colonies, the increase in the means of exchange and in commodities generally, gave to commerce, to navigation, to industry an impulse never before known, and thereby, to the revolutionary element in the tottering feudal society, a rapid development.

The feudal system of industry, under which industrial production was monopolized by closed guilds, now no longer sufficed for the growing wants of the new markets. The manufacturing system took its place. The guild masters were pushed on one side by the manufacturing middle class; division of labor between the different corporate guilds vanished in the face of division of labor in each single workshop.

Meantime the markets kept ever growing, the demand ever rising. Even manufacture no longer sufficed. Thereupon steam and machinery revolutionized industrial production. The place of manufacture was taken by the giant, modern industry, the place of the industrial middle class by industrial millionaires, the leaders of whole industrial armies, the modern bourgeois.

Modern industry has established the world market, for which the discovery of America paved the way. This market has given an immense development to commerce, to navigation, to communication by land. This development has, in its turn, reacted on the extension of industry; and in proportion as industry, commerce, navigation, railways extended, in the same proportion the bourgeoisie developed, increased its capital, and pushed into the background every class handed down from the Middle Ages.

We see, therefore, how the modern bourgeoisie is itself the product of a long course of development, of a series of revolutions in the modes of production and of exchange.

Each step in the development of the bourgeoisie was accompanied by a corresponding political advance of that class. . . . the bourgeoisie has at last, since the establishment of modern industry and of the world market, conquered for itself, in the modern representative state, exclusive political sway. The executive of the modern state is but a committee for managing the common affairs of the whole bourgeoisie.

The bourgeoisie, historically, has played a most revolutionary part.

The bourgeoisie, wherever it has got the upper hand, has put an end to all feudal, patriarchal, idyllic relations. It has pitilessly torn asunder the motley feudal ties that bound man to his "natural superiors," and has left remaining no other nexus between man and man than naked self-interest, than callous "cash payment." It has drowned the most heavenly ecstasies of religious fervor, of chivalrous enthusiasm, of Philistine sentimentalism in the icy water of egotistical calculation. It has resolved personal worth into exchange value and, in place of the numberless indefeasible chartered freedoms, has set up that single, unconscionable freedom—free trade. In one word, for exploitation, veiled by religious and political illusions, it has substituted naked, shameless, direct, brutal exploitation.

The bourgeoisie has stripped of its halo every occupation hitherto honored and looked up to with reverent awe. It has converted the physician, the lawyer, the priest, the poet, the man of science into its paid wage laborers.

The bourgeoisie has torn away from the family its sentimental veil, and has reduced the family relation to a mere money relation.

The bourgeoisie has disclosed how it came to pass that the brutal display of vigor in the Middle Ages, which reactionists so much admire, found its fitting complement in the most slothful indolence. It has been the first to show what man's activity can bring about. It has accomplished wonders far surpassing Egyptian pyramids, Roman aqueducts, and Gothic cathedrals; it has conducted expeditions that put in the shade all former exoduses of nations and crusades.

The bourgeoisie cannot exist without constantly revolutionizing the instruments of production, and thereby the relations of production, and with them the whole relations of society. Conservation of the old modes of production in unaltered form was, on the contrary, the first condition of existence for all earlier industrial classes. Constant revolutionizing of production, uninterrupted disturbance of all social conditions, everlasting uncertainty and agitation distinguished the bourgeois epoch from all earlier ones. All fixed, fast-frozen relations, with their train of ancient and venerable prejudices and opinions, are swept away, all new-formed ones become antiquated before they can ossify. All that is solid melts into air, all that is holy is profaned, and man is at last compelled to face with sober senses his real conditions of life and his relations with his kind.

The need of a constantly expanding market for its products chases the bourgeoisie over the whole surface of the globe. It must nestle everywhere, settle everywhere, establish connections everywhere.

The bourgeoisie has through its exploitation of the world market given a cosmopolitan character to production and consumption in every country. To the great chagrin of reactionists, it has drawn from under the feet of industry the national ground on which it stood. All old-established national industries have been destroyed or are daily being destroyed. They are dislodged by new industries, whose introduction becomes a life and death question for all civilized nations, by industries that no longer work up indigenous raw material, but raw material drawn from the remotest zones; industries whose products are consumed not only at home, but in every quarter of the globe. In place of the old wants, satisfied by the productions of the country, we find new wants, requiring for their satisfaction the products of distant lands and climes. In place of the old local and national seclusion and self-sufficiency we have intercourse in every direction, universal interdependence of nations. And as in material, so also in intellectual production. The intellectual creations of individual nations become common property. National one-sidedness and narrow-mindedness become more and more impossible, and from the numerous national and local literatures there arises a world literature.

The bourgeoisie, by the rapid improvement of all instruments of production, by the immensely facilitated means of communication, draws all, even the most barbarian, nations into civilization. The cheap prices of its commodities are the heavy artillery with which it batters down all Chinese walls, with which it forces the barbarians' intensely obstinate hatred of foreigners to capitulate. It compels all nations, on pain of extinction, to adopt the bourgeois mode of production; it compels them to introduce what it calls civilization into their midst, i.e., to become bourgeois themselves. In one word, it creates a world after its own image.

The bourgeoisie has subjected the country to the rule of the towns. It has created enormous cities, has greatly increased the urban population as compared with the rural, and has thus rescued a considerable part of the population from the idiocy of rural life. Just as it has made the country dependent on the towns, so it has made barbarian and semi-barbarian countries dependent on the civilized ones, nations of peasants on nations of bourgeois, the East on the West.

The bourgeoisie keeps more and more doing away with the scattered state of the population, of the means of production, and of property. It has agglomerated population, centralized means of production, and has concentrated property in a few hands. The necessary consequence of this was political centralization. Independent, or but loosely connected provinces, with separate interests, laws, governments and systems of taxation, became lumped together into one nation, with one government, one code of laws, one national class interest, one frontier, and one customs tariff.

The bourgeoisie, during its rule of scarce one hundred years, has created more massive and more colossal productive forces than have all preceding generations together. Subjection of nature's forces to man, machinery, application of chemistry to industry and agriculture, steam navigation, railways, electric telegraphs, clearing of whole continents for cultivation, canalization of rivers, whole populations conjured out of the ground—what earlier century had even a presentiment that such productive forces slumbered in the lap of social labor?

We see then: the means of production and of exchange, on whose foundation the bourgeoisie built itself up, were generated in feudal society. At a certain stage in the development of these means of production and of exchange, the conditions under which feudal society produced and exchanged, the feudal organization of agriculture and manufacturing industry, in one word, the feudal relations of property, became no longer compatible with the already developed productive forces; they became so many fetters. They had to be burst asunder; they were burst asunder.

Into their place stepped free competition, accompanied by a social and political constitution adapted to it, and by the economic and political sway of the bourgeois class.

A similar movement is going on before our own eyes. Modern bourgeois society with its relations of production, of exchange, and of property, a society that has conjured up such gigantic means of production and of exchange, is like the sorcerer who is no longer able to control the powers of the nether world whom he has called up by his spells. For many a decade past, the history of industry and commerce is but the history of the revolt of modern productive forces against modern conditions of production, against the property relations that are the conditions for the existence of the bourgeoisie and of its rule. It is enough to mention the commercial crises that by their periodic return put on its trial, each time more threateningly, the existence of the entire bourgeois society. In these crises a great part not only of the existing products but also of the previously created productive forces are periodically destroyed. In these crises there breaks out an epidemic that in all earlier epochs would have seemed an absurdity—the epidemic of overproduction. Society suddenly finds itself put back into a state of momentary barbarism; it appears as if a famine, a universal war of devastation had cut off the supply of every means of subsistence; industry and commerce seem to be destroyed; and why? Because there is too much civilization, too much means of subsistence, too much industry, too much commerce. The productive forces at the disposal of society no longer tend to further the development of the conditions of bourgeois property; on the contrary, they have become too powerful for these conditions, by which they are fettered, and as soon as they overcome these fetters they bring disorder into the whole of bourgeois society, endanger the existence of bourgeois property. The conditions of bourgeois society are too narrow to comprise the wealth created by them. And how does the bourgeoisie get over these crises? On the one hand, by enforced destruction of a mass of productive forces; on the other, by the conquest of new markets, and by the more thorough exploitation of the old ones. That is to say, by paving the way for more extensive and more destructive crises, and by diminishing the means whereby crises are prevented.

The weapons with which the bourgeoisie felled feudalism to the ground are now turned against the bourgeoisie itself.

But not only has the bourgeoisie forged the weapons that bring death to itself; it has also called into existence the men who are to wield those weapons—the modern working class— the proletarians.

In proportion as the bourgeoisie, i.e., capital, is developed, in the same proportion is the proletariat, the modern working class, developed—a class of laborers, who live only so long as they find work, and who find work only so long as their labor increases capital. These laborers, who must sell themselves piecemeal, are a commodity, like every other article of commerce, and are consequently exposed to all the vicissitudes of competition, to all the fluctuations of the market.

Owing to the extensive use of machinery and to division of labor, the work of the proletarians has lost all individual character and, consequently, all charm for the workman. He becomes an appendage of the machine, and it is only the simplest, most monotonous, and most easily acquired knack that is required of him. Hence the cost of production of a workman is restricted, almost entirely, to the means of subsistence that he requires for his maintenance and for the propagation of his race. But the price of a commodity, and therefore also of labor, is equal to its cost of production. In proportion, therefore, as the repulsiveness of the work increases, the wage decreases. Nay, more, in proportion as the use of machinery and division of labor increases, in the same proportion the burden of toil also increases, whether by prolongation of the working hours, by increase of the work exacted in a given time, or by increased speed of the machinery, etc.

Modern industry has converted the little workshop of the patriarchal master into the great factory of the industrial capitalist. Masses of laborers, crowded into the factory, are organized like soldiers. As privates of the industrial army they are placed under the command of a perfect hierarchy of officers and sergeants. Not only are they slaves of the bourgeois class, and of the bourgeois state; they are daily and hourly enslaved by the machine, by the overlooker, and, above all, by the individual bourgeois manufacturer himself. The more openly this despotism proclaims gain to be its end and aim, the more petty, the more hateful, and the more embittering it is.

The less the skill and exertion of strength implied in manual labor, in other words, the more modern industry becomes developed, the more is the labor of men superseded by that of women. Differences of age and sex have no longer any distinctive social validity for the working class. All are instruments of labor, more or less expensive to use, according to their age and sex.

No sooner is the exploitation of the laborer by the manufacturer over, to the extent that he receives his wages in cash, than he is set upon by the other portions of the bourgeoisie, the landlord, the shopkeeper, the pawnbroker, etc.

The lower strata of the middle class—the small tradespeople, shopkeepers, and retired tradesmen generally, the handicraftsmen and peasants—all these sink gradually into the proletariat, partly because their diminutive capital does not suffice for the scale on which modern industry is carried on, and is swamped in the competition with the large capitalists, partly because their specialized skill is rendered worthless by new methods of production. Thus the proletariat is recruited from all classes of the population.

The proletariat goes through various stages of development. With its birth begins its struggle with the bourgeoisie. At first the contest is carried on by individual laborers, then by the workpeople of a factory, then by the operatives of one trade, in one locality, against the individual bourgeois who directly exploits them. They direct their attacks not against the bourgeois conditions of production, but against the instruments of production themselves; they destroy imported wares that compete with their labor, they smash to pieces machinery, they set factories ablaze, they seek to restore by force the vanished status of the workman of the Middle Ages.

At this stage the laborers still form an incoherent mass scattered over the whole country and broken up by their mutual competition. If anywhere they unite to form more compact bodies, this is not yet the consequence of their own active union, but of the union of the bourgeoisie, which class, in order to attain its own political ends, is compelled to set the whole proletariat in motion, and is moreover yet, for a time, able to do so. At this stage, therefore, the proletarians do not fight their enemies, but the enemies of their enemies, the remnants of absolute monarchy, the landowners, the non-industrial bourgeois, the petty bourgeoisie. Thus the whole historical movement is concentrated in the hands of the bourgeoisie; every victory so obtained is a victory for the bourgeoisie.

But with the development of industry the proletariat not only increases in number; it becomes concentrated in greater masses, its strength grows, and it feels that strength more. The various interests and conditions of life within the ranks of the proletariat are more and more equalized, in proportion as machinery obliterates all distinctions of labor and nearly

everywhere reduces wages to the same low level. The growing
competition among the bourgeois and the resulting commercial crises makes the wages of the workers ever more fluctuat-
ing. The unceasing improvement of machinery, ever more
rapidly developing, makes their livelihood more and more
precarious; the collisions between individual workmen and
individual bourgeois take more and more the character of
collisions between two classes. Thereupon the workers began
to form combinations (trade unions) against the bourgeois;
they club together in order to keep up the rate of wages; they
found permanent associations in order to make provision beforehand for these occasional revolts. Here and there the contest breaks out into riots.

Now and then the workers are victorious, but only for a
time. The real fruit of their battles lies not in the immediate
result, but in the ever expanding union of the workers. This
union is helped on by the improved means of communication
that are created by modern industry and that place the workers of different localities in contact with one another. It was
just this contact that was needed to centralize the numerous
local struggles, all of the same character, into one national
struggle between classes. But every class struggle is a political
struggle. And that union, to attain which the burghers of the
Middle Ages, with their miserable highways, required centuries, the modern proletarians, thanks to railways, achieve in
a few years.

This organization of the proletarians into a class, and consequently into a political party, is continually being upset
again by the competition between the workers themselves. But
it ever rises up again, stronger, firmer, mightier. It compels
legislative recognition of particular interests of the workers by
taking advantage of the divisions among the bourgeoisie itself.
Thus the ten-hour bill in England was carried.

Altogether collisions between the classes of the old society
further, in many ways, the course of development of the
proletariat. The bourgeoisie finds itself involved in a constant
battle. At first with the aristocracy; later on, with those portions of the bourgeoisie itself whose interests have become
antagonistic to the progress of industry; at all times, with the
bourgeoisie of foreign countries. In all these battles it sees
itself compelled to appeal to the proletariat, to ask for its help,
and thus to drag it into the political arena. The bourgeoisie
itself, therefore, supplies the proletariat with its own elements
of political and general education: in other words, it furnishes
the proletariat with weapons for fighting the bourgeoisie.

Further, as we have already seen, entire sections of the

ruling classes are, by the advance of industry, precipitated
into the proletariat, or are at least threatened in their conditions of existence. These also supply the proletariat with fresh
elements of enlightenment and progress.

Finally, in times when the class struggle nears the decisive
hour, the process of dissolution going on within the ruling
class, in fact within the whole range of old society, assumes
such a violent, glaring character that a small section of the
ruling class cuts itself adrift and joins the revolutionary class,
the class that holds the future in its hands. Just as, therefore,
at an earlier period, a section of the nobility went over to the
bourgeoisie, so now a portion of the bourgeoisie goes over to
the proletariat, and in particular a portion of the bourgeois
ideologists, who have raised themselves to the level of comprehending theoretically the historical movement as a whole.

Of all the classes that stand face to face with the bourgeoisie
today, the proletariat alone is a really revolutionary class. The
other classes decay and finally disappear in the face of modern industry; the proletariat is its special and essential product.

The lower-middle class, the small manufacturer, the shopkeeper, the artisan, the peasant, all these fight against the
bourgeoisie, to save from extinction their existence as fractions of the middle class. They are therefore not revolutionary but conservative. Nay, more, they are reactionary, for
they try to roll back the wheel of history. If by chance they
are revolutionary they are so only in view of their impending
transfer into the proletariat; they thus defend not their present
but their future interests, they desert their own standpoint to
place themselves at that of the proletariat.

The "dangerous class," the social scum, that passively rot-
ting mass thrown off by the lowest layers of old society, may,
here and there, be swept into the movement by a proletarian
revolution; its conditions of life, however, prepare it far more
for the part of a bribed tool of reactionary intrigue.

In the conditions of the proletariat those of old society at
large are already virtually swamped. The proletarian is without property; his relation to his wife and children has no
longer anything in common with the bourgeois family relations; modern industrial labor, modern subjection to capital,
the same in England as in France, in America as in Germany,
has stripped him of every trace of national character. Law,
morality, religion are to him so many bourgeois prejudices,
behind which lurk in ambush just as many bourgeois interests.

All the preceding classes that got the upper hand sought to
fortify their already acquired status by subjecting society at
large to their conditions of appropriation. The proletarians

cannot become masters of the productive forces of society, except by abolishing their own previous mode of appropriation, and thereby also every other previous mode of appropriation. They have nothing of their own to secure and to fortify; their mission is to destroy all previous securities for, and insurances of, individual property.

All previous historical movements were movements of minorities, or in the interest of minorities. The proletarian movement is the self-conscious, independent movement of the immense majority, in the interests of the immense majority. The proletariat, the lowest stratum of our present society, cannot stir, cannot raise itself up, without the whole superincumbent strata of official society being sprung into the air.

Though not in substance, yet in form, the struggle of the proletariat with the bourgeoisie is at first a national struggle. The proletariat of each country must, of course, first of all settle matters with its own bourgeoisie.

In depicting the most general phases of the development of the proletariat, we traced the more or less veiled civil war, raging within existing society, up to the point where that war breaks out into open revolution, and where the violent overthrow of the bourgeoisie lays the foundation for the sway of the proletariat.

Hitherto every form of society has been based, as we have already seen, on the antagonism of oppressing and oppressed classes. But in order to oppress a class certain conditions must be assured to it under which it can, at least, continue its slavish existence. The serf, in the period of serfdom, raised himself to membership in the commune, just as the petty bourgeois, under the yoke of feudal absolutism, managed to develop into a bourgeois. The modern laborer, on the contrary, instead of rising with the progress of industry, sinks deeper and deeper below the conditions of existence of his own class. He becomes a pauper, and pauperism develops more rapidly than population and wealth. And here it becomes evident that the bourgeoisie is unfit any longer to be the ruling class in society, and to impose its conditions of existence upon society as an overriding law. It is unfit to rule because it is incompetent to assure an existence to its slave within his slavery, because it cannot help letting him sink into such a state that it has to feed him instead of being fed by him. Society can no longer live under this bourgeoisie: in other words, its existence is no longer compatible with society.

The essential condition for the existence, and for the sway of the bourgeois class, is the formation and augmentation of capital; the condition for capital is wage labor. Wage labor rests exclusively on competition between the laborers. The advance of industry, whose involuntary promoter is the bourgeoisie, replaces the isolation of the laborers, due to competition, by their revolutionary combination, due to association. The development of modern industry, therefore, cuts from under its feet the very foundation on which the bourgeoisie produces and appropriates products. What the bourgeoisie, therefore, produces, above all, is its own gravediggers. Its fall and the victory of the proletariat are equally inevitable.

The Utopian Socialists

. . . The first direct attempts of the proletariat to attain its own ends, made in times of universal excitement, when feudal society was being overthrown, these attempts necessarily failed, owing to the then undeveloped state of the proletariat, as well as to the absence of the economic conditions for its emancipation, conditions that had yet to be produced, and could be produced by the impending bourgeois epoch alone. The revolutionary literature that accompanied these first movements of the proletariat had necessarily a reactionary character. It inculcated universal asceticism and social leveling in its crudest form.

The socialist and communist systems properly so called, those of St. Simon, Fourier, Owen, and others, spring into existence in the early undeveloped period . . . of the struggle between proletariat and bourgeoisie. . . .

The founders of these systems see, indeed, the class antagonisms as well as the action of the decomposing elements in the prevailing form of society. But the proletariat, as yet in its infancy, offers to them the spectacle of a class without any historical initiative or any independent political movement.

Since the development of class antagonism keeps even pace with the development of industry, the economic situation, as they find it, does not as yet offer to them the material conditions for the emancipation of the proletariat. They therefore search after a new social science, after new social laws that are to create these conditions.

Historical action is to yield to their personal inventive action, historically created conditions of emancipation to fantastic ones, and the gradual, spontaneous class organization of the proletariat to an organization of society specially contrived by these inventors. Future history resolves itself, in their eyes, into the propaganda and the practical carrying out of their social plans.

In the formation of their plans they are conscious of caring

chiefly for the interests of the working class as being the most
suffering class. Only from the point of view of being the most
suffering class does the proletariat exist for them.

The undeveloped state of the class struggle, as well as their
own surroundings, causes socialists of this kind to consider
themselves far superior to all class antagonisms. They want to
improve the condition of every member of society, even that
of the most favored. Hence they habitually appeal to society
at large, without distinction of class; nay, by preference, to
the ruling class. For how can people, when once they understand their system, fail to see in it the best possible plan of the
best possible state of society?

Hence they reject all political, and especially all revolutionary, action; they wish to attain their ends by peaceful means,
and endeavor, by small experiments, necessarily doomed to
failure, and by the force of example, to pave the way for the
new social gospel.

Such fantastic pictures of future society, painted at a time
when the proletariat is still in a very undeveloped state and
has but a fantastic conception of its own position, correspond
with the first instinctive yearnings of that class for a general
reconstruction of society.

But these socialist and communist publications contain also
a critical element. They attack every principle of existing society. Hence they are full of the most valuable materials for
the enlightenment of the working class. The practical measures proposed in them—such as the abolition of the distinction between town and country, of the family, of the carrying
on of industries for the account of private individuals, and of
the wage system, the proclamation of social harmony, the
conversion of the functions of the state into a mere superin-
tendence of production—all these proposals point solely to
the disappearance of class antagonisms which were, at that
time, only just cropping up, and which, in these publications,
are recognized in their earliest, indistinct and undefined forms
only. These proposals, therefore, are of a purely utopian
character.

The significance of critical utopian socialism and communism bears an inverse relation to historical development. In
proportion as the modern class struggle develops and takes
definite shape, this fantastic standing apart from the contest,
these fantastic attacks on it lose all practical value and all
theoretical justification. Therefore, although the originators of
these systems were, in many respects, revolutionary, their disciples have, in every case, formed mere reactionary sects. They
hold fast by the original views of their masters, in opposition

to the progressive historical development of the proletariat. They, therefore, endeavor, and that consistently, to deaden the class struggle and to reconcile the class antagonisms. They still dream of experimental realization of their social utopias, of founding isolated *"phalanstères,"* of establishing "home colonies," of setting up a "Little Icaria"—duodecimo editions of the New Jerusalem—and to realize all these castles in the air they are compelled to appeal to the feelings and purses of the bourgeois. By degrees they sink into the category of the reactionary conservative socialists depicted above, differing from these only by more systematic pedantry, and by their fanatical and superstitious belief in the miraculous effects of their social science.

They, therefore, violently opposed all political action on the part of the working class; such action, according to them, can only result from blind unbelief in the new gospel.

The Owenites in England and the Fourierists in France, respectively, oppose the Chartists and the Réformistes.

*   *   *

World Revolution

The communists fight for the attainment of the immediate aims, for the enforcement of the momentary interests of the working class, but in the movement of the present they also represent and take care of the future of that movement. . . .

But they never cease, for a single instant, to instill into the working class the clearest possible recognition of the hostile antagonism between bourgeoisie and proletariat, in order that the German workers may straightway use, as so many weapons against the bourgeoisie, the social and political conditions that the bourgeoisie must necessarily introduce along with its supremacy, and in order that, after the fall of the reactionary classes in Germany, the fight against the bourgeoisie itself may immediately begin.

The communists turn their attention chiefly to Germany, because that country is on the eve of a bourgeois revolution that is bound to be carried out under more advanced conditions of European civilization, and with a much more developed proletariat, than that of England was in the seventeenth and of France in the eighteenth century, and because the bourgeois revolution in Germany will be but the prelude to an immediately following proletarian revolution.

In short, the communists everywhere support every revolutionary movement against the existing social and political order of things.

In all these movements they bring to the front, as the leading question in each, the property question, no matter what its degree of development at the time.

Finally, they labor everywhere for the union and agreement of the democratic parties of all countries.

The communists disdain to conceal their views and aims. They openly declare that their ends can be attained only by the forcible overthrow of all existing social conditions. Let the ruling classes tremble at a communistic revolution. The proletarians have nothing to lose but their chains. They have a world to win.

Workingmen of All Countries, Unite!

The Dialectic Method

. . . My dialectic method is not only different from the Hegelian, but is its direct opposite. To Hegel the life process of the human brain, i.e., the process of thinking, which, under the name of "the Idea," he even transforms into an independent subject, is the demiurgos of the real world, and the real world is only the external, phenomenal form of "the Idea." With me, on the contrary, the ideal is nothing else than the material world reflected by the human mind and translated into forms of thought.

The mystifying side of Hegelian dialectic I criticized nearly thirty years ago, at a time when it was still the fashion. But just as I was working at the first volume of *Das Kapital*, it was the good pleasure of the peevish, arrogant, mediocre epigoni, who now talk large in cultured Germany, to treat Hegel in the same way as the brave Moses Mendelssohn in Lessing's time treated Spinoza, i.e., as a "dead dog." I therefore openly avowed myself the pupil of that mighty thinker, and even here and there, in the chapter on the theory of value, coquetted with the modes of expression peculiar to him. The mystification which dialectic suffers in Hegel's hand by no means prevents him from being the first to present its general form of working in a comprehensive and conscious manner. With him it is standing on its head. It must be turned right side up again if you would discover the rational kernel within the mystical shell.

In its mystified form dialectic became the fashion in Germany because it seemed to transfigure and to glorify the existing state of things. In its rational form it is a scandal and abomination to bourgeoisdom and its doctrinaire professors because it includes in its comprehension and affirmative recognition of the existing state of things, at the same time also, the recognition of the negation of that state, of its inevitable breaking up; because it regards every historically developed social form as in fluid movement, and therefore takes into account its transient nature not less than its momentary existence; because it lets nothing impose upon it, and is in its essence critical and revolutionary.

The contradictions inherent in the movement of capitalist society impress themselves upon the practical bourgeois most strikingly in the changes of the periodic cycle, through which modern industry runs, and whose crowning point is the universal crisis. That crisis is once again approaching, although as yet but in its preliminary stage; and by the universality of its theater and the intensity of its action it will drum dialectics even into the heads of the mushroom upstarts of the new, holy Prusso-German Empire.

(Extract from the Preface to the Second Edition of *Capital*.)

The Materialist Conception of History

. . . The materialist conception of history starts from the proposition that the production of the means to support human life—and, next to production, the exchange of things produced—is the basis of all social structure; that in every society that has appeared in history, the manner in which wealth is distributed and society divided into classes or orders is dependent upon what is produced, how it is produced, and how the products are exchanged. From this point of view the final causes of all social changes and political revolutions are to be sought not in men's brains, not in man's better insight into eternal truth and justice, but in changes in the modes of production and exchange. They are to be sought not in the *philosophy*, but in the *economics* of each particular epoch. The growing perception that existing social institutions are unreasonable and unjust, that reason has become unreason and right wrong, is only proof that in the modes of production and exchange changes have silently taken place with which the social order, adapted to earlier economic conditions, is no longer in keeping. From this it also follows that the means of getting rid of the incongruities that have been brought to light must also be present, in a more or less developed condition, within the changed modes of production themselves. These means are not to be invented by deduction from fundamental principles, but are to be discovered in the stubborn facts of the existing system of production.

(Extract from Engels' *Socialism: Utopian and Scientific*.)

. . . In the social production which men carry on they enter into definite relations that are indispensable and independent of their will; these relations of production correspond to a definite stage of development of their material powers of production. The sum total of these relations of production constitutes the economic structure of society—the real foundation, on which rise legal and political superstructures and to which correspond definite forms of social consciousness. The mode of production in material life determines the general character of the social, political and spiritual processes of life. It is not the consciousness of men that determines their existence, but, on the contrary, their social existence determines their consciousness. At a certain stage of their development the material forces of production in society come into conflict with the existing relations of production, or—what is but a legal expression for the same thing—with the property relations within which they had been at work before. From forms of development of the forces of production these relations turn into their fetters. Then comes the period of social revolution. With the change of the economic foundation the entire immense superstructure is more or less rapidly transformed. In considering such transformations the distinction should always be made between the material transformation of the economic conditions of production, which can be determined with the precision of natural science, and the legal, political, religious, aesthetic, or philosophic—in short, ideological—forms in which men become conscious of this conflict and fight it out. Just as our opinion of an individual is not based on what he thinks of himself, so can we not judge such a period of transformation by its own consciousness; on the contrary, this consciousness must rather be explained from the contradictions of material life, from the existing conflict between the social forces of production and the relations of production. No social order ever disappears before all the productive forces for which there is room in it have been developed, and new, higher relations of production never appear before the material conditions of their existence have matured in the womb of the old society. Therefore mankind always takes up only such problems as it can solve, since, looking at the matter more closely, we will always find that the problem itself arises only when the material conditions necessary for its solution already exist or are at least in the process of formation. In broad outlines we can designate the Asiatic, the ancient, the feudal, and the modern bourgeois methods of production as so many epochs in the progress of the economic formation of society. The bourgeois relations of production are the last antagonistic form of the social process of production—antagonistic not in the sense of individual antagonism, but of one arising from conditions surrounding the life of individuals in society; at the same time the productive forces developing in the womb of bourgeois society create the material conditions for the solution of that antagonism. This social formation constitutes, therefore, the closing chapter of the prehistoric stage of human society. . . .

(Extract from *Critique of Political Economy*.)

. . . Our conception of history depends on our ability to expound the real process of production, starting out from the simple material production of life, and to comprehend the form of intercourse connected with this and created by this (i.e., civil society in its various stages), as the basis of all history; further, to show it in its action as state, and so, from this starting point, to explain the whole mass of different theoretical products and forms of consciousness, religion, philosophy, ethics, etc., and trace their origins and growth, by which means, of course, the whole thing can be shown in its totality. . . .

Men are the producers of their conceptions, ideas, etc.— real, active men, as they are conditioned by a definite development of their productive forces and of the intercourse corresponding to these, up to its furthest forms. Consciousness can never be anything else than conscious existence, and the existence of men is their actual life process.

. . . we do not set out from what men say, imagine, conceive, nor from men as narrated, thought of, imagined, conceived, in order to arrive at men in the flesh. We set out from real, active men, and on the basis of their real life process we demonstrate the development of the ideological reflexes and echoes of this life process. . . . Morality, religion, metaphysics, all the rest of ideology and their corresponding forms of consciousness, thus no longer retain the semblance of independence. They have no history, no development; but men, developing their material production and their material intercourse, alter, along with this, their real existence, their thinking, and the products of their thinking. Life is not determined by consciousness, but consciousness by life. In the first method of approach the starting point is consciousness taken as the living individual; in the second it is the real, living individuals themselves, as they are in actual life, and consciousness is considered solely as *their* consciousness. . . .

(Extracts from *The German Ideology*.)

. . . According to the materialist conception of history, the *ultimately* determining element in history is the production and reproduction of real life. More than this neither Marx nor I has ever asserted. Hence if somebody twists this into saying that the economic element is the *only* determining one he transforms that proposition into a meaningless, abstract, senseless phrase. The economic situation is the basis, but the various elements of the superstructure—political forms of the class struggle and its results, to wit: constitutions established by the victorious class after a successful battle, etc., juridical forms, and even the reflexes of all these actual struggles in the brains of the participants, political, juristic, philosophical theories, religious views, and their further development into systems of dogmas—also exercise their influence upon the course of the historical struggles and in many cases preponderate in determining their *form*. There is an interaction of all these elements in which, amidst all the endless host of accidents (that is, of things and events whose inner interconnection is so remote or so impossible of proof that we can regard it as non-existent, as negligible), the economic movement finally asserts itself as necessary. Otherwise the application of the theory to any period of history would be easier than the solution of a simple equation of the first degree.

We make our history ourselves, but, in the first place, under very definite assumptions and conditions. Among these the economic ones are ultimately decisive. But the political ones, etc., and indeed even the traditions which haunt human minds also play a part, although not the decisive one. . . .

In the second place, however, history is made in such a way that the final result always arises from conflicts between many individual wills, of which each in turn has been made what it is by a host of particular conditions of life. Thus there are innumerable intersecting forces, an infinite series of parallelograms of forces which give rise to one resultant—the historical event. This may again itself be viewed as the product of a power which works as a whole *unconsciously* and without volition. For what each individual wills is obstructed by everyone else, and what emerges is something that no one willed. Thus history has proceeded hitherto in the manner of a natural process and is essentially subject to the same laws of motion. But from the fact that the wills of individuals—each of whom desires what he is impelled to by his physical constitution and external, in the last resort economic, circumstances (either his own personal circumstances or those of society in general)—do not attain what they want, but are merged into an aggregate mean, a common resultant, it must not be concluded that they are equal to zero. On the contrary, each contributes to the resultant and is to this extent included in it. . . .

Marx and I are ourselves partly to blame for the fact that the younger people sometimes lay more stress on the economic side than is due to it. We had to emphasize the main principle vis-à-vis our adversaries, who denied it, and we had not always the time, the place, or the opportunity to give their due to the other elements involved in the interaction. . . .

(Letter from Engels to Joseph Bloch, September 21-22, 1890.)

The Inevitable Doom of Capitalism

. . . The transformation of the individualized and scattered means of production into socially concentrated ones, of the pygmy property of the many into the huge property of the few, the expropriation of the great mass of the people from the soil, from the means of subsistence, and from the means of labor, this fearful and painful expropriation of the mass of the people forms the prelude to the history of capital. . . . The expropriation of the immediate producers was accomplished with merciless vandalism, and under the stimulus of passions the most infamous, the most sordid, the pettiest, the most meanly odious. Self-earned private property, which is based, so to say, on the fusing together of the isolated, independent laboring individual with the conditions of his labor, is supplanted by capitalistic private property, which rests on exploitation of the nominally free labor of others, i.e., on wage labor.

As soon as this process of transformation has sufficiently decomposed the old society from top to bottom, as soon as the laborers are turned into proletarians, their means of labor into capital, as soon as the capitalist mode of production stands on its own feet, then the further socialization of labor and further transformation of the land and other means of production into socially exploited and, therefore, common means of production, as well as the further expropriation of private proprietors, take a new form. That which is now to be expropriated is no longer the laborer working for himself, but the capitalist exploiting many laborers. This expropriation is accomplished by the action of the immanent laws of capitalistic production itself, by the centralization of capital. One capitalist always kills many. Hand in hand with this centralization, or this expropriation of many capitalists by few, develop, on an ever extending scale, the co-operative form of the labor process, the conscious technical application of science, the methodical cultivation of the soil, the transformation of the instruments of labor into instruments of labor usable only in common, the economizing of all means of production by their use as the means of production of combined, socialized labor, the entanglement of all peoples in the net of the world market, and this, the international character of the capitalistic regime. Along with the constantly diminishing number of the magnates of capital, who usurp and monopolize all advantages of this process of transformation, grows the mass of misery, oppression, slavery, degradation, exploitation; but with this, too, grows the revolt of the working class, a class always increasing in numbers, and disciplined, united, organized by the very mechanism of the process of capitalist production itself. The monopoly of capital becomes a fetter upon the mode of production which has sprung up and flourished along with and under it. Centralization of the means of production and socialization of labor at last reach a point where they become incompatible with their capitalist integument. This integument is burst asunder. The knell of capitalist private property sounds. The expropriators are expropriated.

The capitalist mode of appropriation, the result of the capitalist mode of production, produces capitalist private property. This is the first negation of individual private property, as founded on the labor of the proprietor. But capitalist production begets, with the inexorability of a law of nature, its own negation. It is the negation of negation.

(Extract from *Capital,* chapter 32.)

The Withering Away of the State

. . . The modern state . . . is only the organization that bourgeois society takes on in order to support the external conditions of the capitalist mode of production against the encroachments as well of the workers as of individual capitalists. The modern state, no matter what its form, is essentially a capitalist machine, the state of the capitalists, the ideal personification of the total national capital. The more it proceeds to the taking over of productive forces, the more does it actually become the national capitalist, the more citizens does it exploit. The workers remain wage earners—proletarians. The capitalist relation is not done away with. It is rather brought to a head. But, brought to a head, it topples over. State ownership of the productive forces is not the solution of the conflict, but concealed within it are the technical conditions that form the elements of that solution.

This solution can consist only in the practical recognition of the social nature of the modern forces of production, and therefore in the harmonizing of the modes of production, appropriation, and exchange with the socialized character of the means of production. And this can come about only by society openly and directly taking possession of the productive forces which have outgrown all control except that of society as a whole. The social character of the means of production and of the products today reacts against the producers, periodically disrupts all production and exchange, acts only like a law of nature working blindly, forcibly, destructively. But with the taking over by society of the productive forces, the social character of the means of production and of the products will be utilized by the producers with a perfect understanding of its nature, and instead of being a source of disturbance and periodic collapse will become the most powerful lever of production itself. . . .

With this recognition, at last, of the real nature of the productive forces of today, the social anarchy of production gives place to a social regulation of production upon a definite plan, according to the needs of the community and of each individual. Then the capitalist mode of appropriation, in which the product enslaves first the producer and then the appropriator, is replaced by the mode of appropriation of the products that is based upon the nature of the modern means of production: upon the one hand, direct social appropriation as means to the maintenance and extension of production; on the other, direct individual appropriation as means of subsistence and of enjoyment.

While the capitalist mode of production more and more completely transforms the great majority of the population into proletarians, it creates the power which, under penalty of its own destruction, is forced to accomplish this revolution. While it forces on more and more the transformation of the vast means of production, already socialized, into state property, it shows itself the way to accomplishing this revolution. *The proletariat seizes political power and turns the means of production into state property*.

But in doing this it abolishes itself as proletariat, abolishes all class distinctions and class antagonisms, abolishes also the state as state. Society thus far, based upon class antagonisms, has had need of the state. That is, of an organization of the particular class which was *pro tempore* the exploiting class, an organization for the purpose of preventing any interference from without with the existing conditions of production, and, therefore, especially for the purpose of forcibly keeping the exploited classes in the condition of oppression corresponding with the given mode of production (slavery, serfdom, wage labor). The state was the official representative of society as a whole; the gathering of it together into a visible embodiment. But it was this only in so far as it was the state of that class which itself represented, for the time being, society as a whole: in ancient times, the state of slave-owning citizens; in the Middle Ages, the feudal lords; in our own time, the bourgeoisie. When at last it becomes the real representative of the whole of society it renders itself unnecessary. As soon as there is no longer any social class to be held in subjection, as soon as class rule and the individual struggle for existence based upon our present anarchy in production, with the collisions and excesses arising from these, are removed, nothing more remains to be repressed, and a special repressive force, a state, is no longer necessary. The first act by virtue of which the state really constitutes itself the representative of the whole of society—the taking possession of the means of production in the name of society—this is, at the same time, its last independent act as a state. State interference in social relations becomes, in one domain after another, superfluous, and then dies out of itself; the government of persons is replaced by the administration of things, and by the conduct of processes of production. The state is not "abolished." *It dies out.* . . .

(Extract from Engels' *Socialism: Utopian and Scientific.*)

. . . The state, then, has not existed from all eternity. There have been societies that did without it, that had no conception of the state and state power. At a certain stage of economic development, which was necessarily bound up with the cleavage of society into classes, the state became a necessity, owing to this cleavage. We are now rapidly approaching a stage in the development of production at which the existence of these classes not only will have ceased to be a necessity, but will become a positive hindrance to production. They will fall as inevitably as they arose at an earlier stage. Along with them the state will inevitably fall. The society that will organize production on the basis of a free and equal association of the producers will put the whole machinery of state where it will then belong: into the museum of antiquities, by the side of the spinning wheel and the bronze ax.

(Extract from Engels' *The Origin of the Family, Private Property and the State.*)

SECTION VII

LIBERALISM AND ARISTOCRATIC CONSERVATISM

Stemming from a variety of sources, including individual responsibility associated with the Renaissance and the Reformation, humanism, scientific investigation, the beginning of capitalist economy and the rise of the middle class, liberalism is primarily concerned with freedom or individuality and a rejection of arbitrary authority. Liberalism, since it became prominent in the 19th century, has had a changing meaning given to it by writers, economists or politicians in the context of different historical periods, countries and specific events.

But basic to the liberal tradition are the ideas of freedom of thought and expression, the reduction or elimination of coercion, the toleration of different points of views though differences exist about the limits of toleration, limits on the exercise of power through constitutional arrangements or guarantees of individual rights, an impersonal rule of law, the right of people to choose their political and religious views and the existence of a free opposition to established authority. Liberalism is essentially secular, optimistic, sees history as a generally progressive development, believes in the use of reason and education to solve human problems and in freedom of opportunity, and favors peaceful solutions to international issues.

Early liberalism was identified with the economic concept of laissez-faire—the removal of restrictions or control on economic behavior, and with the market economy. Though some liberals, such as Milton Friedman, still hold this view, most modern liberals, such as Keynes and Beveridge, have accepted the need for state intervention in the economy to a certain degree, and favored the creation of a welfare state. While early liberalism concentrated on freedom from restrictions or "negative liberty", modern liberals tend to emphasize to a greater degree the need for opportunities for people to act and thus pay more attention to the social environment and to economic and political organization.

John Stuart Mill

John Stuart Mill's *On Liberty* (1859) is one of the great statements of classical political liberalism. Mill tackles the perennial issue: what powers should society have over individuals? His essential premise is that the individual is sovereign over his own body and mind. Self-protection is the sole end which justifies interfering with the liberty of others.

Mill can be regarded as a major exponent of negative liberty, the view of freedom as meaning the absence of restraints. He opposes not only coercion and political tyranny but also the tyranny of the majority and the despotism of custom.

Mill argues for freedom of thought and expression which are essential for both individuals and society as a whole. Such freedom allows individuals to mature and develop, and it enables truth to emerge from diverse and conflicting points of view. Mill never resolved the problem of where the line between freedom and government action should be drawn and in later life was more favorable to government authority but in general liberty was for him the basis of relationships between individuals and society.

Herzen

Alexander Herzen (1812–70) left his native Russia in 1847 and spent the rest of his life in exile in West Europe as a constant critic of the Tsarist regime. In *From the Far Shore* Herzen in a series of essays and letters evaluated the 1848 European revolutions he had observed at first hand and on which he wrote a poignant commentary.

Herzen is difficult to classify in a political school since he rejected any general formula as a solution to problems. As a radical he approved the Russian communal organization and attacked royalty and the church as well as the middle class for its orthodoxy. But he also opposed communism, feared the power of the masses and attacked revolutionaries for their willingness to destroy freedom. Herzen rejected ideologies that called for sacrifices of people in the name of an abstract principle, utopian concept or historical destiny. He saw men as free, within certain limits, life as open, and morality as made by men who should not be used for some supposed higher cause or historical force. For Herzen, skeptical of the dangers of idealism, civilized values and individual liberty were of the greatest significance.

Conservatism, historically, has been a response to the principles and activities stemming from the French Revolution. All conservative theorists reject the idea of violent change and uphold the need for order and continuity. They believe that society, institutions and methods of procedure have grown in organic fashion and that therefore social institutions and traditions should be respected. They tend to be pessimistic, or, in their view, realistic, about human capabilities as well as political and social change. Conservatism, its exponents have said, is based chiefly on a proper recognition of human limitation. Critics of conservatism suggest that its real basis is an unwillingness to do anything for the first time.

Throughout the nineteenth century, the democratic principle had been advanced, the political suffrage extended and restrictions removed, the will of the majority increasingly accepted as political wisdom. A number of writers, who might collectively be labeled "aristocratic conservatives," were troubled about these developments and the pace and direction of change. They saw the forces of commercialism and of industrialism, the political reforms, the ideas of egalitarianism, all leading to Jacobinism—power being placed in the hands of the incompetent. Undesirable consequences were stronger central government, the destruction of traditional ways of life, the renunciation of traditional sources of authority, loss of orientation and the prevalence of false values. These writers—Calhoun, de Tocqueville, Burckhardt, Humboldt, and Henry Adams are the most prominent—fearing the increasing levelism and aware of the trend towards conformity, emphasized the need for restrictions on power and the ultimate importance of liberty, although they were inherently pessimistic about the future.

De Tocqueville

Alexis de Tocqueville (1805–1859) is the most graceful stylist and penetrating observer of the fact that a new era dawned with the French Revolution. Lawyer, magistrate at twenty-two, visitor to the United States to study its penal system, member of the legislative opposition to Louis Philippe, and, for a short time, Minister of Foreign Affairs, he was also a gifted historian and political analyst. In 1835, the first volume of *Democracy in America* achieved instantaneous success.

"I am an aristocrat by instinct," he confessed. "That is to say I despise and fear the mass." But de Tocqueville was an aristocrat who had accepted the defeat of his class. The new age was characterized by the movement towards equality, a movement that was ardent, insatiable, incessant and invincible. America was the forerunner of this universal trend; there, all laws derived from this same line of thought, and everything from a single principle.

But the passion for equality would lead to uniformity and might destroy liberty. The power of public opinion would produce conformity rather than individuality, mediocrity rather than outstanding individuals, preoccupation with materialistic rather than spiritual values. Democracy might be as despotic and unstable as any monarchial or aristocratic régime since it was based on majority right, and would lead to centralized government. De Tocqueville argued the need for institutions of local self-government, decentralized administration, widespread ownership of property, and for voluntary associations to maintain political liberties, to obtain stability and to guard against the tyranny of the majority and the demands of authority.

The Anglophile de Tocqueville, friend of J. S. Mill, pointed to England as the only country in the world in which an aristocracy, constantly renewed by wealth, could exercise its political experience and wisdom. Unlike the static and rigid French aristocracy, the English were reformed and perfected.

But the old era was passing. This was an age of revolution, a world in which one had to be ready and prepared for everything, for no one was certain of his destiny. De Tocqueville distrusted "doctrines of necessity" in which theorists tended to interpret history by impersonal laws and inevitable causes; statesmen knew the importance of personality and luck. For de Tocqueville there were no definite conclusions—perhaps it was our destiny to cruise the endless sea for the rest of our lives without reaching an unknown destination.

Burckhardt

Jacob Burckhardt (1818–1897), descendent of a prominent Swiss family, had been attracted by and then estranged from political participation. He was critical both of optimism and radicalism, especially after the renunciation of his political ambitions after 1848. It has taken longer for his political writings to be appreciated than his majestic historical works,

The Civilization of the Renaissance in Italy and The Age of Constantine.

For Burckhardt, the time was one of crisis, the result of which would be complete democracy or absolute, lawless despotism. Mediocrity was the real diabolical force in the world. Civilization had to be protected against the masses gaining ascendancy in society and uninterested in true liberty. *Force and Freedom*, written in 1871, examined the interactions of culture, religion and the state, indicating the dangers inherent in the growth of state power. The preservation of culture was important above all, for this was the real expression of man. It was in the creative energy of the Renaissance that Burckhardt sought for the golden age, the harmony of things.

The Swiss historian clearly saw the dangers of the strong German state, and of uncontrolled authority. Burckhardt forecast the emergence of "the terrible simplifiers," the manner in which discipline would be used to prevent anarchy, and the bogus Messiah, "trampling on law and prosperity," who would emerge in Germany. The competition among all parties for the participation of the masses on all questions would mean more rulers who ignored law, prosperity and enriching work. Like de Tocqueville, he objected to philosophies of history purporting to explain all historical experience; in particular he attacked Hegel's "bold and insolent anticipation of a world plan." He ended a gentle pessimist: "I for one shall choose the cause for which I am going to perish, the culture of Old Europe."

Henry Adams

In America, the most distinguished aristocratic conservative was Henry Adams (1838–1918), erudite historian, Harvard lecturer, amateur diplomat and novelist. A fundamental pessimism runs through his autobiography, *The Education of Henry Adams,* with its belief that his own life was essentially a failure and his own talents insufficiently recognized; that the contemporary political system was corrupt and incompetent, and that the historical process was largely one of continual degradation.

Adams confessed himself bewildered by the vast changes in the world, the engineering products and manifold phenomena of life. He compared this present world of dynamic change, the age of steam and electricity, with its complex and chaotic society, unfavorably with the unity and stable faith of the eleventh century, symbolized by Chartres, Amiens and Mont-

Saint-Michel. Henry Adams, like his brother Brooks, with whom he shared so many ideas, attempted to draw analogies between the social and political worlds, and the physical and mechanical. In both, there were progressive degradation and consumption of energy, change from unity to multiplicity, simplicity to complexity, with consequent dissipation and disorder. Adams' analogy is highly dubious, and his conclusions were depressingly pessimistic. He saw history as the science of human degradation, manifested in the present age by increasing suicide, alcoholism, insanity and revolutionary activity. The complex system of democracy, an infinite mess of finite minds and conflicting interests, would lose its intellectual force and ultimately end in chaos.

JOHN STUART MILL
On Liberty

Negative liberty

The sole end for which mankind are warranted, individually or collectively, in interfering with the liberty of action of any of their number, is self-protection. The only purpose for which power can be rightfully exercised over any member of a civilised community, against his will, is to prevent harm to others. His own good, either physical or moral, is not a sufficient warrant. He cannot rightfully be compelled to do or forbear because it will be better for him to do so, because it will make him happier, because, in the opinions of others, to do so would be wise, or even right. These are good reasons for remonstrating with him, or reasoning with him, or persuading him, or entreating him, but not for compelling him, or visiting him with any evil in case he do otherwise. To justify that, the conduct from which it is desired to deter him must be calculated to produce evil to some one else. The only part of the conduct of any one, for which he is amenable to society, is that which concerns others. In the part which merely concerns himself, his independence is, of right, absolute. Over himself, over his own body and mind, the individual is sovereign.

It is, perhaps hardly necessary to say that this doctrine is meant to apply only to human beings in the maturity of their faculties. We are not speaking of children, or of young persons below the age which the law may fix as that of manhood or womanhood. Those who are still in a state to require being taken care of by others, must be protected against their own actions as well as against external injury. For the same reason, we may leave out of consideration those backward states of society in which the race itself may be considered as in its nonage. The early difficulties in the way of spontaneous progress are so great, that there is seldom any choice of means for overcoming them; and a ruler full of the spirit of improvement is warranted in the use of any expedients that will attain an end, perhaps otherwise unattainable. Despotism is a legitimate mode of government in dealing with barbarians, provided the end be their improvement, and the means justified by actually effecting that end. Liberty, as a principle, has no application to any state of things anterior to the time when mankind have become capable of being improved by free and equal discussion. . . .

But as soon as mankind have attained the capacity of being guided to their own improvement by conviction or persuasion, compulsion, either in the direct form or in that of pains and penalties for non-compliance, is no longer admissible as a means to their own good, and justifiable only for the security of others.

It is proper to state that I forego any advantage which could be derived to my argument from the idea of abstract right, as a thing independent of utility. I regard utility as the ultimate appeal on all ethical questions; but it must be utility in the largest sense, grounded on the permanent interests of man as a progressive being. Those interests, I contend, authorise the subjection of individual spontaneity to external control, only in respect to those actions of each, which concern the interest of other people. If any one does an act hurtful to others, there is a *prima facie* case for punishing him, by law, or, where legal penalties are not safely applicable, by general disapprobation. There are also many positive acts for the benefit of others, which he may rightfully be compelled to perform; such as to give evidence in a court of justice; to bear his fair share in the common defence, or in any other joint work necessary to the interest of the society of which he enjoys the protection; and to perform certain acts of individual beneficence, such as saving a fellow-creature's life, or interposing to protect the defenceless against ill-usage, things which whenever it is obviously a man's duty to do, he may rightfully be made responsible to society for not doing. A person may cause evil to others not only by his actions but by his inaction, and in either case he is justly accountable to them for the injury. The latter case, it is true, requires a much more cautious exercise of compulsion than the former. To make any one answerable for doing evil to others is the rule;

to make him answerable for not preventing evil is, comparatively speaking, the exception. Yet there are many cases clear enough and grave enough to justify that exception. In all things which regard the external relations of the individual, he is *de jure* amenable to those whose interests are concerned, and, if need be, to society as their protector. There are often good reasons for not holding him to the responsibility; but these reasons must arise from the special expediencies of the case: either because it is a kind of case in which he is on the whole likely to act better, when left to his own discretion, than when controlled in any way in which society have it in their power to control him; or because the attempt to exercise control would produce other evils, greater than those which it would prevent. When such reasons as these preclude the enforcement of responsibility, the conscience of the agent himself should step into the vacant judgment seat, and protect those interests of others which have no external protection; judging himself all the more rigidly, because the case does not admit of his being made accountable to the judgment of his fellow-creatures.

But there is a sphere of action in which society, as distinguished from the individual, has, if any, only an indirect interest; comprehending all that portion of a person's life and conduct which affects only himself, or if it also affects others, only with their free, voluntary, and undeceived consent and participation. When I say only himself, I mean directly, and in the first instance; for whatever affects himself, may affect others *through* himself; and the objection which may be grounded on this contingency, will receive consideration in the sequel. This, then, is the appropriate region of human liberty. It comprises, first, the inward domain of consciousness; demanding liberty of conscience in the most comprehensive sense; liberty of thought and feeling; absolute freedom of opinion and sentiment on all subjects, practical or speculative, scientific, moral, or theological. The liberty of expressing and publishing opinions may seem to fall under a different principle, since it belongs to that part of the conduct of an individual which concerns other people; but, being almost of as much importance as the liberty of thought itself, and resting in great part on the same reasons, is practically inseparable from it. Secondly, the principle requires liberty of tastes and pursuits; of framing the plan of our life to suit our own characte.; of doing as we like, subject to such consequences as may follow: without impediment from our fellow-creatures, so long as what we do does not harm them, even though they should think our conduct foolish, perverse, or wrong. Thirdly, from this liberty of each individual, follows the liberty, within the same limits, of combination among individuals; freedom to unite, for any purpose not involving harm to others: the persons combining being supposed to be of full age, and not forced or deceived.

No society in which these liberties are not, on the whole, respected, is free, whatever may be its form of government; and none is completely free in which they do not exist absolute and unqualified. The only freedom which deserves the name, is that of pursuing our own good in our own way, so long as we do not attempt to deprive others of theirs, or impede their efforts to obtain it. Each is the proper guardian of his own health, whether bodily, or mental and spiritual. Mankind are greater gainers by suffering each other to live as seems good to themselves, than by compelling each to live as seems good to the rest.

Though this doctrine is anything but new, and, to some persons, may have the air of a truism, there is no doctrine which stands more directly opposed to the general tendency of existing opinion and practice. Society has expended fully as much effort in the attempt (according to its lights) to compel people to conform to its notions of personal as of social excellence. The ancient commonwealths thought themselves entitled to practise, and the ancient philosophers countenanced, the regulation of every part of private conduct by public authority, on the ground that the State had a deep interest in the whole bodily and mental discipline of every one of its citizens; a mode of thinking which may have been admissible in small republics surrounded by powerful enemies, in constant peril of being subverted by foreign attack or internal commotion, and to which even a short interval of relaxed energy and self-command might so easily be fatal that they could not afford to wait for the salutary permanent effects of freedom. In the modern world, the greater size of political communities, and, above all, the separation between spiritual and temporal authority (which placed the direction of men's consciences in other hands than those which controlled their worldly affairs), prevented so great an interference by law in the details of private life; but the engines of moral repression have been wielded more strenuously against divergence from the reigning opinion in self-regarding, than even in social matters; religion, the most powerful of the elements which have entered into the formation of moral feeling, having almost always been governed either by the ambition of a hierarchy, seeking control over every department of human conduct, or by the spirit of Puritanism.

There is also in the world at large an increasing inclination to stretch unduly the powers of society over the individual, both by the force of opinion and even by that of legislation; and as the tendency of all the changes taking place in the world is to strengthen society, and diminish the power of the individual, this encroachment is not one of the evils which tend spontaneously to disappear, but, on the contrary, to grow more and more formidable. The disposition of mankind, whether as rulers or as fellow-citizens, to impose their own opinions and inclinations as a rule of conduct on others, is so energetically supported by some of the best and by some of the worst feelings incident to human nature, that it is hardly ever kept under restraint by anything but want of power; and as the power is not declining, but growing, unless a strong barrier of moral conviction can be raised against the mischief, we must expect, in the present circumstances of the world, to see it increase.

Liberty of Thought

If all mankind minus one were of one opinion, and only one person were of the contrary opinion, mankind would be no more justified in silencing that one person, than he, if he had the power, would be justified in silencing mankind. Were an opinion a personal possession of no value except to the owner; if to be obstructed in the enjoyment of it were simply a private injury, it would make some difference whether the injury was inflicted only on a few persons or on many. But the peculiar evil of silencing the expression of an opinion is, that it is robbing the human race; posterity as well as the existing generation; those who dissent from the opinion, still more than those who hold it. If the opinion is right, they are deprived of the opportunity of exchanging error for truth: if wrong, they lose, what is almost as great a benefit, the clearer perception and livelier impression of truth, produced by its collision with error.

It is necessary to consider separately these two hypotheses, each of which has a distinct branch of the argument corresponding to it. We can never be sure that the opinion we are endeavouring to stifle is a false opinion; and if we were sure, stifling it would be an evil still.

First: the opinion which it is attempted to suppress by authority may possibly be true. Those who desire to suppress it, of course deny its truth; but they are not infallible. They have no authority to decide the question for all mankind, and exclude every other person from the means of judging. To refuse a hearing to an opinion, because they are sure that it is false, is to assume that *their* certainty is the same thing as *absolute* certainty. All silencing of discussion is an assumption of infallibility. Its condemnation may be allowed to rest on this common argument, not the worse for being common.

Unfortunately for the good sense of mankind, the fact of their fallibility is far from carrying the weight in their practical judgment which is always allowed to it in theory; for while every one well knows himself to be fallible, few think it necessary to take any precautions against their own fallibility, or admit the supposition that any opinion, of which they feel very certain, may be one of the examples of the error to which they acknowledge themselves to be liable. Absolute princes, or others who are accustomed to unlimited deference, usually feel this complete confidence in their own opinions on nearly all subjects. People more happily situated, who sometimes hear their opinions disputed, and are not wholly unused to be set right when they are wrong, place the same unbounded reliance only on such of their opinions as are shared by all who surround them, or to whom they habitually defer; for in proportion to a man's want of confidence in his own solitary judgment, does he usually repose, with implicit trust, on the infallibility of "the world" in general. And the world, to each individual, means the part of it with which he comes in contact; his party, his sect, his church, his class of society; the man may be called, by comparison, almost liberal and large-minded to whom it means anything so comprehensive as his own country or his own age. Nor is his faith in this collective authority at all shaken by his being aware that other ages, countries, sects, churches, classes, and parties have thought, and even now think, the exact reverse. He devolves upon his own world the responsibility of being in the right against the dissentient worlds of other people; and it never troubles him that mere accident has decided which of these numerous worlds is the object of his reliance . . . Yet ages are no more infallible than individuals; every age having held many opinions which subsequent ages have deemed not only false but absurd; and it is as certain that many opinions now general will be rejected by future ages, as it is that many, once general, are rejected by the present.

The objection likely to be made to this argument would probably take some such form as the following. There is no greater assumption of infallibility in forbidding the propagation of error, than in any other thing which is done by public authority on its own judgment and responsibility. Judgment is given to men that they may use it. Because it may be used

erroneously, are men to be told that they ought not to use it at
all? To prohibit what they think pernicious, is not claiming
exemption from error, but fulfilling the duty incumbent on
them, although fallible, of acting on their conscientious conviction. If we were never to act on our opinions, because
those opinions may be wrong, we should leave all our interests
uncared for, and all our duties unperformed. An objection
which applies to all conduct can be no valid objection to any
conduct in particular. It is the duty of governments, and of
individuals, to form the truest opinions they can; to form
carefully, and never impose them upon others unless they are
quite sure of being right. But when they are sure (such rea-
soners may say), it is not conscientiousness but cowardice to
shrink from acting on their opinions, and allow doctrines
which they honestly think dangerous to the welfare of mankind, either in this life or in another, to be scattered abroad
without restraint, because other people, in less enlightened
times, have persecuted opinions now believed to be true. Let us
take care, it may be said, not to make the same mistake: but
governments and nations have made mistakes in other things,
which are not denied to be fit subjects for the exercise of
authority: they have laid on bad taxes, made unjust wars.
Ought we therefore to lay on no taxes, and, under whatever
provocation, make no wars? Men and governments, must act
to the best of their ability. There is no such thing as absolute
certainty, but there is assurance sufficient for the purposes of
human life. We may, and must, assume our opinion to be true
for the guidance of our own conduct: and it is assuming no
more when we forbid bad men to pervert society by the propagation of opinions which we regard as false and pernicious.

I answer, that it is assuming very much more. There is the
greatest difference between presuming an opinion to be true,
because, with every opportunity for contesting it, it has not
been refuted, and assuming its truth for the purpose of not
permitting its refutation. Complete liberty of contradicting
and disproving our opinion is the very condition which justifies us in assuming its truth for purposes of action; and on no
other terms can a being with human faculties have any rational assurance of being right.

. . . he who knows only his own side of the case, knows little
of that. His reasons may be good, and no one may have been
able to refute them. But if he is equally unable to refute the
reasons on the opposite side; if he does not so much as know
what they are, he has no ground for preferring either opinion.
The rational position for him would be suspension of judgment, and unless he contents himself with that, he is either led

by authority, or adopts, like the generality of the world, the side to which he feels most inclination. Nor is it enough that he should hear the arguments of adversaries from his own teachers, presented as they state them, and accompanied by what they offer as refutations. That is not the way to do justice to the arguments, or bring them into real contact with his own mind. He must be able to hear them from persons who actually believe them; who defend them in earnest, and do their very utmost for them. He must know them in their most plausible and persuasive form; he must feel the whole force of the difficulty which the true view of the subject has to encounter and dispose of; else he will never really possess himself of the portion of truth which meets and removes that difficulty. Ninety-nine in a hundred of what are called educated men are in this condition; even of those who can argue fluently for their opinions. Their conclusion may be true, but it might be false for anything they know: they have never thrown themselves into the mental position of those who think differently from them, and considered what such persons may have to say; and consequently they do not, in any proper sense of the word, know the doctrine which they themselves profess. They do not know those parts of it which explain and justify the remainder; the considerations which show that a fact which seemingly conflicts with another is reconcilable with it, or that, of two apparently strong reasons, one and not the other ought to be preferred. All that part of the truth which turns the scale, and decides the judgment of a completely informed mind, they are strangers to; nor is it ever really known, but to those who have attended equally and impartially to both sides, and endeavoured to see the reasons of both in the strongest light. So essential is this dicipline to a real understanding of moral and human subjects, that if opponents of all important truths do not exist, it is indispensable to imagine them, and supply them with the strongest arguments which the most skilful devil's advocate can conjure up.

To abate the force of these considerations, an enemy of free discussion may be supposed to say, that there is no necessity for mankind in general to know and understand all that can be said against or for their opinions by philosophers and theologians. That it is not needful for common men to be able to expose all the misstatements or fallacies of an ingenious opponent. That it is enough if there is always somebody capable of answering them, so that nothing likely to mislead uninstructed persons remains unrefuted. That simple minds, having been taught the obvious grounds of the truths inculcated on them, may trust to authority for the rest, and being aware that they have neither knowledge nor talent to resolve every difficulty which can be raised, may repose in the assurance that all those which have been raised have been or can be answered, by those who are specially trained to the task.

Conceding to this view of the subject the utmost that can be claimed for it by those most easily satisfied with the amount of understanding of truth which ought to accompany the belief of it; even so, the argument for free discussion is no way weakened. For even this doctrine acknowledges that mankind ought to have a rational assurance that all objections have been satisfactorily answered; and how are they to be answered if that which requires to be answered is not spoken? or how can the answers be known to be satisfactory, if the objectors have no opportunity of showing that it is unsatisfactory? If not the public, at least the philosophers and theologians who are to resolve the difficulties, must make themselves familiar with those difficulties in their most puzzling form; and this cannot be accomplished unless they are freely stated, and placed in the most advantageous light which they admit of . . . If, however, the mischievous operation of the absence of free discussion, when the received opinions are true, were confined to leaving men ignorant of the grounds of those opinions, it might be thought that this, if an intellectual, is no moral evil, and does not affect the worth of the opinions, regarded in their influence on the character. The fact, however, is, that not only the grounds of the opinion are forgotten in the absence of discussion, but too often the meaning of the opinion itself. The words which convey it cease to suggest ideas, or suggest only a small portion of those they were originally employed to communicate. Instead of a vivid conception and a living belief there remain only a few phrases retained by rote; or, if any part, the shell and husk only of the meaning is retained, the finer essence being lost. The great chapter in human history which this fact occupies and fills, cannot be too earnestly studied and meditated on.

It is illustrated in the experience of almost all ethical doctrines and religious creeds. They are all full of meaning and vitality to those who originate them, and to the direct disciples of the originators. Their meaning continues to be felt in undiminished strength, and is perhaps brought out into even fuller consciousness, so long as the struggle lasts to give the doctrine or creed an ascendancy over other creeds. At last it either prevails, and becomes the general opinion, or its progress stops; it keeps possession of the ground it has gained, but ceases to spread further. When either of these results has become apparent, controversy on the subject flags, and gradually dies away. The doctrine has taken its place, if not as a received opinion, as one of the admitted sects or divisions of opinion: those who hold it have generally inherited, not adopted it; and conversion from one of these doctrines to another, being now an exceptional fact, occupies little place in the thoughts of their professors. Instead of being, as at first, constantly on the alert either to defend themselves against the world, or to bring the world over to them, they have subsided into acquiescence, and neither listen, when they can help it, to arguments against their creed, nor trouble dissentients (if there be such) with arguments in its favour. From this time may usually be dated the decline in the living power of the doctrine.

In politics, again, it is almost a commonplace, that a party of order or stability, and a party of progress or reform, are both necessary elements of a healthy state of political life; until the one or the other shall have so enlarged its mental grasp as to be a party equally of order and of progress, knowing and distinguishing what is fit to be preserved from what ought to be swept away. Each of these modes of thinking derives its utility from the deficiencies of the other; but it is in a great measure the opposition of the other that keeps each within the limits of reason and sanity. Unless opinions favourable to democracy and to aristocracy, to property and to equality, to co-operation and to competition, to luxury and to abstinence, to sociality and individuality, to liberty and discipline, and all the other standing antagonisms of practical life, are expressed with equal freedom, and enforced and defended with equal talent and energy, there is no chance of both elements obtaining their due; one scale is sure to go up, and the other down. Truth, in the great practical concerns of life, is so much a question of the reconciling and combining of opposites, that very few have minds sufficiently capacious and impartial to make the adjustment with an approach to correctness, and it has to be made by the rough process of a struggle between combatants fighting under hostile banners. On any of the great open questions just enumerated, if either of the two opinions has a better claim than the other, not merely to be tolerated, but to be encouraged and countenanced, it is the one which happens at the particular time and place to be in a minority. That is the opinion which, for the time being, represents the neglected interests, the side of human well-being which is in danger of obtaining less than its share. I am aware that there is not, in this country, any intolerance of differences of opinion on most of these topics.

They are adduced to show, by admitted and multiplied examples, the universality of the fact, that only through diversity of opinion is there, in the existing state of human intellect, a chance of fair play to all sides of the truth. When there are persons to be found who form an exception to the apparent unanimity of the world on any subject, even if the world is in the right, it is always probable that dissentients have something worth hearing to say for themselves, and that truth would lose something by their silence.

We have now recognised the necessity to the mental well-being of mankind (on which all their other well-being depends) of freedom of opinion, and freedom of the expression of opinion, on four distinct grounds;

First, if any opinion is compelled to silence, that opinion may, for aught we can certainly know, be true. To deny this is to assume our own infallibility.

Secondly, though the silenced opinion be an error, it may, and very commonly does, contain a portion of truth; and since the general or prevailing opinion on any subject is rarely or never the whole truth, it is only by the collision of adverse opinions that the remainder of the truth has any chance of being supplied.

Thirdly, even if the received opinion be not only true, but the whole truth; unless it is suffered to be, and actually is, vigorously and earnestly contested, it will, by most of those who receive it, be held in the manner of a prejudice, with little comprehension or feeling of its rational grounds. And not only this, but, fourthly, the meaning of the doctrine itself will be in danger of being lost, or enfeebled, and deprived of its vital effect on the character and conduct; the dogma becoming a mere formal profession, inefficacious for good, but cumbering the ground, and preventing the growth of any real and heartfelt conviction, from reason or personal experience.

Liberty of Action

No one pretends that actions should be as free as opinions. On the contrary, even opinions lose their immunity when the circumstances in which they are expressed are such as to constitute their expression a positive instigation to some mischievous act. An opinion that corn-dealers are starvers of the poor, or that private property is robbery, ought to be unmolested when simply circulated through the press, but may justly incur punishment when delivered orally to an excited mob assembled before the house of a corn-dealer, or when handed about among the same mob in the form of a placard.

Acts, of whatever kind, which, without justifiable cause, do harm to others, may be, and in the more important cases absolutely require to be, controlled by the unfavourable sentiments, and, when needful, by the active interference of mankind. The liberty of the individual must be thus far limited; he must not make himself a nuisance to other people. But if he refrains from molesting others in what concerns them, and merely acts according to his own inclination and judgment in things which concern himself, the same reasons which show that opinion should be free, prove also that he should be allowed, without molestation, to carry his opinions into practice at his own cost. That mankind are not infallible; that their truths, for the most part, are only half-truths; that unity of opinion, unless resulting from the fullest and freest comparison of opposite opinions, is not desirable, and diversity not an evil, but a good, until mankind are much more capable than at present of recognising all sides of the truth, are principles applicable to men's modes of action, not less than to their opinions. As it is useful that while mankind are imperfect there should be different opinions, so it is that there should be different experiments of living; that free scope should be given to varieties of character, short of injury to others; and that the worth of different modes of life should be proved practically, when any one thinks fit to try them. It is desirable, in short, that in things which do not primarily concern others, individuality should assert itself. Where, not the person's own character, but the traditions or customs of other people are the rule of conduct, there is wanting one of the principal ingredients of human happiness, and quite the chief ingredient of individual and social progress.

In maintaining this principle, the greatest difficulty to be encountered does not lie in the appreciation of means towards an acknowledged end, but in the indifference of persons in general to the end itself. If it were felt that the free development of individuality is one of the leading essentials of well-being; that it is not only a coordinate element with all that is designated by the terms civilisation, instruction, education, culture, but is itself a necessary part and condition of all those things; there would be no danger that liberty should be undervalued, and the adjustment of the boundaries between it and social control would present no extraordinary difficulty. But the evil is, that individual spontaneity is hardly recognised by the common modes of thinking as having any intrinsic worth, or deserving any regard on its own account. The majority, being satisfied with the ways of mankind as they now are (for it is they who make them what they are), cannot comprehend why those ways should not be good enough for everybody; and what is more, spontaneity forms no part of the ideal of the majority of moral and social reformers, but is rather looked on with jealousy, as a troublesome and perhaps rebellious obstruction to the general acceptance of what these reformers, in their own judgment, think would be best for mankind. Few persons, out of Germany, even comprehend the meaning of the doctrine which Wilhelm von Humboldt, made the text of a treatise—that "the end of man, or that which is prescribed by the eternal or immutable dictates of reason, and not suggested by vague and transient desires, is the highest and most harmonious development of his powers to a complete and consistent whole;" that, therefore, the object "towards which every human being must ceaselessly direct his efforts, and on which especially those who design to influence their fellow-men must ever keep their eyes, is the individuality of power and development;" that for this there are two requisites, "freedom, and variety of situations;" and that from the union of these arise "individual vigour and manifold diversity," which combine themselves in "originality."

Little, however, as people are accustomed to a doctrine like that of Von Humboldt, and surprising as it may be to them to find so high a value attached to individuality, the question, one must nevertheless think, can only be one of degree. No one's idea of excellence in conduct is that people should do absolutely nothing but copy one another. No one would assert that people ought not to put into their mode of life, and into the conduct of their concerns, any impress whatever of their own judgment, or of their own individual character. On the other hand, it would be absurd to pretend that people ought to live as if nothing whatever had been known in the world before they came into it; as if experience had as yet done nothing towards showing that one mode of existence, or of conduct, is preferable to another. Nobody denies that people should be so taught and trained in youth as to know and benefit by the ascertained results of human experience. But it is the privilege and proper condition of a human being, arrived at the maturity of his faculties, to use and interpret experience in his own way. It is for him to find out what part of recorded experience is properly applicable to his own circumstances and character. The traditions and customs of other people are, to a certain extent, evidence of what their experience has taught *them*; presumptive evidence, and as such, have a claim to his deference: but, in the first place, their experience may be too narrow; or they may not have interpreted it rightly. Secondly, their interpretation of experience may be correct, but unsuitable to him. Customs are made for customary circumstances and customary characters; and his circumstances or his character may be uncustomary. Thirdly, though the customs be both good as customs, and suitable to him, yet to conform to custom, merely *as* custom, does not educate or develop in him any of the qualities which are the distinctive endowment of a human being. The human faculties of perception, judgment, discriminative feeling, mental activity, and even moral preference, are exercised only in making a choice.

The Despotism of Custom

The despotism of custom is everywhere the standing hindrance to human advancement, being in unceasing antagonism to that disposition to aim at something better than customary, which is called, according to circumstances, the spirit of liberty, or that of progress or improvement. The spirit of improvement is not always a spirit of liberty, for it may aim at forcing improvements on an unwilling people; and the spirit of liberty, in so far as it resists such attempts, may ally itself locally and temporarily with the opponents of improvement; but the only unfailing and permanent source of improvement is liberty, since by it there are as many possible independent centres of improvement as there are individuals. The progressive principle, however, in either shape, whether as the love of liberty or of improvement, is antagonistic to the sway of Custom, involving at least emancipation from that yoke; and the contest between the two constitutes the chief interest of the history of mankind. The greater part of the world has, properly speaking, no history, because the despotism of Custom is complete. This is the case over the whole East. Custom is there, in all things, the final appeal; justice and right mean conformity to custom; the argument of custom no one, unless some tyrant intoxicated with power, thinks of resisting. And we see the result. Those nations must once have had originality; they did not start out of the ground populous, lettered, and versed in many of the arts of life; they made themselves all this, and were then the greatest and most powerful nations of the world. What are they now? The subjects or dependents of tribes whose forefathers wandered in the forests when theirs had magnificent palaces and gorgeous temples, but over whom custom exercised only a divided rule with liberty and progress. A people, it appears, may be progressive for a certain length of time, and then stop: when does it stop? When it ceases to possess individuality. If a similar change should befall the nations of Europe, it will not be in exactly the same shape: the despotism of custom with which these nations are threatened is not precisely stationariness. It proscribes singularity, but it does not preclude change, provided all change together. We have discarded the fixed costumes of our forefathers; every one must still dress like other people, but the fashion may change once or twice a year. We thus take care that when there is a change, it shall be for change's sake, and not from any idea of beauty or convenience; for the same idea of beauty or convenience would not strike all the world at the same moment, and be simultaneously thrown aside by all at another moment. But we are progressive as well as changeable: we continually make new inventions in mechanical things, and keep them until they are again superseded by better; we are eager for improvement in politics, in education, even in morals, though in this last our idea of improvement chiefly consists in persuading or forcing other people to be as good as ourselves. It is not progress that we object to; on the contrary, we flatter ourselves that we are the most progressive people who ever lived. It is individuality that we war against: we should think we had done wonders if we had made ourselves all alike; forgetting that the unlikeness of one person to another is generally the first thing which draws the attention of either to the imperfection of his own type, and the superiority of another, or the possibility, by combining the advantages of both, of producing something better than either.

Limits to Authority

What, then, is the rightful limit to the sovereignty of the individual over himself? Where does the authority of society begin? How much of human life should be assigned to individuality, and how much to society?

Each will receive its proper share, if each has that which more particularly concerns it. To individuality should belong the part of life in which it is chiefly the individual that is interested; to society, the part which chiefly interests society.

Though society is not founded on a contract, and though no good purpose is answered by inventing a contract in order to deduce social obligations from it, every one who receives the protection of society owes a return for the benefit, and the fact of living in society renders it indispensable that each should be bound to observe a certain line of conduct towards the rest. This conduct consists, first, in not injuring the interests of one another; or rather certain interests, which, either by express legal provision, or by tacit understanding, ought to be considered as rights; and secondly, in each person's bearing his share (to be fixed on some equitable principle) of the labours and sacrifices incurred for defending the society or its members from injury and molestation. These conditions society is justified in enforcing, at all costs to those who endeavour to withhold fulfilment. Nor is this all that society may do. The acts of an individual may be hurtful to others, or wanting in due consideration for their welfare, without going to the length of violating any of their constituted rights. The offender may then be justly punished by opinion, though not by law. As soon as any part of a person's conduct affects prejudicially the interests of others, society has jurisdiction over it, and the question whether the general welfare will or will not be promoted by interfering with it, becomes open to discussion. But there is no room for entertaining any such question when a person's conduct affects the interests of no persons besides himself, or needs not affect them unless they like (all the persons concerned being of full age, and the ordinary amount of understanding). In all such cases, there should be perfect freedom, legal and social, to do the action and stand the consequences.

The distinction between the part of a person's life which concerns only himself, and that which concerns others, many persons will refuse to admit. How (it may be asked) can any part of the conduct of a member of society be a matter of indifference to the other members? No person is an entirely isolated being; it is impossible for a person to do anything seriously or permanently hurtful to himself, without mischief reaching at least to his near connections, and often far beyond them. If he injures his property, he does harm to those who directly or indirectly derived support from it, and usually diminishes, by a greater or less amount, the general resources of the community. If he deteriorates his bodily or mental faculties, he not only brings evil upon all who depended on him for any portion of their happiness, but disqualifies himself for rendering the services which he owes to his fellow-creatures generally; perhaps becomes a burthen on their affection or benevolence; and if such conduct were very frequent, hardly any offence that is committed would detract more from the general sum of good. Finally, if by his vices or follies a person does no direct harm to others, he is nevertheless (it may be said) injurious by his example; and ought to be compelled to control himself, for the sake of those whom the sight of knowledge of his conduct might corrupt or mislead.

And even (it will be added) if the consequences of misconduct could be confined to the vicious or thoughtless individual, ought society to abandon to their own guidance those who are manifestly unfit for it? If protection against themselves is confessedly due to children and persons under age, is not society equally bound to afford it to persons of mature years who are equally incapable of self-government? If gambling, or drunkenness, or incontinence, or idleness, or uncleanliness, are as injurious to happiness, and as great a hindrance to improvement, as many or most of the acts prohibited by law, why (it may be asked) should not law, so far as is consistent with practicability and social convenience, endeavour to repress these also? And as a supplement to the unavoidable imperfections of law, ought not opinion at least to organise a powerful police against these vices, and visit rigidly with social penalties those who are known to practise them? There is no question here (it may be said) about restricting individuality, or impeding the trial of new and original experiments in living. The only things it is sought to prevent are things which have been tried and condemned from the beginning of the world until now; things which experience has shown not to be useful or suitable to any person's individuality. There must be some length of time and amount of experience after which a moral or prudential truth may be regarded as established: and it is merely desired to prevent generation after generation from falling over the same precipice which has been fatal to their predecessors.

I fully admit that the mischief which a person does to himself may seriously affect, both through their sympathies and their interests, those nearly connected with him and, in a minor degree, society at large. When, by conduct of this sort, a person is led to violate a distinct and assignable obligation to any other person or persons, the case is taken out of the self-regarding class, and becomes amenable to moral disapprobation in the proper sense of the term. If, for example, a man, through intemperance or extravagance, becomes unable to pay his debts, or, having undertaken the moral responsibility of a family, becomes from the same cause incapable of supporting or educating them, he is deservedly reprobated, and might be justly punished; but it is for the breach of duty to his family or creditors, not for the extravagance. . . . Again, in the frequent case of a man who causes grief to his family by addiction to bad habits, he deserves reproach for his unkindness or ingratitude; but so he may for cultivating habits not in themselves vicious, if they are painful to those with whom he passes his life, or who from personal ties are depen-

dent on him for their comfort. Whoever fails in the consideration generally due to the interests and feelings of others, not
being compelled by some more imperative duty, or justified by
allowable self-preference, is a subject of moral disapprobation
for that failure, but not for the cause of it, nor for the errors,
merely personal to himself, which may have remotely led to
it. In like manner, when a person disables himself, by conduct purely self-regarding, from the performance of some definite duty incumbent on him to the public, he is guilty of a
social offence. No person ought to be punished simply for
being drunk; but a soldier or a policeman should be punished
for being drunk on duty. Whenever, in short, there is a definite damage, or a definite risk of damage, either to an individual or to the public, the case is taken out of the province of
liberty, and placed in that of morality or law.

But with regard to the merely contingent, or, as it may be
called, constructive injury which a person causes to society,
by conduct which neither violates any specific duty to the
public, nor occasions perceptible hurt to any assignable individual except himself; the inconvenience is one which society
can afford to bear, for the sake of the greater good of human
freedom. If grown persons are to be punished for not taking
proper care of themselves, I would rather it were for their
own sake, than under pretence of preventing them from im-
paring their capacity of rendering to society benefits which
society does not pretend it has a right to exact. But I cannot
consent to argue the point as if society had no means of
bringing its weaker members up to its ordinary standard of
rational conduct, except waiting till they do something irrational, and then punishing them, legally or morally, for it.
Society has had absolute power over them during all the early
portion of their existence: it has had the whole period of
childhood and nonage in which to try whether it could make
them capable of rational conduct in life.

If society lets any considerable number of its members grow
up mere children, incapable of being acted on by rational consideration of distant motives, society has itself to blame for
the consequences. Armed not only with all the powers of education, but with the ascendancy which the authority of a received opinion always exercises over the minds who are least
fitted to judge for themselves; and aided by the *natural* penalties which cannot be prevented from falling on those who
incur the distaste or the contempt of those who know them;
let not society pretend that it needs, besides all this, the power
to issue commands and enforce obedience in the personal
concerns of individuals, in which, on all principles of justice

and policy, the decision ought to rest with those who are to abide the consequences.

With respect to what is said of the necessity of protecting society from the bad example set to others by the vicious or the self-indulgent; it is true that bad example may have a pernicious effect, especially the example of doing wrong to others with impunity to the wrong-doer. But we are now speaking of conduct which, while it does no wrong to others, is supposed to do great harm to the agent himself: and I do not see how those who believe this can think otherwise than that the example, on the whole, must be more salutary than hurtful, since, if it displays the misconduct, it displays also the painful or degrading consequences which, if the conduct is justly censured, must be supposed to be in all or most cases attendant on it.

But the strongest of all the arguments against the interference of the public with purely personal conduct is that, when it does interfere, the odds are that it interferes wrongly, and in the wrong place. On questions of social morality, of duty to others, the opinion of the public, that is, of an overruling majority, though often wrong, is likely to be still oftener right; because on such questions they are only required to judge of their own interests; of the manner in which some mode of conduct, if allowed to be practised, would affect themselves. But the opinion of a similar majority, imposed as a law on the minority, on questions of self-regarding conduct, is quite as likely to be wrong as right; for in these cases public opinion means, at the best, some people's opinion of what is good or bad for other people; while very often it does not even mean that; the public, with the most perfect indifference, passing over the pleasure or convenience of those whose conduct they censure, and considering only their own preference.

(Extracts from *On Liberty,* chapters 1, 2, 3 and 4.)

ALEXANDER HERZEN
From the Other Shore

Human Dignity and Freedom

The liberty of the individual is the greatest thing of all, it is *on this and on this alone* that the true will of the people can develop. Man must respect liberty in himself, and he must esteem it in himself no less than in his neighbour, than in the entire nation. If you are convinced of that, then you will agree that to remain here is my right, my duty; it is the only protest that an individual can make amongst us; he must offer up this sacrifice to his human dignity. If you call my withdrawal an escape and will forgive me only out of your love, this will mean that you yourselves are not wholly free.

I know all the answers that can be made from the point of view of romantic patriotism and formal civil responsibility, but I cannot allow these antiquated attitudes. I have outlived them, left them behind, and it is precisely against them that I am fighting. These *réchauffé* remnants of the Roman and Christian heritage are the greatest obstacles to the establishment of true ideas of freedom, ideas that are healthy, clear, mature. Fortunately, in Europe, custom and a long process of development partly counterbalance these absurd theories and absurd laws. The people who live here are living on a soil fertilized by two civilizations; the path traversed by their ancestors for the past two and a half thousand years was not in vain, many human virtues have developed independently of the external organization and the official order.

Even in the worst periods of European history, we encounter some respect for the individual, some recognition of independence, some rights conceded to talent and genius. Vile as were the German rulers of that time, Spinoza was not sentenced to transportation, Lessing was not flogged or conscripted. This respect not merely for material but also for moral force, this unquestioning recognition of the individual —is one of the great human principles in European life.

In Europe a man who lives abroad has never been considered a criminal, nor one who emigrates to America a traitor.

We have nothing similar. With us the individual has always been crushed, absorbed, he has never even tried to emerge. Free speech with us has always been considered insolence, independence, subversion; man was engulfed in the State, dissolved in the community. The revolution of Peter the Great replaced the obsolete squirearchy of Russia—with a European bureaucracy; everything that could be copied from the Swedish and German codes, everything that could be taken over from the free municipalities of Holland into our half-communal, half-absolutist country, was taken over; but the unwritten, the moral check on power, the instinctive recognition of the rights of man, of the rights of thought, of truth, could not be and were not imported.

With us slavery increased with education; the State grew and improved but the individual reaped nothing from it; on the contrary, the stronger the State, the weaker the individual.

European forms of administration and justice, of military and
civil organization, developed with us into a kind of monstrous
and inescapable despotism.

Were it not that Russia was so vast, that the alien system of
power was so chaotically established, so incompetently administered, one might have said without exaggeration that no
human being with any sense of his own dignity could live in
Russia . . .

Nature and Freedom

'How is it that while everything in Nature is so purposive,
civilization, its highest effort, the crown of the age, emerges
from it as if by accident, drops out of life and finally fades
away, leaving behind only a dim memory? Meanwhile mankind moves backward, leaves the high road, and then again
begins to strain upwards, to end once more in the same gorgeous flower—magnificent, but without seed. . . . In your
philosophy of history there is something that revolts the soul.
Why all these efforts? The life of peoples becomes mere idle
play, it piles grain on grain, pebble on pebble, until once again
everything comes tumbling down to earth and men begin to
crawl out from under the ruins, to clear a space and build
huts for themselves out of moss, boards and fallen capitals,
only to achieve, after centuries of long effort, destruction once
more. It was not for nothing that Shakespeare said that history was a tale told by an idiot, signifying nothing.' . . .

'That is just your melancholy view of things. You are like
those monks who have nothing better to say to each other
when they meet than a gloomy *memento mori*, or like those
excessively sentimental souls who cannot recall that "man is
born but to die" without shedding a tear. To look at the end
and not at the action itself is the greatest of errors. Of what
use to the plant is its bright, gorgeous flower, its intoxicating
scent which will pass away? None at all. But nature is not so
miserly, and does not disdain what is transient, what lives
only in the moment. At every point she attains all that she can
attain, she achieves the impossible—fragrance, delight, an
idea . . . she goes on until she reaches the frontiers of development, reaches death itself, which cools her ardour, checks
her poetic fantasy, her unbridled creative passion. Who will
blame nature because flowers that bloom in the morning fade
in the evening, because she has not bestowed on the rose or
the lily the hardness of flint? And yet it is this mean and prosy
attitude that we want to carry over into the world of history!
Who has ventured to restrict civilization to the practical

alone? What barrier does it know? It is boundless, like thought, like art; it traces the ideals of life, it dreams the apotheosis of its own being, but life is under no obligation to realize such fantasies and ideas, the more so since this would be only an improved edition of what was there before, and life loves novelty. Roman civilization was far higher, far more humane than the barbarian world, but in the very confusion of barbarism were the seeds of things not to be found in the civilization of Rome, and so barbarism triumphed despite the *Corpus Juris Civilis* and the wisdom of Roman philosophers. Nature rejoices in what has been attained, and reaches out beyond it; she has no desire to wrong what exists; let it live as long as it can, while the new is still growing. That is why it is so difficult to fit the work of nature into a straight line; nature hates regimentation, she casts herself in all directions and never marches forward in step. The German barbarians were, in their untutored spontaneity *potentialiter* higher than the civilized Romans.'

'I'm beginning to think that you're expecting a new barbarian invasion and migration of peoples.'

'I don't like prophesying. The future does not exist; it is created by the combination of a thousand causes, some necessary, some accidental, plus human will, which adds unexpected dramatic *dénouements* and *coups de théâtre*. History improvises, she rarely repeats herself . . . she uses every chance, every coincidence, she knocks simultaneously at a thousand gates . . . Who knows which may open?' . . .

'. . . All in all, is the game worth the candle?'

'Of course it is! Especially as it isn't you who pay for it. You're dismayed because not all games are played to the end, but if they were they would be intolerably tedious. Long, long ago, Goethe used to tell us that beauty is transient because only the transient can be beautiful; this offends people. Man has an instinctive desire to preserve all that delights him; he is born, *ergo* he wants to live for ever; he falls in love, he wants to love and be loved all his life as in the first moment of avowal. He is angry with life when he notices that at fifty his feelings haven't the freshness or sharpness they had at twenty. But such a stagnant immobility is repugnant to the spirit of life; life cares nothing for the survival of anything personal, individual; she always pours the whole of herself into the present moment, and while endowing people with a capacity for the fullest possible pleasure, insures neither existence nor pleasure, and accepts no responsibility for their continuance. In this ceaseless movement of all living things, in this universal change, nature renews herself and lives on; in them she is eternally young. That is why each historical moment is complete and self-contained, like each year with its spring and summer, its winter and autumn, its storms and fine weather. That is why each period is new, fresh, full of its own hopes, carrying within itself its own joys and sorrows. The present belongs to it. But human beings are not satisfied with this. They want the future to be theirs as well.'

'It is painful for man that he cannot see even in the future the harbour towards which he is moving. With melancholy anxiety, he contemplates the infinite road ahead of him and sees that he is just as far from his end after all efforts as he was a thousand, two thousand years ago!'

'And what, pray, is the end of the song that the singer sings? . . . The sounds that burst from her throat, the melody that dies as soon as it has resounded? If you look beyond your pleasure in them for something else, for some other end, you will find that the singer has stopped singing, and then you will have only memories, and regrets, and remorse because, instead of listening, you were waiting for something else. You are misled by categories not fitted to catch the flow of life. Think carefully: is this end that you seek—a programme, an order? Who conceived it, who declared it? Is it something inevitable or not? If it is, are we mere puppets? . . . Are we morally free beings, or wheels in a machine? I prefer to think of life, and therefore of history, as an end attained than as a means to something else.'

'You mean, in short, that the end of nature and history is just—you and me? . . .'

'Partly; plus the present state of everything existing. Everything is included in this: the legacy of past efforts and the seeds of all that is to come; the inspiration of the artist, the energy of the citizen, and the rapture of the youth who, at this very moment, somewhere or other, is stealing his way towards some secret arbour where his shy love awaits him—giving herself completely to the present, with no thought of the future or of an aim . . . and the joy of a fish splashing—there —in the moonlight . . . and the harmony of the entire solar system . . . in short, I could add "and so forth . . . and so forth . . . and so forth . . ." three times—as after some feudal title.'

'You are quite right when you speak of nature, but it seems to me that you have forgotten that throughout all the changes and confusions of history there runs a single red thread binding it into one aim. This thread—is progress, or perhaps you do not acknowledge progress?'

'Progress is the inalienable quality of uninterrupted conscious development: it consists in a retentive memory and the physiological perfection of man through social life.'

'Is it possible that in all this you do not see a goal?'

'Quite the opposite, I see here only a consequence. If progress is the end, for whom are we working? Who is this Moloch who, as the toilers approach him, instead of rewarding them, only recedes, and as a consolation to the exhausted, doomed multitudes crying "morituri te salutant", can give back only the mocking answer that after their death all will be beautiful on earth. Do you truly wish to condemn all human beings alive to-day to the sad role of caryatids supporting a floor for others some day to dance on . . . or of wretched galley slaves, up to their knees in mud, dragging a barge filled with some mysterious treasure and with the humble words "progress in the future" inscribed on its bows? Those who are exhausted fall in their tracks; others, with fresh forces take up the ropes; but there remains, as you said yourself, as much ahead as there was at the beginning, because progress is infinite. This alone should serve as a warning to people: an end that is infinitely remote is not an end, but, if you like, a trap; an end must be nearer—it ought to be, at the very least, the labourer's wage, or pleasure in the work done. Each age, each generation, each life had and has its own fullness; *en route*, new demands arise, new experiences, new methods; some capacities improve at the expense of others; finally, the cerebral tissue improves. . . .

'. . . We talk so much about free will; we are so proud of it and, at the same time, annoyed that nobody leads us by the hand and that we stumble and must take the consequences of our actions. I am ready to repeat your words that the brain has grown one-sidedly because of idealism; people have begun to notice this and are now moving in another direction. They will be cured of idealism as they have been of other historical diseases—chivalry, Catholicism, Protestantism. . . .'

'But you must agree that the path of development through deviation and disease is a very strange one.'

'Yes, but the path is not determined. . . . Nature has hinted only vaguely, in the most general terms, at her intentions, and has left all the details to the will of man, circumstances, climate, and a thousand conflicts. The struggle, the reciprocal action of natural forces and the forces of will, the consequences of which one cannot know in advance, give an overwhelming interest to every historical epoch. If humanity marched straight towards some kind of result, then there would be no history, only logic; humanity would have come to rest, a finished article, in an absolute *status quo*, like animals. But all this is fortunately impossible, unnecessary, and worse than the existing situation. The organism of the animal gradually develops an instinct; in man the development goes further. He develops *reason* and does so painfully, slowly: it exists neither in nature nor outside nature; one has to achieve it and come to terms with it as best one may, because there is no *libretto*. If there was a *libretto*, history would lose all interest, become unnecessary, boring, ludicrous; the grief of Tacitus and the joy of Columbus would turn into a game, into buffoonery; great men would be so many heroes strutting on a stage who, whether they acted well or badly, would inevitably move towards and reach a definite dénouement. In history, all is improvisation, all is will, all is *ex tempore*; there are no frontiers, no itineraries. There exist conditions, sacred discontent; the flame of life and the eternal challenge to the fighters to try their strength, to go where they will, where there is a road; and where there is none, genius will blast a path.

'. . . Life—is both the means and the end, the cause and the effect. It is the eternal restlessness of active, tense matter striving for equilibrium only to lose it again, it is perpetual motion, the *ultima ratio*, beyond which one cannot go. In the past people used to look for answers in the clouds or in the depths, upwards or downwards, but they found nothing, because all that is essential, and important, is here on the surface. Life does not try to reach an aim, but realizes all that is possible, continues all that has been realized. It is always ready to go one step further in order to live more completely, to live more, if possible. There is no other aim. Very often we take as an aim what are the consecutive phases of some single development to which we have become accustomed. We believe that the aim of a child is its coming of age, because he does come of age; but the aim of a child is rather to play and enjoy himself, to be himself. If one looks for the final aim, then the purpose of everything living is—death.'

The Need for Free Choice

Man is freer than is usually believed.

He depends a great deal on his environment, but not as much as he surrenders to it. A large part of our destiny lies in our hands. One should grasp it and not let it go. But understand this, people allow the external world to overcome them, to captivate them against their will; they renounce their independence, depending on all occasions not on themselves but on the world, pulling ever tigher the knots that bind them to it. They expect from the world all the good and evil in life, the last thing they rely on is themselves. With such childish submission, the fatal power of the external becomes invincible; to enter into battle with it seems madness. Yet this terrible power wanes from the moment when in a man's soul, instead of self-sacrifice and despair, instead of fear and submission, there arises the simple question: 'Am I really so fettered to my environment in life and death that I have no possibility of freeing myself from it even when I have in fact lost all touch with it, when I want nothing from it and am indifferent to its bounty?'

I am not saying that this protest in the name of the independence and self-reliance of the individual is easy. It is not freely torn from the breast of man; either long, personal trials and misfortunes precede it, or else, those hard times when the more man understands the world, the more he is at odds with it, when all the bonds that link him to the external world have become chains, when he feels that he is right in despite of events and the masses, when he realizes that he is an enemy, a stranger, and not a member of a large family to which he belongs.

Outside us everything changes, everything vacillates. We are standing on the edge of a precipice and we see it crumbling. Twilight descends and no guiding star appears in the sky. We shall find no haven but in ourselves, in the consciousness of our unlimited freedom, of our autocratic independence. Saving ourselves in such a fashion, we take our stand on that open, manly ground which alone makes possible the development of a free existence in society—if it is at all possible for humanity.

If only people wanted to save themselves instead of saving the world, to liberate themselves instead of liberating humanity, how much they would do for the salvation of the world and the liberation of humanity! . . .

The world will not know liberty until everything religious and political is transformed into something simple, human, susceptible to criticism and denial. Logic, when it comes of age, detests canonized truths; it demotes them from angelic rank to human status, it converts holy mysteries into plain truths; it holds nothing sacrosanct and if the Republic arrogates to itself the same rights as the Monarchy, it will despise it as much as it did the Monarchy; nay, even more. Monarchy has no meaning; it is maintained by force, whereas the word 'republic' makes the heart beat faster. Monarchy is itself a religion; the republic has no mystical saving-clauses, no Divine Right, it stands on the same level with us all. It is not enough to despise the crown, one must give up respecting the

Phrygian cap; it is not enough not to consider *lèse majesté* a crime, one must look on *salus populi* as being one.

An End to Sacrifice

The submission of the individual to society, to the people, to humanity, to the Idea, is merely a continuation of human sacrifice, of the immolation of the lamb to pacify God, of the crucifixion of the innocent for the sake of the guilty. All religions have based morality on obedience, that is to say, on voluntary slavery. That is why they have always been more pernicious than any political organization. For the latter makes use of violence, the former—of the corruption of the will. Obedience means the transference of all that is most individual in a man on to an impersonal, generalized sphere independent of him. Christianity, the religion of contradictions, recognized on the one hand the infinite worth of the individual, as if only for the purpose of destroying him all the more solemnly before Redemption, the church, the Father in Heaven! These notions impregnated the whole of social life, were elaborated into a complete system of moral subjection, into a perverted but completely consistent dialectic. The world becoming more worldly or, better, noticing at last that it was actually just as worldly as ever, introduced its own elements into the Christian moral doctrine, but the foundation remained the same. The individual, who is the true, real monad of society, has always been sacrificed to some social concept, some collective noun, some banner or other. For whose sake this was done, to whom the sacrifice was made, who profited by it, who was liberated at the price of the individual's freedom, no one ever asked. Everyone sacrificed (at least in words) himself and everyone else.

This is not the place to examine how far the backwardness of the people justified such educational measures. Probably these measures were natural and indispensable, we come across them everywhere, but we can boldly say that even if they achieved large results, they certainly retarded the course of development, at least as much, distorting the mind with a false vision.

A century ago, the preaching of individualism awakened people from the heavy slumber into which they had sunk under the influence of the Catholic opiate. It led to freedom just as humility leads to submission. The writings of the egoist Voltaire did more for liberation than those of the loving Rousseau did for brotherhood.

Moralists talk of egoism as of a bad habit, without asking

whether man can remain man, having lost a living sense of personality, and without explaining what kind of a substitute 'brotherhood' and 'love of humanity' will prove. They do not even explain why one should be a brother of all and sundry and what is this duty of loving everyone in the world. We equally see no reason to love or hate anything merely because it exists. Leave man free in his emotions. He will find whom to love and whom to be a brother to; for that he does not need commandments or orders and if he doesn't find anyone, that is his affair and his misfortune.

Christianity at least did not stop at such trifles, but boldly ordered men to love not merely everyone but especially enemies. For eighteen hundred years men found this deeply touching; now it is time to admit that this rule is not absolutely clear. . . . Why should we love our enemies? Or if they are so amiable, why be their enemies?

The fact is quite simply that egoism and social sense (brotherhood and love) are not virtues or vices. They are the basic elements of human life, without which there would be no history, no development, but either the scattered life of wild beasts or else a herd of tame troglodytes. Kill the social sense in man—and you will get a savage orangoutang; kill egoism in him, and he will become a tame monkey. Slaves have the least egoism of anyone. The very word 'egoism' hasn't a precise meaning. There is a narrow, bestial, filthy egoism just as there is a filthy, bestial, narrow love. The real point is not to fulminate against egoism and extol brotherhood, for the one will never overcome the other, but to unite freely and harmoniously these two ineradicable elements of human life.

As a social being, man strives to love and needs no commandment to do so. To hate oneself is not at all necessary. Moralists consider all moral action to be so repugnant to human nature that they attribute great merit to every good action. That is why they make brotherhood a duty, like keeping Lent or mortifying the flesh. The last form of the religion of slavery is based on the divorce between society and the individual, on the fictitious hostility between them. As long as there is on one side the Archangel-Brotherhood and on the other Lucifer-Egoism, there will be a government to reconcile them and keep them in leash, there will be judges to punish, executioners to execute, the church to pray God for forgiveness, a God to inspire fear, and the commissar of police to put people in prison.

The harmony between society and the individual is not established once and for all. It *comes into being* in each period, almost in each country, and it changes with circumstances, like everything living. There can be no universal norm, no universal decision in the matter. We have seen how easy it is at some periods for man to surrender to his milieu and how at others he can *preserve* the tie only by exile, by withdrawal—*taking his all with him*. It is not in our power to change the historical relationship of the individual to society, nor unfortunately is it in the power of society itself, but it depends on us whether we are contemporary, in harmony with our development, in a word, whether we *mould* our conduct in response to circumstances.

Indeed, the truly free man *creates* his own morality. That was what the Stoics meant when they said: 'There are no laws for the wise.' What was admirable behaviour yesterday may be abominable to-day. There is no eternal, immutable morality, just as there are no eternal rewards and punishments. That which is really immutable in morality can be reduced to such generalities that almost everything personal in them is lost; for instance, that every action contrary to our convictions is a crime, or, as Kant said, that an act that man cannot universalize or elevate to a rule is immoral.

My advice is not to quarrel with the world, but to begin an independent, self-reliant life, which would find salvation within itself even were the whole world around us to perish.

(Extracts from *From the Other Shore*, introduction and sections 2, 5, and 6.)

DE TOCQUEVILLE
Democracy in America

The Irresistible Revolution

. . . If the men of our time should be convinced, by attentive observation and sincere reflection, that the gradual and progressive development of social equality is at once the past and the future of their history, this discovery alone would confer upon the change the sacred character of a divine decree. To attempt to check democracy would be in that case to resist the will of God; and the nations would then be constrained to make the best of the social lot awarded to them by Providence.

The Christian nations of our day seem to me to present a most alarming spectacle; the movement which impels them is already so strong that it cannot be stopped, but it is not yet so rapid that it cannot be guided. Their fate is still in their own hands; but very soon they may lose control.

The first of the duties that are at this time imposed upon those who direct our affairs is to educate democracy, to re-awaken, if possible, its religious beliefs; to purify its morals; to mold its actions; to substitute a knowledge of statecraft for its inexperience, and an awareness of its true interest for its blind instincts, to adapt its government to time and place, and to modify it according to men and to conditions. A new science of politics is needed for a new world.

This, however, is what we think of least; placed in the middle of a rapid stream, we obstinately fix our eyes on the ruins that may still be descried upon the shore we have left while the current hurries us away and drags us backward towards the abyss.

In no country in Europe has the great social revolution that I have just described made such rapid progress as in France; but it has always advanced without guidance. The heads of the state have made no preparation for it, and it has advanced without their consent or without their knowledge. The most powerful, the most intelligent, and the most moral classes of the nation have never attempted to control it in order to guide it. Democracy has consequently been abandoned to its wild instincts. . . . Its existence was seemingly unknown when suddenly it acquired supreme power. All then servilely sub-mitted to its caprices; it was worshipped as the idol of strength; and when afterwards it was enfeebled by its own excesses, the legislator conceived the rash project of destroying it, instead of instructing it and correcting its vices. No attempt was made to fit it to govern, but all were bent on excluding it from the government.

The result has been that the democratic revolution has taken place in the body of society without that concomitant change in the laws, ideas, customs, and morals which was necessary to render such a revolution beneficial. Thus we have a democracy without anything to lessen its vices and bring out its natural advantages; and although we already perceive the evils it brings, we are ignorant of the benefits it may confer. . . .

The social state [in the past] might [have] boast[ed] of its stability, its power, and, above all, its glory.

But the scene is now changed. Gradually the distinctions of rank are done away with; the barriers that once severed man-kind are falling; property is divided, power is shared by many, the light of intelligence spreads, and the capacities of all classes tend towards equality. Society becomes democratic, and the empire of democracy is slowly and peaceably introduced into institutions and customs.

I can conceive of a society in which all men would feel an equal love and respect for the laws of which they consider themselves the authors; in which the authority of the government would be respected as necessary, and not divine; and in which the loyalty of the subject to the chief magistrate would not be a passion, but a quiet and rational persuasion. With every individual in the possession of rights which he is sure to retain, a kind of manly confidence and reciprocal courtesy would arise between all classes, removed alike from pride and servility. The people, well acquainted with their own true interests, would understand that, in order to profit from the advantages of the state, it is necessary to satisfy its requirements. The voluntary association of the citizens might then take the place of the individual authority of the nobles, and the community would be protected from tyranny and license.

I admit that, in a democratic state thus constituted, society would not be stationary. But the impulses of the social body might there be regulated and made progressive. If there were less splendor than in an aristocracy, misery would also be less prevalent; the pleasures of enjoyment might be less excessive, but those of comfort would be more general; the sciences might be less perfectly cultivated, but ignorance would be less common; the ardor of the feelings would be constrained, and the habits of the nation softened; there would be more vices and fewer crimes.

In the absence of enthusiasm and ardent faith, great sacrifices may be obtained from the members of a commonwealth by an appeal to their understanding and their experience; each individual will feel the same necessity of union with his fellows to protect his own weakness; and as he knows that he can obtain their help only on condition of helping them, he will readily perceive that his personal interest is identified with the interests of the whole community. The nation, taken as a whole, will be less brilliant, less glorious, and perhaps less strong; but the majority of the citizens will enjoy a greater degree of prosperity, and the people will remain peaceable, not because they despair of a change for the better, but because they are conscious that they are well off already.

If all the consequences of this state of things were not good or useful, society would at least have appropriated all such as were useful and good; and having once and forever renounced the social advantages of aristocracy, mankind would enter into possession of all the benefits that democracy can offer.

But here it may be asked what we have adopted in the place

of those institutions, those ideas, and those customs of our forefathers which we have abandoned.

The spell of royalty is broken, but it has not been succeeded by the majesty of the laws. The people have learned to despise all authority, but they still fear it; and fear now extorts more than was formerly paid from reverence and love.

I perceive that we have destroyed those individual powers which were able, single-handed, to cope with tyranny; but it is the government alone that has inherited all the privileges of which families, guilds, and individuals have been deprived; to the power of a small number of persons, which if it was sometimes oppressive was often conservative, has succeeded the weakness of the whole community.

The division of property has lessened the distance which separated the rich from the poor; but it would seem that, the nearer they draw to each other, the greater is their mutual hatred and the more vehement the envy and the dread with which they resist each other's claims to power; the idea of right does not exist for either party, and force affords to both the only argument for the present and the only guarantee for the future.

The poor man retains the prejudices of his forefathers without their faith, and their ignorance without their virtues; he has adopted the doctrine of self-interest as the rule of his actions without understanding the science that puts it to use; and his selfishness is no less blind than was formerly his devotion to others.

If society is tranquil, it is not because it is conscious of its strength and its well-being, but because it fears its weakness and its infirmities; a single effort may cost it its life. Everybody feels the evil, but no one has courage or energy enough to seek the cure. The desires, the repinings, the sorrows, and the joys of the present time lead to nothing visible or permanent, like the passions of old men, which terminate in impotence.

We have, then, abandoned whatever advantages the old state of things afforded, without receiving any compensation from our present condition; we have destroyed an aristocracy, and we seem inclined to survey its ruins with complacency and to accept them. . . .

(Extract from the Introduction.)

The Power of the Majority

The very essence of democratic government consists in the absolute sovereignty of the majority; for there is nothing in democratic states that is capable of resisting it. Most of the American constitutions have sought to increase this natural strength of the majority by artificial means.

Of all political institutions, the legislature is the one that is most easily swayed by the will of the majority. The Americans determined that the members of the legislature should be elected by the people *directly,* and for a *very brief term,* in order to subject them, not only to the general convictions, but even to the daily passions, of their constituents. The members of both houses are taken from the same classes in society and nominated in the same manner; so that the movements of the legislative bodies are almost as rapid, and quite as irresistible, as those of a single assembly. It is to a legislature thus constituted that almost all the authority of the government has been entrusted. . . .

Several particular circumstances combine to render the power of the majority in America not only preponderant, but irresistible. The moral authority of the majority is partly based upon the notion that there is more intelligence and wisdom in a number of men united than in a single individual, and that the number of the legislators is more important than their quality. The theory of equality is thus applied to the intellects of men; and human pride is thus assailed in its last retreat by a doctrine which the minority hesitate to admit, and to which they will but slowly assent. Like all other powers, and perhaps more than any other, the authority of the many requires the sanction of time in order to appear legitimate. At first it enforces obedience by constraint; and its laws are not *respected* until they have been long maintained.

The right of governing society, which the majority supposes itself to derive from its superior intelligence, was introduced into the United States by the first settlers; and this idea, which of itself would be sufficient to create a free nation, has now been amalgamated with the customs of the people and the minor incidents of social life.

The French under the old monarchy held it for a maxim that the king could do no wrong; and if he did do wrong, the blame was imputed to his advisers. This notion made obedience very easy; it enabled the subject to complain of the law without ceasing to love and honor the lawgiver. The Americans entertain the same opinion with respect to the majority.

The moral power of the majority is founded upon yet another principle, which is that the interests of the many are to be preferred to those of the few. It will readily be perceived that the respect here professed for the rights of the greater number must naturally increase or diminish according to the state of parties. When a nation is divided into several great irreconcilable interests, the privilege of the majority is often overlooked, because it is intolerable to comply with its demands.

If there existed in America a class of citizens whom the legislating majority sought to deprive of exclusive privileges which they had possessed for ages and to bring down from an elevated station to the level of the multitude, it is probable that the minority would be less ready to submit to its laws. But as the United States was colonized by men holding equal rank, there is as yet no natural or permanent disagreement between the interests of its different inhabitants.

There are communities in which the members of the minority can never hope to draw the majority over to their side, because they must then give up the very point that is at issue between them. Thus an aristocracy can never become a majority while it retains its exclusive privileges, and it cannot cede its privileges without ceasing to be an aristocracy.

In the United States, political questions cannot be taken up in so general and absolute a manner; and all parties are willing to recognize the rights of the majority, because they all hope at some time to be able to exercise them to their own advantage. The majority in that country, therefore, exercise a prodigious actual authority, and a power of opinion which is nearly as great; no obstacles exist which can impede or even retard its progress, so as to make it heed the complaints of those whom it crushes upon its path. This state of things is harmful in itself and dangerous for the future.

. . . the mutability of the laws is an evil inherent in a democratic government, because it is natural to democracies to raise new men to power. But this evil is more or less perceptible in proportion to the authority and the means of action which the legislature possesses.

In America the authority exercised by the legislatures is supreme; nothing prevents them from accomplishing their wishes with celerity and with irresistible power, and they are supplied with new representatives every year. That is to say, the circumstances which contribute most powerfully to democratic instability, and which admit of the free application of caprice to the most important objects, are here in full operation. Hence America is, at the present day, the country beyond all others where laws last the shortest time. . . .

The omnipotence of the majority and the rapid as well as absolute manner in which its decisions are executed in the United States not only render the law unstable, but exercise the same influence upon the execution of the law and the conduct of the administration. As the majority is the only power that it is important to count, all its projects are taken up with the greatest ardor; but no sooner is its attention distracted than all this ardor ceases; while in the free states of Europe, where the administration is at once independent and secure, the projects of the legislature continue to be executed even when its attention is directed to other objects.

In America certain improvements are prosecuted with much more zeal and activity than elsewhere; in Europe the same ends are promoted by much less social effort more continuously applied. . . .

I hold it to be an impious and detestable maxim that, politically speaking, the people have a right to do anything; and yet I have asserted that all authority orginates in the will of the majority. Am I, then, in contradiction with myself?

A general law,. which bears the name of justice, has been made and sanctioned, not only by a majority of this or that people, but by a majority of mankind. The rights of every people are therefore confined within the limits of what is just. A nation may be considered as a jury which is empowered to represent society at large and to apply justice, which is its law. Ought such a jury, which represents society, to have more power than the society itself whose laws it executes?

When I refuse to obey an unjust law, I do not contest the right of the majority to command, but I simply appeal from the sovereignty of the people to the sovereignty of mankind. Some have not feared to assert that a people can never outstep the boundaries of justice and reason in those affairs which are peculiarly its own; and that consequently full power may be given to the majority by which it is represented. But this is the language of a slave.

A majority taken collectively is only an individual, whose opinions, and frequently whose interests, are opposed to those of another individual, who is styled a minority. If it be admitted that a man possessing absolute power may misuse that power by wronging his adversaries, why should not a majority be liable to the same reproach? Men do not change their characters by uniting with one another; nor does their patience in the presence of obstacles increase with their strength. For my own part, I cannot believe it; the power to do everything, which I should refuse to one of my equals, I will never grant to any number of them.

I do not think that, for the sake of preserving liberty, it is possible to combine several principles in the same government so as really to oppose them to one another. The form of government that is usually termed *mixed* has always appeared to me a mere chimera. Accurately speaking, there is no such thing as a *mixed government,* in the sense usually given to that word, because in all communities some one principle of action may be discovered which preponderates over the others. . . .

I am therefore of the opinion that social power superior to all others must always be placed somewhere; but I think that liberty is endangered when this power finds no obstacle which can retard its course and give it time to moderate its own vehemence.

Unlimited power is in itself a bad and dangerous thing. Human beings are not competent to exercise it with discretion. God alone can be omnipotent, because his wisdom and his justice are always equal to his power. There is no power on earth so worthy of honor in itself or clothed with rights so sacred that I would admit its uncontrolled and all-predominant authority. When I see that the right and the means of absolute command are conferred on any power whatever, be it called a people or a king, an aristocracy or a democracy, a monarchy or a republic, I say there is the germ of tyranny, and I seek to live elsewhere, under other laws.

In my opinion, the main evil of the present democratic institutions of the United States does not arise, as is often asserted in Europe, from their weakness, but from their irresistible strength. I am not so much alarmed at the excessive liberty which reigns in that country as at the inadequate securities which one finds there against tyranny.

When an individual or a party is wronged in the United States, to whom can he apply for redress? If to public opinion, public opinion constitutes the majority; if to the legislature, it represents the majority and implicitly obeys it; if to the executive power, it is appointed by the majority and serves as a passive tool in its hands. The public force consists of the majority under arms; the jury is the majority invested with the right of hearing judicial cases; and in certain states even the judges are elected by the majority. However iniquitous or absurd the measure of which you complain, you must submit to it as well as you can.

If, on the other hand, a legislative power could be so constituted as to represent the majority without necessarily being the slave of its passions, an executive so as to retain a proper share of authority, and a judiciary so as to remain independent of the other two powers, a government would be formed which would still be democratic while incurring scarcely any risk of tyranny.

I do not say that there is a frequent use of tyranny in

America at the present day; but I maintain that there is no sure barrier against it, and that the causes which mitigate the government there are to be found in the circumstances and the manners of the country more than in its laws.

(Extract from chapter 15.)

BURCKHARDT

Force and Freedom

The Growth of the Power of the State

[In the nineteenth century] it might [have] appear[ed] as if the State were merely a police force protecting this multitudinous activity [i.e. industrialization in England, world trade, extension of colonization, etc.—*the Author*], which at one time looked to the State for co-operation in many directions, but ultimately only required of it the abolition of restrictions. Further, it aimed at extending its customs radius as far as possible, and therefore desired the State to be as powerful as possible.

At the same time, however, the ideas of the French Revolution were still actively at work, politically and socially. Constitutional, radical, social claims were being put forward, supported by the general equalization of rights, and, by way of the press, were reaching the public on a gigantic scale. Political science became common property, statistics and political economy the arsenal from which everybody took the weapons he could best wield. Every movement was oecumenical. The Church, however, seemed to be nothing but an irrational force; religion was desired, but without the Church.

And on the other hand the State, as independently of all this development as the temporary circumstances permitted, proclaimed its power as a heritage to be increased with might and main. Wherever possible, it reduced the rights of the lower orders to a mere fiction. There were and still are dynasties, bureaucracies and militarisms which are firmly resolved to establish their own programmes, and not to submit to dictation.

All these things have co-operated to produce the great crisis in the idea of the State through which we are now living.

No class of society now admits that the State has any special rights. Everything is open to question. Indeed, political thought expects the State to be as mutable as its own caprices.

At the same time, political thought claims for the State an

ever-increasing and more comprehensive power of coercion, so that it may be in a position to put into practice the completely theoretical political programmes which political thinkers periodically draw up, the most turbulent individuals demanding the most extreme control of the individual and the community.

The State is thus, on the one hand, the realization and expression of the cultural ideas of every party; on the other, merely the visible vestures of civic life and only *ad hoc* almighty. It should be able to do everything, yet allowed to do nothing. In particular, it must not defend its existing form in any crisis—and after all, what men want more than anything else is to retrieve their share of its exercise of power.

Thus the *form* of the State is increasingly questionable and its radius of power increasingly great. The latter also holds good in the geographical sense; the State must now embrace at least the whole nation and something over. The unity of the State's power and its mere area have become a cult.

The more radically the sacred right of the State (its once arbitrary power over life and property) dies out, the more its secular rights expand. The rights of corporations are in any case extinct; nothing now exists which can cause any inconvenience. In the end, people become exceedingly sensitive to any differentiation; the simplifications and standardizations secured by the great State suffice no longer. Money-making, the main force of present-day culture, postulates the universal State, if only for the sake of communications, though that demand finds a powerful counterpoise in the specific character of the individual peoples and their sense of power.

And through it all there can occasionally be heard complaining undertones in favor of decentralization, American simplifications, etc.

The most important point, however, is that the boundaries between the respective duties of State and Society threaten to shift entirely.

The strongest impetus in this direction came from the French Revolution and the Rights of Man, while the State might well be thankful if its constitution survived with a reasonable definition of the rights of the *citizen*.

In any case, as Carlyle rightly points out, some thought should have been spent on the duties and capacities of man, on the natural resources of the country.

The modern version of the Rights of Man includes the right to work and subsistence. For men are no longer willing to leave the most vital matters to Society, because they want the impossible and imagine that it can only be secured under compulsion from the State.

Not only is everything of the nature of an "institution" or a "foundation" promptly noised abroad by the literary and journalistic intercourse of the day, so that there is a general demand for it, but absolutely everything that people know or feel Society will not undertake is simply heaped on to the daily growing burden of the State. At every turn, needs grow, bearing their theories with them, and not only needs, but debt, the chief, miserable folly of the nineteenth century. This habit of flinging away the fortune of future generations is of itself enough to show that a heartless pride is the peculiar characteristic of our time.

(Extract from *The State Determined by Culture*.)

The Tendencies of the Present Age

The long peace dating from 1815 had created an optical illusion, namely that a permanent balance of power had been established. In any case, from the very outset too little account was taken of the mutability of national temperaments.

The Restoration and its ostensible principle of Legitimacy, which was in effect a reaction against the spirit of the French Revolution, restored in most unequal fashion a number of former modes of life and law and a series of national frontiers; on the other hand, it was impossible to banish from the world the continuing after-effects of the French Revolution, namely, the actual and far-reaching equality before the law (in taxation, qualification for office, the division of inheritances), the transferability of landed property, the placing of all property at the disposal of industry, and religious parity in a number of countries whose populations were now very mixed.

The State itself, moreover, was determined not to relinquish one of the results of the Revolution, namely the great expansion in the idea of its power which had come about in the interim and was due, among other things, to the Napoleonic Caesarism which had been imitated everywhere. The Power State of its very nature postulated equality, even where it abandoned places at Court and in the army as spoils to its aristocracy.

Opposing this, there stood the spirit of those peoples who had waged the wars of 1812–1815 in a state of extreme national fervor. A spirit of criticism had awakened which, however much men needed rest, could no longer lie still, and henceforth applied a new standard to life as a whole. . . .

In Western Europe, during the Thirties, politics developed into a general radicalism, namely that way of thinking which attributed all evils to existing political conditions and their representatives, and thought to find salvation in demolishing and rebuilding the whole structure from the foundations with the help of abstract principles which already revealed a much closer kinship with North America.

With the Forties there set in a development of Socialistic and Communistic theories, in part the project of conditions in the great English and French industrial towns; they embraced the whole social edifice, an inevitable result of untrammelled traffic. The freedom actually existing was ample for such ideas to spread unchecked, so that, according to Renan, after 1840 a deterioration of their quality was distinctly perceptible. At the same time, nobody had any idea of what and how strong the opposing forces might be. How far the right of defence was misunderstood became evident in February 1848.

This state of affairs was reflected in the literature and poetry of the time. Derision, loud snarling and *Weltschmerz* chairacterized its new, post-Byronic attitude.

Then came the February Revolution of 1848. In the midst of the general upheaval, it caused a sudden clearing of the horizon. By far its most important, though only ephemeral, result was the proclamation of union in Germany and Italy. Socialism proved far less powerful than people had imagined, for the June days in Paris almost at once restored the monarchist and constitutional party to power, and the sense of property and money-making was more intense than ever. . . .

With dynasties, bureaucracies and militarisms continuing to exist, the *inward* crisis in men's minds had to be left almost entirely out of account. Public opinion, the press, the swiftly rising tide of traffic, won the day everywhere and were already so intrinsic a part of money-making that any check on the one meant damage to the other. Everywhere industry was striving for a place in world industry.

At the same time, the events of 1848 had given the ruling classes a deeper insight into the people. Louis Napoleon had risked universal suffrage for the elections, and others followed his lead. The conservative strain in the rural populations had been recognized, though no attempt had been made to assess precisely how far it might be extended from the elections to everything and everybody (institutions, taxes, etc.).

With all business swelling into big business, the views of the business man took the following line: on the one hand, the State should be no more than the protective guarantor of his interests and of his type of intelligence, henceforth assumed to be the main purpose of the world. Indeed, it was his desire that his type of intelligence should obtain possession of the State by means of constitutional adjustments. On the other hand, there prevailed a profound distrust of constitutional liberty in practice, since it was more likely to be used by destructive forces.

For at the same time the ideas of the French Revolution and the reform principles of modern times were both finding active expression in democracy, so-called, a doctrine nourished by a thousand springs, and varying greatly with the social status of its adherents. Only in one respect was it consistent, namely, in the insatiability of its demand for State control of the individual. Thus it effaces the boundaries between State and Society, and looks to the State for the things that Society will most likely refuse to do, while maintaining a permanent condition of argument and change and ultimately vindicating the right to work and subsistence for certain castes. . . .

March 1873. The first great phenomenon to follow the war of 1870–1871 was a further extraordinary intensification of money-making. . . .

The spiritual results, however, of which some are already visible, and some about to become so, are that the so-called "best minds" are going into business or are actually being educated to that end by their parents. Bureaucracy, like the army in France and other countries, is no longer a career. In Prussia the most strenuous efforts are necessary in order to keep it as such.

Art and science have the greatest difficulty in preventing themselves from sinking into a mere branch of urban money-making and from being carried away on the stream of general unrest. The utmost effort and self-denial will be necessary if they are to remain creatively independent in view of the relation to which they stand to the daily press, to cosmopolitan traffic, to world exhibitions. A further menace is the decay of local patriotism, with its advantages and disadvantages, and a great decrease even in national patriotism.

What classes and strata of society will now become the real representatives of culture, will give us our scholars, artists and poets, our creative personalities?

Or is everything to turn into big business, as in America?

Now for the political results. Two great nations, Germany and Italy, have been founded, partly with the help of public opinion, long since in a state of extreme agitation, partly by means of great wars. A further factor is the spectacle of rapid demolition and reconstruction in countries whose established polity had long been regarded as immutable. Hence political adventure has become a matter of daily occurrence among the nations, and the opposing convictions, which tended to defend any existing institutions, grow steadily weaker. Statesman no longer seek to combat "democracy," but in some way or other to reckon with it, to eliminate risks as far as possible from the transition to what is now regarded as inevitable. The form of a State is to all intents and purposes no longer defended, but only its area and power, democracy for the time being lending a helping hand. The sense of power and democratic feeling are for the most part indistinguishable. The Socialist systems have been the first to abandon the quest for power and to place their specific aims before anything else.

The republics of France and Spain may very well subsist as republics by sheer force of habit and from fear of the terrible moment of change, and if, from time to time, they take on some other form, it will tend to be a Caesarian rather than a dynastic monarchy.

One wonders how soon the other countries will follow suit.

These ferments, however, conflict with the money-making current, and ultimately the latter proves the stronger. The masses want their peace and their pay. If they get them from a republic or a monarchy, they will cling to either. If not, without much ado they will support the first constitution to promise them what they want. A decision of the kind, of course, is never taken directly, but is always influenced by passion, personalities and the lingering effects of former situations. . . .

And finally, the question of the Church. In the whole of Western Europe the philosophy issuing from the French Revolution is in conflict with the Church, particularly the Catholic Church, a conflict ultimately springing from the optimism of the former and the pessimism of the latter.

Of late, that pessimism has been deepened by the Syllabus, the *Concilium* and the doctrine of infallibility, the Church, for obscure reasons, having decided to offer a conscious opposition to modern ideas on a wide front. . . .

The great decision can only come from the mind of men. Will optimism, under the guise of power and money, continue to survive, and how long? Or, as the pessimist philosophy of today might seem to suggest, will there be a general change in

thought such as took place in the third and fourth centuries?
(Extract from *Supplementary Notes on the Origin and Nature of the Present Crisis.*)

HENRY ADAMS
The Education of Henry Adams

The Dynamo and the Virgin

Until the Great Exposition of 1900 closed its doors in November, Adams haunted it, aching to absorb knowledge, and helpless to find it. He would have liked to know how much of it could have been grasped by the best-informed man in the world. . . .

Nothing in education is so astonishing as the amount of ignorance it accumulates in the form of inert facts. Adams had looked at most of the accumulations of art in the storehouses called Art Museums; yet he did not know how to look at the art exhibits of 1900. He had studied Karl Marx and his doctrines of history with profound attention, yet he could not apply them at Paris. Langley, with the ease of a great master of experiment, threw out of the field every exhibit that did not reveal a new application of force, and naturally threw out, to begin with, almost the whole art exhibit. Equally, he ignored almost the whole industrial exhibit. He led his pupil directly to the forces. His chief interest was in new motors to make his airship feasible, and he taught Adams the astonishing complexities of the new Daimler motor, and of the automobile, which, since 1893, had become a nightmare at a hundred kilometres an hour, almost as destructive as the electric tram which was only ten years older; and threatening to become as terrible as the locomotive steam-engine itself, which was almost exactly Adams's own age.

Then he showed his scholar the great hall of dynamos, and explained how little he knew about electricity or force of any kind, even of his own special sun, which spouted heat in inconceivable volume, but which, as far as he knew, might spout less or more, at any time, for all the certainty he felt in it. To him, the dynamo itself was but an ingenious channel for conveying somewhere the heat latent in a few tons of poor coal hidden in a dirty engine-house carefully kept out of sight; but to Adams the dynamo became a symbol of infinity. As he grew accustomed to the great gallery of machines, he began to feel the forty-foot dynamos as a moral force, much as the early Christians felt the Cross. The planet itself seemed less impressive, in its old-fashioned, deliberate, annual or daily revolution, than this huge wheel, revolving within arm's-length at some vertiginous speed, and barely murmuring— scarcely humming an audible warning to stand a hair's-breadth further for respect of power—while it would not wake the baby lying close against its frame. Before the end, one began to pray to it; inherited instinct taught the natural expression of man before silent and infinite force. Among the thousand symbols of ultimate energy, the dynamo was not so human as some, but it was the most expressive.

Yet the dynamo, next to the steam-engine, was the most familiar of exhibits. For Adams's objects its value lay chiefly in its occult mechanism. Between the dynamo in the gallery of machines and the engine-house outside, the break of continuity amounted to abysmal fracture for a historian's objects. No more relation could he discover between the steam and the electric current than between the Cross and the cathedral. The forces were interchangeable if not reversible, but he could see only an absolute *fiat* in electricity as in faith. Langley could not help him. Indeed, Langley seemed to be worried by the same trouble, for he constantly repeated that the new forces were anarchical, and specially that he was not responsible for the new rays, that were little short of parricidal in their wicked spirit towards science. His own rays, with which he had doubled the solar spectrum, were altogether harmless and beneficent; but Radium denied its God—or, what was to Langley the same thing, denied the truths of his Science. The force was wholly new. . . .

Historians undertake to arrange sequences,—called stories, or histories—assuming in silence a relation of cause and effect. These assumptions, hidden in the depths of dusty libraries, have been astounding, but commonly unconscious and childlike; so much so, that if any captious critic were to drag them to light, historians would probably reply, with one voice, that they had never supposed themselves required to know what they were talking about. Adams, for one, had toiled in vain to find out what he meant. He had even published a dozen volumes of American history for no other purpose than to satisfy himself whether, by the severest process of stating, with the least possible comment, such facts as seemed sure, in such order as seemed rigorously consequent, he could fix for a familiar moment a necessary sequence of human movement. The result had satisfied him as little as at Harvard College. Where he saw sequence, other men saw something quite different, and no one saw the same unit of measure. He cared little about his experiments and less about his statesmen, who seemed to him quite as ignorant as himself and, as a rule, no more honest; but he insisted on a relation of sequence, and if he could not reach it by one method, he would try as many methods as science knew. Satisfied that the sequence of men led to nothing and that the sequence of their society could lead no further, while the mere sequence of time was artificial, and the sequence of thought was chaos, he turned at last to the sequence of force; and thus it happened that, after ten years' pursuit, he found himself lying in the Gallery of Machines at the Great Exposition of 1900, his historical neck broken by the sudden irruption of forces totally new. . . .

Here opened another totally new education, which promised to be by far the most hazardous of all. The knife-edge along which he must crawl, like Sir Lancelot in the twelfth century, divided two kingdoms of force which had nothing in common but attraction. They were as different as a magnet is from gravitation, supposing one knew what a magnet was, or gravitation, or love. The force of the Virgin was still felt at Lourdes, and seemed to be as potent as X-rays; but in America neither Venus nor Virgin ever had value as force—at most as sentiment. No American had ever been truly afraid of either.

This problem in dynamics gravely perplexed an American historian. The Woman had once been supreme; in France she still seemed potent, not merely as a sentiment, but as a force. Why was she unknown in America? For evidently America was ashamed of her, and she was ashamed of herself, otherwise they would not have strewn fig-leaves so profusely all over her. When she was a true force, she was ignorant of fig-leaves, but the monthly-magazine-made American female had not a feature that would have been recognized by Adam. The trait was notorious, and often humorous, but any one brought up among Puritans knew that sex was sin. In any previous age, sex was strength. Neither art nor beauty was needed. Every one, even among Puritans, knew that neither Diana of the Ephesians nor any of the Oriental goddesses was worshipped for her beauty. She was goddess because of her force; she was the animated dynamo; she was reproduction—the greatest and most mysterious of all energies; all she needed was to be fecund. . . . The true American knew something of the facts, but nothing of the feelings; he read the letter, but he never felt the law. Before this historical chasm, a mind like that of Adams felt itself helpless; he turned from the Virgin to the Dynamo as though he were a Branly coherer. On one side, at the Louvre and at Chartres, as he knew by the record of

work actually done and still before his eyes, was the highest
energy ever known to man, the creator of four-fifths of his
noblest art, exercising vastly more attraction over the human
mind than all the steam-engines and dynamos ever dreamed
of; and yet this energy was unknown to the American mind.
An American Virgin would never dare command; an American Venus would never dare exist. . . .

Great men before great monuments express great truths,
provided they are not taken too solemnly. Adams never tired
of quoting the supreme phrase of his idol Gibbon, before the
Gothic cathedrals: "I darted a contemptuous look on the
stately monuments of superstition." Even in the footnotes of
his history, Gibbon had never inserted a bit of humor more
human than this, and one would have paid largely for a
photograph of the fat little historian, on the background of
Notre Dame of Amiens, trying to persuade his readers—
perhaps himself—that he was darting a contemptuous look on
the stately monument, for which he felt in fact the respect
which every man of his vast study and active mind always
feels before objects worthy of it; but besides the humor, one
felt also the relation. Gibbon ignored the Virgin, because in
1789 religious monuments were out of fashion. In 1900 his
remark sounded fresh and simple as the green fields to ears
that had heard a hundred years of other remarks, mostly no
more fresh and certainly less simple. Without malice, one
might find it more instructive than a whole lecture of Ruskin.
One sees what one brings, and at that moment Gibbon
brought the French Revolution. Ruskin brought reaction
against the Revolution. St. Gaudens had passed beyond all.
He liked the stately monuments much more than he liked
Gibbon or Ruskin; he loved their dignity; their unity; their
scale; their lines; their lights and shadows; their decorative
sculpture; but he was even less conscious than they of the
force that created it all—the Virgin, the Woman—by whose
genius "the stately monuments of superstition" were built,
through which she was expressed. He would have seen more
meaning in Isis with the cow's horns, at Edfoo, who expressed
the same thought. The art remained, but the energy was lost
even upon the artist.

Yet in mind and person St. Gaudens was a survival of the
1500; he bore the stamp of the Renaissance, and should have
carried an image of the Virgin round his neck, or stuck in his
hat, like Louis XI. In mere time he was a lost soul that had
strayed by chance into the twentieth century, and forgotten
where it came from. He writhed and cursed at his ignorance,
much as Adams did at his own, but in the opposite sense. St.

Gaudens was a child of Benvenuto Cellini, smothered in an American cradle. Adams was a quintessence of Boston, devoured by curiosity to think like Benvenuto, St. Gaudens's art was starved from birth, and Adams's instinct was blighted from babyhood. Each had but half of a nature, and when they came together before the Virgin of Amiens they ought both to have felt in her the force that made them one; but it was not so. To Adams she became more than ever a channel of force; to St. Gaudens she remained as before a channel of taste.

. . . St. Gaudens at Amiens was hardly less sensitive to the force of the female energy than Matthew Arnold at the Grande Chartreuse. Neither of them felt goddesses as power —only as reflected emotion, human expression, beauty, purity, taste, scarcely even as sympathy. They felt a railway train as power; yet they, and all other artists, constantly complained that the power embodied in a railway train could never be embodied in art. All the steam in the world could not, like the Virgin, build Chartres.

Yet in mechanics, whatever the mechanicians might think, both energies acted as interchangeable forces on man, and by action on man all known force may be measured. Indeed, few men of science measured force in any other way. After once admitting that a straight line was the shortest distance between two points, no serious mathematician cared to deny anything that suited his convenience, and rejected no symbol, unproved or unproveable, that helped him to accomplish work. The symbol was force, as a compass needle or a triangle was force, as the mechanist might prove by losing it, and nothing could be gained by ignoring their value. Symbol or energy, the Virgin had acted as the greatest force the Western world ever felt, and had drawn man's activities to herself more strongly than any other power, natural or supernatural, had ever done; the historian's business was to follow the track of the energy; to find where it came from and where it went to; its complex source and shifting channels; its values, equivalents, conversions. It could scarcely be more complex than radium; it could hardly be deflected, diverted, polarized, absorbed more perplexingly than other radiant matter. Adams knew nothing about any of them, but as a mathematical problem of influence on human progress, though all were occult, all reacted on his mind, and he rather inclined to think the Virgin easiest to handle.

The pursuit turned out to be long and tortuous, leading at last into the vast forests of scholastic science. From Zeno to Descartes, hand in hand with Thomas Aquinas, Montaigne, and Pascal, one stumbled as stupidly as though one were still a German student of 1860. Only with the instinct of despair could one force one's self into his old thicket of ignorance after having been repulsed at a score of entrances more promising and more popular. Thus far, no path had led anywhere, unless perhaps to an exceedingly modest living. Forty-five years of study had proved to be quite futile for the pursuit of power; one controlled no more force in 1900 than in 1850, although the amount of force controlled by society had enormously increased. The secret of education still hid itself somewhere behind ignorance, and one fumbled over it as feebly as ever. . . .

(Extract from chapter 25.)

SECTION VIII

NATIONALISM

The French Revolution not only provoked revolutionary and counterrevolutionary theories; it also produced modern nationalism. Its heritage held that states and nations ought to coincide, that a unity could be created in a nation and that the nation could be freed from foreign control. Aspiration towards personal liberty was accompanied by the demand for popular sovereignty, and with this was associated the claim for national self-determination. A temporary alliance of democracy and nationalism had been created. Rousseau had stimulated the love of one's country. For Renan, a nation was a soul, a spiritual principle; for J. S. Mill, a necessary condition of free institutions was that the boundaries of government should coincide in the main with those of nationalities.

But if in England and France the state had created the nation, in Germany and eastern Europe the nation was attempting to create the state. Nationalism was helping to cement unity. As dreams of universal brotherhood faded in the nineteenth century, nationalism became an increasingly divisive element in politics as each nation claimed the right to form an independent state. Before long, Lord Acton was arguing that the principle of nationality was a retrograde step. By the end of the century, nationalism, in the older unified states, was almost exclusively associated with right-wing political sentiment and with imperialistic expansion based on various motives.

In the contemporary world, a new upsurge by countries claiming to be both nations and states, is performing the double function of liberation from former colonial control and creation of a unifying sentiment. At a time when Western

nations increasingly recognize that the nation-state is neither
self-sufficient nor capable of dealing with certain problems,
and are moving hesitatingly toward closer ties and schemes
of confederation, it is the newer nations which display not
only an intense nationalism, but also a suspicious xenophobia,
and an attitude of neutralism in international relations.

Mazzini

Giuseppe Mazzini (1805–1872) was the most influential
prophet of liberal nationalism, its visionary agitator and conscience. If he was a conspirator in a highly romantic fashion
—complete with swordstick, invisible ink, secret rooms and
manuals on guerrilla warfare—he was also an effective publicist, of whose works one hundred volumes have been issued
so far.

Nationality, for Mazzini, was the ruling principle of the
future; each nation would live happily within the exact
boundaries drawn up for it. His Italian patriotism led him to
emphasize the restoration of Italian greatness and unification
because "Italy is perhaps nearer than are other countries to
the sacred altar on which God will descend." But Mazzini, the
fighter for Italian freedom, exhorted his disciples to love humanity.

A liberal in his view that a nation must be responsible for
its own liberation, a democrat in his belief that sovereignty
resided in the whole people, a republican in his dislike of
monarchy, a religious idealist who appealed to God and duty,
an optimist in his belief that the future belonged to the common people, Mazzini became a European symbol for national
independence. Part of the irony of history is that this Italian
exile, founder of the Young Italy and the Young Europe
movements, should have been distrusted by Cavour and Garibaldi, forced to sneak into his native country in disguise and
die under an assumed name after independence had been
gained. It is even more tragic that the land to which the
liberal Mazzini devoted his genius, should have been the setting for the first modern totalitarian state.

Right-wing Nationalism

In the middle of the nineteenth century, nationalism had
been liberal in orientation, becoming the focal point for opposition to oppressive or autocratic régimes and foreign control.
In the latter part of the century, nationalism became increasingly associated with the right. Liberal nationalism disap-

peared before the development of militarism, suspicion of foreign nations, protectionism and rejection of free trade, and the tendency to exalt the nation at the expense of the individual and to suppress opposition.

In Germany, Herder had argued for the national spirit and Fichte for the closed, autarkic state. Representatives of the more bellicose nationalism were Treitschke in Germany and Taine, Barrès and Maurras in France. Treitschke, popular writer and lecturer and member of the Reichstag, viewed history as the development of the spirits of nations and of states which were their personified expression. Not surprisingly, the 1870 Prussian victory over France and the unification of Germany became desirable stages along the road of historical development. The unifying force of the nation was a powerful state, actively responsible for shaping culture and character, exerting strong leadership in a hierarchical society based on social and economic inequality.

In France, Taine, the proponent of positivism and of scientific investigation, was equally a traditionalist, believing in the importance of deep-seated, invisible roots beneath the visible trunk and foliage of a nation, and a nationalist, emphasizing the soil and the heritage of France. Maurice Barrès, with his deterministic acceptance of nationalism, his cult of the earth and the dead and his emphasis on the tradition and continuity in the *enraciné*, and Charles Maurras, with his integral nationalism and support of the traditional authorities of church and monarchy, signified the departure of nationalism from its liberal associations.

Zionism

The Dreyfus Affair of 1898 caused great articulation and agitation by the anti-revisionist nationalists in defending the army against all slights, of whom Barrès and Maurras were leading figures. But the same event led to a different kind of nationalism. For Theodor Herzl (1860–1904), elegant and brilliant Viennese journalist in Paris, the obvious injustice of the affair, the hatred shown to its leading Jewish figure and the general civil disabilities of Jews, stimulated his interest in a Jewish homeland. His book, *The Jewish State*, was the effective beginning of Zionism.

Zionism is the belief in the restoration of the Jewish people to the Holy Land of Palestine. In general, nationalist movements are based on achieving political control of the territory in which members of the group live. Since the Jewish people were scattered, Zionism was always culturally as well as nationally oriented. Whereas for Herzl, a new territorial settlement was vital, others, such as Ahad Ha'am (Asher Ginzberg), concentrated on the survival of Jewish culture because of the increasing assimilation of Jews in the Diaspora. The problem, and the differences of approach, remain even after the foundation of the state of Israel in 1948.

Racist Nationalism

The greatest enemy of the Jewish people, Adolf Hitler (1889–1945), influenced by the racist writers Gobineau and H. S. Chamberlain, linked racism with nationalism. In 1924 he dictated the first part of *Mein Kampf* to Rudolf Hess while in prison, and the following year wrote the second part. Some seven million copies of the work have been sold. Few will claim Hitler as a great political philosopher, but his book announced his future intentions: emphasizing blood as the determinant of human value, stressing the *Volk*, anti-Semitism and a crude Darwinism. The work heralded the violence, nihilism and rejection of civilized values of the Nazi era; its extreme nationalism emphasized unity, the need for *Lebensraum* and the destiny of the German people, as the master race.

Hitler argued the need to end the parliamentary system, exterminate the Jewish-materialist spirit, introduce strong, centralized government, reunite all Germans in a greater Germany, provide equality of rights for the German nation, end the subjection caused by the Versailles Treaty and restore the German colonies. Nationalism for Hitler resulted in a conception of a totalitarian state—anti-liberal, anti-parliamentary, hierarchical, ordered and dominated by a supreme leader.

MAZZINI
The Duties of Man

Duties to Country

Your first Duties—first, at least, in importance—are, as I have told you, to Humanity. You are *men* before you are *citizens* or *fathers*. If you do not embrace the whole human family in your love, if you do not confess your faith in its unity—consequent on the unity of God—and in the brotherhood of the Peoples who are appointed to reduce that unity to fact—if wherever one of your fellow-men groans, wherever the dignity of human nature is violated by falsehood or tyranny, you are not prompt, being able, to succour that wretched one, or do not feel yourself called, being able, to fight for the purpose of relieving the deceived or oppressed— you disobey your law of life, or do not comprehend the religion which will bless the future.

But what can *each* of you, with his isolated powers *do* for the moral improvement, for the progress of Humanity? You can, from time to time, give sterile expression to your belief; you may, on some rare occasion, perform an act of *charity* to a brother not belonging to your own land, no more. Now, *charity* is not the watchword of the future faith. The watchword of the future faith is *association,* fraternal cooperation towards a common aim, and this is as much superior to *charity* as the work of many uniting to raise with one accord a building for the habitation of all together would be superior to that which you would accomplish by raising a separate hut each for himself, and only helping one another by exchanging stones and bricks and mortar. But divided as you are in language tendencies, habits, and capacities, you cannot attempt this common work. The *individual* is too weak, and Humanity too vast. *My God*, prays the Breton mariner as he puts out to sea, *protect me, my ship is so little, and Thy ocean so great!* And this prayer sums up the condition of each of you, if no means is found of multiplying your forces and your powers of action indefinitely. But God gave you this means when he gave you a Country, when, like a wise overseer of labour, who distributes the different parts of the work according to the capacity of the workmen, he divided Humanity into distinct groups upon the face of our globe, and thus planted the seeds of nations. Bad governments have disfigured the design of God, which you may see clearly marked out, as far, at least, as regards Europe, by the courses of the great rivers, by the lines of the lofty mountains, and by other geographical conditions; they have disfigured it by conquest, by greed, by jealousy of the just sovereignty of others; disfigured it so much that today there is perhaps no nation except England and France whose confines correspond to this design. They did not, and they do not, recognise any country except their own families and dynasties, the egoism of caste. But the divine design will infallibly be fulfilled. Natural divisions, the innate spontaneous tendencies of the peoples will replace the arbitrary divisions sanctioned by bad governments. The map of Europe will be remade. The Countries of the People will rise, define by the voice of the free, upon the ruins of the Countries of Kings and privileged castes. Between these Countries there will be harmony and brotherhood. And then the work of

Humanity for the general amelioration, for the discovery and application of the real law of life, carried on in association and distributed according to local capacities, will be accomplished by peaceful and progressive development; then each of you, strong in the affections and in the aid of many millions of men speaking the same language, endowed with the same tendencies, and educated by the same historic tradition, may hope by your personal effort to benefit the whole of Humanity. . . .

Without Country you have neither name, token, voice, nor rights, no admission as brothers into the fellowship of the Peoples. You are the bastards of Humanity. Soldiers without a banner, Israelites among the nations, you will find neither faith nor protection; none will be sureties for you. Do not beguile yourselves with the hope of emancipation from unjust social conditions if you do not first conquer a Country for yourselves; where there is no Country there is no common agreement to which you can appeal; the egoism of self-interest rules alone, and he who has the upper hand keeps it, since there is no common safeguard for the interests of all. Do not be led away by the idea of improving your material conditions without first solving the national question. . . . you are not the working-class of Italy; you are only fractions of that class; powerless, unequal to the great task which you propose to yourselves. Your emancipation can have no practical beginning until a National Government, understanding the signs of the times, shall, seated in Rome, formulate a Declaration of Principles to be the guide for Italian progress, and shall insert into it these words, *Labour is sacred, and is the source of the wealth of Italy.*

Do not be led astray, then, by hopes of material progress which in your present conditions can only be illusions. Your Country alone, the vast and rich Italian Country, which stretches from the Alps to the farthest limit of Sicily, can fulfil these hopes. You cannot obtain your *rights* except by obeying the commands of *Duty*. Be worthy of them, and you will have them. O my Brothers! love your Country. Our Country is our home, the home which God has given us, placing therein a numerous family which we love and are loved by, and with which we have a more intimate and quicker communion of feeling and thought than with others; a family which by its concentration upon a given spot, and by the homogeneous nature of its elements, is destined for a special kind of activity. Our Country is our field of labour; the products of our activity must go forth from it for the benefit of the whole earth; but the instruments of labour which we can use best and most effectively exist in it, and we may not reject them without being unfaithful to God's purpose and diminishing our own strength. In labouring according to true principles for our Country we are labouring for Humanity; our Country is the fulcrum of the lever which we have to wield for the common good. If we give up this fulcrum we run the risk of becoming useless to our Country and to Humanity. Before *associating* ourselves with the Nations which compose Humanity we must exist as a Nation. There can be no association except among equals; and you have no recognized collective existence.

Humanity is a great army moving to the conquest of unknown lands, against powerful and wary enemies. The Peoples are the different corps and divisions of that army. Each has a post entrusted to it; each a special operation to perform; and the common victory depends on the exactness with which the different operations are carried out. Do not disturb the order of the battle. Do not abandon the banner which God has given you. Wherever you may be, into the midst of whatever people circumstances may have driven you, fight for the liberty of that people if the moment calls for it; but fight as Italians, so that the blood which you shed may win honour and love, not for you only, but for your Country. And may the constant thought of your soul be for Italy, may all the acts of your life be worthy of her, and may the standard beneath which you arrange yourselves to work for Humanity be Italy's. Do not say I; say *we*. Be every one of you an incarnation of your Country, and feel himself and make himself responsible for his fellow-countrymen; let each one of you learn to act in such a way that in him men shall respect and love his Country.

Your Country is one and indivisible. . . .

Your Country is the token of the mission which God has given you to fulfil in Humanity. The faculties, the strength of *all* its sons should be united for the accomplishment of this mission. . . . A Country must have a single government. The politicians who call themselves federalists, and who would make Italy into a brotherhood of different states, would dismember the Country, not understanding the idea of Unity. . . .

A Country is a fellowship of free and equal men bound together in a brotherly concord of labour towards a single end. You must make it and maintain it such. A Country is not an aggregation, it is an *association*. There is no true Country without a uniform right. There is no true Country where the uniformity of that right is violated by the existence of caste, privilege, and inequality—where the powers and faculties of a large number of individuals are suppressed or dormant—where there is no common principle accepted, recognised, and developed by all. In such a state of things there can be no Nation, no People, but only a multitude, a fortuitous agglomeration of men whom circumstances have brought together and different circumstances will separate. In the name of your love for your Country you must combat without truce the existence of every privilege, every inequality, upon the soil which has given you birth. One privilege only is lawful—the privilege of Genius when Genius reveals itself in brotherhood with Virtue; but it is a privilege conceded by God and not by men, and when you acknowledge it and follow its inspirations, you acknowledge it freely by the exercise of your own reason and your own choice. Whatever privilege claims your submission in virtue of force or heredity, or any right which is not a common right, is a usurpation and a tyranny, and you ought to combat it and annihilate it. Your Country should be your Temple. God at the summit, a People of equals at the base. . . .

The law must express the general aspiration, promote the good of all, respond to a beat of the nation's heart. The whole nation therefore should be, directly or indirectly, the legislator. By yielding this mission to a few men, you put the egoism of one class in the place of the Country, which is the union of *all* the classes.

A Country is not a mere territory; the particular territory is only its foundation. The Country is the idea which rises upon that foundation; it is the sentiment of love, the sense of fellowship which binds together all the sons of that territory. So long as a single one of your brothers is not represented by his own vote in the development of the national life—so long as a single one vegetates uneducated among the educated—so long as a single one able and willing to work languishes in poverty for want of work—you have not got a Country such as it ought to be, the Country of all and for all. *Votes, education, work* are the three main pillars of the nation; do not rest until your hands have solidly erected them.

And when they have been erected—when you have secured for every one of you food for both body and soul—when freely united, entwining your right hands like brothers round a beloved mother, you advance in beautiful and holy concord towards the development of your faculties and the fulfilment of the Italian mission—remember that that mission is the moral unity of Europe; remember the immense duties which it imposes upon you. . . .

Your duties to your Country are proportioned to the loftiness of this mission. You have to keep it pure from egoism, uncontaminated by falsehood and by the arts of that political Jesuitism which they call diplomacy.

The government of the country will be based through your labours upon the worship of principles, not upon the idolatrous worship of interests and of opportunity. . . . Through you Italy will have, with one only God in the heavens, one only truth, one only faith, one only rule of political life upon earth. Upon the edifice, sublimer than Capitol or Vatican, which the people of Italy will raise, you will plant the banner of Liberty and of Association, so that it shines in the sight of all the nations, nor will you lower it ever for terror of despots or lust for the gains of a day. You will have boldness as you have faith. You will speak out aloud to the world, and to those who call themselves the lords of the world, the thought which thrills in the hearts of Italy. You will never deny the sister nations. The life of the Country shall grow through you in beauty and in strength, free from servile fears and the hesitations of doubt, keeping as its *foundation* the people, as its *rule* the consequences of its principles logically deduced and energetically applied, as its *strength* the strength of all, as its *outcome* the amelioration of all, as its *end* the fulfilment of the mission which God has given it. And because you will be ready to die for Humanity, the life of your Country will be immortal.

(Extracts from chapter 5.)

HERZL

The Jewish State

The Need for a Jewish State

The idea which I have developed in this pamphlet is an ancient one: It is the restoration of the Jewish State.

The world resounds with clamor against the Jews, and this has revived the dormant idea. . . .

•The decisive factor is our propelling force. And what is that force? The plight of the Jews. . . .

Now everyone knows how steam is generated by boiling water in a kettle, but such steam only rattles the lid. The current Zionist projects and other associations to check anti-Semitism are teakettle phenomena of this kind. But I say that this force, if properly harnessed, is powerful enough to propel a large engine and to move passengers and goods, let the engine have whatever form it may. . . .

I . . . state, clearly and emphatically, that I believe in the achievement of the idea, though I do not profess to have discovered the shape it may ultimately take. The world needs the Jewish State; therefore it will arise.

The plan would seem mad enough if a single individual were to undertake it; but if many Jews simultaneously agree on it, it is entirely reasonable, and its achievement presents no difficulties worth mentioning. The idea depends only on the number of its adherents. Perhaps our ambitious young men, to whom every road of advancement is now closed, and for whom the Jewish State throws open a bright prospect of freedom, happiness, and honor—perhaps they will see to it that this idea is spread. . . .

It depends on the Jews themselves whether this political document remains for the present a political romance. If this generation is too dull to understand it rightly, a future, finer, more advanced generation will arise to comprehend it. The Jews who will try it shall achieve their State; and they will deserve it. . . .

The technical achievements of our century have brought about a remarkable renaissance; but we have not yet seen this fabulous advance applied for the benefit of humanity. Distance has ceased to be an obstacle, yet we complain of the problem of congestion. Our great steamships carry us swiftly and surely over hitherto uncharted seas. Our railways carry us safely into a mountain world hitherto cautiously scaled on foot. Events occurring in countries undiscovered when Europe first confined Jews in ghettos are known to us in a matter of an hour. That is why the plight of the Jews is an anachronism—not because over a hundred years ago there was a period of enlightenment which in reality affected only the most elevated spirits.

To my mind, the electric light was certainly not invented so that the drawing rooms of a few snobs might be illuminated, but rather to enable us to solve some of the problems of humanity by its light. One of these problems, and not the least of them, is the Jewish question. In solving it we are working not only for ourselves, but also for many other downtrodden and oppressed beings.

The Jewish question still exists. It would be foolish to deny it. It is a misplaced piece of medievalism which civilized nations do not even yet seem able to shake off, try as they will. They proved they had this high-minded desire when they emancipated us. The Jewish question persists wherever Jews live in appreciable numbers. Wherever it does not exist, it is brought in together with Jewish immigrants. We are naturally drawn into those places where we are not persecuted, and our appearance there gives rise to persecution. This is the case, and will inevitably be so, everywhere, even in highly civilized countries—see, for instance, France—so long as the Jewish question is not solved on the political level. The unfortunate Jews are now carrying the seeds of anti-Semitism into England; they have already introduced it into America.

Anti-Semitism is a highly complex movement, which I think I understand. I approach this movement as a Jew, yet without fear or hatred. I believe that I can see in it the elements of cruel sport, of common commercial rivalry, of inherited prejudice, of religious intolerance—but also of a supposed need for self-defense. I consider the Jewish question neither a social nor a religious one, even though it sometimes takes these and other forms. It is a national question, and to solve it we must first of all establish it as an international political problem to be discussed and settled by the civilized nations of the world in council.

We are a people—*one* people.

We have sincerely tried everywhere to merge with the national communities in which we live, seeking only to preserve the faith of our fathers. It is not permitted us. In vain are we loyal patriots, sometimes superloyal; in vain do we make the same sacrifices of life and property as our fellow citizens; in vain do we strive to enhance the fame of our native lands in the arts and sciences, or her wealth by trade and commerce. In our native lands where we have lived for centuries we are still decried as aliens, often by men whose ancestors had not yet come at a time when Jewish sighs had long been heard in the country. The majority decide who the "alien" is; this, and all else in the relations between peoples, is a matter of power. I do not surrender any part of our prescriptive right when I make this statement merely in my own name, as an individual. In the world as it now is and will probably remain, for an indefinite period, might takes precedence over right. It is without avail, therefore, for us to be loyal patriots, as were the Huguenots, who were forced to emigrate. If we were left in peace . . .

But I think we shall not be left in peace.

Oppression and persecution cannot exterminate us. No nation on earth has endured such struggles and sufferings as we have. Jew-baiting has merely winnowed out our weaklings; the strong among us defiantly return to their own whenever persecution breaks out. This was most clearly apparent in the period immediately following the emancipation of the Jews. Those Jews who rose highest intellectually and materially entirely lost the sense of unity with their people. Wherever we remain politically secure for any length of time, we assimilate. I think this is not praiseworthy. Hence, the statesman who would wish to see a Jewish strain added to his nation must see to it that we continue politically secure. But even a Bismarck could never achieve that.

For old prejudices against us are still deeply ingrained in the folk ethos. He who would have proof of this need only listen to the people where they speak candidly and artlessly: folk wisdom and folklore both are anti-Semitic. The people is everywhere a great child, which can be readily educated; but even in the most favorable circumstances its education would be such a long-drawn-out process that we could far sooner, as already mentioned, help ourselves by other means. . . .

A . . . serious objection would be that I am giving aid and comfort to the anti-Semites when I say we are a people—*one* people. Or that I am hindering the assimilation of Jews where there are hopes of achieving it, and endangering it where it is already an accomplished fact, insofar as it is possible for a solitary writer to hinder or endanger anything. . . .

However much I may esteem personality—powerful individual personality in statesmen, inventors, artists, philosophers, or leaders, as well as the collective personality of a historic group of human beings, which we designate "nation" —however much I may esteem personality, I do not mourn its decline. Whoever can, will, and must perish, let him perish. But the distinctive nationality of the Jews neither can, will, nor must perish. It cannot, because external enemies consolidate it. It does not wish it; this it has proved through two millennia of appalling suffering. It need not; that, as a descendant of countless Jews who refused to despair, I am trying once more to prove in this pamphlet. Whole branches of Jewry may wither and fall away. The tree lives on. . . .

But the attempts at colonization made even by truly well-meaning men, interesting attempts though they were, have so far been unsuccessful. . . .

No human being is wealthy or powerful enough to transplant a people from one place of residence to another. Only an idea can achieve that. The State idea surely has that power. The Jews have dreamed this princely dream throughout the long night of their history. "Next year in Jerusalem" is our age-old motto. It is now a matter of showing that the vague dream can be transformed into a clear and glowing idea.

For this, our minds must first be thoroughly cleansed of many old, outworn, muddled, and shortsighted notions. The unthinking might, for example, imagine that this exodus would have to take its way from civilization into the desert. That is not so! It will be carried out entirely in the framework of civilization. We shall not revert to a lower stage; we shall rise to a higher one. We shall not dwell in mud huts; we shall build new, more beautiful, and more modern houses, and possess them in safety. We shall not lose our acquired possessions; we shall realize them. We shall surrender our well-earned rights for better ones. We shall relinquish none of our cherished customs; we shall find them again. We shall not leave our old home until the new one is available. Those only will depart who are sure thereby to improve their lot; those who are now desperate will go first, after them the poor, next the well to do, and last of all the wealthy. Those who go first will raise themselves to a higher grade, on a level with that whose representatives will shortly follow. The exodus will thus at the same time be an ascent in class.

The departure of the Jews will leave no wake of economic disturbance, no crises, no persecutions; in fact, the countries of emigration will rise to a new prosperity. There will be an inner migration of Christian citizens into the positions relinquished by Jews. The outflow will be gradual, without any disturbance, and its very inception means the end of anti-Semitism. The Jews will leave as honored friends, and if some of them later return they will receive the same favorable welcome and treatment at the hands of civilized nations as is accorded all foreign visitors. Nor will their exodus in any way be a flight, but it will be a well-regulated movement under the constant check of public opinion. The movement will not only be inaugurated in absolute accordance with the law, but it can nowise be carried out without the friendly co-operation of the interested governments, who will derive substantial benefits. . . .

The whole plan is essentially quite simple, as it must necessarily be if it is to be comprehensible to all.

Let sovereignty be granted us over a portion of the globe adequate to meet our rightful national requirements; we will attend to the rest.

To create a new State is neither ridiculous nor impossible. Haven't we witnessed the process in our own day, among nations which were not largely middle class as we are, but poorer, less educated, and consequently weaker than ourselves? The governments of all countries scourged by anti-Semitism will be keenly interested in obtaining sovereignty for us.

The plan, simple in design but complicated in execution,

will be executed by two agencies: the Society of Jews and the Jewish Company.

The scientific plan and political policies which the Society of Jews will establish will be carried out by the Jewish Company.

The Jewish Company will be the liquidating agent for the business interests of departing Jews, and will organize trade and commerce in the new country.

We must not visualize the exodus of the Jews as a sudden one. It will be gradual, proceeding over a period of decades. The poorest will go first and cultivate the soil. They will construct roads, bridges, railways, and telegraph installations, regulate rivers, and provide themselves with homesteads, all according to predetermined plans. Their labor will create trade, trade will create markets, and markets will attract new settlers—for every man will go voluntarily, at his own expense and his own risk. The labor invested in the soil will enhance its value. The Jews will soon perceive that a new and permanent frontier has been opened up for that spirit of enterprise which has heretofore brought them only hatred and obloquy. . . .

Will people say, again, that the venture is hopeless, because even if we obtain the land with sovereignty over it, the poor only will go along? It is precisely they whom we need at first! Only desperate men make good conquerors.

Will some one say: If it were feasible it would have been done long ago?

It has never yet been possible. Now it is possible. A hundred, even fifty, years ago it would have been sheer fantasy. Today it is reality. The rich, who enjoy a comprehensive acquaintance with all technical advances, know full well how much can be done for money. And this is how it will go: precisely the poor and simple, who have no idea what power man already exercises over the forces of Nature, will have the staunchest faith in the new message. For these have never lost their hope of the Promised Land.

Here you have it, Jews! Not fiction, nor yet fraud! Every man may convince himself of it, for every man will carry over with him a portion of the Promised Land—one in his head, another in his arms, another in his acquired possessions.

Now, all this may appear to be a drawn-out affair. Even in the most favorable circumstances, many years might elapse before the founding of the State is under way. In the meantime, Jews in a thousand different places will suffer insult, mortification, abuse, drubbings, depredation, and death. But no; once we begin to execute the plan, anti-Semitism will cease at once and everywhere. For it is the conclusion of peace. When the Jewish Company has been formed, the news will be carried in a single day to the utmost ends of the globe by the lightning speed of our telegraph wires.

And immediate relief will ensue. The intellectuals whom we produce so superabundantly in our middle classes will find an immediate outlet in our organizations, as our first technicians, officers, professors, officials, lawyers, physicians. And so it will continue, swiftly but smoothly.

Prayers will be offered up in the temples for the success of the project. And in the churches as well! It is the relief from the old burden, under which all have suffered.

But first the minds must be enlightened. The idea must make its way into the uttermost miserable holes where our people dwell. They will awaken from barren brooding. For into all our lives will come a new meaning. Every man need think only of himself, and the movement will become an overwhelming one.

And what glory awaits the selfless fighters for the cause!

Therefore I believe that a wondrous breed of Jews will spring up from the earth. The Maccabees will rise again.

Let me repeat once more my opening words: The Jews who will it shall achieve their State.

We shall live at last as free men on our own soil, and in our own homes peacefully die.

The world will be liberated by our freedom, enriched by our wealth, magnified by our greatness.

And whatever we attempt there for our own benefit will redound mightily and beneficially to the great of all mankind.

(Extracts from chapter 1 and the conclusion.)

HITLER
Mein Kampf

The Aryan Race

It is idle to argue which race or races were the original representative of human culture and hence the real founders of all that we sum up under the word 'humanity.' It is simpler to raise this question with regard to the present, and here an easy, clear answer results. All the human culture, all the results of art, science, and technology that we see before us today, are almost exclusively the creative product of the Aryan. This very fact admits of the not unfounded inference that he alone was the founder of all higher humanity, therefore representing the prototype of all that we understand by the word 'man.' He is the Prometheus of mankind from whose bright forehead the divine spark of genius has sprung at all times, forever kindling anew that fire of knowledge which illumined the night of silent mysteries and thus caused man to climb the path to mastery over the other beings of this earth. Exclude him—and perhaps after a few thousand years darkness will again descend on the earth, human culture will pass, and the world turn to a desert.

If we were to divide mankind into three groups, the founders of culture, the bearers of culture, the destroyers of culture, only the Aryan could be considered as the representative of the first group. From him originate the foundations and walls of all human creation, and only the outward form and color are determined by the changing traits of character of the various peoples. He provides the mightiest building stones and plans for all human progress and only the execution corresponds to the nature of the varying men and races. . . . Creatively active peoples always have a fundamental creative gift, even if it should not be recognizable to the eyes of superficial observers. Here, too, outward recognition is possible only in consequence of accomplished deeds, since the rest of the world is not capable of recognizing genius in itself, but sees only its visible manifestations in the form of inventions, discoveries, buildings, pictures, etc.; here again it often takes a long time before the world can fight its way through to this knowledge. Just as in the life of the outstanding individual, genius or extraordinary ability strives for practical realization only when spurred on by special occasions, likewise in the life of nations the creative forces and capacities which are present can often be exploited only when definite preconditions invite.

We see this most distinctly in connection with the race which has been and is the bearer of human cultural development—the Aryans. As soon as Fate leads them toward special conditions, their latent abilities begin to develop in a more and more rapid sequence and to mold themselves into tangible forms. The cultures which they found in such cases are nearly always decisively determined by the existing soil, the given climate, and—the subjected people. This last item, to be sure, is almost the most decisive. The more primitive the technical foundations for a cultural activity, the more necessary is the presence of human helpers who, organizationally assembled and employed, must replace the force of the machine. Without this possibility of using lower human beings, the Aryan would never have been able to take his first steps toward his future culture; just as without the help of various suitable beasts which he knew how to tame, he would not have arrived at a technology which is now gradually permitting him to do without these beasts. . . .

Thus, for the formation of higher cultures the existence of lower human types was one of the most essential preconditions, since they alone were able to compensate for the lack of technical aids without which a higher development is not conceivable. It is certain that the first culture of humanity was based less on the tamed animal than on the use of lower human beings. . . .

The progress of humanity is like climbing an endless ladder; it is impossible to climb higher without first taking the lower steps. Thus, the Aryan had to take the road to which reality directed him and not the one that would appeal to the imagination of a modern pacifist. . . .

Hence it is no accident that the first cultures arose in places where the Aryan, in his encounters with lower peoples, subjugated them and bent them to his will. They then became the first technical instrument in the service of a developing culture. . . .

But in directing them to a useful, though arduous activity, he not only spared the life of those he subjected; perhaps he gave them a fate that was better than their previous so-called 'freedom.' As long as he ruthlessly upheld the master attitude, not only did he really remain master, but also the preserver and increaser of culture. For culture was based exclusively on his abilities and hence on his actual survival. As soon as the subjected people began to raise themselves up and probably approached the conqueror in language, the sharp dividing wall between master and servant fell. The Aryan gave up the purity of his blood and, therefore, lost his sojourn in the paradise which he had made for himself. He became submerged in the racial mixture, and gradually, more and more, lost his cultural capacity, until at last, not only mentally but also physically, he began to resemble the subjected aborigines more than his own ancestors. For a time he could live on the existing cultural benefits, but then petrifaction set in and he fell a prey to oblivion.

Thus cultures and empires collapsed to make place for new formations.

Blood mixture and the resultant drop in the racial level is the sole cause of the dying out of old cultures; for men do not perish as a result of lost wars, but by the loss of that force of resistance which is contained only in pure blood.

All who are not of good race in this world are chaff.

And all occurrences in world history are only the expression of the races' instinct of self-preservation, in the good or bad sense.

In opposition to [Marxist doctrine], the folkish philosophy finds the importance of mankind in its basic racial elements. In the state it sees on principle only a means to an end and construes its end as the preservation of the racial existence of man. Thus, it by no means believes in an equality of the races, but along with their difference it recognizes their higher or lesser value and feels itself obligated, through this knowledge, to promote the victory of the better and stronger, and demand the subordination of the inferior and weaker in accordance with the eternal will that dominates this universe. Thus, in principle, it serves the basic aristocratic idea of Nature and believes in the validity of this law down to the last individual. It sees not only the different value of the races, but also the different value of individuals. From the mass it extracts the importance of the individual personality, and thus, in contrast to disorganizing Marxism, it has an organizing effect. It believes in the necessity of an idealization of humanity, in which alone it sees the premise for the existence of humanity. . . .

Human culture and civilization on this continent are inseparably bound up with the presence of the Aryan. If he dies out or declines, the dark veils of an age without culture will again descend on this globe. . . .

. . . the folkish philosophy of life corresponds to the innermost will of Nature, since it restores that free play of forces which must lead to a continuous mutual higher breeding, until at last the best of humanity, having achieved possession of this earth, will have a free path for activity in domains which will lie partly above it and partly outside it.

We all sense that in the distant future humanity must be faced by problems which only a highest race, become master people and supported by the means and possibilities of an entire globe, will be equipped to overcome.

A philosophy can only be organizationally comprehended on the basis of a definite formulation of that philosophy, and what dogmas represent for religious faith, party principles are for a political party in the making.

Hence an instrument must be created for the folkish world

*view which enables it to fight, just as the Marxist party or-
ganization creates a free path for internationalism.*

This is the goal pursued by the National Socialist German
Workers' Party. . . .

. . . *the state represents no end, but a means. It is, to be
sure, the premise for the formation of a higher human culture, but not its cause, which lies exclusively in the existence
of a race capable of culture.* Hundreds of exemplary states
might exist on earth, but if the Aryan culture-bearer died out,
there would be no culture corresponding to the spiritual level
of the highest peoples of today. We can go even farther and say
that the fact of human state formation would not in the least
exclude the possibility of the destruction of the human race,
provided that superior intellectual ability and elasticity would
be lost due to the absence of their racial bearers. . . .

*The state is a means to an end. Its end lies in the preserva-
tion and advancement of a community of physically and
psychically homogeneous creatures. This preservation itself
comprises first of all existence as a race and thereby permits
the free development of all the forces dormant in this race. Of
them a part will always primarily serve the preservation of
physical life, and only the remaining part the promotion of a
further spiritual development. Actually the one always creates
the precondition for the other.*

*States which do not serve this purpose are misbegotten,
monstrosities in fact. The fact of their existence changes this
no more than the success of a gang of bandits can justify
robbery.*

We National Socialists as champions of a new philosophy
of life must never base ourselves on so-called 'accepted facts'
—and false ones at that. If we did, we would not be the
champions of a new great idea, but the coolies of the present-
day lie. We must distinguish in the sharpest way between the
state as a vessel and the race as its content. This vessel has
meaning only if it can preserve and protect the content; otherwise it is useless.

*Thus, the highest purpose of a folkish state is concern for
the preservation of those original racial elements which bestow culture and create the beauty and dignity of a higher
mankind. We, as Aryans, can conceive of the state only as the
living organism of a nationality which not only assures the
preservation of this nationality, but by the development of its
spiritual and ideal abilities leads it to the highest freedom. . . .*

*Anyone who speaks of a mission of the German people on
earth must know that it can exist only in the formation of a
state which sees its highest task in the preservation and pro-*

motion of the most noble elements of our nationality, indeed of all mankind, which still remain intact.

Thus, for the first time the state achieves a lofty inner goal. Compared to the absurd catchword about safeguarding law and order, thus laying a peaceable groundwork for mutual swindles, the task of preserving and advancing the highest humanity, given to this earth by the benevolence of the Almighty, seems a truly high mission.

From a dead mechanism which only lays claim to existence for its own sake, there must be formed a living organism with the exclusive aim of serving a higher idea.

The German Reich as a state must embrace all Germans and has the task, not only of assembling and preserving the most valuable stocks of basic racial elements in this people, but slowly and surely of raising them to a dominant position. . . .

SECTION IX

SOCIAL DARWINISM, HISTORY AND NEO-IDEALISM

In the latter half of the nineteenth century, the biological ideas of Darwin began penetrating political theory. His theses—the process of natural selection, the struggle for existence, the need for adaptation—were applied to human society, mainly to emphasize varying aspects of competition and struggle, to justify political control by a minority and the capitalistic economic system. Evolution was equated with social progress.

The chief representatives of Social Darwinism, particularly Herbert Spencer and William Graham Sumner, asserted the value of the struggle for life which resulted in improvement, since it meant the survival of the fittest. But other writers—Pearson and Gumplowicz, and politicians like Bismarck, Joseph Chamberlain and Theodore Roosevelt—justifying eugenic or racial differences, imperialist expansion, colonialism or war, stressed the competitive relationship and struggle, not between individuals of the same group, but between nations, races and groups, resulting in the survival of the physically and mentally fittest people.

Spencer and Bagehot

Herbert Spencer (1820–1903), product of a nonconformist background, was always an individualist, believing that the functions of the state were limited to protection, that no restrictions should be placed on commerce and no provision made for social welfare or education. His individualistic conclusions were reinforced by his application of evolutionary concepts to social relationships. Spencer used the analogy of the social and individual organism, but at the same time warned that it was only a metaphor. All existence grew through a series of transformations from the simple to the complex, by successive differentiations. Civilization was a process in which man adjusted to an increasingly complex environment. The evolutionary process, in the absence of interference, led inevitably to social improvement.

Spencer equated the poor and the "unfit." All efforts to help them, through legislation, public charity and social reconstruction, were undesirable, since this might allow them to mature and pass on their weakness. His conclusion was logical and ruthless. The whole effort of nature was to get rid of the inefficient and to make room for better. If they were not sufficiently complete to live, they died, and it was best that they should die.

Another version of the use of biology for political analysis was provided by Walter Bagehot (1826–1877), banker, distinguished journalist and editor of the *Economist*, who wrote with urbanity and charm on political institutions, social behavior and literature, as well as on economics. His *Lombard Street* is a classical analysis of the British banking system, and *The English Constitution* was the first realistic examination of the operation of British political institutions.

The oddly-titled *Physics and Politics* (1875), was Bagehot's attempt to apply psychological, biological and anthropological knowledge to the understanding of political and social affairs, and to political development. He stressed the influence of imitation in behavior, which in primitive societies allowed the fittest to survive, and which cemented civilized societies. Before men could innovate and break "the cake of custom," they had first to learn to imitate it. Bagehot traced historical development from relationships of force to social cooperation, the manner in which each generation transmitted certain new qualities to its successor and the way in which national character was formed. Bagehot propounded a somewhat questionable theory of three historical stages: the preliminary age, the fighting age, and the present age of discussion, in which the socially desirable type of character was strengthened. This was the age of choice, the age in which intellectual and political liberty was encouraged and which would lead to social progress.

His political outlook was conservative, based on fear of "the rule of mere numbers" and of democracy, especially the American kind. He opposed the 1867 extension of the British suffrage as mischievous, since it would lead to the supremacy of ignorance over instruction and of numbers over knowledge.

The great days were passing; permit the ignorant classes to rule, and "farewell to deference forever."

Maine and the Historical Method

This fear of the extension of the suffrage, of the likelihood that it might lead to apathy and mediocrity, and belief in oligarchical control was shared by Sir Henry Maine (1822–1888), professor of law in England and civil servant in India. In *Ancient Law,* written in 1861, two years after Darwin's *Origin of Species,* Maine used the historical method of Savigny and Montesquieu's comparative method of studying institutions, to trace the development of law and the manner in which different societies had produced different legal codes. Early law contained elements of all future law. Maine held that the Hobbes-Utilitarian concept of law was relatively new, was parochial and limited to the West. Their simplified explanation of law as an expression of sovereignty neglected the whole enormous aggregate of opinions, sentiments, beliefs, superstitions and prejudices of all kinds.

Most societies never got beyond customary law and the era of codes. Members of the family were tied to the family, dominated by paterfamilias. Law was changed through fictions, equity and legislation—the most systematic method of lawmaking, and one that came late in most societies. In the developing, progressive societies, the individual was substituted for the family; there was greater freedom for the individual. The abolition of slavery, the gradual breakdown of the power of paterfamilias over children, and the emancipation of women led to more freedom in making contracts. Maine was a conservative, yet his ideas on law coincided with the economic demands of his time for a free labor force.

British Idealism

Idealism in England was both a qualification of the German original and a philosophy that, in general, drew more liberal and humane political conclusions than its predecessor. It attracted poets like Browning, the later Wordsworth and Coleridge, theologians like Maurice and Martineau, as well as philosophers like Harris, Bradley, McTaggart and Bosanquet. The most significant philosophic idealist was T. H. Green (1836–1882), Oxford don, town councillor, member of the school board and of the temperance movement. Due to his premature death, his major writings, *Prolegomena to Ethics* and *Lectures on the Principles of Political Obligation,* edited

by friends and students, were left in perhaps a more ambiguous and obscure form than might otherwise have been the
case.

Green revised and broadened the idea of liberalism. The
aim of liberal society must be to create the conditions necessary for the higher moral development of its citizens. The
basis for social action, legislation and the standard for judgment was the common good. The function of the state, therefore, was to create opportunity and freedom for the individual, to maintain those conditions conducive to the moral life
and to allow the expression of a system of rights in the interests of all.

There was a mutual relationship between the individual and
society, since personality was fully realized in playing a significant role in the life of the society. Individual rights were
related to function and to the common well-being of society.
There could be no rights against the state, since a right existed
only if it were conducive to the common good.

Green was concerned with positive freedom, "a positive
power or capacity of doing or enjoying something worth
doing or enjoying." This involved not only a scale of ethical
values, but also, government action in industrial affairs, housing, education, alcoholism and health. With Green, neo-idealism and liberalism met at the frontiers of Fabian socialism.

SPENCER

The Study of Sociology, 1873
and
Social Statics, 1850

The Social Organism and Adaptation

That there is a real analogy between an individual organism
and a social organism, becomes undeniable when certain
necessities determining structure are seen to govern them in
common.

Mutual dependence of parts is that which initiates and
guides organization of every kind. So long as, in a mass of
living matter, all parts are alike, and all parts similarly live
and grow without aid from one another, there is no organization: the undifferentiated aggregate of protoplasm thus characterized, belongs to the lowest grade of living things. Without
distinct faculties, and capable of but the feeblest movements,
it cannot adjust itself to circumstances; and is at the mercy of
environing destructive actions. The changes by which this

structureless mass becomes a structured mass, having the characters and powers possessed by what we call an organism, are changes through which its parts lose their original likeness; and do this while assuming the unlike kinds of activity for which their respective positions towards one another and surrounding things fit them. These differences of function, and consequent differences of structure, at first feebly marked, slight in degree, and few in kind, become, as organization progresses, definite and numerous; and in proportion as they do this the requirements are better met. Now structural traits expressible in the same language, distinguish lower and higher types of societies from one another; and distinguish the earlier stages of each society from the later. Primitive tribes show no established contrasts of parts. At first all men carry on the same kind of activities, with no dependence on one another; or but occasional dependence. There is not even a settled chieftainship; and only in times of war is there a spontaneous and temporary subordination to those who show themselves the best leaders. From the small unformed social aggregates thus characterized, the progress is towards social aggregates of increased size, the parts of which acquire unlikenesses that become ever greater, more definite, and more multitudinous. The units of the society as it evolves, fall into different orders of activities, determined by differences in their local conditions or their individual powers; and there slowly result permanent social structures, of which the primary ones become decided while they are being complicated by secondary ones, growing in their turns decided, and so on.

Even were this all, the analogy would be suggestive; but it is not all. These two metamorphoses have a cause in common. Beginning with an animal composed of like parts, severally living by and for themselves, on what condition only can there be established a change, such that one part comes to perform one kind of function, and another part another kind? Evidently each part can abandon that original state in which it fulfilled for itself all vital needs, and can assume a state in which it fulfills in excess some single vital need, only if its other vital needs are fulfilled for it by other parts that have meanwhile undertaken other special activities. One portion of a living aggregate cannot devote itself exclusively to the respiratory function, and cease to get nutriment for itself, unless other portions that have become exclusively occupied in absorbing nutriment give it a due supply. That is to say, there must be exchange of services. Organization in an individual creature is made possible only by dependence of each part on all, and of all on each. Now this is obviously true also of social organization. A member of a primitive society cannot devote himself to an order of activity which satisfies one only of his personal wants, thus ceasing the activities required for satisfying his other personal wants, unless those for whose benefit he carries on his special activity in excess, give him in return the benefits of their special activities. If he makes weapons instead of continuing a hunter, he must be supplied with the produce of the chase on condition that the hunters are supplied with his weapons. If he becomes a cultivator of the soil, no longer defending himself, he must be defended by those who have become specialized defenders. That is to say, mutual dependence of parts is essential for the commencement and advance of social organization, as it is for the commencement and advance of individual organization.

Even were there no more to be pointed out, it would be clear enough that we are not here dealing with a figurative resemblance, but with a fundamental parallelism in principles of structure. . . . What . . . is implied by mutual dependence —by exchange of services? There is implied some mode of communication between mutually-dependent parts. Parts that perform functions for one another's benefit, must have appliances for conveying to one another the products of their respective functions, or for giving to one another the benefits (when these are not material products) which their respective functions achieve. And obviously, in proportion as the organization becomes high, the appliances for carrying on the intercourse must become involved. This we find to hold in both cases. In the lowest types of individual organisms, the exchange of services between the slightly-differentiated parts is effected in a slow, vague way, by an irregular diffusion of the nutrient matters jointly elaborated, and by an irregular propagation of feeble stimuli, causing a rude co-ordination in the actions of the parts. It is thus, also, with small and simple social aggregates. No definite arrangements for interchanging services exist; but only indefinite ones. Barter of products— food, skins, weapons, or what not—takes place irregularly between individual producers and consumers throughout the whole social body; there is no trading or distributing system, as, in the rudimentary animal, there is no vascular system. So, too, the social organism of low type, like the individual organism of low type, has no appliances for combining the actions of its remoter parts. When co-operation of them against an enemy is called for, there is nothing but the spread of an alarm from man to man throughout the scattered population; just as in an undeveloped kind of animal, there is merely a slow undirected diffusion of stimulus from one point to all others. In either case, the evolution of a larger, more complex, more active organism, implies an increasingly-efficient set of agencies for making the parts co-operate, so that the times and amounts of their activities may be kept in fit relations. And this, the facts everywhere show us. In the individual organism as it advances to a high structure, no matter of what class, there arises an elaborate system of channels through which the common stock of nutritive matters . . . is distributed throughout the body for the feeding of the various parts, severally occupied in their special actions; while in the social organism as it advances to a high structure, no matter of what political type, there develops an extensive and complicated trading organization for the distribution of commodities, which, sending its heterogeneous currents through the kingdom by channels that end in retailers' shops, brings within reach of each citizen the necessaries and luxuries that have been produced by others, while he has been producing his commodity or small part of a commodity, or performing some other function or small part of a function, beneficial to the rest. Similarly, development of the individual organism, be its class what it may, is always accompanied by development of a nervous system which renders the combined actions of the parts prompt and duly proportioned, so making possible the adjustments required for meeting the varying contingencies; while, along with the development of the social organism, there always goes development of directive centres, general and local, with established arrangements for inter-changing information and instigation, serving to adjust the rates and kinds of activities going on in different parts.

Along with the proofs thus furnished that the biological law of adaptation, holding of all other species, holds of the human species, and that the change of nature undergone by the human species since societies began to develop, has been an adaptation of it to the conditions implied by harmonious social life, we receive the lesson, that the one thing needful is a rigorous maintenance of these conditions. While all see that the immediate function of our chief social institutions is the securing of an orderly social life by making these conditions imperative, very few see that their further function, and in one sense more important function, is that of fitting men to fulfill these conditions spontaneously. The two functions are inseparable. From the biological laws we have been contemplating, it is, on the one hand, an inevitable corollary that if these conditions are maintained, human nature will slowly adapt itself to them; while, on the other hand, it is an inevitable corollary that by no other discipline than subjection to these conditions, can fitness to the social state be produced. Enforce these conditions, and adaptation to them will continue. Relax these conditions, by so much there will be a cessation of the adaptive changes. Abolish these conditions, and after the consequent social dissolution, there will commence (unless they are re-established) an adaptation to the conditions then resulting—those of savage life. These are conclusions from which there is no escape, if Man is subject to the laws of life in common with living things in general.

It may, indeed, be rightly contended that if those who are but little fitted to the social state are rigorously subjected to these conditions, evil will result: intolerable restraint, if it does not deform or destroy life, will be followed by violent reaction. We are taught by analogy, that greatly-changed circumstances from which there is no escape, fail to produce adaptation because they produce death. Men having constitutions fitted for one climate, cannot be fitted to an extremely-different climate by persistently living in it, because they do not survive, generation after generation. Such changes can be brought about only by slow spreadings of the race through intermediate regions having intermediate climates, to which successive generations are accustomed little by little. And doubtless the like holds mentally. The intellectual and emotional natures required for high civilization, are not to be obtained by thrusting on the completely-uncivilized, the needful activities and restraints in unqualified forms: gradual decay and death, rather than adaptation, would result. . . . The merciful policy, no less than the just policy, is that of insisting that all-essential requirements of self-support and nonaggression, shall be conformed to . . . the just policy, because failing to insist is failing to protect the better or more-adapted natures against the worse or less-adapted; the merciful policy, because the pains accompanying the process of adaptation to the social state must be gone through, and it is better that they should be gone through once than gone through twice, as they have to be when any relaxation of these conditions permits retrogression.

Thus, that which sundry precepts of the current religion embody—that which ethical systems, intuitive or utilitarian, equally urge, is also that which Biology, generalizing the laws of life at large, dictates. All further requirements are unimportant compared with this primary requirement, that each shall so live as neither to burden others nor to injure others. And all further appliances for influencing the actions and the natures of men, are unimportant compared with those serving to maintain and increase the conformity to this primary requirement. But unhappily, legislators and philanthropists, busy with schemes which, instead of aiding adaptation, indirectly hinder it, give little attention to the enforcing and improving of those arrangements by which adaptation is effected.

And here, on behalf of the few who uphold this policy of natural discipline, let me emphatically repudiate the name of 'laissez-faire' as applied to it, and emphatically condemn the counter-policy as involving a 'laissez-faire' of the most vicious kind. While holding that, when the State leaves each citizen to get what food for himself he can, and to suffer what evil he brings on himself, such a let-alone policy is both immediately and remotely injurious. When a Legislature takes from the worthy the things they have laboured for, that it may give to the unworthy the things they have not earned—when cause and consequence, joined in the order of Nature, are thus divorced by law-makers; then may properly come the suggestion—"Cease your interference." But when, in any way, direct or indirect, the unworthy deprive the worthy of their dues, or impede them in the quiet pursuit of their ends, then may properly come the demand—"Interfere promptly; and be, in fact, the protectors you are in name." Our politicians and philanthropists, impatient with a salutary 'laissez-faire,' tolerate and even defend 'laissez-faire' that is in the highest degree mischievous.

(Extracts from *The Study of Sociology*, chapter 14.)

Social Darwinism

Other evils, no less serious, are entailed by legislative actions and by actions of individuals, single and combined, which overlook or disregard a kindred biological truth. Besides an habitual neglect of the fact that the quality of a society is physically lowered by the artificial preservation of its feeblest members, there is an habitual neglect of the fact that the quality of a society is lowered morally and intellectually, by the artificial preservation of those who are least able to take care of themselves.

If anyone denies that children bear likenesses to their progenitors in character and capacity—if he holds that men whose parents and grandparents were habitual criminals, have tendencies as good as those of men whose parents and grandparents were industrious and upright, he may consistently hold that it matters not from what families in a society the successive generations descend. He may think it just as well if the most active, and capable, and prudent, and conscientious people die without issue; while many children are left by the reckless and dishonest. But whoever does not espouse so insane a proposition, must admit that social arrangements which retard the multiplication of the mentally-best, and facilitate the multiplication of the mentally-worst, must be extremely injurious.

For if the unworthy are helped to increase, by shielding them from that mortality which their unworthiness would naturally entail, the effect is to produce, generation after generation, a greater unworthiness. From diminished use of self-conserving faculties already deficient, there must result, in posterity, still smaller amounts of self-conserving faculties. The general law which we traced above in its bodily applications, may be traced here in its mental applications. Removal of certain difficulties and dangers which have to be met by intelligence and activity, is followed by a decreased ability to meet difficulties and dangers. Among children born to the more capable who marry with the less capable, thus artificially preserved, there is not simply a lower average power of self-preservation than would else have existed, but the incapacity reaches in some cases a greater extreme. Smaller difficulties and dangers become fatal in proportion as greater ones are warded off. . . . For such members of a population as do not take care of themselves, but are taken care of by the rest, inevitably bring on the rest extra exertion; either in supplying them with the necessaries of life, or in maintaining over them the required supervision, or in both. That is to say, in addition to self-conservation and conservation of their own offspring, the best, having to undertake the conservation of the worst, and of their offspring, are subject to an overdraw upon their energies. In some cases this stops them from marrying; in other cases it diminishes the numbers of their children; in other cases it causes inadequate feeding of their children; in other cases it brings their children to orphanhood—in every way tending to arrest the increase of the best, to deteriorate their constitutions, and to pull them down towards the level of the worst.

Fostering the good-for-nothing at the expense of the good, is an extreme cruelty. It is a deliberate storing-up of miseries for future generations. There is no greater curse to posterity than that of bequeathing them an increasing population of imbeciles and idlers and criminals. To aid the bad in multiplying, is, in effect, the same as maliciously providing for our descendants a multitude of enemies. It may be doubted whether the maudlin philanthropy which, looking only at direct mitigations, persistently ignores indirect mischiefs, does not inflict a greater total of misery than the extremest selfishness inflicts. Refusing to consider the remote influences of his incontinent generosity, the thoughtless giver stands but a degree above the drunkard who thinks only of today's pleasure and ignores to-morrow's pain, or the spendthrift who seeks immediate delights at the cost of ultimate poverty. In one respect, indeed, he is worse; since, while getting the present pleasure produced in giving pleasure, he leaves the future miseries to be borne by others—escaping them himself. And calling for still stronger reprobation is that scattering of money prompted by misinterpretation of the saying that "charity covers a multitude of sins." . . .

How far the mentally-superior may, with a balance of benefit to society, shield the mentally-inferior from the evil results of their inferiority, is a question too involved to be here discussed at length. Doubtless it is in the order of things that parental affection, and regard of relatives, and the spontaneous sympathy of friends and even of strangers, should mitigate the pains which incapacity has to bear, and the penalties which unfit impulses bring around. Doubtless, in many cases the reactive influence of this sympathetic care which the better take of the worse, is morally beneficial, and in a degree compensates by good in one direction for evil in another. It may be fully admitted that individual altruism, left to itself, will work advantageously—wherever, at least, it does not go to the extent of helping the unworthy to multiply. But an unquestionable injury is done by agencies which undertake in a wholesale way to foster good-for-nothings: putting a stop to that natural process of eliminations by which society continually purifies itself. For not only by such agencies is this preservation of the worst and destruction of the best carried further than it would else be, but there is scarcely any of that compensating advantage which individual altruism implies. A mechanically-working State-apparatus, distributing money drawn from grumbling ratepayers, produces little or no moralizing effect on the capables to make up for multiplication of the incapables. Here, however, it is needless to dwell on the perplexing questions hence arising. My purpose is simply to show that a rational policy must recognize certain general truths of Biology; and to insist that only when study of these general truths, as illustrated throughout the living world, has woven them into the conceptions of things, is there gained a strong conviction that disregard of them must cause enormous mischiefs. . . .

(Extract from *The Study of Sociology,* chapter 14.)

Pervading all nature we may see at work a stern discipline, which is a little cruel that it may be very kind. That state of universal welfare maintained throughout the lower creation, to the great perplexity of many worthy people, is at bottom the most merciful provision which the circumstances admit of. It is much better that the ruminant animal, when deprived by age of the vigor which made its existence a pleasure, should be killed by some beast of prey than that it should linger out a life made painful by infirmities, and eventually die of starvation. By the destruction of all such, not only is existence ended before it becomes burdensome, but room is made for a younger generation capable of the fullest enjoyment; and, moreover, out of the very act of substitution happiness is derived for a tribe of predatory creatures. Note further, that their carnivorous enemies not only remove from herbivorous herds individuals past their prime, but also weed out the sickly, the malformed, and the least fleet or powerful. By the aid of which purifying process, as well as by the fighting, so universal in the pairing season, all vitiation of the race through the multiplication of its inferior samples is prevented; and the maintenance of a constitution completely adapted to surrounding conditions, and therefore most productive of happiness, is insured.

The development of the higher creation is a progress toward a form of being capable of a happiness undiminished by these drawbacks. It is in the human race that the consummation is to be accomplished. Civilization is the last stage of its accomplishment. And the ideal man is the man in whom all the conditions of that accomplishment are fulfilled. Meanwhile the well-being of existing humanity and the unfolding of it into this ultimate perfection, are both secured by that same beneficient, though severe, discipline to which the animate creation at large is subject: a discipline which is pitiless in the working out of good: a felicity-pursuing law which never swerves for the avoidance of partial and temporary suffering. The poverty of the incapable, the distresses that come upon the imprudent, the starvation of the idle, and those shoulderings aside of the weak by the strong, which leave so many "in shallows and in miseries," are the decrees of a large, far-seeing benevolence. It seems hard that an unskillfulness which with all his efforts he cannot overcome, should entail hunger upon the artisan. It seems hard that a laborer incapacitated by sickness from competing with his stronger fellows, should have to bear the resulting privations. It seems hard that widows and orphans should be left to struggle for life or death. Nevertheless, when regarded not separately, but in connection with the interests of universal humanity, these harsh fatalities are seen to be full of the highest beneficence—the same beneficence which brings to early graves the children of diseased parents, and singles out the low-spirited, the intemperate, and the debilitated as the victims of an epidemic.

There are many very amiable people—people over whom in so far as their feelings are concerned we may fitly rejoice—who have not the nerve to look this matter fairly in the face. Disabled as they are by their sympathies with present suffering, from duly regarding ultimate consequences, they pursue a course which is very injudicious and in the end even cruel. We do not consider it true kindness in a mother to gratify her child with sweetmeats that are certain to make it ill. We should think it a very foolish sort of benevolence which led a surgeon to let his patient's disease progress to a fatal issue, rather than inflict pain by an operation. Similarly, we must call those spurious philanthropists, who, to prevent misery, would entail greater misery upon future generations. All defenders of a poor-law must, however, be classed amongst such. That rigorous necessity which, when allowed to act on them, becomes so sharp a spur to the lazy and so strong a bridle to the random, these paupers' friends would repeal, because of the wailings it here and there produces. Blind to the fact, that under the natural order of things, society is constantly excreting its unhealthy, imbecile, slow, vacillating, faithless members, these unthinking, though well-meaning, men advocate an interference which not only stops the purifying process, but even increases the vitiation—absolutely encourages the multiplication of the reckless and incompetent by offering them an unfailing provision, and *dis*courages the multiplication of the competent and provident by heightening the prospective difficulty of maintaining a family. And thus, in their eagerness to prevent the really salutary sufferings that surround us, these sigh-wise and groan-foolish people bequeath to posterity a continually increasing curse.

Returning again to the highest point of view, we find that there is a second and still more injurious mode in which law-enforced charity checks the process of adaptation. To become fit for the social state, man has not only to lose his savageness, but he has to acquire the capacities needful for civilized life. Power of application must be developed; such modification of the intellect as shall qualify it for its new tasks must take place; and, above all, there must be gained the ability to sacrifice a small immediate gratification for a future great one. The state of transition will of course be an unhappy state. Misery inevitably results from incongruity between constitution and conditions. All these evils, which afflict us, and seem to the uninitiated the obvious consequences of this or that removable cause, are unavoidable attendants on the adaptation now in progress. Humanity is being pressed against the inexorable necessities of its new position—is being molded into harmony with them, and has to bear the resulting unhappiness as best it can. The process *must* be undergone, and the sufferings *must* be endured. No power on earth, no cunningly-devised laws of statesmen, no world-rectifying schemes of the humane, no communist panaceas, no reforms that men ever did broach or ever will broach, can diminish them one jot. Intensified they may be, and are; and in preventing their intensification, the philanthropic will find ample scope for exertion. But there is bound up with the change a *normal* amount of suffering, which cannot be lessened without altering the very laws of life. Every attempt at mitigation of this eventuates in exacerbation of it.

(Extract from *Social Statics*, chapter 25.)

BAGEHOT
Physics and Politics

The Age of Discussion

. . . If fixity is an invariable ingredient in early civilizations, how then did any civilization become unfixed? No doubt most civilizations stuck where they first were; no doubt we see now why stagnation is the rule of the world, and why progress is the very rare exception; but we do not learn what it is which has caused progress in these few cases, or the absence of what it is which has denied it in all others.

To this question history gives a very clear and very remarkable answer. It is that the change from the age of status to the age of choice was first made in states where the government was to a great and a growing extent a government by discussion, and where the subjects of that discussion were in some degree abstract or, as we should say, matters of principle. It was in the small republics of Greece and Italy that the chain of custom was first broken. "Liberty said, Let there be light, and, like a sunrise on the sea, Athens arose," says Shelley, and his historical philosophy is in this case far more correct that is usual with him. A free state—a state with liberty—means a state, call it republic or call it monarchy, in which the sovereign power is divided between many persons, and in which there is a discussion among those persons. Of these the Greek republics were the first in history, if not in time, and Athens was the greatest of those republics.

After the event it is easy to see why the teaching of history should be this and nothing else. It is easy to see why the common discussion of common actions or common interests should become the root of change and progress. In early society, originality in life was forbidden and repressed by the fixed rule of life. . . . An ordinary man who wished to strike out a new path, to begin a new and important practice by himself, would have been peremptorily required to abandon his novelties on pain of death; he was deviating, he would be told, from the ordinances imposed by the gods on his nation, and he must not do so to please himself. . . . The quaking bystanders in a superstitious age would soon have slain an isolated bold man in the beginning of his innovations. What Macaulay so relied on as the incessant source of progress—the desire of man to better his condition—was not then permitted to work; man was required to live as his ancestors had lived.

Still further away from those times were the "free thought" and the "advancing sciences" of which we now hear so much. The first and most natural subject upon which human thought concerns itself is religion; the first wish of the half-emancipated thinker is to use his reason on the great problems of human destiny—to find out whence he came and whither he goes, to form for himself the most reasonable idea of God which he can form. But, as Mr. Grote happily said, "This is usually what ancient times would not let a man do." . . . Toleration is of all ideas the most modern. . . . Physical science, as we conceive it—that is, the systematic investigation of external nature in detail—did not then exist. . . . It is indeed a modern idea, and is peculiar to a few European countries even yet. . . .

But a government by discussion, if it can be borne, at once breaks down the yoke of fixed custom. The idea of the two is inconsistent. As far as it goes, the mere putting up of a subject to discussion, with the object of being guided by that discussion, is a clear admission that that subject is in no degree settled by established rule, and that men are free to choose in it. It is an admission too that there is no sacred authority—no one transcendent and divinely appointed man whom in that matter the community is bound to obey. And if a single subject or group of subjects be once admitted to discussion, ere long the habit of discussion comes to be established, the sacred charm of use and wont to be dissolved. . . . The same is true of "discussion." Once effectually submit a subject to that ordeal, and you can never withdraw it again; you can never again clothe it with mystery, or fence it by consecration; it remains forever open to free choice and exposed to profane deliberation.

The only subjects which can be first submitted, or which till a very late age of civilization can be submitted, to discussion in the community are the questions involving the visible and pressing interests of the community; they are political questions of high and urgent import. If a nation has in any considerable degree gained the habit, and exhibited the capacity, to discuss these questions with freedom, and to decide them with discretion, to argue much on politics and not to argue ruinously, an enormous advance in other kinds of civilization may confidently be predicted for it. And the reason is a plain deduction from the principles which we have found to guide early civilization. The first pre-historic men were passionate savages, with the greatest difficulty coerced into order and compressed into a state. For ages were spent in beginning that order and founding that state; the only sufficient and effectual agent in so doing was consecrated custom; but then that custom gathered over everything, arrested all onward progress, and stayed the originality of mankind. If, therefore, a nation is able to gain the benefit of custom without the evil—if after ages of waiting it can have order and choice together—at once the fatal clog is removed, and the ordinary springs of progress, as in a modern community we conceive them, begin their elastic action.

Discussion, too, has incentives to progress peculiar to itself. It gives a premium to intelligence. To set out the arguments required to determine political action with such force and effect that they really should determine it is a high and great exertion of intellect. Of course, all such arguments are produced under conditions; the argument abstractedly best is not necessarily the winning argument. Political discussion must move those who have to act; it must be framed in the ideas, and be consonant with the precedent, of its time, just as it must speak its language. But within these marked conditions good discussion is better than bad; no people can for a day bear a government of discussion which does not, within the foundaries of its prejudices and its ideas, prefer good reasoning to bad reasoning, sound argument to unsound. A prize for argumentative mind is given in free states, to which no other states have anything to compare.

Tolerance too is learned in discussion and, as history shows, is only so learned. In all customary societies bigotry is the ruling principle. In rude places to this day, anyone who says anything new is looked on with suspicion, and is persecuted by opinion if not injured by penalty. One of the greatest pains to human nature is the pain of a new idea. . . . Naturally, therefore, common men hate a new idea, and are disposed more or less to ill-treat the original man who brings it. Even nations with long habits of discussion are intolerant enough. . . . If we know that a nation is capable of enduring continuous discussion, we know that it is capable of practicing with equanimity continuous tolerance.

The power of a government by discussion as an instrument of elevation plainly depends—other things being equal—on the greatness or littleness of the things to be discussed. There are periods when great ideas are "in the air," and when, from some cause or other, even common persons seem to partake of an unusual elevation. The age of Elizabeth in England was conspicuously such a time . . . the temper of the age encouraged originality, and in consequence original men started into prominence, went hither and thither where they liked, arrived at goals which the age never expected, and so made it ever memorable.

In this manner all the great movements of thought in ancient and modern times have been nearly connected in time with government by discussion. Athens, Rome, the Italian republics of the Middle Ages, the communes and states-general of feudal Europe have all had a special and peculiar quickening influence, which they owed to their freedom, and which states without that freedom have never communicated. And it has been at the time of great epochs of thought—at the Peloponnesian War, at the fall of the Roman Republic, at the Reformation, at the French Revolution—that such liberty of speaking and thinking have produced their full effect. . . .

Why did discussions in some cases relate to prolific ideas, and why did discussions in other cases relate only to isolated transactions? The reply which history suggests is very clear and very remarkable. Some races of men at our earliest knowledge of them have already acquired the basis of a free constitution; they have already the rudiments of a complex polity—a monarch, a senate, and a general meeting of citizens. The Greeks were one of those races, and it happened, as was natural, that there was in process of time a struggle, the earliest that we know of, between the aristocratic party, originally represented by the senate, and the popular party, represented by the "general meeting." . . . the effect of fundamental political discussion was the same in ancient as in modern times. The whole customary ways of thought were at once shaken by it, and shaken not only in the closets of philosophers but in the common thought and daily business of ordinary men. The "liberation of humanity," as Goethe used to call it—the deliverance of men from the yoke of inherited usage, and of rigid, unquestionable law—was begun in Greece, and had many of its greatest effects, good and evil, on Greece. It is just because of the analogy between the controversies of that time and those of our times that some one has said, "Classical history is a part of modern history; it is medieval history only which is ancient. . . ."

Every page of Aristotle and Plato bears ample and indelible trace of the age of discussion in which they lived; and thought cannot possibly be freer. The deliverance of the speculative intellect from traditional and customary authority was altogether complete.

. . . as far as the intellectual and cultivated part of society is concerned, the triumph of reason was complete; the minds of the highest philosophers were then as ready to obey evidence and reason as they have ever been since; probably they were more ready. The rule of custom over them at least had been wholly broken, and the primary conditions of intellectual progress were in that respect satisfied. . . .

But though in the earliest and in the latest time government by discussion has been a principal organ for improving mankind, yet, from its origin, it is a plant of singular delicacy. At first the chances are much against its living. In the beginning, the members of a free state are of necessity few. The essence of it requires that discussion shall be brought home to those members. But in early time, when writing is difficult, reading rare, and representation undiscovered, those who are to be guided by the discussion must hear it with their own ears, must be brought face to face with the orator, and must feel his influence for themselves. The first free states were little towns, smaller than any political division which we now have, except the republic of Andorra, which is a sort of vestige of them. It is in the market place of the country town, as we should now speak, and in petty matters concerning the market town, that discussion began, and thither all the long train of its consequences may be traced back. . . .

The following conditions may, I think, be historically traced to the nation capable of a polity which suggests principles for discussion, and so leads to progress. First, the nation must possess the *patria potestas* in some form so marked as to give family life distinctness and precision, and to make a home education and a home discipline probable and possible. While descent is traced only through the mother, and while the family is therefore a vague entity, no progress to a high polity is possible. Secondly, that polity would seem to have been created very gradually; by the aggregation of families into clans of *gentes,* and of clans into nations, and then again by the widening of nations, so as to include circumjacent outsiders, as well as the first compact and sacred group—the number of parties to a discussion was at first augmented very slowly. Thirdly, the number of "open" subjects, as we should say nowadays—that is, of subjects on which public opinion was optional, and on which discussion was admitted—was at first very small. Custom ruled everything originally, and the area of free argument was enlarged but very slowly. If I am at all right, that area could only be enlarged thus slowly, for custom was in early days the cement of society, and if you suddenly questioned such custom you would destroy society. . . .

(Extract from chapter 5.)

MAINE
Ancient Law

Custom and Law

. . . Bentham in his *Fragment on Government,* and Austin, in his *Province of Jurisprudence Determined,* resolve every law into a *command* of the lawgiver, an *obligation* imposed thereby on the citizen, and a *sanction* threatened in the event of disobedience; and it is further predicated of the *command,* which is the first element in a law, that it must prescribe, not a single act, but a series or number of acts of the same class or kind. The results of this separation of ingredients tally exactly with the facts of mature jurisprudence; and, by a little straining of language, they may be made to correspond in form with all law, of all kinds, at all epochs. . . . It is curious that, the farther we penetrate into the primitive history of thought, the farther we find ourselves from a conception of law which at all resembles a compound of the elements which Bentham determined. It is certain that, in the infancy of mankind, no sort of legislature, not even a distinct author of law, is contemplated or conceived of. Law has scarcely reached the footing of custom; it is rather a habit. It is, to use a French phrase, "in the air." The only authoritative statement of right and wrong is a judicial sentence after the facts, not one presupposing a law which has been violated, but one which is breathed for the first time by a higher power into the judge's mind at the moment of adjudication. . . .

The epoch of Customary Law, and of its custody by a privileged order, is a very remarkable one. The condition of the jurisprudence which it implies has left traces which may still be detected in legal and popular phraseology. The law, thus known exclusively to a privileged minority, whether a caste, an aristocracy, a priestly tribe, or a sacerdotal college, is true unwritten law. Except this, there is no such thing as unwritten law in the world. . . .

From the period of Customary Law we come to another sharply defined epoch in the history of jurisprudence. We arrive at the era of Codes, those ancient codes of which the Twelve Tables of Rome were the most famous specimen. . . .

Among the chief advantages which the Twelve Tables and similar codes conferred on the societies which obtained them, was the protection which they afforded against the frauds of the privileged oligarchy and also against the spontaneous depravation and debasement of the national institutions. The Roman Code was merely an enunciation in words of the existing customs of the Roman people. . . . The usages which a particular community is found to have adopted in its infancy and in its primitive seats are generally those which are on the whole best suited to promote its physical and moral well-being; and, if they are retained in their integrity until new social wants have taught new practices, the upward march of society is almost certain. But unhappily there is a law of development which ever threatens to operate upon unwritten usage. The customs are of course obeyed by multitudes who are incapable of understanding the true ground of their expediency, and who are therefore left inevitably to invent superstitious reasons for their permanence. A process then commences which may be shortly described by saying that usage which is reasonable generates usage which is unreasonable. . . .

(Extracts from chapter 1.)

Theories of Jurisprudence

The necessity of submitting the subject of jurisprudence to scientific treatment has never been entirely lost sight of in modern times, and the essays which the consciousness of this necessity has produced have proceeded from minds of very various calibre, but there is not much presumption, I think, in asserting that what has hitherto stood in the place of a science has for the most part been a set of guesses. . . .

The Lockeian theory of the origin of Law in a Social Compact scarcely conceals its Roman derivation, and indeed is only the dress by which the ancient views were rendered more attractive to a particular generation of the moderns; but on the other hand the theory of Hobbes on the same subject was purposely devised to repudiate the reality of a law of nature as conceived by the Romans and their disciples. Yet these two theories, which long divided the reflecting politicians of England into hostile camps, resemble each other strictly in their fundamental assumption of a non-historic, unverifiable condition of the race. Their authors differed as to the characteristics of the præ-social state, and as to the nature of the abnormal action by which men lifted themselves out of it into that social organisation with which alone we are acquainted, but they agreed in thinking that a great chasm separated man in his primitive condition from man in society, and this notion we cannot doubt that they borrowed, consciously or unconsciously, from the Romans. If indeed the phenomena of law be regarded in the way in which these theorists regarded them —that is, as one vast complex whole—it is not surprising that the mind should often evade the task it has set to itself by falling back on some ingenious conjecture which (plausibly interpreted) will seem to reconcile everything, or else that it should sometimes abjure in despair the labour of systematization.

From the theories of jurisprudence which have the same speculative basis as the Roman doctrine two of much celebrity must be excepted. The first of them is that associated with the great name of Montesquieu. Though there are some ambiguous expressions in the early part of the *Esprit des Lois*, which seem to show its writer's unwillingness to break quite openly with the views hitherto popular, the general drift of the book is certainly to indicate a very different conception of its subject from any which had been entertained before. It has often been noticed that, amidst the vast variety of examples which, in its immense width of survey, it sweeps together from supposed systems of jurisprudence, there is an evident anxiety to thrust into especial prominence those manners and institutions which astonish the civilised reader by their uncouthness, strangeness, or indecency. The inference constantly suggested is, that laws are the creatures of climate, local situation, accident, or imposture—the fruit of any causes except those which appear to operate with tolerable constancy. Montesquieu seems, in fact, to have looked on the nature of man as entirely plastic, as passively reproducing the impressions, and submitting implicitly to the impulses, which it receives from without. And here no doubt lies the error which vitiates his system as a system. He greatly underrates the stability of human nature. He pays little or no regard to the inherited qualities of the race, those qualities which each generation receives from its predecessors, and transmits but slightly altered to the generation which follows it. It is quite true, indeed, that no complete account can be given of social phenomena, and consequently of laws, till due allowance has been made for those modifying causes which are noticed in the *Esprit des Lois;* but their number and their force appear to have been overestimated by Montesquieu. Many of the anomalies which he parades have since been shown to rest on false report or erroneous construction, and of those which remain not a few prove the permanence rather than the variableness of man's nature, since they are relics of older stages of the race which have obstinately defied the influences that have elsewhere had effect. The truth is that the stable part of our mental, moral, and physical constitution is the largest part of it, and the resistance it opposes to change is such that, though the variations of human society in a portion of the world are plain enough, they are neither so rapid nor so extensive that their amount, character, and general direction cannot be ascertained. . . .

(Extract from chapter 5.)

From Status to Contract

There is such wide-spread dissatisfaction with existing theories of jurisprudence, and so general a conviction that they do not really solve the questions they pretend to dispose of, as to justify the suspicion that some line of inquiry necessary to a perfect result has been incompletely followed or altogether omitted by their authors. And indeed there is one remarkable omission with which all these speculations are chargeable, except perhaps those of Montesquieu. They take no account of what law has actually been at epochs remote from the particular period at which they made their appearance. Their originators carefully observed the institutions of their own age and civilisation, and those of other ages and civilisations with which they had some degree of intellectual sympathy, but, when they turned their attention to archaic states of society which exhibited much superficial difference from their own, they uniformly ceased to observe and began guessing. The mistake which they committed is therefore analogous to the error of one who, in investigating the laws of the material universe, should commence by contemplating the existing physical world as a world, instead of beginning with the particles which are its simplest ingredients. One does not certainly see why such a scientific solecism should be more defensible in jurisprudence than in any other region of thought. It would seem antecedently that we ought to commence with the simplest social forms in a state as near as possible to their rudimentary condition. In other words, if we followed the course usual in such inquiries, we should penetrate as far up as we could in the history of primitive societies. The phenomena which early societies present us with are not easy at first to understand, but the difficulty of grappling with them bears no proportion to the perplexities which beset us in considering the baffling entanglement of modern social organisation. It is a difficulty arising from their strangeness and uncouthness, not from their number and complexity. . . . But, even if they gave more trouble than they do, no pains would be wasted in ascertaining the germs out of which has assuredly been unfolded every form of moral restraint which controls our actions and shapes our conduct at the present moment.

The rudiments of the social state, so far as they are known to us at all, are known through testimony of three sorts—accounts by contemporary observers of civilisations less advanced than their own, the records which particular races have preserved concerning their primitive history, and ancient law. . . .

The movement of the progressive societies has been uniform in one respect. Through all its course it has been distinguished by the gradual dissolution of family dependency and the growth of individual obligation in its place. The Individual is steadily substituted for the Family, as the unit of which civil laws take account. The advance has been accomplished at varying rates of celerity. . . . Nor is it difficult to see what is the tie between man and man which replaces by degrees those forms of reciprocity in right and duties which have their origin in the Family. It is Contract. Starting, as from one terminus of history, from a condition of society in which all the relations of Persons are summed up in the relations of Family, we seem to have steadily moved towards a phase of social order in which all these relations arise from the free agreement of Individuals. In Western Europe the progress achieved in this direction has been considerable. Thus the status of the Slave has disappeared—it has been superseded by the contractual relation of the servant to his master. The status of the Female under Tutelage, if the tutelage be understood of persons other than her husband, has also ceased to exist; from her coming of age to her marriage all the relations she may form are relations of contract. So too the status of the Son under Power has no true place in the law of modern European societies. . . .

The word Status may be usefully employed to construct a formula expressing the law of progress thus indicated, which, whatever be its value, seems to me to be sufficiently ascertained. All the forms of Status taken notice of in the Law of Persons were derived from, and to some extent are still coloured by, the powers and privileges anciently residing in the Family. If then we employ Status, agreeably with the usage of the best writers, to signify these personal conditions only, and avoid applying the term to such conditions as are the immediate or remote result of agreement, we may say that the movement of the progressive societies has hitherto been a movement *from Status to Contract*.

(Extracts from chapter 5.)

GREEN

The Principles of Political Obligation

Will, Not Force, Is the Basis of the State

. . . it is only as members of a society, as recognising common interests and objects, that individuals come to have [moral] attributes and rights [of humanity]; and the power, from the development and systematisation of those institutions for the regulation of a common life without which they would have no rights at all.

To ask why I am to submit to the power of the state, is to ask why I am to allow my life to be regulated by that complex of institutions without which I literally should not have a life to call my own, nor should be able to ask for a justification of what I am called on to do. For that I may have a life which I can call my own, I must not only be conscious of myself and of ends which I present to myself as mine; I must be able to reckon on a certain freedom of action and acquisition for the attainment of those ends, and this can only be secured through common recognition of this freedom on the part of each other by members of a society, as being for a common good. Without this, the very consciousness of having ends of his own and a life which he can direct in a certain way, a life of which he can make something, would remain dormant in a

man. It is true that slaves have been found to have this consciousness in high development; but a slave even at his lowest
has been partly made what he is by an ancestral life which
was not one of slavery pure and simple, a life in which certain
elementary rights were secured to the members of a society
through their recognition of a common interest. . . . Thus the
appearance in slaves of the conception that they should be
masters of themselves, does not conflict with the proposition
that only so far as a certain freedom of action and acquisition
is secured to a body of men through their recognition of the
exercise of that freedom by each other as being for the
common good, is there an actualisation of the individual's
consciousness of having life and ends of his own. The exercise, manifestation, expression of this consciousness through a
freedom secured in the way described is necessary to its real
existence, just as language of some sort is necessary to the real
existence of thought, and bodily movement to that of the
soul.

The demand, again, for a justification of what one is called
on by authority to do presupposes some standard of right,
recognised as equally valid for and by the person making the
demand and others who form a society with him, and such a
recognised standard in turn implies institutions for the regulation of men's dealings with each other, institutions of which
the relation to the consciousness of right may be compared, as
above, to that of language to thought. It cannot be said that
the most elementary consciousness of right is prior to them,
or they to it. They are the expressions in which it becomes
real. As conflicting with the momentary inclinations of the
individual, these institutions are a power which he obeys unwillingly; which he has to, or is made to, obey. But it is only
through them that the consciousness takes shape and form
which expresses itself in the question, 'Why should I thus be
constrained? By what right is my natural right to do as I like
overborne?'

The doctrine that the rights of government are founded on
the consent of the governed is a confused way of stating the
truth, that the institutions by which man is moralised, by
which he comes to do what he sees that he must, as distinct
from what he would like, express a conception of a common
good; that through them that conception takes form and
reality; and that it is in turn through its presence in the
individual that they have a constraining power over him, a
power which is not that of mere fear, still less a physical
compulsion, but which leads him to do what he is not inclined
to because there is a law that he should.

Rousseau, it will be remembered, speaks of the 'social pact' not merely as the foundation of sovereignty or civil government, but as the foundation of morality. Through it man becomes a moral agent; for the slavery to appetite he substitutes the freedom of subjection to a self-imposed law. If he had seen at the same time that rights do not begin till duties begin, and that if there was no morality prior to the pact there could not be rights, he might have been saved from the error which the notion of there being natural rights introduces into his theory. But though he does not seem himself to have been aware of the full bearing of his own conception, the conception itself is essentially true. Setting aside the fictitious representation of an original covenant as having given birth to that common 'ego' or general will, without which no such covenant would have been possible, and of obligations arising out of it, as out of a bargain made between one man and another, it remains true that only through a recognition by certain men of a common interest, and through the expression of that recognition in certain regulations of their dealings with each other, could morality originate, or any meaning be gained for such terms as 'ought' and 'right' and their equivalents.

Morality, in the first instance, is the observance of such regulations, and though a higher morality, the morality of the character governed by 'disinterested motives,' i.e. by interest in some form of human perfection, comes to differentiate itself from this primitive morality consisting in the observance of rules established for a common good, yet this outward morality is the presupposition of the higher morality. Morality and political subjection thus have a common source, *political* subjection' being distinguished from that of a slave, as a subjection which secures rights to the subject. That common source is the rational recognition by certain human beings—it may be merely by children of the same parent—of a common well-being which is their well-being . . . and the embodiment of that recognition in rules by which the inclinations of the individuals are restrained, and a corresponding freedom of action for the attainment of well-being on the whole is secured. . . .

What is certain is, that a habit of subjection founded upon such fear could not be a basis of political or free society; for to this it is necessary, not indeed that everyone subject to the laws should take part in voting them, still less that he should consent to their application to himself, but that it should represent an idea of common good, which each member of the society can make his own so far as he is rational, i.e. capable of the conception of a common good, however much

particular passions may lead him to ignore it and thus neces-
sitate the use of force to prevent him from doing that which,
so far as influenced by the conception of a common good, he
would willingly abstain from.

Whether the legislative and administrative agencies of society can be kept in the main free from bias by private interests, and true to the idea of common good, without popular
control; whether again, if they can, that 'civil sense,' that
appreciation of common good on the part of the subjects,
which is as necessary to a free or political society as the
direction of law to the maintenance of a common good, can
be kept alive without active participation of the people in
legislative functions; these are questions of circumstances
which perhaps do not admit of unqualified answers. The views
of those who looked mainly to the highest development of
political life in a single small society, have to be modified if
the object sought for is the extension of political life to the
largest number of people. The size of modern states renders
necessary the substitution of a representative system for one
in which the citizens shared directly in legislation, and this so
far tends to weaken the active interest of the citizens in the
common weal, though the evil may partly be counteracted by
giving increased importance to municipal or communal administration. In some states, from the want of homogeneity or
facilities of communication, a representative legislature is
scarcely possible. In others, where it exists, a great amount of
power, virtually exempt from popular control, has to be left
with what Rousseau would have called the 'prince or magistrate.' In all this there is a lowering of civil vitality as compared with that of the ancient, and perhaps of some excep-
tionally developed modern, commonwealths. But perhaps this
is a temporary loss that we have to bear as the price of having
recognised the claim to citizenship as the claim of all men.
Certainly all political ideals, which require active and direct
participation by the citizens in the functions of the sovereign
state, fail us as soon as we try to conceive their realisation on
the wide area even of civilised mankind. . . .

The idea of a common good which the state fulfills has
never been the sole influence actuating those who have been
agents in the historical process by which states have come to
be formed. . . .

This is equally true of those who contribute to the formation and maintenance of states rather as agents, and of those
who do so rather as patients. No one could pretend that even
the most thoughtful and dispassionate publicist is capable of
the idea of the good served by the state to which he belongs,

in all its fulness. He apprehends it only in some of its bearings; but it is as a common good that he apprehends it, i.e. not as a good for himself or for this man or that more than another, but for all members equally in virtue of their relation to each other and their common nature. The idea which the ordinary citizen has of the common good served by the state is much more limited in content. Very likely he does not think of it at all in connection with anything that the term 'state' represents to him. But he has a clear understanding of certain interests and rights common to himself with his neighbours, if only such as consist in getting his wages paid at the end of the week, in getting his money's worth at the shop, in the inviolability of his own person and that of his wife. Habitually and instinctively, i.e. without asking the reason why, he regards the claim which in these respects he makes for himself as conditional upon his recognizing a like claim in others, and thus as in the proper sense a right,—a claim of which the essence lies in its being common to himself with others. Without this instinctive recognition he is one of the 'dangerous classes,' virtually outlawed by himself. With it, though he have no reverence for the 'state' under that name, no sense of an interest shared with others in maintaining it, he has the needful elementary conception of a common good maintained by law. It is the fault of the state if this conception fails to make him a loyal subject, if not an intelligent patriot. It is a sign that the state is not a true state; that it is not fulfilling its primary function of maintaining law equally in the interest of all, but is being administered in the interest of classes; whence it follows that the obedience which, if not rendered willingly, the state compels the citizen to render, is not one that he feels any spontaneous interest in rendering, because it does not present itself to him as the condition of the maintenance of those rights and interests, common to himself with his neighbours, which he understands. . . .

That active interest in the service of the state, which makes patriotism in the better sense, can hardly arise while the individual's relation to the state is that of a passive recipient of protection in the exercise of his rights of person and property. While this is the case, he will give the state no thanks for the protection which he will come to take as a matter of course, and will only be conscious of it when it descends upon him with some unusual demand for service or payment, and then he will be conscious of it in the way of resentment. If he is to have a higher feeling of political duty, he must take part in the work of the state. He must have a share, direct or indirect, by himself acting as a member or by voting for the members of supreme or provincial assemblies, in making and maintaining the laws which he obeys. Only thus will he learn to regard the work of the state as a whole, and to transfer to the whole the interest which otherwise his particular experience would lead him to feel only in that part of its work that goes to the maintenance of his own and his neighbour's rights. . . .

It is admitted that the outward visible sign of a state is the presence of a supreme or independent coercive power, to which habitual obedience is rendered by a certain multitude of people, and that this power may often be exercised in a manner apparently detrimental to the general well-being. It may be the case, as we have tried to show that it is, that a power which is in the main so exercised, and is generally felt to be so, is not likely long to maintain its supremacy; but this does not show that a state cannot exist without the promotion of the common good of its subjects, or that (in any intelligible way) the promotion of such good belongs to the idea of a state. A short-lived state is not therefore not a state, and if it were, it is rather the active interference with the subject's well-being, than a failure to promote it, that is fatal to the long life of a state. How, finally, can the state be said to exist for the sake of an end, or to fulfil an idea, the contemplation of which, it is admitted, has had little to do with the actions which have had most to do with bringing states into existence?

The assertion . . . that an idea of social good is represented by, or realised in, the formation of states, is not to be met by pointing to the selfishness and bad passions of men who have been instrumental in forming them, if there is reason to think that the influences, under the direction of which these passions become thus instrumental, are due to the action of such an idea. And when we speak thus we do not refer to any action of the idea otherwise than in the consciousness of men. It may be legitimate, as we have seen, to consider ideas as existing and acting otherwise, and perhaps, on thinking the matter out, we should find ourselves compelled to regard the idea of social good as a communication to the human consciousness, a consciousness developing itself in time, from an eternally complete consciousness. But here we are considering it as a source of the moral action of men, and therefore necessarily as having its seat in their consciousness, and the proposition advanced is that such an idea is a determining element in the consciousness of the most selfish men who have been instrumental in the formation or maintenance of states; that only through its influence in directing and controlling their actions could they be so instrumental; and that, though its active presence in their consciousness is due to the institutions, the organisation of life, under which they are born and bred, the existence of these institutions is in turn due to the action, under other conditions, of the same idea in the minds of men. . . .

It is not . . . supreme coercive power, simply as such, but supreme coercive power exercised in a certain way and for certain ends, that makes a state; viz. exercised according to law, written or customary, and for the maintenance of rights. The abstract consideration of sovereignty has led to these qualifications being overlooked. Sovereignty=supreme coercive power, indeed, but such power as exercised in and over a state, which means with the qualifications specified; but the mischief of beginning with an inquiry into sovereignty before the idea of a state has been investigated, is that it leads us to adopt this abstract notion of sovereignty, as merely supreme coercive power, and then, when we come to think of the state as distinguished by sovereignty, makes us suppose that supreme coercive power is all that is essential to a state, forgetting that it is rather the state that makes the sovereign, than the sovereign that makes the state. . . . A power that altered laws otherwise than according to law, according to a constitution, written or unwritten, would be incompatible with the existence of a state, which is a body of persons, recognised by each other as having rights, and possessing certain institutions for the maintenance of those rights. The office of the sovereign, as an institution of such a society, is to protect those rights from invasion, either from without, from foreign nations, or from within, from members of the society who cease to behave as such. Its supremacy is the society's independence of such attacks from without or within. It is an agency of the society, or the society itself acting for this end. If the power, existing for this end, is used on the whole otherwise than in conformity either with a formal constitution or with customs which virtually serve the purpose of a constitution, it is no longer an institution for the maintenance of rights and ceases to be the agent of a state. We only count Russia a state by a sort of courtesy on the supposition that the power of the Czar, though subject to no constitutional control, is so far exercised in accordance with a recognised tradition of what the public good requires as to be on the whole a sustainer of rights.

It is true, just as in a state, all law being derived from the sovereign, there is a sense in which the sovereign is not bound by any law, so there is a sense in which all rights are derived from the sovereign, and no power which the sovereign refuses to allow can be a right; but it is only in the sense that, the sovereign being the state acting in a certain capacity, and the state being an institution for the more complete and harmonious maintenance of the rights of its members, a power, claimed as a right, but which the state or sovereign refuses to allow, cannot be really compatible with the general system of rights. In other words, it is true only on the supposition that a state is made a state by the functions which it fulfils of maintaining the rights of its members as a whole or a system, in such a way that none gains at the expense of another (no one has any power guaranteed to him through another's being deprived of that power). Thus the state, or the sovereign as a characteristic institution of the state, does not create rights, but gives fuller reality to rights already existing. It secures and extends the exercise of powers, which men, influenced in dealing with each other by an idea of common good, had recognised in each other as being capable of direction to that common good, and had already in a certain measure secured to each other in consequence of that recognition. It is not a state unless it does so. . . .

(Extracts from sections 113-119, 121-122, 124, 131-132.)

SECTION **X**

IRRATIONALISM AND PSYCHOLOGY

The deepest error of our political thinking, Walter Lippmann has said, is to talk of politics without reference to human beings. In the latter part of the nineteenth century, criticism was directed at idealism as abstract and almost completely remote from political reality, at positivism as wishing to impose a rational order on society, and at scientific rationalism as providing no valid explanation of phenomena, but resulting rather in determinism. Philosophers like Nietzsche, Bergson and Croce, writers and economists like Sorel and Pareto, those interested in psychology like Freud, Le Bon and Wallas, wanted a fresh approach to the study of human nature in which new truths such as the role of intuition, the unconscious or myths, would be recognized. Direct action and inner drives were stressed, rather than intellect or traditional behavior. Religion was examined more as commentary on human behavior than for any theological significance.

Nietzsche

Friedrich Nietzsche (1844–1900) became Professor of Classical Philology and colleague of Burckhardt at Basle when only twenty-four, resigned after ten years and spent the latter part of his life in poor health or near madness. He was poet, artist and psychologist as much as philosopher; he leaves no one inheritance to politics, but his works are full of extraordinary psychological insights, poetic imagery and symbols, and daring prophecies. Many of his ideas have entered the coinage of philosophical discussion: the superman, the will to power, self-mastery, the eternal recurrence, the tension between the Dionysian and Apollonian spirits, between frenzy and passion and ordered calm, the inadequacy of rationalism, the aristocratic distaste for modern vulgarity, the herd morality, the influence of myth for motivating action, the need for leadership to instill purpose in life, the death of God and the transvaluation of values.

The sick and gentle scholar despised weakness, praised the "strong virtues"—nobility and courage—and attacked Christianity for being the enemy of vital living, for upholding meekness and charity. But much of the legend of Nietzsche as a racist, nationalist and violent anti-Semite has been dispelled in recent years. Nietzsche has been influential in modern philosophical schools, especially existentialism, because of his conviction of nihilism and his insistence on the need for creativity and regeneration: "launch the arrow of longing towards the other shore." Since good and evil had no roots in existence, they had to be discarded; man must be strong enough to accept a world truly beyond good and evil. Nietzsche heralded the importance of the artist—the true artist, not the charlatan posing as an artist, like Wagner—for only after the death of religion would the imagination be able to luxuriate again in divine spheres.

The Myth in France

Bergson was a philosophical essayist of great charm and elegance, not a political writer. It is difficult to extract from his writings any concrete, positive proposals. But his criticism of the inadequacy of positivism, materialism and purely scientific explanations of evolution, and his advocacy of creativity, the *élan vital*, intuition and a somewhat nebulous philosophical mysticism, gained considerable popular or fashionable appeal as well as influence on those, like Sorel, William James and Charles Péguy, who were dissatisfied with purely rationalistic explanations of phenomena.

Georges Sorel (1847–1922), the engineer who retired to write at forty-five, was a prolific, if unsystematic, writer, with extensive intellectual interests—little of his output is concerned with political problems as such. Sorel was essentially a moralist, believing in the need for regeneration in a society becoming decadent, and seeking to produce the autonomous man who would become free by participating in that which he loved. He attacked both the role played by intellectuals in human affairs and intellectualism, which he regarded as extreme rationalism, incapable of understanding the complexity of phenomena. The bourgeois conception of life was lacking in sublimity; it could not give rise to the vital noble instincts and heroism. To introduce the sublime and to transform society meant action, tension and struggle.

The idea for which Sorel is best known is the myth, the appeal to a deeper consciousness and the expression of the determination to act. All great historical movements were motivated by a social myth, a non-rational idea that created an epic state in its adherents. Sorel, attracted temporarily to the syndicalist movement, believed that a general strike was the contemporary method to regenerate society through the proletariat.

Sorel, opposed to bourgeois plutocracy and commerce, and to optimism, inherited Proudhon's distaste for state enterprise, political institutions and political parties. Politicians, corrupt and incompetent, were as empty of ideas as of grandeur of soul. Communists and fascists have both claimed Sorel as a sympathizer at least, but, in spite of some praise for Lenin at the end of his life, he remained aloof from political movements.

Psychology and Politics

Graham Wallas (1858–1932) was, like T. H. Green, an academic who participated in practical politics. His interests included early membership in the Fabian Society in 1886, membership in the London School Board and the London County Council and intellectual interest in the syndicalist movement. Wallas was dissatisfied with easy or rationalistic assumptions about the nature of man, pointing out the minor role played by reason in politics and denying that all human actions were produced by intellectual processes.

The political scientist had to study society in a scientific fashion. He should be capable of deliberate invention and the organization of expedients for making common action effective. But although Wallas was continually concerned with the exploration of thought, the way in which ideas were produced and the need to foster such invention, he produced singularly few ideas of a concrete nature.

His *Human Nature in Politics* of 1908 is a pioneer work in social psychology, indicating the place of instinct and impulse. But he drew from this the conclusion, not of irrationality, but that the rational must guide the irrational in the interests of the common good.

It was through Freud, and his great contemporaries Jung and Adler, that psychology penetrated social thought to any considerable degree. Freud's concepts of personality, man's sex habits, unconscious behavior, physiological motivations, have been questioned for their scientific accuracy, but, as Auden has written,

> "To us he is no more a person
> Now but a climate of opinion"[1]

NIETZSCHE

Beyond Good and Evil (1886)
and
Thus Spoke Zarathustra (1883–85)

The Will to Power

"In moderation, according to nature" you wish to live? Oh noble Stoics! How your words deceive! Think of a being like Nature, immoderately wasteful, immoderately indifferent, devoid of intentions and considerateness, devoid of compassion and a sense of justice, fruitful and desolate and uncertain at the same time; think of indifference on the throne—how could you live in moderation according to this indifference? Living—isn't it precisely a wishing-to-be-different from this Nature? Doesn't living mean evaluating, preferring, being unjust, being limited, wanting to be different? But supposing your imperative "to live in moderation, according to nature" only means "to live in moderation, according to life"—how then could you live *otherwise?* Why make a principle of something that you are and have to be? The truth is quite another matter: while rapturously pretending to read the canon of your law out of nature, you actually want the opposite—you strange play-actors and self-deceivers! Your pride wants to dictate your morality, your ideal, to nature (even to nature!). It wants to incorporate itself in nature; you demand that nature be nature "in moderation, according to the Stoa"; you want to remake all existence to mirror your own existence; you want an enormous everlasting glorification of stoicism! With all your love for truth, you force yourselves to see nature *falsely*, i.e. stoically—so long, so insistently, so hypnotically petrified, until you can no longer see it any other way. And in the end some abysmal arrogance gives you the insane hope that, *because* you know how to tyrannize over

[1] From W. H. Auden, "In Memory of Sigmund Freud," appearing in *The Collected Poetry of W. H. Auden* (New York: Random House, 1945).

yourselves (stoicism is self-tyranny), you can also tyrannize over nature—for isn't the Stoic a *part* of nature? . . . But all this is an old, everlasting story. What happened to the Stoics still happens today, as soon as a philosophy begins to have faith in itself. It always creates the world in its own image; it cannot do otherwise, for philosophy *is* the tyrannical desire; it is the most spiritual will to power, to "creation of the world," to the *causa prima*. . . .

All psychology hitherto has become stuck in moral prejudices and fears: none has ventured into the depths. To consider psychology as the morphology and evolutionary doctrine of the will to power—as I consider it—this no one has touched upon even in thought (insofar as it is allowable to recognize in what has been written the symptoms of what has been kept dark). The force of moral prejudices has penetrated deeply into the most spiritual, the seemingly coldest and most open-minded world, and, as one may imagine, with harmful, obstructionist, blinding, and distorting results. A proper physio-psychology must battle with unconscious resistances in the heart of the investigator; his "heart" sides against it. Even a doctrine of the reciprocally limiting interaction of the "good" and "wicked" impulses causes, as being a subtle form of immorality, some distress and aversion in a still strong and hearty conscience. Even worse is a doctrine that all the good impulses are derived from the wicked ones. But imagine someone who takes the very passions—hatred, envy, greed, domineering—to be the passions upon which life is conditioned, as things which must be present in the total household of life. Takes them to be necessary in order to preserve the very nature of life, to be further developed if life is to be further developed! Such a man suffers from the inclination of his judgment as though from seasickness! But even this hypothesis is by no means the most painful or the strangest in this enormous, almost totally unknown domain of dangerous insights. Indeed, there are a hundred good reasons for staying away from it if one—can! On the other hand, if our ship has once taken us there—very well, let us go ahead, grit our teeth, open our eyes, grip the rudder and—ride out morality! Perhaps we will crush and destroy our own remaining morality, but what do *we* matter! Never yet had a *deeper* world of insight been opened to bold travellers and adventurers. And the psychologist who can make this sort of "sacrifice" (it is not the *sacrifizio dell' intelletto*—on the contrary!) will at least be in a position to demand that psychology be acknowledged once more as the mistress of the sciences, for whose service and preparation the other sciences exist. For psychology is now again the road to the basic problems. . . .

Let us assume that nothing is "given" as real except our world of desires and passions, that we cannot step down or step up to any kind of "reality" except the reality of our drives—for thinking is nothing but the interrelation and interaction of our drives. Would we not be allowed to experiment with the question whether these "givens" are not *sufficient* for understanding the so-called mechanistic (or material) world? I mean not as an illusion, "a semblance," an "idea" (in Berkeley's or Schopenhauer's sense), but as equal in reality-stature to our passions? To understand it as a more primitive form of the world of passions in which everything, still contained in a powerful unison, later branches off and develops (also, as is fair enough, weakens and is refined) in the organic processes? As a sort of primitive life in which all the organic functions, together with self-regulation, assimilation, nutrition, secretion and metabolism, are still synthetically bound up with one another? To understand the material world as a *preform* of life? In the end this experimental question is not merely allowed; it is demanded by the conscience of *methodology*. Not to assume several types of causality until the experiment of getting along with a single one has been followed to its utmost conclusion (to the point of absurdity, if I may be permitted to say so): this is the morality of methodology which one may not escape today. It follows "from its definition" as a mathematician would say. In the end, the question is whether we really acknowledge the will as *effective;* whether we believe in that causality of the will. If we do (and basically our faith in the causality of the will amounts to our belief in causality itself), we *must* experiment with taking will-causality as our only hypothesis. Will, of course, can only act on will, not on matter (on "nerves," for example). Enough said: we must risk the hypothesis that everywhere we recognize "effects" there is an effect of will upon will; that all mechanical happenings, insofar as they are activated by some energy, are will-power, will-effects.—Assuming, finally, that we succeeded in explaining our entire instinctual life as the development and ramification of one basic form of will (of the will to power, as I hold); assuming that one could trace back all the organic functions to this will to power, including the solution of the problem of generation and nutrition (they are one problem) —if this were done, we should be justified in defining *all* effective energy unequivocally as *will to power*. The world seen from within, the world designated and defined according to its "intelligible character"—this world would be *will to power* and nothing else. . . .

Whether it is hedonism, pessimism, utilitarianism, or eudemonism—all these ways of thinking which measure the value of things according to *pleasure* and *pain*, i.e. according to subsidiary circumstances and secondary considerations, are superficial ways of thinking. They are naïvetés upon which anyone who is conscious of *formative* powers and of an artist's conscience will look with scorn and not without some compassion. Compassion for *you!* That is, to be sure, not the compassion you have in mind. It is not compassion with "social distress," with "society" and its sick and maimed, with those who are vice-laden and broken from their very beginnings, as they lie strewn on the ground around us; even less is it compassion with grumbling, oppressed, revolutionary slave strata who seek domination and call it "freedom." *Our* compassion is a superior, more farsighted compassion. We see how *mankind* is depreciating, how *you* are depreciating mankind. There are moments in which we look with indescribable anxiety at *your* compassion, when we defend ourselves against what you call compassion, when we find your earnestness more dangerous than any wantonness. You want, if possible (and there is no more insane "if possible") to *do away with suffering*. And we—it seems that *we* want it worse and more than it ever was! Well-being as you think of it is no aim; to us it seems more like an *end*—a finish! A condition which makes men ridiculous and contemptible, which creates the *desire* that man might perish. The discipline of suffering, of suffering in the *great* sense: don't you know that all the heightening of man's powers has been created by only this discipline? That tension of the soul in misfortune which trains it to strength, its shudders at the sight of great perdition, its inventiveness and courageousness in enduring, maintaining itself in, interpreting, and utilizing, misfortune—whatever was given to the soul by way of depth, mystery, mask, mind, guile, and greatness: was it not given through suffering, through the discipline of great suffering? In man there is united both *creature* and *creator;* in man there is material, fragment, excess, clay, filth, nonsense, and chaos. But in man there is also creator, imagemaker, hammer-hardness, spectator-divinity, and day of rest: do you understand this antithesis? And do you understand that *your* compassion is spent on the "creature" in man, on that which must be formed, broken, forged, torn, burnt, brought to white heat, purified, on all that which must necessarily suffer and *ought* to suffer! And our compassion—don't you comprehend on whom our *opposite* compassion is spent, when it defends itself against your compassion, as though against the worst coddling and weakness? Compassion, in other words, against compassion!—But, as I said before, there are problems higher than any pleasure and pain problems, including that of the pain of compassion; any philosophy which seeks to culminate here is a naïveté. . . .

(Extracts from *Beyond Good and Evil*, sections 9, 23, 36 and 225.)

The Transvaluation of Values

Many lands and many peoples did Zarathustra see; thus he discovered the goods and evils of many peoples. No greater force did Zarathustra find on earth than good and evil.

No people could live unless it had values; but if it wants to preserve itself it must not have the same values as its neighbor.

Many things that one people called good, another called ridiculous and shameful: that is how I found things. Many things I found which in one place were called evil but which in another place were adorned with purple honors.

Never has one neighbor understood the other; always has his soul wondered at his neighbor's illusion and wickedness.

Over each people there hangs a tablet of values. Behold, it is the tablet of its self-mastery; behold, it is the voice of its will to power.

Whatever comes hard to a people is praiseworthy; whatever is irremissible and difficult for them is called good; and that which liberates them from deepest necessity, whatever is most difficult and most rare—they call holy.

Whatever makes them rule and triumph and shine, whatever appalls their neighbors and makes them envious—they consider sublime, primal, the test and the aim of all things.

Truly, my brother, when you have recognized the necessities, the land, the sky, and the neighbors of a people, you can infer the principles of its self-mastery and why it uses this ladder to climb toward its hopes.

"Always shall you be the first and tower over all others; no one shall your jealous soul love, except your friend"—this principle caused a Greek soul to tremble and pursue his path toward greatness.

"To speak the truth and be skillful with bow and arrow"— is what seemed equally dear and difficult to that people from whom my name comes—my name which is equally dear and difficult to me.

"To honor father and mother and to do their will down to the last fibres of one's soul"—another people suspended this tablet of self-mastery over itself and grew mighty and everlasting because of it.

"To be loyal and for the sake of loyalty to risk honor and blood even in dangerous and evil causes"—another people mastered itself by teaching thus, and, having mastered itself, it became pregnant and heavy with great hopes.

Truly—men gave themselves all their good and evil. Truly —they did not take it, they did not find it; it did not drop down on them as a voice from the heavens.

Things had no value until man put them there for his self-preservation; he created an aim, a meaning for things—a human aim and meaning! That is why he calls himself "man," that is, "value-giver."

To give values is to create: note it, you creators! Value-giving itself is the most valuable and precious jewel of all things that have value.

Values are the result only of value-giving; without value-giving the nutshell of existence would be hollow. Note it, you creators!

Transformation of values—means transformation of creators. Whoever of necessity creates, of necessity destroys.

First it was whole peoples who created; only very late did individuals create; in fact, the individual himself is the most recent creation.

Once it was peoples who suspended over themselves a tablet of what is good. Love which would rule and love which would obey together created such tablets.

Pleasure in being part of a herd is older than pleasure in being an individual; as long as good conscience rests in the herd, only the bad conscience says "I."

Truly, the individual, shrewd, unloving, wanting to seek his profit in the profit of many—is not the beginning but the decline of the herd.

Always it was lovers and creators who created good and evil. Burning love and burning anger radiate from the names of all the virtues.

Zarathustra saw many lands and many peoples; he found no force on earth greater than the creations designated "good" and "evil"—the creations of lovers.

Truly—a monster is the force of such praise and blame. Tell me, my brothers, who can master it? Who will throw the yoke over the thousand necks of this beast?

There have been a thousand aims up to now, for there were a thousand peoples. Only the yoke for the thousand necks was still lacking—the one aim was still lacking. Humanity has no aim as yet.

But tell me, my brothers, if the aim of humanity is still lacking—is not humanity itself still lacking?

Self-Mastery

"Will to Truth" you call it, you wisest of men, that which drives you on and makes you ardent?

"Will to rationalize all things which have being"—is what *I* call your will!

You want to *make* rational all things which have being, for you doubt with good reason that they are rational.

But things are supposed to bend toward and accommodate themselves to you! That is what your will wants. They are supposed to become smooth and subservient to reason, as reason's mirror and image.

That is your whole will, you wisest of men; it is a will to power, even if you talk about good and evil and value judgments.

You want to create a world before which you may kneel: that is your last hope and frenzy.

The unwise men, to be sure, the people—they are like the stream down which a boat is floating; and in the boat, solemnly shrouded, sit the value judgments.

You have placed your will and your values on the stream of Becoming; what the people believe to be "good" and "evil" reveals to me an ancient will to power.

It was you, you wisest of men, who set up such guests in the boat and surrounded them with pomp and proud names—you and your dominant will!

Now the stream is carrying your boat: it *must* carry it. It makes little difference that the broken waves are churning and opposing the keel!

Your danger and the end of your good and evil is not the stream, you wisest of men, but your danger is that will itself, the will to power, the inexhaustible, creative Life-will.

So that you may understand my talk about good and evil, I'll say a word to you about Life and the nature of living things.

I have pursued living things, pursued them by the greatest and smallest paths, that I might know the nature of life.

With a hundred-fold mirror I have caught Life's glance, so that when its mouth was silent, its eyes might speak. And its eyes did speak to me:

Wherever I found living things, I heard talk about obedience. All things alive are things which obey.

And this is the second thing: Whoever cannot obey himself, receives commands. That is the way of living things.

And this is the third thing I heard: That to command is more difficult than to obey. Not only because whoever commands carries the load of all who obey him and that this load can easily crush him—

But also because all commanding seemed an experiment and a risk to me; whenever something alive commands, it is risking itself.

Even when it commands itself, it must atone for its command. It must become judge and avenger and sacrifice to its own law.

How can this happen? I asked myself. What impels living things to obey and to command and to obey as they are commanding?

Now hear my words, oh wisest of men! Test them earnestly to see whether I have crept to the heart of Life and even to the very roots of Life's heart!

Wherever I found Life, I found will to power, and even in the will of the servant I found the will to be master.

That the weaker should serve the stronger is the persuasive will of the weaker, which wants to be master over the still weaker: this joy is the only thing it will not give up.

And just as the smaller gives itself up to the greater so that it can have joy in its power over the smallest—just so the greatest gives itself up and risks for the sake of power—its very life.

Therein lies the yielding of the greatest—it is risk and danger and a cast of the dice with death at stake.

And where there are sacrifices and service and loving looks —even there is the will to be master. By a round-about path the weaker sneaks into the fort—into the very heart of the stronger—and steals his power.

Life itself told me this secret: "Look," it said, "I am that which *must ever master itself*.

"You call it will to create, or impulse toward an end, something higher, farther, more greatly varied—but all these are one, one secret.

"I would rather descend to the depths than give up this One, and wherever there is descent and falling of leaves, there you may see Life sacrificing itself—for power!

"I must be Battle and Becoming and Purpose and Cross-purpose. Ah, whoever knows my will, surely knows what crooked paths it must take!

"No matter what I create or how much I love it—soon I

must be its opponent and must oppose my own love—thus wills my will.

"You too, you aware man, you too are only a path or a footprint of my will: truly, my will to power walks on the feet of your will to truth, too!

"He who shot the phrase 'Will to existence' at truth, did not bring it down. There is no such will!

"For what is not cannot will; but how could that which exists, will existence!

"Only where there is Life, there is will—but not 'Will to life' but—as I am teaching you—'Will to power!'

"One who is alive, values many things higher than Life, but his valuation itself bespeaks—Will to power!"—

That is what Life once taught me, and with it I'll solve the riddle of your hearts, you wisest of men.

I tell you in truth: There are no goods and evils which last forever. They must ever master themselves out of their own energies.

You exert energy with your values, your words of good and evil, you value judgers; that is your hidden love, the gleam and tremor and overflow of your souls.

But a stronger energy grows from your values themselves, and a new mastery. Egg and eggshell break on it.

And whoever must be a creator of good and evil, must first be a destroyer and break up values.

Thus the highest evil is part of the highest good, which is creative.

Let us at least *talk* about it, you wisest of men, even if it seems bad. Silence is worse; all truths suppressed become poisonous.

(Extracts from *Thus Spoke Zarathustra*, Part I, section 15.)

The Superior Man

1

When I went among men for the first time, I committed the anchorite's folly, the great folly: I stood in the marketplace.

And when I talked to all, I talked to no one. In the evening, rope-dancers and corpses were my companions. I myself was almost a corpse.

But with the new morning, a new truth came to me. I learned to say, "What do I care for marketplace and rabble and rabble-noise and long rabble-ears!"

You superior men! Learn this from me: No one in the marketplace believes in superior men. If you must speak there, very well. But the rabble, squinting, will say, "We are all equal."

"You superior men," the rabble will squint, "there are no superior men. We are all equal; man is man; before God—we are all equal!"

Before God! But now this God is dead. And before the rabble we do not wish to be equal. You superior men, go away from the marketplace.

2

Before God! But now this God is dead. You superior men, this God was your greatest danger.

Only since he is in his grave, have you risen again. Only now comes the great noontide; only now the superior man will be—lord!

Did you understand this word, oh my brothers? You are shocked—are your hearts reeling? Do you see the abyss sprawling? Do you hear the hell-hound brawling?

Onward! Upward! You superior men! Only now the mountain of man's future screams in labor. God died: now *we* want—the Superman to live.

3

The most worried men today ask, "How can we preserve man?" But Zarathustra is the first and only one who asks, "How can we *master* man?"

The Superman is close to my heart; *he* is my first and only—*not* man. Not the nearest, not the poorest, not the greatest sufferer, not the best—

Oh my brothers, what I can love in man is that he is a transcending and a descending into the depths. In you, too, there is much to make me love and hope.

That you have contempt, you superior men, makes me hope. For those who have great contempt have great reverence.

That you despair is greatly to be honored. For you have not learned to give in; you have not learned small clevernesses.

Today, you see, the small people have become lords; they all preach giving in and doing without, and cleverness and diligence and considerateness and the whole long etcetera of the small virtues.

Whatever is of female and servile origin, especially the rabble-hodge-podge—*they* now want to be lord over all human destiny! Oh nausea! Nausea! Nausea!

They now ask and peer and don't grow weary: "How can man be preserved best, longest, most pleasantly?" With that—they are lords of today.

Master these lords of today, oh my brothers! These small people—*they* are the greatest danger to the Superman!

Master the small virtues, you superior men, the small clevernesses, the grain-of-sand considerations, the ant-swarmings, the wretched creature-comforts, the "happiness of the greatest number!"

Despair rather than give in! Truly, I love you, you superior men, for not knowing how to live today. For that way *you* live best!

4

Have you courage, oh my brothers? Have you staunch hearts? *Not* courage before witnesses, but anchorite-courage, eagle-courage, when even gods no longer look on?

Cold souls, moles, the blind, the drunk—I do not call them staunch-hearted! Having a heart means knowing fear but compelling it to one's own ends; seeing the abyss but looking with *pride*.

Whoever sees the abyss—but with an eagle's eyes, whoever grasps the abyss—but with an eagle's talons: *he* has courage.—

5

"Man is evil"—so the wisest men told me to console me. Ah, if it were only still true! For evil is man's best strength.

"Man must grow stronger in good and in evil"—that is *my* teaching. The worst is necessary for the Superman's best.

Suffering and taking sin upon himself might have been right for that preacher of small people. But I rejoice in great sin as my great *solace*.—

But such things are not said for long ears. Not every word belongs in every snout. These are delicate distant things—not made for sheeps' paws to paw at!

6

You superior men, do you think I exist to make good what you did badly?

Or that I shall bed you sufferers more comfortably from

now on? Or show you unsteady wanderers who have gone astray a new, easier footpath?

No! No! Thrice No! More and more, better and better your type shall descend to the depths—for your life shall be worse and worse and more and more difficult. Only thus—

—only thus man grows to his height where the lightning strikes and destroys him: tall enough to be struck!

My mind, my longing, reach toward the few, the enduring, the far away; what do I care for your small, brief multitudes of misery!

You have not suffered enough to suit me. For you have always suffered from yourselves—you have not yet suffered from *mankind*. You would be lying if you denied it. None of you suffers my sufferings.—

7

It is not enough for me to know that the lightning no longer does harm. I do not want to conduct it into the ground. I want it to work for me.

My wisdom has long been piling up like a cloud, growing stiller and darker. All wisdom does this, if it is to give birth to the *lightning* some day.—

I do not wish to be a light for today's men, nor to be thought a light. Rather I would blind them—Lightning of my wisdom! Stab into their eyes!

8

Do not will beyond your capacity! There is a terrible falseness in those who will beyond their capacity.

Especially if they will great things! For they awaken suspicion against great things, these subtle counterfeiters and play-actors—

—until at last they are false even in their own estimation: squint-eyed, white-washed worm-fodder, cloaked with strong words, show-virtues, splendid false works.

Do be cautious, you superior men! For nothing today seems more precious and rare to me than candor.

Does Today not belong to the rabble? The rabble, however, does not know what is great, what is small, what is straight and what is honest. They are innocently crooked; they always lie.

9

Keep a healthy suspicion about you, today, you superior men!

You stout-hearted, openhearted men! And keep your reasons secret. For Today belongs to the rabble.

What rabble once learned to believe without reasons—who could overthrow it with reasons!

And in the marketplace they persuade with gestures. But reasons make the rabble suspicious.

And if truth for once prevails in the marketplace, ask yourselves with healthy suspicion, "Which strong error was fighting on its side?"

Beware also of the learned! They hate you because they are barren. They have cold dried-up eyes; any birds lie before them stripped of their feathers.

They boast that they do not lie; but inability to lie is far from being love of truth. Beware!

Being free of fever is far from being aware. I do not believe what chill spirits have to say. Whoever cannot lie does not know what truth is.

10

If you would climb high, use your own legs! Do not let yourselves be *carried* upward, do not squat on other backs or heads!

You made the climb on horseback, did you? You are riding swiftly toward your goal? Very good, my friend! But your lame foot is riding along with you!

When you have reached your goal, when you leap from your horse: precisely on your superior height, you superior man—you will stumble.

11

You creators, you superior men! One can be pregnant only with one's own child.

Don't let anyone talk you into anything or anything into you! Who is *your* neighbor anyway? And if you do act "for your neighbor"—you don't create for him!

Why don't you unlearn this "for," you creators! Precisely your virtue will not let you do anything "for" or "because." Glue your ears shut against these false little words.

"For one's neighbor" is the virtue of small people only.

With them it's "birds of a feather" and "one hand washes the other"—they have neither the right to nor the strength for *your* self-interest!

In your self-interest, you creators, lies the cautiousness and providence of the pregnant. What no one has ever seen with his eyes—the fruit—is what your whole love guards and protects and nourishes.

Where your whole love is, in your child, there is your whole virtue! Your work, your will, is *your* neighbor: don't let them talk any false values into you!

12

You creators, you superior men! Whoever has to give birth is sick; whoever has just given birth is unclean.

Ask women: no one gives birth because giving birth is fun. The pains make hens and poets cluck.

You creators, there is much in you that is unclean. That's because you had to be mothers.

A new baby: oh, how much new uncleanness came into the world with it! Step aside for a while! Whoever has given birth should wash his soul clean!

13

Do not be virtuous beyond your power! And do not want anything from yourselves that is improbable!

Walk in the footprints of your fathers' virtues! How could you climb except together with the will of your fathers?

But if you would be a firstling—beware that you do not turn out to be a lastling. And where the vices of your fathers are, you cannot expect to be saints!

If your fathers dealt with women and strong wines and wild boars—how could you expect chastity of yourself!

It would be utter foolishness! It would be a good deal, it seems to me, if such a man were content to be one or two or three women's man.

And if he were to found monasteries and were to write above the door "The road to saintliness"—I should say, "What for? It is another foolishness!"

He has but founded a work-house and shirk-house for himself. I hope he likes it! But I don't believe in it.

Solitude will grow whatever one brings into it, including the inner beasts. That's what makes solitude inadvisable for many. Has there been anything filthier in the world than desert-saints? Not only was the devil turned loose in them—but also the swine.

14

Shy, shame-faced, awkward—like a tiger who has missed his leap—thus I have often seen you creep away, you superior men. You had missed a cast.

But what does it matter, you dice-players! You haven't yet learned to play and to mock as it is necessary to play and to mock. Are we not always sitting at a great play-table and mock-table?

Even if you missed a great cast—are you therefore mis-cast? And if you were mis-cast, is mankind therefore mis-cast? And if mankind were mis-cast—very well, then: On with it!

15

The higher a type, the rarer a happy cast. You superior men—aren't you all mis-cast?

Be of good cheer: what does it matter! How much is still possible! Learn to laugh at yourselves as it is necessary to laugh!

No wonder that you are mis-cast and half-cast, you half-broken men! Isn't the *future of man* crowding and kicking in your bellies?

Man's farthest, deepest, star-highest—his enormous energy: isn't it all furiously foaming in your pot?

No wonder that many a pot cracks! Learn to laugh at yourselves, as it is necessary to laugh! Oh you superior men, how much is still possible!

And truly, how many a good cast already exists! How rich this earth is in small, good, perfect things, in things that are happily cast!

Surround yourselves with small, good, perfect things, you superior men! Their golden ripeness heals the heart. Perfection teaches hope.

16

What has been the greatest sin on earth so far? Was it not the words of him who said, "Woe to those who laugh here!"

Did he never find reasons for laughter here on earth? Then he didn't look very well. Even a child can find them.

He—did not love enough; if he had, he would have loved

us who laugh. But he hated us and jeered at us: he prophesied weeping and gnashing of teeth for us.

Must one curse where one does not love? That—seems bad taste to me. But that's what he did, this absolutist. He came from the rabble.

And he himself didn't love enough; if he had, he would have been less angry that he wasn't loved enough. All great love does not *want* love—it wants more.

Avoid all such absolutists! They are a poor, sick type, a rabble-type. They look ill-tempered on this life; they have the evil eye turned on this earth.

Avoid all such absolutists! Their feet drag; their hearts are sultry: they do not know how to dance. How could the earth be easy on them!

17

Crookedly all good things approach their goal. Like cats they arch their backs and purr inwardly at their close-approaching bliss—all good things laugh.

When a man is walking on *his* road, even his steps reveal it: watch me walk! But when a man is approaching his goal, he dances.

Truly, I was not made to be a statue. I'm not standing stiff, stifled, stony, like a pillar, I love swift running.

And even if there are moors and soggy afflictions on this earth: if you have light feet, you'll run over swamps and dance on them as if they were swept ice.

Lift up your hearts, my brothers—high, still higher! And don't forget your feet, either. Lift up your feet too, you good dancers, and—better yet—stand on your heads!

18

This crown of laughter, this rosy-wreathed crown: I have placed it on my own head; I myself have pronounced my laughter holy. I've found no one else today who is strong enough to do it.

Zarathustra the dancer, Zarathustra the light-footed, who beckons with his wings, ready to fly, greeting all birds, ready and prepared, a blissful, reckless, ready creature—

Zarathustra the soothsayer, Zarathustra the sooth-laugher, neither impatient nor absolutist, one who loves leaps and roundabout ways: I myself have placed this crown upon my head!

19

Lift up your hearts, my brothers—high, still higher! And don't forget your feet, either. Lift up your feet too, you good dancers, and—better yet—stand on your heads!

In bliss, too, there are heavy creatures; there are flat-feet from time immemorial. They make strange attempts to be blissful, like an elephant trying to stand on his head.

But it's still better to be foolishly blissful than foolishly wretched. Better to dance clumsily than to walk lamely. Learn my wisdom, why don't you: even the worst things have two good sides—

—even the worst things have good legs to dance on. Why don't you learn, you superior men, to get on your proper feet!

Why don't you unlearn your moping and all your rabble-sadness. Oh how sad even the rabble's buffoons seem to me today. But this Today belongs to the rabble.

20

Be like the Wind when he rushes out of his mountain-caverns; he would dance to his own piping; the seas are trembling and skipping under his foot-prints.

Who gives wings to the ass, who milks the lioness—praised be this good, unfettered spirit who comes like a hurricane to all Today and all the rabble,—

—who is hostile to thistle-heads and hair-splitters and to all dead leaves and weeds; praised be to this wild, good, free storm-spirit who dances over moors and mopers as if over meadows!

Who hates the consumptive rabble-dogs and all the mis-cast, gloomy breed; praised be this spirit of all free spirits, the laughing storm who blows sand in the eyes of all who are gloomy-eyed and bleary-eyed!

You superior men! Your worst is this: you have not learned to dance as it is necessary to dance—to dance over yourselves. What does it matter if you were mis-cast!

How much is still possible! Then learn—do learn to laugh over and beyond yourselves! Lift up your hearts, you good dancers! High! Still higher! And don't forget good laughter!

This crown of laughter, this rosy-wreathed crown: I toss it toward you, oh my brothers! I have pronounced laughter holy, you superior men. Learn, do learn—how to laugh!

(Extracts from *Thus Spoke Zarathustra*, Part 4, section 13.)

GEORGES SOREL
Reflections on Violence

The Fallacy of Optimism

The optimist in politics is an inconstant and even dangerous man, because he takes no account of the great difficulties presented by his projects; these projects seem to him to possess a force of their own, which tends to bring about their realisation all the more easily as they are, in his opinion, destined to produce the happiest results. He frequently thinks that small reforms in the political constitution, and, above all, in the personnel of the government, will be sufficient to direct social development in such a way as to mitigate those evils of the contemporary world which seem so harsh to the sensitive mind. As soon as his friends come into power, he declares that it is necessary to let things alone for a little, not to hurry too much, and to learn how to be content with whatever their own benevolent intentions prompt them to do. It is not always self-interest that suggests these expressions of satisfaction, as people have often believed; self-interest is strongly aided by vanity and by the illusions of philosophy. The optimist passes with remarkable facility from revolutionary anger to the most ridiculous social pacifism.

If he possesses an exalted temperament, and if unhappily he finds himself armed with great power, permitting him to realise the ideal he has fashioned, the optimist may lead his country into the worst disasters. He is not long in finding out that social transformations are not brought about with the ease that he had counted on; he then supposes that this is the fault of his contemporaries, instead of explaining what actually happens by historical necessities; he is tempted to get rid of people whose obstinacy seems to him to be so dangerous to the happiness of all. During the Terror, the men who spilt most blood were precisely those who had the greatest desire to let their equals enjoy the golden age they had dreamt of, and who had the most sympathy with human wretchedness: optimists, idealists, and sensitive men, the greater desire they had for universal happiness the more inexorable they showed themselves.

Pessimism is quite a different thing from the caricatures of it which are usually presented to us; it is a philosophy of conduct rather than a theory of the world; it considers the *march towards deliverance* as narrowly conditioned, on the one hand, by the experimental knowledge that we have acquired from the obstacles which opposed themselves to the satisfaction of our imaginations (or, if we like, by the feeling of social determinism), and, on the other, by a profound conviction of our natural weakness. These two aspects of pessimism should never be separated, although, as a rule, scarcely any attention is paid to their close connection. . . .

The pessimist regards social conditions as forming a system bound together by an iron law which cannot be evaded, so that the system is given, as it were, in one block, and cannot disappear except in a catastrophe which involves the whole. If this theory is admitted, it then becomes absurd to make certain wicked men responsible for the evils from which society suffers; the pessimist is not subject to the sanguinary follies of the optimist, infatuated by the unexpected obstacles that his projects meet with; he does not dream of bringing about the happiness of future generations by slaughtering existing egoists.

The most fundamental element of pessimism is its method of conceiving the path towards deliverance. A man would not go very far in the examination either of the laws of his own wretchedness or of fate, which so much shock the ingenuousness of our pride, if he were not borne up by the hope of putting an end to these tyrannies by an effort, to be attempted with the help of a whole band of companions. . . .

(Extract from the Introduction.)

The Myth and Anti-intellectualism

In the course of this study one thing has always been present in my mind . . . that men who are participating in a great social movement always picture their coming action as a battle in which their cause is certain to triumph. These constructions, knowledge of which is so important for historians, I propose to call myths; the syndicalist "general strike" and Marx's catastrophic revolution are such myths. As remarkable examples of such myths, I have given those which were constructed by primitive Christianity, by the Reformation, by the Revolution and by the followers of Mazzini. I now wish to show that we should not attempt to analyse such groups of images in the way that we analyse a thing into its elements, but that they must be taken as a whole, as historical forces, and that we should be especially careful not to make any comparison between accomplished fact and the picture people had formed for themselves before action.

I could have given one more example which is perhaps still more striking: Catholics have never been discouraged even in the hardest trials, because they have always pictured the history of the Church as a series of battles between Satan and the hierarchy supported by Christ; every new difficulty which arises is only an episode in a war which must finally end in the victory of Catholicism.

At the beginning of the nineteenth century the revolutionary persecutions revived this myth of the struggle with Satan, which inspired so many of the eloquent pages in Joseph de Maistre; this rejuvenation explains to a large extent the religious renascence which took place at that epoch. If Catholicism is in danger at the present time, it is to a great extent owing to the fact that the myth of the Church militant tends to disappear. . . .

I have always tried to escape the influence of that intellectualist philosophy, which seems to me a great hindrance to the historian who allows himself to be dominated by it. . . .

The intellectualist philosophy finds itself unable to explain phenomena like the following—the sacrifice of his life which the soldier of Napoleon made in order to have had the honour of taking part in "immortal deeds" and of living in the glory of France, knowing all the time that "he would always be a poor man"; then, again, the extraordinary virtues shown by the Romans who resigned themselves to a frightful inequality and who suffered so much to conquer the world; "the belief in glory (which was) a value without equal," created by Greece, and as a result of which "a selection was made from the swarming masses of humanity, life acquired an incentive and there was a recompense here for those who had pursued the good and the beautiful." The intellectualist philosophy, far from being able to explain these things, leads, on the contrary, to an admiration for the fifty-first chapter of Jeremiah, "the lofty though profoundly sad feeling with which the peaceful man contemplates these falls of empires, and the pity excited in the heart of the wise man by the spectacle of the nations *labouring for vanity,* victims of the arrogance of the few." . . .

The intellectualist philosophy would have vainly endeavoured to convince the ardent Catholics, who for so long struggled successfully against the revolutionary traditions, that the myth of the Church militant was not in harmony with the scientific theories formulated by the most learned authors according to the best rules of criticism; it would never have succeeded in persuading them. It would not have been possible to shake the faith that these men had in the promises made to the Church by any argument; and so long as this faith remained, the myth was, in their eyes, incontestable. Similarly, the objections urged by philosophy against the rev-

olutionary myths would have made an impression only on
those men who were anxious to find a pretext for abandoning
any active rôle, for remaining revolutionary in words only. . . .

As long as there are no myths accepted by the masses, one
may go on talking of revolts indefinitely, without ever provoking any revolutionary movement; this is what gives such importance to the general strike and renders it so odious to
socialists who are afraid of a revolution; they do all they can
to shake the confidence felt by the workers in the preparations
they are making for the revolution; and in order to succeed in
this they cast ridicule on the idea of the general strike—the
only idea that could have any value as a motive force. One of
the chief means employed by them is to represent it as a
Utopia; this is easy enough, because there are very few myths
which are perfectly free from any Utopian element.

The revolutionary myths which exist at the present time are
almost free from any such mixture; by means of them it is
possible to understand the activity, the feelings and the ideas
of the masses preparing themselves to enter on a decisive
struggle; the myths are not descriptions of things, but expressions of a determination to act. A Utopia is, on the contrary,
an intellectual product; it is the work of theorists who, after
observing and discussing the known facts, seek to establish a
model to which they can compare existing society in order to
estimate the amount of good and evil it contains. It is a
combination of imaginary institutions having sufficient analogies to real institutions for the jurist to be able to reason about
them; it is a construction which can be taken to pieces, and
certain parts of it have been shaped in such a way that they
can (with a few alterations by way of adjustment) be fitted
into approaching legislation. Whilst contemporary myths lead
men to prepare themselves for a combat which will destroy
the existing state of things, the effect of Utopias has always
been to direct men's minds towards reforms which can be
brought about by patching up the existing system; it is not
surprising, then, that so many makers of Utopias were able to
develop into able statesmen when they had acquired a greater
experience of political life. A myth cannot be refuted, since it
is, at bottom, identical with the convictions of a group, being
the expression of these convictions in the language of movement; and it is, in consequence, unanalysable into parts which
could be placed on the plane of historical descriptions. A
Utopia, on the contrary, can be discussed like any other social
constitution; the spontaneous movements it presupposes can
be compared with the movements actually observed in the
course of history, and we can in this way evaluate its verisi-

militude; it is possible to refute Utopias by showing that the economic system on which they have been made to rest is incompatible with the necessary conditions of modern production. . . .

For a long time Socialism was scarcely anything but a Utopia; the Marxists were right in claiming for their master the honour of bringing about a change in this state of things; Socialism has now become the preparation of the masses employed in great industries for the suppression of the State and property; and it is no longer necessary, therefore, to discuss how men must organise themselves in order to enjoy future happiness; everything is reduced to the *revolutionary apprenticeship* of the proletariat. . . .

People who are living in this world of "myths," are secure from all refutation; this has led many to assert that Socialism is a kind of religion. For a long time people have been struck by the fact that religious convictions are unaffected by criticism, and from that they have concluded that everything which claims to be beyond science must be a religion. It has been observed also that Christianity tends at the present day to be less a system of dogmas than a Christian life, *i.e.* a moral reform penetrating to the roots of one's being; consequently, a new analogy has been discovered between religion and the revolutionary Socialism which aims at the apprenticeship, preparation, and even reconstruction of the individual,— a gigantic task. But Bergson has taught us that it is not only religion which occupies the profounder region of our mental life; revolutionary myths have their place there equally with religion. . . .

To-day the confidence of the Socialists is greater than ever since the myth of the general strike dominates all the truly working-class movement. No failure proves anything against Socialism since the latter has become a work of preparation (for revolution); if they are checked, it merely proves that the apprenticeship has been insufficient; they must set to work again with more courage, persistence, and confidence than before; their experience of labour has taught workmen that it is by means of patient apprenticeship that a man may become a true comrade, and it is also the only way of becoming a true revolutionary.

(Extract from the Introduction.)

Myth and the General Strike

. . . The revolutionary Syndicates argue about Socialist action exactly in the same manner as military writers argue about war; they restrict the whole of Socialism to the general strike; they look upon every combination as one that should culminate in this catastrophe; they see in each strike a reduced facsimile, an essay, a preparation for the great final upheaval.

The *new school,* which calls itself Marxist, Syndicalist, and revolutionary, declared in favour of the idea of the general strike as soon as it became clearly conscious of the true sense of its own doctrine, of the consequences of its activity, and of its own originality. It was thus led to leave the old official, Utopian, and political tabernacles, which hold the general strike in horror, and to launch itself into the true current of the proletarian revolutionary movement. . . .

Parliamentary Socialists can only obtain great influence if they can manage, by the use of a very confused language, to impose themselves on very diverse groups; for example, they must have working-men constituents simple enough to allow themselves to be duped by high-sounding phrases about future collectivism; they are compelled to represent themselves as profound philosophers to stupid middle-class people who wish to appear to be well informed about social questions; it is very necessary also for them to be able to exploit rich people who think that they are earning the gratitude of humanity by taking shares in the enterprises of Socialist politicians. This influence is founded on balderdash, and our bigwigs endeavour—sometimes only too successfully—to spread confusion among the ideas of their readers; they detest the general strike because all propaganda carried on from that point of view is too socialistic to please philanthropists.

In the mouths of these self-styled representatives of the proletariat all socialistic formulas lose their real sense. The class war still remains the great principle, but it must be subordinated to national solidarity. Internationalism is an article of faith about which the most moderate declare themselves ready to take the most solemn oaths; but patriotism also imposes sacred duties. The emancipation of the workers must be the work of the workers themselves—their newspapers repeat this every day,—but real emancipation consists in voting for a professional politician, in securing for him the means of obtaining a comfortable situation in the world, in subjecting oneself to a leader. In the end the State must disappear—and they are very careful not to dispute what Engels has written on this subject—but this disappearance will take place only in a future so far distant that you must prepare yourself for it by using the State meanwhile as a means of providing the politicians with tidbits; and the best means of bringing about the disappearance of the State consists in strengthening meanwhile the Governmental machine. . . .

Against this noisy, garrulous, and lying Socialism, which is exploited by ambitious people, of every description, which amuses a few buffoons, and which is admired by decadents—revolutionary Syndicalism takes its stand, and endeavours, on the contrary, to leave nothing in a state of indecision; its ideas are honestly expressed, without trickery and without mental reservations; no attempt is made to dilute doctrines by a stream of confused commentaries. Syndicalism endeavours to employ methods of expression which throw a full light on things, which put them exactly in the place assigned to them by their nature, and which bring out the whole value of the forces in play. Oppositions, instead of being glozed over, must be thrown into sharp relief if we desire to obtain a clear idea of the Syndicalist movement; the groups which are struggling one against the other must be shown as separate and as compact as possible; in short, the movements of the revolted masses must be represented in such a way that the soul of the revolutionaries may receive a deep and lasting impression.

These results could not be produced in any very certain manner by the use of ordinary language; use must be made of a body of images which, *by intuition alone,* and before any considered analyses are made, is capable of evoking as an undivided whole the mass of sentiments which corresponds to the different manifestations of the war undertaken by Socialism against modern society. The Syndicalists solve this problem perfectly, by concentrating the whole of Socialism in the drama of the general strike; there is thus no longer any place for the reconciliation of contraries in the equivocations of the professors; everything is clearly mapped out, so that only one interpretation of Socialism is possible. This method has all the advantages which "integral" knowledge has over analysis, according to the doctrine of Bergson; and perhaps it would not be possible to cite another example which would so perfectly demonstrate the value of the famous professor's doctrines. . . .

The attempt to construct hypotheses about the nature of the struggles of the future and the means of suppressing capitalism, on the model furnished by history, is a return to the old methods of the Utopists. There is no process by which the future can be predicted scientifically, nor even one which enables us to discuss whether one hypothesis about it is better than another; it has been proved by too many memorable examples that the greatest men have committed prodigious errors in thus desiring to make predictions about even the least distant future.

And yet without leaving the present, without reasoning about this future, which seems for ever condemned to escape our reason, we should be unable to act at all. Experience shows that the *framing of a future, in some indeterminate time,* may, when it is done in a certain way, be very effective, and have very few inconveniences; this happens when the anticipations of the future take the form of those myths, which enclose with them, all the strongest inclinations of a people, of a party or of a class, inclinations which recur to the mind with the insistence of instincts in all the circumstances of life: and which give an aspect of complete reality to the hopes of immediate action by which, more easily than by any other method, men can reform their desires, passions, and mental activity. We know, moreover, that these social myths in no way prevent a man profiting by the observations which he makes in the course of his life, and form no obstacle to the pursuit of his normal occupations. . . .

A knowledge of what the myths contain in the way of details which will actually form part of the history of the future is of small importance; they are not astrological almanacs; it is even possible that nothing which they contain will ever come to pass,—as was the case with the catastrophe expected by the first Christians. . . .

The myth must be judged as a means of acting on the present; any attempt to discuss how far it can be taken literally as future history is devoid of sense. *It is the myth in its entirety which is alone important;* its parts are only of interest in so far as they bring out the main idea. No useful purpose is served, therefore, in arguing about the incidents which may occur in the course of a social war, and about the decisive conflicts which may give victory to the proletariat; even supposing the revolutionaries to have been wholly and entirely deluded in setting up this imaginary picture of the general strike, this picture may yet have been, in the course of the preparation for the Revolution, a great element of strength, if it has embraced all the aspirations of Socialism, and if it has given to the whole body of Revolutionary thought a precision and a rigidity which no other method of thought could have given.

To estimate, then, the significance of the idea of the general strike, all the methods of discussion which are current among politicians, sociologists, or people with pretensions to political science, must be abandoned. Everything which its opponents endeavour to establish may be conceded to them, without reducing in any way the value of the theory which they think they have refuted. The question whether the general strike is a partial reality, or only a product of popular imagination, is of little importance. All that it is necessary to know is, whether the general strike contains everything that the Socialist doctrine expects of the revolutionary proletariat.

. . . the general strike is indeed what I have said: the *myth* in which Socialism is wholly comprised, *i.e.* a body of images capable of evoking instinctively all the sentiments which correspond to the different manifestations of the war undertaken by Socialism against modern society. Strikes have engendered in the proletariat the noblest, deepest, and most moving sentiments that they possess; the general strike groups them all in a co-ordinated picture, and, by bringing them together, gives to each one of them its maximum of intensity; appealing to their painful memories of particular conflicts, it colours with an intense life all the details of the composition presented to consciousness. We thus obtain that intuition of Socialism which language cannot give us with perfect clearness—and we obtain it as a whole, perceived instantaneously. . . .

[Our politicians] struggle against the conception of the general strike, because they recognise, in the course of their propagandist rounds, that this conception is so admirably adapted to the working-class mind that there is a possibility of its dominating the latter in the most absolute manner, thus leaving no place for the desires which the Parliamentarians are able to satisfy. They perceive that this idea is so effective as a motive force that once it has entered the minds of the people they can no longer be controlled by leaders, and that thus the power of the deputies would be reduced to nothing. In short, they feel in a vague way that the whole Socialist movement might easily be absorbed by the general strike, which would render useless all those compromises between political groups in view of which the Parliamentary régime has been built up. . . .

The Syndicalist general strike presents a very great number of analogies with the first conception of war: the proletariat organises itself for battle, separating itself distinctly from the other parts of the nation, and regarding itself as the great motive power of history, all other social considerations being subordinated to that of combat; it is very clearly conscious of the glory which will be attached to its historical rôle and of the heroism of its militant attitude; it longs for the final contest in which it will give proof of the whole measure of its valour. Pursuing no conquest, it has no need to make plans for utilising its victories: it counts on expelling the capitalists from the productive domain, and on taking their place in the workshop created by capitalism.

This conception of the general strike manifests in the clearest manner its indifference to the material profits of conquest by affirming that it proposes to suppress the State. The State has always been, in fact, the organiser of the war of conquest, the dispenser of its fruits, and the *raison d'être* of the dominating groups which profit by the enterprises—the cost of which is borne by the general body of society.

Politicians adopt the other point of view; they argue about social conflicts in exactly the same manner as diplomats argue about international affairs; all the actual fighting apparatus interests them very little; they see in the combatants nothing but instruments. The proletariat is their army, which they love in the same way that a colonial administrator loves the troops which enable him to bring large numbers of negroes under his authority; they apply themselves to the task of training the proletariat, because they are in a hurry to win quickly the great battles which will deliver the State into their hands; they keep up the ardour of their men, as the ardour of troops of mercenaries has always been kept up, by promises of pillage, by appeals to hatred, and also by the small favours which their occupancy of a few political places enables them to distribute already. But the proletariat for them is *food for cannon*, and nothing else, as Marx said in 1873.

The reinforcement of power of the State is at the basis of all their conceptions; in the organisations which they at present control, the politicians are already preparing the framework of a strong, centralised and disciplined authority, which will not be hampered by the criticism of an opposition, which will be able to enforce silence, and which will give currency to its lies. . . .

(Extracts from chapters 4 and 5.)

GRAHAM WALLAS
Human Nature in Politics

Impulse and Instinct in Politics

Whoever sets himself to base his political thinking on a reexamination of the working of human nature, must begin by trying to overcome his own tendency to exaggerate the intellectuality of mankind.

We are apt to assume that every human action is the result of an intellectual process, by which a man first thinks of some end which he desires, and then calculates the means by which that end can be attained. An investor, for instance, desires good security combined with five per cent. interest. He spends an hour in studying with an open mind the price-list of stocks, and finally infers that the purchase of Brewery Debentures will enable him most completely to realise his desire. Given the original desire for good security, his act in purchasing the Debentures appears to be the inevitable result of his inference. The desire for good security itself may further appear to be merely an intellectual inference as to the means of satisfying some more general desire, shared by all mankind, for 'happiness,' our own 'interest,' or the like. The satisfaction of this general desire can then be treated as the supreme 'end' of life, from which all our acts and impulses, great and small, are derived by the same intellectual process as that by which the conclusion is derived from the premises of an argument.

This way of thinking is sometimes called 'common sense.' A good example of its application to politics may be found in a sentence from Macaulay's celebrated attack on the Utilitarian followers of Bentham in the *Edinburgh Review* of March 1829. This extreme instance of the foundation of politics upon dogmatic psychology is, curiously enough, part of an argument intended to show that 'it is utterly impossible to deduce the science of government from the principles of human nature.' 'What proposition,' Macaulay asks, 'is there respecting human nature which is absolutely and universally true? We know of only one: and that is not only true, but identical; that men always act from self-interest. . . . *When we see the actions of a man, we know with certainty what he thinks his interest to be.*' Macaulay believes himself to be opposing Benthamism root and branch, but is unconsciously adopting and exaggerating [its] assumption . . . that all motives result from the idea of some pre-conceived end. . . .

Impulse . . . has an evolutionary history of its own earlier than the history of those intellectual processes by which it is often directed and modified. Our inherited organisation inclines us to re-act in certain ways to certain stimuli because such reactions have been useful in the past in preserving our species. Some of the reactions are what we call specifically 'instincts,' that is to say, impulses towards definite acts or series of acts, independent of any conscious anticipation of their probable effects. Those instincts are sometimes unconscious and involuntary; and sometimes, in the case of ourselves and apparently of other higher animals, they are conscious and voluntary. But the connection between means and ends which they exhibit is the result not of any contrivance by the actor, but of the survival, in the past, of the 'fittest' of many varying tendencies to act. Indeed the instinct persists when it is obviously useless. . . .

The politician, however, is still apt to intellectualise impulse as completely as the schoolmaster did fifty years ago. He has two excuses, that he deals entirely with adults, whose impulses are more deeply modified by experience and thought than those of children, and that it is very difficult for any one who thinks about politics not to confine his consideration to those political actions and impulses which are accompanied by the greatest amount of conscious thought, and which therefore come first into his mind. But the politician thinks about men in large communities that the intellectualist fallacy is most misleading. The results of experience and thought are often confined to individuals or small groups, and when they differ may cancel each other as political forces. The original human impulses are, with personal variations, common to the whole race, and increase in their importance with an increase in the number of those influenced by them.

. . . in politics we are dealing not with such clear-cut separate instincts as we may find in children and animals, but with tendencies often weakened by the course of human evolution, still more often transferred to new uses, and acting not simply but in combination or counteraction.

Aristotle, for instance, says that it is 'affection' . . . which 'makes political union possible,' and 'which law-givers consider more important than justice.' It is, he says, a hereditary instinct among animals of the same race, and particularly among men. If we look for this political affection in its simplest form, we see it in our impulse to feel 'kindly' towards any other human being of whose existence and personality we become vividly aware. . . .

The tactics of an election consist largely of contrivances by which this immediate emotion of personal affection may be set up. The candidate is advised to 'show himself' continually, to give away prizes, to 'say a few words' at the end of other people's speeches—all under circumstances which offer little or no opportunity for the formation of a reasoned opinion of his merits, but many opportunities for the rise of purely instinctive affection among those present. His portrait is periodically distributed, and is more effective if it is a good, that is to say, a distinctive, than if it is a flattering likeness. Best of all is a photograph which brings his ordinary existence sharply forward by representing him in his garden smoking a pipe or reading a newspaper. . . .

(Extracts from chapter 1.)

Non-rational Inference in Politics

The assumption—which is so closely interwoven with our habits of political and economic thought—that men always act on a reasoned opinion as to their interests, may be divided into two separate assumptions: first, that men always act on some kind of inference as to the best means of reaching a preconceived end, and secondly, that all inferences are of the same kind, and are produced by a uniform process of 'reasoning.'

. . . it is important for a politician to realise that men do not always act on inferences as to means and ends . . . men often act in politics under the immediate stimulus of affection and instinct; that affection and interest may be directed towards political entities which are very different from those facts in the world around which we can discover by deliberate observation and analysis.

. . . how far is it true that men, when they do form inferences as to the result of their political actions, always form them by a process of reasoning? . . .

Any one who watches the working of his own mind will find that it is by no means easy to trace these sharp distinctions between various mental states, which seem so obvious when they are set out in little books on psychology. The mind of man is like a harp, all of whose strings throb together; so that emotion, impulse, inference, and the special kind of inference called reasoning, are often simultaneous and intermingled aspects of a single mental experience.

This is especially true in moments of action and excitement; but when we are sitting in passive contemplation we would often find it hard to say whether our successive states of consciousness are best described as emotions or inferences. And when our thought clearly belongs to the type of inference it is often hard to say whether its steps are controlled by so definite a purpose of discovering truth that we are entitled to call it reasoning.

Even when we think with effort and with a definite purpose, we do not always draw inferences or form beliefs of any kind.

The political importance of all this consists in the fact that most of the political opinions of most men are the result, not of reasoning tested by experience, but of unconscious or half-conscious inference fixed by habit. It is indeed mainly in the formation of tracks of thought that habit shows its power in politics. In our other activities habit is largely a matter of muscular adaptation, but the bodily movements of politics

occur so seldom that nothing like a habit can be set up by
them. One may see a respectable voter, whose political opinions have been smoothed and polished by the mental habits of
thirty years, fumbling over the act of marking and folding his
ballot paper like a child with its first copybook.

. . . as a complete science of politics Benthamism is no
longer possible. Pleasure and pain are indeed facts about
human nature, but they are not the only facts which are
important to the politician. The Benthamites, by straining the
meaning of words, tried to classify such motives as instinctive
impulse, ancient tradition, habit, or personal and racial idio-
syncrasy as being forms of pleasure and pain. But they failed;
and the search for a basis of valid political reasoning has to
begin again, among a generation more conscious than were
Bentham and his disciples of the complexity of the problem,
and less confident of absolute success.

In that search one thing at least is becoming clear. We must
aim at finding as many relevant and measurable facts about
human nature as possible, and we must attempt to make all of
them serviceable in political reasoning. In collecting, that is to
say, the material for a political science, we must adopt the
method of the biologist, who tries to discover how many
common qualities can be observed and measured in a group
of related beings, rather than that of the physicist, who con-
structs, or used to construct, a science out of a single quality
common to the whole material world.

The facts when collected must, because they are many, be
arranged. I believe that it would be found convenient by the
political student to arrange them under three main heads:
descriptive facts as to the human type; quantitative facts as to
inherited variations from that type observed either in individuals or groups of individuals; and facts, both quantitative
and descriptive, as to the environment into which men are
born, and the observed effect of that environment upon their
political actions and impulses. . . .

It is the extreme instability and uncertainty of this [last]
element which constitutes the special difficulty of politics. The
human type and the quantitative distribution of its variations
are for the politician, who deals with a few generations only,
practically permanent. Man's environment changes with ever-
increasing rapidity. The inherited nature of every human
being varies indeed from that of every other, but the relative
frequency of the most important variations can be forecasted
for each generation. The difference, on the other hand, between one man's environment and that of other men can be
arranged on no curve and remembered or forecasted by no

expedient. Buckle, it is true, attempted to explain the present and prophesy the future intellectual history of modern nations by the help of a few generalisations as to the effect of that small fraction of their environment which consisted of climate. But Buckle failed, and no one has attacked the problem again with anything like his confidence. . . .

The traditional method of political reasoning has inevitably shared the defects of its subject-matter. In thinking about politics we seldom penetrate behind those simple entities which form themselves so easily in our minds, or approach in earnest the infinite complexity of the actual world. Political abstractions, such as Justice, or Liberty, or the State, stand in our minds as things having a real existence. The names of political species, 'governments,' or 'rights,' or 'Irishmen,' suggest to us the idea of single 'type specimens'; and we tend, like medieval naturalists, to assume that all the individual members of a species are in all respects identical with the type specimen and with each other.

(Extracts from chapters 3, 4 and 5.)

SECTION XI

THE ELITISTS

Around the turn of the twentieth century, a number of writers, dissatisfied with the metaphysical preoccupations of political thinkers and influenced by new scientific and psychological theories, asserted that politics must be understood in a more realistic fashion. For these writers—Vilfredo Pareto (1848–1923), Gaetano Mosca (1858–1941) and Roberto Michels (1876–1936)—this meant primarily the study of power and of the elitist groups who controlled the making of decisions. They studied the manner in which power was obtained and maintained, the interaction between the ruling group and the masses and the use made of force, myth and symbols.

In *The Ruling Class*, Mosca argued the existence in all societies of a political class, a minority wielding power, no matter what the formal political organization. Sharing a common outlook and based on a political formula, the members of the class managed the affairs of the nation, controlled the possession of power and occupied the places of honor. This did not imply irresponsibility, since the position of the political class depended not only on its ideology, but on the support it obtained from the vast unorganized majority to whose demands it adapted itself. Moreover, Mosca's theory did not imply autocracy, for it also advocated the importance of juridical defense, the desirability not only of institutional checks, but also of a plurality of social forces, including a separation of church and state, and of economic and political power.

Pareto's treatment of an elitist ruling class in *The Mind and Society* (1916) was based on psychological analysis of human behavior into the basic human impulses, "the residues," the unvarying instincts, and "the derivatives," or rationalizations of behavior. The different residues characterized the different and successive elites throughout history. But the distinction between residues and derivatives, and the further distinctions that Pareto made between actions based on reason and actions based on emotion, and between "logical" and "non-logical" conduct, are often imprecise and unenlightening. The avowed scientific and positivistic approach of Pareto often takes on a rather homilistic tone, emotional and propagandist in character and anti-liberal in nature, foreign to impartial investigation.

The great contribution of Michels in *Political Parties* (1915), was his iron law of oligarchy, based primarily on his analysis of the German Social-Democratic Party, but equally applicable to all organizations. Like Mosca and Pareto, Michels held that power was always controlled by a minority, that government and organizations were inherently oligarchical and that struggles took place largely because of disputes between groups dominated by minorities. Conceptions such as popular sovereignty, egalitarianism or rule by the people were inadequate or meaningless descriptions of political reality.

Hierarchy and domination were inevitable, but not rigidity or static relationships. Mosca saw the interaction, the ebb and flow, "the ferment of endosmosis and exosmosis," between the upper and certain parts of the lower classes, as the history of civilized man. Pareto's most celebrated ideas are those of social equilibrium—a concept which this engineer turned-economist borrowed from mechanics and applied to politics—and the circulation of elites. All elites inevitably declined; the governing class was always in a state of slow and continuous transformation. Elites became increasingly incapable or unwilling to defend their power; a new elite arose out of the former ruled group. Different qualities were needed at different times in the rulers, sometimes the lion, sometimes the fox, sometimes the *rentier,* sometimes the speculator.

All three writers were interested in the way in which control was maintained. Michels explained that the elite was concerned with power while the mass was interested only in better material conditions. Not only were the masses satisfied if their material demands were met—they also bore a superstitious reverence toward the elite because of its cultural superiority. Pareto held that an elite employed a myth that convinced its subjects that it was worthy of ruling and made them prepared to die on behalf of their country. For Mosca, political rule rested on the political formula. Illusions and myths inspired historical myths. All revolutions were based on sentiment, not on reason; if men were not convinced that things would be better, if they even suspected that they might be worse, it would be difficult to get them to the barricades.

The elitist theories of the three writers did not lead to uniformity of political convictions. Mosca was a conservative deputy and senator, fearing the tyranny of both a sovereign and the people. Michels was sympathetic to both syndicalism and socialism. Pareto attacked political liberalism, pacifism and ideas of international brotherhood. But, though the fascists claimed him as one of their own, and Mussolini said that he had attended some of Pareto's lectures, Pareto was, in economics, an advocate of *laissez-faire,* and his elitism included no racist element.

The examination of the role of elites in politics has attracted an increasingly large number of modern writers and publicists. They include Croce, with his concept of the classless class, Walter Lippmann in his early studies of public opinion, Harold Lasswell and the school of behavior analysis he has influenced, C. Wright Mills in his controversial idea of a power elite, and Joseph Schumpeter, as well as a host of lesser luminaries.

PARETO

The Mind and Society

Social Elites and Circulation

2027. Let us assume that in every branch of human activity each individual is given an index which stands as a sign of his capacity, very much the way grades are given in the various subjects in examinations in school. The highest type of lawyer, for instance, will be given 10. The man who does not get a client will be given 1—reserving zero for the man who is an out-and-out idiot. To the man who has made his millions—honestly or dishonestly as the case may be—we will give 10. To the man who has earned his thousands we will give 6; to such as just manage to keep out of the poor-house, 1, keeping zero for those who get in. To the woman "in politics," such as the Aspasia of Pericles, the Maintenon of Louis XIV, the Pompadour of Louis XV, who has managed to infatuate a man of power and play a part in the man's career, we shall give some higher number, such as 8 or 9; to the strumpet who merely satisfies the senses of such a man and exerts no influence on public affairs, we shall give zero. To a clever rascal who knows how to fool people and still keep clear of the penitentiary, we shall give 8, 9, or 10, according to the number of geese he has plucked and the amount of money he has been able to get out of them. To the sneak-thief who snatches a piece of silver from a restaurant table and runs away into the arms of a policeman, we shall give 1. To a poet like Carducci we shall give 8 or 9 according to our tastes; to a scribbler who puts people to rout with his sonnets we shall give zero. For chess-players we can get very precise indices, noting what matches, and how many, they have won. And so on for all the branches of human activity.

2031. So let us make a class of the people who have the highest indices in their branch of activity, and to that class give the name of *élite*.

2032. For the particular investigation with which we are engaged, a study of social equilibrium, it will help if we further divide that class into two classes: a *governing élite*, comprising individuals who directly or indirectly play some considerable part in government, and a *non-governing élite*, comprising the rest.

2033. A class champion is certainly a member of the *élite*, but it is no less certain that his merits as a chess-player do not open the doors to political influence for him; and hence unless he has other qualities to win him that distinction, he is not a member of the governing *élite*. Mistresses of absolute monarchs have oftentimes been members of the *élite*, either because of their beauty or because of their intellectual endowments; but only a few of them, who have had, in addition, the particular talents required by politics, have played any part in government.

2034. So we get two strata in a population: (1) A lower stratum, the *non-élite*, with whose possible influence on government we are not just here concerned; then (2) a higher stratum, the *élite*, which is divided into two: (*a*) a governing *élite*, (*b*) a non-governing *élite*.

2035. In the concrete, there are no examinations whereby each person is assigned to his proper place in these various classes. That deficiency is made up for by other means, by various sorts of labels that serve the purpose after a fashion. Such labels are the rule even where there are examinations. The label "lawyer" is affixed to a man who is supposed to know something about the law and often does, though sometimes again he is an ignoramus. So, the governing *élite* contains individuals who wear labels appropriate to political offices of a certain altitude—ministers, Senators, Deputies, chief justices, generals, colonels, and so on—making the apposite exceptions for those who have found their way into that exalted company without possessing qualities corresponding to the labels they wear.

2041. Furthermore, the manner in which the various groups in a population intermix has to be considered. In moving from one group to another an individual generally brings with him certain inclinations, sentiments, attitudes, that he has acquired in the group from which he comes, and that circumstance cannot be ignored.

2042. To this mixing, in the particular case in which only two groups, the *élite* and the *non-élite*, are envisaged, the term "circulation of *élites*" has been applied—in French, *circulation des élites* [or in more general terms "class-circulation"].

2043. In conclusion we must pay special attention (1), in the case of one single group, to the proportions between the total of the group and the number of individuals who are nominally members of it but do not possess the qualities requisite for effective membership; and then (2), in the case of various groups, to the ways in which transitions from one group to the other occur, and to the intensity of that movement—that is to say, to the velocity of the circulation.

2044. Velocity in circulation has to be considered not only absolutely but also in relation to the supply of and the demand for certain social elements. A country that is always at peace does not require many soldiers in its governing class, and the production of generals may be overexuberant as compared with the demand. But when a country is in a state of continuous warfare many soldiers are necessary, and though production remains at the same level it may not meet the demand. That, we might note in passing, has been one of the causes for the collapse of many aristocracies.

2045. Another example. In a country where there is little industry and little commerce, the supply of individuals possessing in high degree the qualities requisite for those types of activity exceeds the demand. Then industry and commerce develop and the supply, though remaining the same, no longer meets the demand.

2046. We must not confuse the state of law with the state of fact. The latter alone, or almost alone, has a bearing on the social equilibrium. There are many examples of castes that are legally closed, but into which, in point of fact, new-comers make their way, and often in large numbers. On the other hand, what difference does it make if a caste is legally open, but conditions *de facto* prevent new accessions to it? If a person who acquires wealth thereby becomes a member of the governing class, but no one gets rich, it is as if the class were closed; and if only a few get rich, it is as if the law erected serious barriers against access to the caste. Something of that sort was observable towards the end of the Roman Empire. People who acquired wealth entered the order of the curials. But only a few individuals made any money. Theoretically we might examine any number of groups. Practically we have to confine ourselves to the more important. We shall proceed by successive approximations, starting with the simple and going on to the complex.

2047. *Higher class and lower class in general*. The least we can do is to divide society into two strata: a higher stratum, which usually contains the rulers, and a lower stratum, which usually contains the ruled. That fact is so obvious that it has always forced itself even upon the most casual observation, and so far the circulation of individuals between the two strata. Even Plato had an inkling of class-circulation and tried to regulate it artificially. The "new man," the upstart, the *parvenu*, has always been a subject of interest, and literature has analyzed him unendingly. Here, then, we are merely giving a more exact form to things that have long been perceived more or less vaguely. We [have] noted a varying distribution of residues in the various social groupings, and chiefly in the higher and the lower class. Such heterogeneousness is a fact perceived by the most superficial glance.

2051. The upper stratum of society, the *élite*, nominally contains certain groups of people, not always very sharply definited, that are called aristocracies. There are cases in which the majority of individuals belonging to such aristocracies actually possess the qualities requisite for remaining there; and then again there are cases where considerable numbers of the individuals making up the class do not possess those requisites. Such people may occupy more or less important places in the governing *élite* or they may be barred from it.

2052. In the beginning, military, religious, and commercial aristocraries and plutocracies—with a few exceptions not worth considering—must have constituted parts of the governing *élite* and sometimes have made up the whole of it. The victorious warrior, the prosperous merchant, the opulent plutocrat, were men of such parts, each in his own field, as to be superior to the average individual. Under those circumstances the label corresponded to an actual capacity. But as time goes by, considerable, sometimes very considerable, differences arise between the capacity and the label; while on the other hand, certain aristocracies orginally figuring prominently in the rising *élite* end by constituting an insignificant element in it. That has happened especially to military aristocracies.

2053. Aristocracies do not last. Whatever the causes, it is an incontestable fact that after a certain length of time they pass away. History is a graveyard of aristocracies. The Athenian "People" was an aristocracy as compared with the remainder of a population of resident aliens and slaves. It vanished without leaving any descent. The various aristocracies of Rome vanished in their time. So did the aristocracies of the Barbarians. Where, in France, are the descendants of the Frankish conquerors? The genealogies of the English nobility have been very exactly kept; and they show that very few families still remain to claim descent from the comrades of William the Conqueror. The rest have vanished. In Germany the aristocracy of the present day is very largely made up of descendants of vassals of the lords of old. The populations of European countries have increased enormously during the past few centuries. It is as certain as certain can be that the aristocracies have not increased in proportion.

2054. They decay not in numbers only. They decay also in quality, in the sense that they lose their vigour, that there is a decline in the proportions of the residues which enabled them to win their power and hold it. The governing class is restored not only in numbers, but—and that is the more important thing—in quality, by families rising from the lower classes and bringing with them the vigour and the proportions of residues necessary for keeping themselves in power. It is also restored by the loss of its more degenerate members.

2055. If one of those movements comes to an end, or worse still, if they both come to an end, the governing class crashes to ruin and often sweeps the whole of a nation along with it. Potent cause of disturbance in the equilibrum is the accumulation of superior elements in the lower classes and, conversely, of inferior elements in the higher classes. If human aristocracies were like thorough-breds among animals, which reproduce themselves over long periods of time with approximately the same traits, the history of the human race would be something altogether different from the history we know.

2056. In virtue of class-circulation, the governing *élite* is always in a state of slow and continuous transformation. It flows on like a river, never being today what it was yesterday. From time to time sudden and violent disturbances occur. There is a flood—the river overflows its banks. Afterwards, the new governing *élite* again resumes its slow transformation. The flood has subsided, the river is again flowing normally in its wonted bed.

2057. Revolutions come about through accumulations in

the higher strata of society—either because of a slowing-down in class-circulation, or from other causes—of decadent elements no longer possessing the residues suitable for keeping them in power, and shrinking from the use of force; while meantime in the lower strata of society elements of superior quality are coming to the fore, possessing residues suitable for exercising the functions of government and willing enough to use force.

2058. In general, in revolutions the members of the lower strata are captained by leaders from the higher strata because the latter possess the intellectual qualities required for outlining a tactic, while lacking the combative residues supplied by the individuals from the lower strata.

2059. Violent movements take place by fits and starts, and effects therefore do not follow immediately on their causes. After a governing class, or a nation, has maintained itself for long periods of time on force and acquired great wealth, it may subsist for some time still without using force, buying off its adversaries and paying not only in gold, but also in terms of the dignity and respect that it had formerly enjoyed and which constitute, as it were, a capital. In the first stages of decline, power is maintained by bargainings and concessions, and people are so deceived into thinking that that policy can be carried on indefinitely. So the decadent Roman Empire bought peace of the Barbarians with money and honours. So Louis XVI, in France, squandering in a very short time an ancestral inheritance of love, respect, and almost religious reverence for the monarchy, managed, by making repeated concessions, to be the King of the Revolution. So the English aristocracy managed to prolong its term of power in the second half of the nineteenth century down to the dawn of its decadence, which was heralded by the "Parliament Bill" in the first years of the twentieth.

The Use of Force

2174. To ask whether or not force ought to be used in a society, whether the use of force is or is not beneficial, is to ask a question that has no meaning; for force is used by those who wish to preserve certain uniformities and by those who wish to overstep them; and the violence of the ones stands in contrast and in conflict with the violence of the others. In truth, if a partisan of a governing class disavows the use of force, he means that he disavows the use of force by insurgents trying to escape from the norms of the given uniformity. On the other hand, if he says he approves of the use of force,

what he really means is that he approves of the use of force,
by the public authority to constrain insurgents to conformity.
Conversely, if a partisan of the subject class says he detests
the use of force in society, what he really detests is the use of
force by constituted authorities in forcing dissidents to conform; and if, instead, he lauds the use of force, he is thinking
of the use of force by those who would break away from
certain social uniformities.

2176. What we have just said serves to explain, along with
the theoretical difficulties, how it comes about that the solutions that are usually found for the general problem have so
little and sometimes no bearing on realities. Solutions of particular problems come closer to the mark because, situated as
they are in specific places and times, they present fewer theoretical difficulties; and because practical empiricism implicitly takes account of many circumstances that theory, until it
has been carried to a state of high perfection, cannot explicitly appraise.

Considering violations of material conformities among
modern civilized peoples, we see that, in general, the use of
violence in repressing them is the more readily condoned in
proportion as the violation can be regarded as an individual
anomaly designed to attain some individual advantage, and
the less readily condoned in proportion as the violation appears as a collective act aiming at some collective advantage,
and especially if its apparent design be to replace general
norms prevailing with certain other general norms.

2177. That states all that there is in common between the
large numbers of facts in which a distinction is drawn between so-called private and so-called political crimes. A distinction, and often a very sharp distinction, is drawn between
the individual who kills or steals for his own benefit and the
individual who commits murder or theft with the intent of
benefiting a party. In general, civilized countries grant extra-
dition for the former, but refuse it for the latter. In the same
way one notes a continually increasing leniency towards
crimes committed during labour strikes or in the course of
other economic, social, or political struggles. There is a more
and more conspicuous tendency to meet such aggressions with
merely passive resistance, the police power being required not
to use arms, or else permitted to do so only in cases of
extreme necessity. Such cases never arise in practice. . . . So
long as the policeman is alive, the necessity is held not to be
extreme, and it is bootless, after all, to recognize the extremity
after he is in his grave and no longer in a position to profit by
the considerate permission to use his revolver. Punishment by

judicial process is also becoming less and less vigorous. Criminals are either not convicted or, being convicted, are released in virtue of some probation law, failing of which, they can still rely on commutations, individual pardons, or general amnesties, so that, sum total, they have little or nothing to fear from the courts. In a word, in a vague, cloudy, confused sort of way, the notion is coming to the fore that an existing government may make some slight use of force against its enemies, but no great amount of force, and that it is under all circumstances to be condemned if it carries the use of force so far as to cause the death of considerable numbers, of a small number, a single one, of its enemies; nor can it rid itself of them, either, by putting them in prison or otherwise,

2178. What now are the correlations that subsist between this method of applying force and other social facts? We note, as usual, a sequence of actions and reactions, in which the use of force appears now as cause, now as effect. As regards the governing class, one gets, in the main, five groups of facts to consider: 1. A mere handful of citizens, so long as they are willing to use violence, can force their will upon public officials who are not inclined to meet violence with equal violence. If the reluctance of the officials to resort to force is primarily motivated by humanitarian sentiments, that result ensues very readily; but if they refrain from violence because they deem it wiser to use some other means, the effect is often the following: 2. To prevent or resist violence, the governing class resorts to "diplomacy," fraud, corruption—governmental authority passes, in a word, from the lions to the foxes. The governing class bows its head under the threat of violence, but it surrenders only in appearances, trying to turn the flank of the obstacle it cannot demolish in frontal attack. In the long run that sort of procedure comes to exercise a far-reaching influence on the selection of the governing class, which is now recruited only from the foxes, while the lions are blackballed. The individual who best knows the arts of sapping the strength of the foes of "graft" and of winning back by fraud and deceit what seemed to have been surrendered under pressure of force, is now leader of leaders. The man who has bursts of rebellion, and does not know how to crook his spine at the proper times and places, is the worst of leaders, and his presence is tolerated among them only if other distinguished endowments offset that defect. 3. So it comes about that the residues of the combination-instinct (Class I) are intensified in the governing class, and the residues of group-persistence (Class II) debilitated; for the combination-residues supply, precisely, the artistry and resourcefulness required for evolving ingenious expedients as substitutes for open resistance, while the residues of group-persistence stimulate open resistance, since a strong sentiment of group-persistence cures the spine of all tendencies to curvature. 4. Policies of the governing class are not planned too far ahead in time. Predominance of the combination instincts and enfeeblement of the sentiments of group-persistence result in making the governing class more satisfied with the present and less thoughtful of the future. The individual comes to prevail, and by far, over family, community, nation. Material interests and interests of the present or a near future come to prevail over the ideal interests of community or nation and interests of the distant future. The impulse is to enjoy the present without too much thought for the morrow. 5. Some of these phenomena become observable in international relations as well. Wars become essentially economic. Efforts are made to avoid conflicts with the powerful and the sword is rattled only before the weak. Wars are regarded more than anything else as speculations. A country is often unwittingly edged towards war by nursings of economic conflicts which, it is expected, will never get out of control and turn into armed conflicts. Not seldom, however, a war will be forced upon a country by peoples who are not so far advanced in the evolution that leads to the predominance of Class I residues.

2179. As regards the subject class, we get the following relations, which correspond in part to the preceding: 1. When the subject class contains a number of individuals disposed to use force and with capable leaders to guide them, the governing class is, in many cases, overthrown and another takes its place. That is easily the case where governing classes are inspired by humanitarian sentiments primarily, and very very easily if they do not find ways to assimilate the exceptional individuals who come to the front in the subject classes. A humanitarian aristocracy that is closed or stiffly exclusive represents the maximum of insecurity. 2. It is far more difficult to overthrow a governing class that is adept in the shrewd use of chicanery, fraud, corruption; and in the highest degree difficult to overthrow such a class when it successfully assimilates most of the individuals in the subject class who show those same talents, are adept in those same arts, and might therefore become the leaders of such plebeians as are disposed to use violence. Thus left without leadership, without talent, disorganized, the subject class is almost always powerless to set up any lasting régime. 3. So the combination-residues (Class I) become to some extent enfeebled in the subject class. But that phenomenon is in no way comparable to the corresponding reinforcement of those same residues in the governing class; for the governing class, being composed, as it is, of a much smaller number of individuals, changes considerably in character from the addition to it or withdrawal from it of relatively small numbers of individuals; whereas shifts of identical number produce but slight effects in the enormously greater total of the subject class. For that matter the subject class is still left with many individuals possessed of combination-instincts that are applied not to politics or activities connected with politics but to arts and trades independent of politics. That circumstance lends stability to societies, for the governing class is required to absorb only a small number of new individuals in order to keep the subject class deprived of leadership. However, in the long run the differences in temperament between the governing class and the subject class become gradually accentuated, the combination-instincts tending to predominate in the ruling class, and instincts of group-persistence in the subject class. When that difference becomes sufficiently great, revolution often occurs. 4. Revolution often transfers power to a new governing class, which exhibits a reinforcement in its instincts of group-persistence and so adds to its designs of present enjoyment aspirations towards ideal enjoyments presumably attainable at some future time—scepticism in part gives way to faith. 5. These considerations must to some extent be applied to international relations. If the combination-instincts are reinforced in a given country beyond a certain limit, as compared with the instincts of group-persistence, that country may be easily vanquished in war by another country in which that change in relative proportions has not occurred. The potency of an ideal as a pilot to victory is observable in both civil and international strife. People who lose the habit of applying force, who acquire the habit of considering policy from a commercial standpoint and of judging it only in terms of profit and loss, can readily be induced to purchase peace; and it may well be that such a transaction taken by itself is a good one, for war might have cost more money than the price of peace. Yet experience shows that in the long run, and taken in connexion with the things that inevitably go with it, such practice leads a country to ruin. The combination-instincts rarely come to prevail in the whole of a population. More commonly that situation arises in the upper strata of society, there being few if any traces of it in the lower and more populous classes. So when a war breaks out one gazes in amazement on the energies that are suddenly manifested by the masses at large, something that could in no way have been foreseen by studying the

upper classes only. Sometimes, as happened in the case of
Carthage, the burst of energy may not be sufficient to save a
country, because a war may have been inadequately prepared
for and be incompetently led by the ruling classes, and
soundly prepared for and wisely led by the ruling classes of
the enemy country. Then again, as happened in the wars of
the French Revolution, the energy in the masses may be great
enough to save a country because, though the war may have
been badly prepared for by its ruling classes, preparations and
leadership have been even worse in the ruling classes of the
enemy countries, a circumstance that gives the constituent
members of the lower strata of society time to drive their
ruling class from power and replace it with another of greater
energy and possessing the instincts of group-persistence in
greater abundance. Still again, as happened in Germany after
the disaster at Jena, the energy of the masses may spread to
the higher classes and spur them to an activity that proves
most effective as combining able leadership with enthusiastic
faith.

MOSCA

The Ruling Class

Rule by Minority

1. Among the constant facts and tendencies that are to be
found in all political organisms, one is so obvious that it is
apparent to the most casual eye. In all societies—from societies that are very meagerly developed and have barely attained the dawnings of civilization, down to the most advanced and powerful societies—two classes of people appear
—a class that rules and a class that is ruled. The first class,
always the less numerous, performs all political functions,
monopolizes power and enjoys the advantages that power
brings, whereas the second, the more numerous class, is directed and controlled by the first, in a manner that is now
more or less legal, now more or less arbitrary and violent, and
supplies the first, in appearance at least, with material means
of subsistence and with the instrumentalities that are essential
to the vitality of the political organism.

In practical life we all recognize the existence of this ruling
class (or political class, as we have elsewhere chosen to define
it). We all know that, in our own country, whichever it may
be, the management of public affairs is in the hands of a
minority of influential persons, to which management, willingly or unwillingly, the majority defer. We know that the

same thing goes on in neighboring countries, and in fact we should be put to it to conceive of a real world otherwise organized—a world in which all men would be directly subject to a single person without relationships of superiority or subordination, or in which all men would share equally in the direction of political affairs. If we reason otherwise in theory, that is due partly to inveterate habits that we follow in our thinking and partly to the exaggerated importance that we attach to two political facts that loom far larger in appearance than they are in reality.

The first of these facts—and one has only to open one's eyes to see it—is that in every political organism there is one individual who is chief among the leaders of the ruling class as a whole and stands, as we say, at the helm of the state. That person is not always the person who holds supreme power according to law. At times, alongside of the hereditary king or emperor there is a prime minister or a major-domo who wields an actual power that is greater than the sovereign's. At other times, in place of the elected president the influential politician who has procured the president's election will govern. Under special circumstances there may be, instead of a single person, two or three who discharge the functions of supreme control.

The second fact, too, is readily discernible. Whatever the type of political organization, pressures arising from the discontent of the masses who are governed, from the passions by which they are swayed, exert a certain amount of influence on the policies of the ruling, the political, class.

But the man who is at the head of the state would certainly not be able to govern without the support of a numerous class to enforce respect for his orders and to have them carried out; and granting that he can make one individual, or indeed many individuals, in the ruling class feel the weight of his power, he certainly cannot be at odds with the class as a whole or do away with it. Even if that were possible, he would at once be forced to create another class, without the support of which action on his part would be completely paralyzed. On the other hand, granting that the discontent of the masses might succeed in deposing a ruling class, inevitably, as we shall later show, there would have to be another organized minority within the masses themselves to discharge the functions of a ruling class. Otherwise all organization, and the whole social structure, would be destroyed.

2. From the point of view of scientific research the real superiority of the concept of the ruling, or political, class lies

in the fact that the varying structure of ruling classes has a preponderant importance in determining the political type, and also the level of civilization, of the different peoples. According to a manner of classifying forms of government that is still in vogue, Turkey and Russia were both, up to a few years ago, absolute monarchies, England and Italy were constitutional, or limited, monarchies, and France and the United States were classed as republics. The classification was based on the fact that, in the first two countries mentioned, headship in the state was hereditary and the chief was nominally omnipotent; in the second two, his office is hereditary but his powers and prerogatives are limited; in the last two, he is elected.

That classification is obviously superficial. Absolutisms though they were, there was little in common between the manners in which Russia and Turkey were managed politically, the levels of civilization in the two countries and the organization of their ruling classes being vastly different. On the same basis, the regime in Italy, a monarchy, is much more similar to the regime in France, a republic, than it is to the regime in England, also a monarchy; and there are important differences between the political organizations of the United States and France, though both countries are republics.

As we have already suggested, ingrained habits of thinking have long stood, as they still stand, in the way of scientific progress in this matter. The classification mentioned above, which divides governments into absolute monarchies, limited monarchies and republics, was devised by Montesquieu and was intended to replace the classical categories of Aristotle, who divided governments into monarchies, aristocracies and democracies. What Aristotle called a democracy was simply an aristocracy of fairly broad membership. Aristotle himself was in a position to observe that in every Greek state, whether aristocratic or democratic, there was always one person or more who had a preponderant influence. Between the day of Polybius and the day of Montesquieu, many writers perfected Aristotle's classification by introducing into it the concept of "mixed" governments. Later on the modern democratic theory, which had its source in Rousseau, took its stand upon the concept that the majority of the citizens in any state can participate, and in fact *ought* to participate, in its political life, and the doctrine of popular sovereignty still holds sway over many minds in spite of the fact that modern scholarship is making it increasingly clear that democratic, monarchical and aristocratic principles function side by side in every political organism. We shall not stop to refute this democratic theory here, since that is the task of this work as a whole. Besides, it would be hard to destroy in a few pages a whole system of ideas that has become firmly rooted in the human mind. . . .

3. We think it may be desirable, nevertheless, to reply at this point to an objection which might very readily be made to our point of view. If it is easy to understand that a single individual cannot command a group without finding within the group a minority to support him, it is rather difficult to grant, as a constant and natural fact, that minorities rule majorities, rather than majorities minorities. But that is one of the points—so numerous in all the other sciences—where the first impression one has of things is contrary to what they are in reality. In reality the dominion of an organized minority, obeying a single impulse, over the unorganized majority is inevitable. The power of any minority is irresistible as against each single individual in the majority, who stands alone before the totality of the organized minority. At the same time, the minority is organized for the very reason that it is a minority. A hundred men acting uniformly in concert, with a common understanding, will triumph over a thousand men who are not in accord and can therefore be dealt with one by one. Meanwhile it will be easier for the former to act in concert and have a mutual understanding simply because they are a hundred and not a thousand. It follows that the larger the political community, the smaller will the proportion of the governing minority to the governed majority be, and the more difficult will it be for the majority to organize for reaction against the minority.

However, in addition to the great advantage accruing to them from the fact of being organized, ruling minorities are usually so constituted that the individuals who make them up are distinguished from the mass of the governed by qualities that give them a certain material, intellectual or even moral superiority; or else they are the heirs of individuals who possessed such qualities. In other words, members of a ruling minority regularly have some attribute, real or apparent, which is highly esteemed and very influential in the society in which they live.

(Extract from chapter 2.)

The Political Formula

1. . . . in fairly populous societies that have attained a certain level of civilization, ruling classes do not justify their

power exclusively by *de facto* possession of it, but try to find a moral and legal basis for it, representing it as the logical and necessary consequence of doctrines and beliefs that are generally recognized and accepted. So if a society is deeply imbued with the Christian spirit the political class will govern by the will of the sovereign, who, in turn, will reign because he is God's anointed. So too in Mohammedan societies political authority is exercised directly in the name of the caliph, or vicar, of the Prophet, or in the name of someone who has received investiture, tacit or explicit, from the caliph. The Chinese mandarins ruled the state because they were supposed to be interpreters of the will of the Son of Heaven, who had received from heaven the mandate to govern paternally, and in accordance with the rules of the Confucian ethic, "the people of the hundred families." The complicated hierarchy of civil and military functionaries in the Roman Empire rested upon the will of the emperor, who, at least down to Diocletian's time, was assumed by a legal fiction to have received from the people a mandate to rule the commonwealth. The powers of all lawmakers, magistrates and government officials in the United States emanate directly or indirectly from the vote of the voters, which is held to be the expression of the sovereign will of the whole American people.

This legal and moral basis, or principle, on which the power of the political class rests, is what we have elsewhere called, and shall continue here to call, the "political formula." (Writers on the philosophy of law generally call it the "principle of sovereignty.") The political formula can hardly be the same in two or more different societies; and fundamental or even notable similarities between two or more political formulas appear only where the peoples professing them have the same type of civilization (or . . . belong to the same social type). According to the level of civilization in the peoples among whom they are current, the various political formulas may be based either upon supernatural beliefs or upon concepts which, if they do not correspond to positive realities, at least appear to be rational. We shall not say that they correspond in either case to scientific truths. A conscientious observer would be obliged to confess that, if no one has ever seen the authentic document by which the Lord empowered certain privileged persons or families to rule his people on his behalf, neither can it be maintained that a popular election, however liberal the suffrage may be, is ordinarily the expression of the will of a people, or even of the will of the majority of a people.

And yet that does not mean that political formulas are

mere quackeries aptly invented to trick the masses into obedience. Anyone who viewed them in that light would fall into grave error. The truth is that they answer a real need in man's social nature; and this need, so universally felt, of governing and knowing that one is governed not on the basis of mere material or intellectual force, but on the basis of a moral principle, has beyond any doubt a practical and a real importance.

Spencer wrote that the divine right of kings was the great superstition of past ages, and that the divine right of elected assemblies is the great superstition of our present age. The idea cannot be called wholly mistaken, but certainly it does not consider or exhaust all aspects of the question. It is further necessary to see whether a society can hold together without one of these "great superstitions"—whether a universal illusion is not a social force that contributes powerfully to consolidating political organization and unifying peoples or even whole civilizations.

2. Mankind is divided into social groups each of which is set apart from other groups by beliefs, sentiments, habits and interests that are peculiar to it. The individuals who belong to one such group are held together by a consciousness of common brotherhood and held apart from other groups by passions and tendencies that are more or less antagonistic and mutually repellent. As we have already indicated, the political formula must be based upon the special beliefs and the strongest sentiments of the social group in which it is current, or at least upon the beliefs and sentiments of the particular portion of that group which holds political pre-eminence. . . .

(Extract from chapter 3.)

Representative Government and Political Reality

1. Many doctrines that advocate liberty and equality, as the latter terms are still commonly understood—doctrines which the eighteenth century thought out, which the nineteenth perfected and tried to apply and which the twentieth will probably dispense with or modify substantially—are summed up and given concrete form in the theory that views universal suffrage as the foundation of all sound government. It is commonly believed that the only free, equitable and legitimate government is a government that is based upon the will of the majority, the majority by its vote delegating its powers for a specified length of time to men who represent it. Down to a few generations ago—and even today in the eyes

of many writers and statesmen—all flaws in representative government were attributed to incomplete or mistaken applications of the principles of representation and suffrage. . . .

We shall simply refer to some of the main considerations that most seriously undermine the foundations on which universal suffrage as an intellectual edifice rests. We deem it sufficient for our purposes here to demonstrate that the assumption that the elected official is the mouthpiece of the majority of his electors is as a rule not consistent with the facts; and we believe that this can be proved by facts of ordinary experience and by certain practical observations that anyone can make on the manner in which elections are conducted.

What happens in other forms of government—namely, that an organized minority imposes its will on the disorganized majority—happens also and to perfection, whatever the appearances to the contrary, under the representative system. When we say that the voters "choose" their representative, we are using a language that is very inexact. The truth is that the representative *has himself elected* by the voters, and, if that phrase should seem too inflexible and too harsh to fit some cases, we might qualify it by saying that *his friends have him elected*. In elections, as in all other manifestations of social life, those who have the will and, especially, the moral, intellectual and material *means* to force their will upon others take the lead over the others and command them.

The political mandate has been likened to the power of attorney that is familiar in private law. But in private relationships, delegations of powers and capacities always presuppose that the principal has the broadest freedom in choosing his representative. Now in practice, in popular elections, that freedom of choice, though complete theoretically, necessarily becomes null, not to say ludicrous. If each voter gave his vote to the candidate of his heart, we may be sure that in almost all cases the only result would be a wide scattering of votes. When very many wills are involved, choice is determined by the most various criteria, almost all of them subjective, and if such wills were not coordinated and organized it would be virtually impossible for them to coincide in the spontaneous choice of one individual. If his vote is to have any efficacy at all, therefore, each voter is forced to limit his choice to a very narrow field, in other words to a choice among the two or three persons who have some chance of succeeding; and the only ones who have any chance of succeeding are those whose candidacies are championed by groups, by committees, by *organized minorities*. In order to simplify the situation for purposes of proof, we have assumed a uninominal ballot, where one name only is to be voted for. But the great majority of voters will necessarily have a very limited freedom in the choice of their representative, and the influence of committees will necessarily be preponderant, whatever the system of balloting. When the list ballot is used and the voter votes for a list of candidates, it turns out that the number of candidates with some chance of succeeding is less than double the number of representatives to be elected.

How do these organized minorities form about individual candidates or groups of candidates? As a rule they are based on considerations of property and taxation, on common material interests, on ties of family, class, religion, sect or political party. Whether their component personnels be good or bad, there can be no doubt that such committees—and the representatives who are now their tools, now their leaders or "bosses"—represent the organization of a considerable number of social values and forces. In practice, therefore, the representative system results not at all in government by the majority; it results in the participation of a certain number of social values in the guidance of the state, in the fact that many political forces which in an absolute state, a state ruled by a bureaucracy alone, would remain inert and without influence upon government become organized and so exert an influence on government.

2. In examining the relations between the representative system and juridical defense, a number of distinctions and observations have to be borne in mind.

The great majority of voters are passive, it is true, in the sense that they have not so much freedom to choose their representatives as a limited right to exercise an option among a number of candidates. Nevertheless, limited as it may be, that capacity has the effect of obliging candidates to try to win a weight of votes that will serve to tip the scales in their direction, so that they make every effort to flatter, wheedle and obtain the good will of the voters. In this way certain sentiments and passions of the "common herd" come to have their influence on the mental attitudes of the representatives themselves, and echoes of a widely disseminated opinion, or of any serious discontent, easily come to be heard in the highest spheres of government.

It may be objected that this influence of the majority of voters is necessarily confined to the broad lines of political policy and makes itself felt only on a very few topics of a very general character, and that within limits as narrow as that even in absolute governments the ruling classes are obliged to take account of mass sentiments. In fact the most despotic of governments has to proceed very cautiously when it comes to shocking the sentiments, convictions or prejudices of the majority of the governed, or to requiring of that majority pecuniary sacrifices to which they are not accustomed. But wariness about giving offense will be much greater when every single representative, whose vote may be useful or necessary to the executive branch of government, knows that the discontent of the masses may at almost any moment bring about the triumph of a rival. We are aware that this is a two-edged argument. The masses are not always any wiser in discerning and protecting their interests than their representatives are; and we are acquainted with regions where public discontent has created greater obstacles to desirable reforms than the mistakes of parliamentary representatives and ministries.

The representative system, furthermore, has widely different effects according as the molecular composition of the electoral body varies. If all the voters who have some influence, because of education or social position, are members of one or another of the organized minorities, and if only a mass of poor and ignorant citizens are left outside of them, it is impossible for the latter to exercise their right of option and control in any real or effective manner. In these circumstances, of the various organized minorities that are disputing the field, that one infallibly wins which spends most money or lies most persuasively.

The same thing happens if persons of ability and economic independence represent only a slender minority within the electing group and so have no way of influencing the vote of majorities directly. Then, as ordinarily happens in large cities, the majorities do not feel the moral and material influence of the "better elements." But when the "better elements" do succeed in withdrawing the majority from the influence of committees and "ward heelers" and win its vote, their control over the conduct of the organized minorities becomes effective. It follows, therefore, that the comparison of the merits and platforms of the various candidates will be relatively serious and dispassionate only when electoral forces are not entirely under the control of men who make a regular profession or trade of electioneering.

The real juridical safeguard in representative governments lies in the public discussion that takes place within representative assemblies. Into those assemblies the most disparate political forces and elements make their way, and the existence of a small independent minority is often enough to control the conduct of a large majority and, especially, to prevent the bureaucratic organization from becoming omnipotent. But when, beyond being organs of discussion and publicizing, assemblies come to concentrate all the prestige and power of legitimate authority in their own hands, as regularly happens in parliamentary governments, then in spite of the curb of public discussion the whole administrative and judiciary machine falls prey to the irresponsible and anonymous tyranny of those who win in the elections and speak in the name of the people, and we get one of the worst types of political organization that the real majority in a modern society can possibly be called upon to tolerate.

In governments that are based very largely on the representative principle the referendum is in some respects a fairly effective instrument. By it the mass of likes and dislikes, enthusiasms and angers, which, when they are truly widespread and truly general, constitute what may quite plausibly be called public opinion, is enabled to react against the conduct and enterprise of the governing minority. In a referendum it is a question not of making a choice, or an election, but of pronouncing a "yes" or a "no" upon a specific question. No single vote, therefore, is lost, and each single vote has its practical importance independently of any coordination or organization along lines of sect, party or committee. However, the democratic ideal of majority government is not realized even by the referendum. Governing is not altogether a matter of allowing or prohibiting modifications in constitutions or laws. It is quite as much a matter of managing the whole military, financial, judiciary and administrative machine, or of influencing those who manage it. Then again, even if the referendum does serve to limit the arbitrariness of the governing class, it is no less true that often it seriously hampers improvements in the political organism.

(Extract from chapter 6.)

MICHELS

Political Parties

The Power of Leaders

The bureaucrat identifies himself completely with the organization, confounding his own interests with its interests. All objective criticism of the party is taken by him as a personal affront. This is the cause of the obvious incapacity of all party leaders to take a serene and just view of hostile criticism. The leader declares himself personally offended, doing this partly in good faith, but in part deliberately, in order to shift the battleground, so that he can present himself as the harmless object of an unwarrantable attack, and arouse in the minds of the masses towards his opponents in matters of theory that antipathy which is always felt for those whose actions are dictated by personal rancour. If, on the other hand, the leader is attacked personally, his first care is to make it appear that the attack is directed against the party as a whole. He does this not only on diplomatic grounds, in order to secure for himself the support of the party and to overwhelm the aggressor with the weight of numbers, but also because he quite ingenuously takes the part for the whole. This is frequently the outcome, not merely of blind fanaticism, but of firm conviction. According to Netchajeff, the revolutionary has the right of exploiting, deceiving, robbing, and in case of need utterly ruining, all those who do not agree unconditionally with his methods and his aims, for he need consider them as nothing more than *chair à conspiration*. His sole objective must be to ensure the triumph of his essentially individual ideas, without any respect for persons—*La Révolution c'est moi!* Bakunin uttered a sound criticism of this mode of reasoning when he said that its hidden source was to be found in Netchajeff's unconscious but detestable ambition.

The despotism of the leaders does not arise solely from a vulgar lust of power or from uncontrolled egoism, but is often the outcome of a profound and sincere conviction of their own value and of the services which they have rendered to the common cause. The bureaucracy which is most faithful and most efficient in the discharge of its duties is also the most dictatorial. . . . Where we have to do with excellent and incorruptible state officials like those of the German empire, the megalomaniac substitution of thing for person is partly due to the upright consciences of the officials and to their great devotion to duty. Among the members of such a bureaucracy, there is hardly one who does not feel that a pinprick directed against his own person is a crime committed against the whole state. It is for the same reason that they all hold together *comme les doigts de la main*. Each one of them regards himself as an impersonation of a portion of the whole state, and feels that this portion will suffer if the authority of any other portion is impaired. Further, the bureaucrat is apt to imagine that he knows the needs of the masses better than these do themselves, an opinion which may be sound enough in individual instances, but which for the most part is no more than a form of megalomania. Undoubtedly the party official is less exposed than the state official to the danger of becoming fossilized, for in most cases he has work as a public speaker, and in this way he maintains a certain degree of contact with the masses. On the other hand, the applause which he seeks and receives on these occasions cannot fail to stimulate his personal vanity.

When in any organization the oligarchy has attained an advanced stage of development, the leaders begin to identify with themselves, not merely the party institutions, but even the party property, this phenomenon being common both to the party and to the state. In the conflict between the leaders and the rank and file of the German trade unions regarding the right to strike, the leaders have more than once maintained that the decision in this matter is morally and legally reserved for themselves, because it is they who provide the financial resources which enable the workers to remain on strike. This view is no more than the ultimate consequence of that oligarchical mode of thought which inevitably leads to a complete forgetfulness of true democratic principles. . . .

(Extract from Part 3, chapter 3.)

The Iron Law of Oligarchy

. . . society cannot exist without a "dominant" or "political" class, and the ruling class, whilst its elements are subject to a frequent partial renewal, nevertheless constitutes the only factor of sufficiently durable efficacy in the history of human development. According to this view, the government, or, if the phrase be preferred, the state, cannot be anything other than the organization of a minority. It is the aim of this minority to impose upon the rest of society a "legal order," which is the outcome of the exigencies of dominion and of the exploitation of the mass of helots effected by the ruling minority, and can never be truly representative of the majority. The majority is thus permanently incapable of self-government. Even when the discontent of the masses culminates in a successful attempt to deprive the bourgeoisie of power, this is after all, so Mosca contends, effected only in appearance; always and necessarily there springs from the masses a new organized minority which raises itself to the rank of a governing class. Thus the majority of human beings, in a condition of eternal tutelage, are predestined by tragic necessity to submit to the dominion of a small minority, and must be content to constitute the pedestal of an oligarchy.

The principle that one dominant class inevitably succeeds to another, and the law deduced from that principle that oligarchy is, as it were, a preordained form of the common life of great social aggregates, far from conflicting with or replacing the materialist conception of history, completes that conception and reinforces it. There is no essential contradiction between the doctrine that history is the record of a continued series of class struggles and the doctrine that class struggles invariably culminate in the creation of new oligarchies which undergo fusion with the old. The existence of a political class does not conflict with the essential content of Marxism, considered not as an economic dogma but as a philosophy of history; for in each particular instance the dominance of a political class arises as the resultant of the relationships between the different social forces competing for supremacy, these forces being of course considered dynamically and not quantitatively. . . .

Thus the social revolution would not effect any real modification of the internal structure of the mass. The socialists might conquer, but not socialism, which would perish in the moment of its adherents' triumph. We are tempted to speak of this process as a tragicomedy in which the masses are content to devote all their energies to effecting a change of masters. . . . The result seems a poor one, especially if we take into account the psychological fact that even the purest of idealists who attains to power for a few years is unable to escape the corruption which the exercise of power carries in its train. In France, in working-class circles, the phrase is current, *homme élu, homme foutu*. . . .

Fourier defined modern society as a mechanism in which the extremest individual license prevailed, without affording any guarantee to the individual against the usurpations of the mass, or to the mass against the usurpations of the individual. History seems to teach us that no popular movement, however energetic and vigorous, is capable of producing profound and permanent changes in the social organism of the civilized world. The preponderant elements of the movement, the men who lead and nourish it, end by undergoing a gradual detachment from the masses, and are attracted within the orbit of the "political class." They perhaps contribute to this class a certain number of "new ideas," but they also endow it with more creative energy and enhanced practical intelligence, thus providing for the ruling class an ever-renewed youth. The "political class" (continuing to employ Mosca's convenient phrase) has unquestionably an extreme fine sense of its possibilities and its means of defence. It displays a remarkable force of attraction and a vigorous capacity for absorption

which rarely fail to exercise an influence even upon the most
embittered and uncompromising of its adversaries. . . .

Leadership is a necessary phenomenon in every form of
social life. Consequently it is not the task of science to inquire
whether this phenomenon is good or evil, or predominantly
one or the other. But there is great scientific value in the
demonstration that every system of leadership is incompatible
with the most essential postulates of democracy. We are now
aware that the law of the historic necessity of oligarchy is
primarily based upon a series of facts of experience. Like all
other scientific laws, sociological laws are derived from empirical observation. In order, however, to deprive our axiom
of its purely descriptive character, and to confer upon it that
status of analytical explanation which can alone transform a
formula into a law, it does not suffice to contemplate from a
unitary outlook those pheonomena which may be empirically
established; we must also study the determining causes of
these phenomena. . . .

Now, if we leave out of consideration the tendency of the
leaders to organize themselves and to consolidate their interests, and if we leave also out of consideration the gratitude of
the led towards the leaders, and the general immobility and
passivity of the masses, we are led to conclude that the principal cause of oligarchy in the democratic parties is to be
found in the technical indispensability of leadership.

The process which has begun in consequence of the differentiation of functions in the party is completed by a complex
of qualities which the leaders acquire through their detachment from the mass. At the outset, leaders arise SPONTANE-
OUSLY; their functions are ACCESSORY and GRATUITOUS. Soon,
however, they become PROFESSIONAL leaders, and in this second stage of development they are STABLE and IRREMOVABLE.

It follows that the explanation of the oligarchical phenomenon which thus results is partly PSYCHOLOGICAL; oligarchy derives, that is to say, from the psychical transformations which the leading personalties in the parties undergo in
the course of their lives. But also, and still more, oligarchy
depends upon what we may term the PSYCHOLOGY OF ORGA-
NIZATION ITSELF, that is to say, upon the tactical and technical
necessities which result from the consolidation of every disciplined political aggregate. Reduced to its most concise expression, the fundamental sociological law of political parties
(the term "political" being here used in its most comprehensive significance) may be formulated in the following terms:

"It is organization which gives birth to the dominion of the elected over the electors, of the mandataries over the mandators, of the delegates over the delegators. Who says organization, says oligarchy."

Every party organization represents an oligarchical power grounded upon a democratic basis. We find everywhere electors and elected. Also we find everywhere that the power of the elected leaders over the electing masses is almost unlimited. The oligarchical structure of the building suffocates the basic democratic principle. That which IS oppresses THAT WHICH OUGHT TO BE. For the masses, this essential difference between the reality and the ideal remains a mystery. Socialists often cherish a sincere belief that a new *élite* of politicians will keep faith better than did the old. The notion of the representation of popular interests, a notion to which the great majority of democrats, and in especial the working-class masses of the German-speaking lands, cleave with so much tenacity and confidence, is an illusion engendered by a false illumination, is an effect of mirage. . . . the modern proletariat, enduringly influenced by glib-tongued persons intellectually superior to the mass, ends by believing that by flocking to the poll and entrusting its social and economic cause to a delegate, its direct participation in power will be assured.

The formation of oligarchies within the various forms of democracy is the outcome of organic necessity, and consequently affects every organization, be it socialist or even anarchist. Haller long ago noted that in every form of social life relationships of dominion and of dependence are created by Nature herself. The supremacy of the leaders in the democratic and revolutionary parties has to be taken into account in every historic situation present and to come, even though only a few and exceptional minds will be fully conscious of its existence. The mass will never rule except *in abstracto*. Consequently the question we have to discuss is not whether ideal democracy is realizable, but rather to what point and in what degree democracy is desirable, possible, and realizable at a given moment. In the problem as thus stated we recognize the fundamental problem of politics as a science. Whoever fails to perceive this must, as Sombart says, either be so blind and fanatical as not to see that the democratic current daily makes undeniable advance, or else must be so inexperienced and devoid of critical faculty as to be unable to understand that all order and all civilization must exhibit aristocratic features. The great error of socialists, an error committed in consequence of their lack of adequate psychological knowledge, is to be found in their combination of pessimism regarding the present, with rosy optimism and immeasurable confidence regarding the future. A realistic view of the mental condition of the masses shows beyond question that even if we admit the possibility of moral improvement in mankind, the human materials with whose use politicians and philosophers cannot dispense in their plans of social reconstruction are not of a character to justify excessive optimism. Within the limits of time for which human provision is possible, optimism will remain the exclusive privilege of utopian thinkers.

(Extracts from Part 6, chapters 2 and 4.)

SECTION XII

ANARCHISM, DEMOCRATIC SOCIALISM AND MARXISM

Capitalism had led to remarkable economic advances, but also to increasing expressions of social discontent. Liberalism was essentially bound up with industrial and commercial expansion, the product of individual enterprise and initiative. But the Tory Disraeli, spoke of England divided into two nations, and the imperialist Joseph Chamberlain, recognized the need for social services, the ransom that owners of property must pay for the security they enjoyed.

Movements for social reform in opposition to the capitalist system took a variety of forms, primarily anarchism and differing concepts of socialism: Christian, ethical, moral and humanitarian, as well as Marxian.

Popularly, anarchism evokes the image of fanatical revolutionaries devoted to the art of bomb-throwing. Philosophically, anarchism has a respectable intellectual pedigree going back to the Greeks. The most significant exponents in the nineteenth century were William Godwin (1756–1836), Pierre Joseph Proudhon (1809–1865), who invented the word "anarchist," Max Stirner (1806–1856), Mikhail Bakunin (1814–1876) and Prince Pëtr Kropotkin (1842–1921), who invented the term "anarchist-communism."

Anarchist thought has taken different directions: the anarcho-syndicalist stressed the economic struggle and the syndicate as the unit of organization, the religious anarchist stressed love as the basis of human relationships, others emphasized the freedom of individuals. All groups opposed coercive authority, all rejected state power, all believed that individuals should be free both economically and politically, all assumed that such freedom would result in a social, peaceful and harmonious existence. If their ultimate aims—the free society and the absence of government—are similar to those of socialism, as both Kropotkin and Lenin argued, they differed completely on the means by which these ends were to be reached.

Revisionist Socialism

The two strongest currents of left-wing thought have been democratic socialism and Marxism. Democratic socialism has been practiced in the Scandinavian countries and in England. Its principle theorists have been the Revisionists, of whom Eduard Bernstein (1850–1932) is the most prominent representative, and the European humanitarian socialists, of whom the most significant are Jean Jaurès, G. D. H. Cole, August Bebel, Émile Vandervelde, Harold Laski and R. H. Tawney. Marxists argue that capitalism will inevitably collapse because of the inherent contradictions within it. Tawney is typical of the religious socialists in believing that capitalism is not so much unworkable as wicked. The economic evils of society were due primarily to the unregulated operation of the institutions of private property. Industry and society had to be organized to promote social ends. Inequalities of wealth and, above all, of opportunity, must be removed. Irresponsible economic power must be subjected to democratic control. For British and French socialists of this type, socialism was, in Émile Durkheim's words, not a science, but a cry of pain, sometimes of rage.

Bernstein became the object of fierce attacks by Lenin and Kautsky for his qualifications of a rigid Marxist position. According to Bernstein, Marxism was an insight, not a recipe. He accepted the Marxian theory of history, but criticized the dialectic and rejected its prophecies. Marx had been wrong about the doctrine of increasing misery, the worsening of crises, the growing inequality of incomes, the disappearance of intermediate classes. The rapid industrial development of German capitalism led Bernstein to conclude that there would be no catastrophic fall for capitalism, and to advocate cooperation among the different classes. History was not deterministic—man had a moral will which enabled him to ease class antagonisms and establish socialism peacefully. Neither the class struggle nor revolution was inevitable. Socialism was possible through democratic, parliamentary means. Social legislation could raise the proletariat to the level of the middle class.

Bernstein asserted that "What is generally called the goal of socialism is nothing to me, the movement, everything." It was unimportant whether the classless society would ever be reached. But the socialist movement was continuously enriching the lives of the workers, raising their standard of living, improving housing and stimulating education. Socialism was a way of life for workers to experience and enjoy.

Marxism

The most successful, if not the greatest, of the Marxist epigoni was Lenin [Vladimir Ilyich Ulyanov] (1870–1924), the son of a tsarist official, who became the chief theoretician and leader of the Russian Social Democratic Party and the inspirer of the Bolshevik capture of power in 1917. Lenin was a revolutionary applying Marxism to contemporary political struggles, an activist in whom practical, tactical considerations predominated over doctrinal consistency. Marx's style, as Trotsky commented, showed the influence of German socialistic literature; Lenin's style was simple and ascetic.

Lenin's major ideas were the emphasis he placed on the dictatorship of the proletariat as the transitional form for the state before the final socialist era, the role of the small revolutionary party as the leading group of the proletariat and maker of the revolution, its organization on the basis of democratic centralism, and the theory of imperialism, largely plagiarized from Hobson, as "the last stage of capitalism," and the explanation for the delay in the growth of misery among the workers of the West.

Lenin believed that the working class could not spontaneously develop a class consciousness sufficiently revolutionary to overthrow the capitalist system. Nor was economic struggle alone capable of producing a revolution. With occasional hesitation and qualification, Lenin argued that only the small, secret and strictly selected party, with its politically conscious ideologists and dedicated revolutionaries could solve the theoretical, political, tactical and organizational questions, instill the necessary class consciousness and act as the vanguard of the proletariat. But it was the supreme opportunism of Lenin that enabled power to be captured in 1917, when the Bolsheviks took advantage of the spontaneous outbreaks whose significance he had always denied.

An even greater irony was the fate of Leon Trotsky [Lev Bronstein] (1879–1940), the magnetic leader of the revolution with Lenin. In 1904 he had criticized Lenin's authoritarian view of the party, and asserted that the organization would take the place of the party, the central committee would take the place of the organization and the dictator would take the place of the central committee. In 1940 he was assassinated by an agent of the dictator whose emergence he had prophesied.

In 1905 Trotsky outlined his concept of the permanent revolution, a phrase he took from Marx. The backwardness of Russian industry convinced him that the *bourgeoisie* was not strong enough to overthrow tsarism, and therefore the workers must make both the bourgeois and proletarian revolutions. The socialist revolution could be consolidated only by an international revolution, and the revolution must therefore be uninterrupted, permanent and universal. Nearly twenty years later, it became the theoretical basis of the dispute with Stalin, in which differences of personality and of policy merged with those of theory.

Trotsky's *The Revolution Betrayed,* written while exiled in Norway in 1936, is a polemical discussion of the Stalinist system and its bureaucratic apparatus, which he explained by the objective conditions and economic backwardness of Russia and the isolation of the Russian revolution. The basis of bureaucratic rule in Russia was the poverty of society in objects of consumption, and therefore the struggle of each against all, and the strengthening of the state. But the whip of a bureaucracy would have to be broken in pieces before one could speak of socialism without a blush of shame. Full of false prophecies, the book is still a remarkably perceptive commentary, written within the Marxist framework, on the Stalinist régime. Its influence on later critics, including George Orwell, Edward Kardelj, and Milovan Djilas, has been considerable.

Antonio Gramsci (1891–1917) is one of the most original and influential of 20th century Marxists. His writings are fragmentary and unsystematic in nature but they are prolific and show his wide acquaintance with philosophy, culture and Italian history.

Gramsci rejected an economic determinist view of Marxism, arguing that a social and economic system was based not only on domination through economic control and physical coercion but also on the hegemony of the ruling class which was able to persuade the population to accept its system of values, attitudes and beliefs and to support the established order.

The revolutionary struggle in the West must be based not on the idea of an immediate crisis or a quick overthrow of the existing system which might have been appropriate for Russia but on an ideological process by which a counter-hegemony could lead to the transformation of consciousness of the people and to the change of all relationships, economic, cultural and political. Gramsci advocated the importance of politics in this struggle, the role of intellectuals in preparing the new cultural changes, the role of the revolutionary party in leading and educating the people, and the formation of a broad coalition between the party and other social forces.

BAKUNIN

God and the State

Liberty and Authority

What is authority? Is it the inevitable power of the natural laws which manifest themselves in the necessary concatenation and succession of phenomena in the physical and social worlds? Indeed, against these laws revolt is not only forbidden —it is even impossible. We may misunderstand them or not know them at all, but we cannot disobey them; because they constitute the basis and fundamental conditions of our existence; they envelop us, penetrate us, regulate all our movements, thoughts, and acts: even when we believe that we disobey them, we only show their omnipotence.

Yes, we are absolutely the slaves of these laws. But in such slavery there is no humiliation, or, rather, it is not slavery at all. For slavery supposes an external master, a legislator outside of him whom he commands, while these laws are not outside of us; they are inherent in us; they constitute our being, our whole being, physically, intellectually, and morally: we live, we breathe, we act, we think, we wish only through these laws. Without them we are nothing, *we are not*. Whence, then, could we derive the power and the wish to rebel against them?

In his relation to natural laws but one liberty is possible to man—that of recognizing and applying them on an ever-extending scale in conformity with the object of collective and individual emancipation or humanization which he pursues. These laws, once recognized, exercise an authority which is never disputed by the mass of men. . . .

The great misfortune is that a large number of natural laws, already established as such by science, remain unknown to the masses, thanks to the watchfulness of these tutelary governments that exist, as we know, only for the good of the people. There is another difficulty—namely, that the major portion of the natural laws connected with the development of human society, which are quite as necessary, invariable, fatal, as the laws that govern the physical world, have not been duly established and recognized by science itself.

Once they shall have been recognized by science, and then from science, by means of an extensive system of popular education and instruction, shall have passed into the consciousness of all, the question of liberty will be entirely solved. The most stubborn authorities must admit that then there will be no need either of political organization or direction or legislation, three things which, whether they emanate from the will of the sovereign or from the vote of a parliament elected by universal suffrage, and even should they conform to the system of natural laws—which has never been the case and never will be the case—are always equally fatal and hostile to the liberty of the masses from the very fact that they impose upon them a system of external and therefore despotic laws.

The liberty of man consists solely in this: that he obeys natural laws because he has *himself* recognized them as such, and not because they have been externally imposed upon him by any extrinsic will whatever, divine or human, collective or individual.

Suppose a learned academy, composed of the most illustrious representatives of science; suppose this academy charged with legislation for and the organization of society, and that, inspired only by the purest love of truth, it frames none but laws in absolute harmony with the latest discoveries of science. Well, I maintain, for my part, that such legislation and such organization would be a monstrosity, and that for two reasons: first, that human science is always and necessarily imperfect, and that, comparing what it has discovered with what remains to be discovered, we may say that it is still in its cradle. So that were we to try to force the practical life of men, collective as well as individual, into strict and exclusive conformity with the latest data of science, we should condemn society as well as individuals to suffer martyrdom on a bed of Procrustes, which would soon end by dislocating and stifling them, life ever remaining an infinitely greater thing than science.

The second reason is this: a society which should obey legislation emanating from a scientific academy, not because it understood itself the rational character of this legislation (in which case the existence of the academy would become useless), but because this legislation, emanating from the academy, was imposed in the name of a science which it venerated without comprehending—such a society would be a society, not of men, but of brutes. . . . It would surely and rapidly descend to the lowest stage of idiocy.

But there is still a third reason which would render such a government impossible—namely that a scientific academy invested with a sovereignty, so to speak, absolute, even if it were composed of the most illustrious men, would infallibly and soon end in its own moral and intellectual corruption. Even today, with the few privileges allowed them, such is the history of all academies. The greatest scientific genius, from the moment that he becomes an academician, an officially licensed *savant*, inevitably lapses into sluggishness. He loses his spontaneity, his revolutionary hardihood, and that troublesome and savage energy characteristic of the grandest geniuses, ever called to destroy old tottering worlds and lay the foundations of new. He undoubtedly gains in politeness, in utilitarian and practical wisdom, what he loses in power of thought. In a word, he becomes corrupted.

It is the characteristic of privilege and of every privileged position to kill the mind and heart of men. The privileged man, whether politically or economically, is a man depraved in mind and heart. That is a social law which admits of no exception, and is as applicable to entire nations as to classes, corporations, and individuals. It is the law of equality, the supreme condition of liberty and humanity. The principal object of this treatise is precisely to demonstrate this truth in all the manifestations of human life.

A scientific body to which had been confided the government of society would soon end by devoting itself no longer to science at all, but to quite another affair; and that affair, as in the case of all established powers, would be its own eternal perpetuation by rendering the society confided to its care ever more stupid and consequently more in need of its government and direction.

But that which is true of scientific academies is also true of all constituent and legislative assemblies, even those chosen by universal suffrage. In the latter case they may renew their composition, it is true, but this does not prevent the formation in a few years' time of a body of politicians, privileged in fact though not in law, who, devoting themselves exclusively to the direction of the public affairs of a country, finally form a sort of political aristocracy or oligarchy. Witness the United States of America and Switzerland.

Consequently, no external legislation and no authority—one, for that matter, being inseparable from the other, and both tending to the servitude of society and the degradation of the legislators themselves.

Does it follow that I reject all authority? Far from me such a thought. In the matter of boots, I refer to the authority of the bootmaker; concerning houses, canals, or railroads, I consult that of the architect or engineer. For such or such special knowledge I apply to such or such a *savant*. But I allow neither the bootmaker nor the architect nor the *savant* to impose his authority upon me. I listen to them freely and with all the respect merited by their intelligence, their character, their knowledge, reserving always my incontestable right of criticism and censure. I do not content myself with consulting a single authority in any special branch; I consult several; I compare their opinions, and choose that which seems to me the soundest. But I recognize no infallible authority, even in special questions; consequently, whatever respect I may have for the honesty and the sincerity of such or such an individual, I have no absolute faith in any person. Such a faith would be fatal to my reason, to my liberty, and even to the success of my undertakings; it would immediately transform me into a stupid slave, an instrument of the will and interests of others. . . .

I bow before the authority of special men because it is imposed upon me by my own reason. I am conscious of my inability to grasp, in all its details and positive developments, any very large portion of human knowledge. The greatest intelligence would not be equal to a comprehension of the whole. Thence results, for science as well as for industry, the necessity of the division and association of labor. I receive and I give—such is human life. Each directs and is directed in his turn. Therefore there is no fixed and constant authority, but a continual exchange of mutual, temporary, and, above all, volunatry authority and subordination.

This same reason forbids me, then, to recognize a fixed, constant, and universal authority, because there is no universal man, no man capable of grasping in that wealth of detail, without which the application of science to life is impossible, all the sciences, all the branches of social life. And if such universality could ever be realized in a single man, and if he wished to take advantage thereof to impose his authority upon us, it would be necessary to drive this man out of society, because his authority would inevitably reduce all the others to slavery and imbecility. . . .

We recognize, then, the absolute authority of science, because the sole object of science is the mental reproduction, as well-considered and systematic as possible, of the natural laws inherent in the material, intellectual, and moral life of both the physical and the social worlds, these two worlds constituting, in fact, but one and the same natural world. Outside of this only legitimate authority, legitimate because rational and in harmony with human liberty, we declare all other authorities false, arbitrary and fatal.

We recognize the absolute authority of science, but we reject the infallibility and universality of the *savant*. In our church—if I may be permitted to use for a moment an expression which I so detest: Church and State are my two *bêtes noires*—in our church, as in the Protestant church, we have a chief, an invisible Christ, science; and, like the Protestants, more logical even than the Protestants, we will suffer neither pope, nor council, nor conclaves of infallible cardinals, nor bishops, nor even priests. Our Christ differs from the Protestant and Christian Christ in this—that the latter is a personal being, ours impersonal; the Christian Christ, already completed in an eternal past, presents himself as a perfect being, while the completion and perfection of our Christ, science, are ever in the future: which is equivalent to saying that they will never be realized. Therefore, in recognizing *absolute science* as the only absolute authority, we in no way compromise our liberty.

I mean by the words "absolute science," the truly universal science which would reproduce ideally, to its fullest extent and in all its infinite detail, the universe, the system or coordination of all the natural laws manifested by the incessant development of the world. . . .

But, while rejecting the absolute, universal, and infallible authority of men of science, we willingly bow before the respectable, although relative, quite temporary, and very restricted authority of the representatives of special sciences, asking nothing better than to consult them by turns, and very grateful for such precious information as they may extend to us, on condition of their willingness to receive from us on occasions when, and concerning matters about which, we are more learned than they. In general, we ask nothing better than to see men endowed with great knowledge, great experience, great minds, and, above all, great hearts, exercise over us a natural and legitimate influence, freely accepted, and never imposed in the name of any official authority whatsoever, celestial or terrestrial. We accept all natural authorities and all influences of fact, but none of right; for every authority or every influence of right, officially imposed as such, becoming directly an oppression and a falsehood, would inevitably impose upon us, as I believe I have sufficiently shown, slavery and absurdity.

In a word, we reject all legislation, all authority, and all privileged, licensed, official, and legal influence, even though arising from universal suffrage, convinced that it can turn only to the advantage of a dominant minority of exploiters against the interests of the immense majority in subjection to them.

This is the sense in which we are really Anarchists. . . .

KROPOTKIN
Anarchist Communism

The Basis of Anarchism

Anarchy, the No-Government system of Socialism, has a double origin. It is an outgrowth of the two great movements of thought in the economical and the political fields which characterise our century, and especially its second part. In common with all Socialists, the Anarchists hold that the private ownership of land, capital, and machinery has had its time; that it is condemned to disappear; and that all requisites for production must, and will, become the common property of society, and be managed in common by the producers of wealth. And, in common with the most advanced representatives of political Radicalism, they maintain that the ideal of the political organisation of society is a condition of things where the functions of government are reduced to a minimum, and the individual recovers his full liberty of initiative and action for satisfying, by means of free groups and federations—freely constituted—all the infinitely varied needs of the human being. As regards Socialism, most of the Anarchists arrive at its ultimate conclusion, that is, at a complete negation of the wage-system and at Communism. And with reference to political organisation, by giving a further development to the above-mentioned part of the Radical programme, they arrive at the conclusion that the ultimate aim of society is the reduction of the functions of government to *nil*—that is, to a society without government, to An-archy. The Anarchists maintain, moreover, that such being the ideal of social and political organisation, they must not remit it to future centuries, but that only those changes in our social organisation which are in accordance with the above double ideal, and constitute an approach to it, will have a chance of life and be beneficial for the commonwealth.

As to the method followed by the Anarchist thinker, it entirely differs from that followed by the Utopists. The Anarchist thinker does not resort to metaphysical conceptions (like "natural rights," the "duties of the State," and so on) to establish what are, in his opinion, the best conditions for realising the greatest happiness of humanity. He follows, on the contrary, the course traced by the modern philosophy of evolution—without entering, however, the slippery route of mere analogies so often resorted to by Herbert Spencer. He studies human society as it is now and was in the past; and, without either endowing men altogether, or separate individuals, with superior qualities which they do not possess, he merely considers society as an aggregation of organisms trying to find out the best ways of combining the wants of the individual with those of co-operation for the welfare of the species. He studies society and tries to discover its *tendencies,* past and present, its growing needs, intellectual and economical, and in his ideal he merely points out in which direction evolution goes. He distinguishes between the real wants and tendencies of human aggregations and the accidents (want of knowledge, migrations, wars, conquests) which have prevented these tendencies from being satisfied, or temporarily paralysed them. And he concludes that the two most prominent, although often unconscious, tendencies throughout our history have been: a tendency towards integrating labour for the production of all riches in common, so as finally to render it impossible to discriminate the part of the common production due to the separate individual; and a tendency towards the fullest freedom of the individual in the prosecution of all aims, beneficial both for himself and for society at large. The ideal of the Anarchist is thus a mere summing-up of what he considers to be the next phase of evolution. It is no longer a matter of faith; it is a matter for scientific discussion. . . .

Taking all this into account, and still more the practical aspects of the question as to how private property *might* become common property, most of the Anarchists maintain that the very next step to be made by society, as soon as the present *régime* of property undergoes a modification, will be in a Communist sense. We are Communists. But our Communism is not that of either the Phalanstery or the authoritarian school: it is Anarchist Communism, Communism without government, free Communism. It is a synthesis of the two chief aims prosecuted by humanity since the dawn of its history—economical freedom and political freedom. . . .

BERNSTEIN

Evolutionary Socialism

The Need to Revise Socialism

It has been maintained in a certain quarter that the practical deductions from my treatises would be the abandonment of the conquest of political power by the proletariat organised politically and economically. That is quite an arbitrary deduction, the accuracy of which I altogether deny.

I set myself against the notion that we have to expect shortly a collapse of the bourgeois economy, and that social democracy should be induced by the prospect of such an imminent, great, social catastrophe to adapt its tactics to that assumption. That I maintain most emphatically.

The adherents of this theory of a catastrophe, base it especially on the conclusions of the *Communist Manifesto*. This is a mistake in every respect.

The theory which the *Communist Manifesto* sets forth of the evolution of modern society was correct as far as it characterised the general tendencies of that evolution. But it was mistaken in several special deductions, above all in the estimate of the *time* the evolution would take. The last has been unreservedly acknowledged by Friedrich Engels, the joint author with Marx of the *Manifesto,* in his preface to the *Class War in France.* But it is evident that if social evolution takes a much greater period of time than was assumed, it must also take upon itself *forms* and lead to forms that were not foreseen and could not be foreseen then.

Social conditions have not developed to such an acute opposition of things and classes as is depicted in the *Manifesto.* It is not only useless, it is the greatest folly to attempt to conceal this from ourselves. The number of members of the possessing classes is to-day not smaller but larger. The enormous increase of social wealth is not accompanied by a decreasing number of large capitalists but by an increasing number of capitalists of all degrees. The middle classes change their character but they do not disappear from the social scale.

The concentration in productive industry is not being accomplished even to-day in all its departments with equal thoroughness and at an equal rate. In a great many branches of production it certainly justifies the forecasts of the socialist critic of society; but in other branches it lags even today behind them. The process of concentration in agriculture proceeds still more slowly. Trade statistics show an extraordinarily elaborated graduation of enterprises in regard to size. No rung of the ladder is disappearing from it. The significant changes in the inner structure of these enterprises and their inter-relationship cannot do away with this fact.

In all advanced countries we see the privileges of the capitalist bourgeoisie yielding step by step to democratic organisations. Under the influence of this, and driven by the movement of the working classes which is daily becoming stronger, a social reaction has set in against the exploiting tendencies of capital, a counteraction which, although it still proceeds timidly and feebly, yet does exist, and is always drawing more departments of economic life under its influence. Factory legislation, the democratising of local government, and the extension of its area of work, the freeing of trade unions and systems of co-operative trading from legal restrictions, the consideration of standard conditions of labour in the work undertaken by public authorities—all these characterise this phase of the evolution.

But the more the political organisations of modern nations are democratised the more the needs and opportunities of great political catastrophes are diminished. He who holds firmly to the catastrophic theory of evolution must, with all his power, withstand and hinder the evolution described above, which, indeed, the logical defenders of that theory formerly did. But is the conquest of political power by the proletariat simply to be by a political catastrophe? Is it to be the appropriation and utilisation of the power of the State by the proletariat exclusively against the whole non-proletarian world?

He who replies in the affirmative must be reminded of two things. In 1872 Marx and Engels announced in the preface to the new edition of the *Communist Manifesto* that the Paris Commune had exhibited a proof that "the working classes cannot simply take possession of the ready-made State machine and set it in motion for their own aims." And in 1895 Friedrich Engels stated in detail in the preface to *War of the Classes* that the time of political surprises, of the "revolutions of small conscious minorities at the head of unconscious masses" was to-day at an end, that a collision on a large scale with the military would be the means of checking the steady growth of social democracy and of even throwing it back for a time—in short, that social democracy would flourish far better by lawful than by unlawful means and by violent revolution. And he points out in conformity with this opinion that the next task of the party should be "to work for an uninterrupted increase of its votes" or to carry on a slow *propaganda of parliamentary activity*.

Thus Engels, who, nevertheless, as his numerical examples show, still somewhat over-estimated the rate of process of the evolution! Shall we be told that he abandoned the conquest of political power by the working classes, because he wished to avoid the steady growth of social democracy secured by lawful means being interrupted by a political revolution?

If not, and if one subscribes to his conclusions, one cannot reasonably take any offence if it is declared that for a long time yet the task of social democracy is, instead of speculating on a great economic crash, "to organise the working classes politically and develop them as a democracy and to fight for all reforms in the State which are adapted to raise the working classes and transform the State in the direction of democracy."

That is what I have said in my impugned article and what I still maintain in its full import. As far as concerns the question propounded above it is equivalent to Engels' dictum, for democracy is, at any given time, as much government by the working classes as these are capable of practising according to their intellectual ripeness and the degree of social development they have attained. Engels, indeed, refers at the place just mentioned to the fact that the *Communist Manifesto* has "proclaimed the conquest of the democracy as one of the first and important tasks of the fighting proletariat."

In short, Engels is so thoroughly convinced that the tactics based on the presumption of a catastrophe have had their day, that he even considers a revision of them necessary in the Latin countries where tradition is much more favourable to them than in Germany. "If the conditions of war between nations have altered," he writes, "no less have those for the war between classes." Has this already been forgotten?

No one has questioned the necessity for the working classes to gain the control of government. The point at issue is between the theory of a social cataclysm and the question whether with the given social development in Germany and the present advanced state of its working classes in the towns and the country, a sudden catastrophe would be desirable in the interest of the social democracy. I have denied it and deny it again, because in my judgment a greater security for lasting success lies in a steady advance than in the possibilities offered by a catastrophic crash.

And as I am firmly convinced that important periods in the development of nations cannot be leapt over I lay the greatest value on the next tasks of social democracy, on the struggle for the political rights of the working man, on the political activity of working men in town and country for the interests of their class, as well as on the work of the industrial organisation of the workers.

In this sense I wrote the sentence that the movement means everything for me and that what is *usually* called "the final aim of socialism" is nothing; and in this sense I write it down again to-day. Even if the word "usually" had not shown that the proposition was only to be understood conditionally, it was obvious that it *could* not express indifference concerning the final carrying out of socialist principles, but only indifference—or, as it would be better expressed, carelessness—as to the form of the final arrangement of things. I have at no time had an excessive interest in the future, beyond general principles; I have not been able to read to the end any picture of the future. My thoughts and efforts are concerned with the duties of the present and the nearest future, and I only busy myself with the perspectives beyond so far as they give me a line of conduct for suitable action now.

The conquest of political power by the working classes, the expropriation of capitalists, are no ends in themselves but only means for the accomplishment of certain aims and endeavours. As such they are demands in the programme of social democracy and are not attacked by me. Nothing can be said beforehand as to the circumstances of their accomplishment; we can only fight for their realisation. But the conquest of political power necessitates the possession of political *rights;* and the most important problem of tactics which German social democracy has at the present time to solve, appears to me to be to devise the best ways for the extension of the political and economic rights of the German working classes.

(Extract from the Introduction.)

LENIN

What Is to Be Done?
1902

Spontaneous and Revolutionary Activity

We said that *there could not yet be* Social-Democratic consciousness among the workers. This consciousness could only be brought to them from without. The history of all countries shows that the working class, exclusively by its own effort, is able to develop only trade-union consciousness, *i.e.*, it may itself realise the necessity for combining in unions, to fight against the employers and to strive to compel the government to pass necessary labour legislation, etc.

The theory of Socialism, however, grew out of the philosophic, historical and economic theories that were elaborated by the educated representatives of the propertied classes, the intellectuals. The founders of modern scientific Socialism,

Marx and Engels, themselves belonged to the bourgeois intelligentsia. Similarly, in Russia, the theoretical doctrine of Social-Democracy arose quite independently of the spontaneous growth of the labour movement; it arose as a natural and inevitable outcome of the development of ideas among the revolutionary Socialist intelligentsia. . . .

. . . it is possible to "raise the activity of the masses of the workers" *only* provided this activity *is not restricted entirely* to "political agitation on an economic basis." And one of the fundamental conditions for the necessary expansion of political agitation is the organisation of *all-sided* political exposure. In *no other way* can the masses be trained in political consciousness and revolutionary activity except by means of such exposures. Hence, to conduct such activity is one of the most important functions of international Social-Democracy as a whole even in countries where political liberty exists. . . . Working-class consciousness cannot be genuinely political consciousness unless the workers are trained to respond to all cases of tyranny, oppression, violence and abuse, no matter *what class* is affected. Moreover, that response must be a Social-Democratic response, and not one from any other point-of-view. The consciousness of the masses of the workers cannot be genuine class consciousness, unless the workers learn to observe from concrete, and above all from topical, political facts and events, *every* other social class and *all* the manifestations of the intellectual, ethical and political life of these classes; unless they learn to apply practically the materialist analysis and the materialist estimate of *all* aspects of the life and activity of *all* classes, strata and groups of the population. . . .

The workers can acquire class political consciousness *only from without,* that is, only outside of the economic struggle, outside of the sphere of relations between workers and employers. The sphere from which alone it is possible to obtain this knowledge is the sphere of relationships between *all* classes and the state and the government—the sphere of the inter-relations between *all* classes. . . .

The Social-Democrat's ideal should not be a trade-union secretary, but *a tribune of the people,* able to react to every manifestation of tyranny and oppression, no matter where it takes place, no matter what stratum or class of the people it affects; he must be able to group all these manifestations into a single picture of police violence and capitalist exploitation; he must be able to take advantage of every petty event in order to explain his Socialistic convictions and his Social-

Democratic demands *to all*, in order to explain to *all* and every one the world historical significance of the struggle for the emancipation of the proletariat. . . .

. . . subservience to the spontaneity of the mass movement and any degrading of Social-Democratic politics to trade-union politics means precisely to prepare the ground for converting the labour movement into an instrument of bourgeois democracy. The spontaneous labour movement is able by itself to create (and inevitably will create) only trade union-ism, and working-class trade-union politics are precisely working-class bourgeois politics. The fact that the working class participates in the political struggle and even in political revolution does not in itself make its politics Social-Democratic politics. . . .

(Extracts from chapter 3.)

The Need for a Revolutionary Party

. . . workers, average people of the masses, are capable of displaying enormous energy and self-sacrifice in strikes and in street battles, with the police and troops, and are capable (in fact, are alone capable) of *determining* the whole outcome of our movement—but the struggle against the *political* police requires special qualities; it can be conducted only by *professional* revolutionists. And we must not only see to it that the masses "advance" concrete demands, but also that the masses of the workers "advance" an increasing number of such professional revolutionists from their own ranks. . . .

The workers' organisations must in the first place be trade organisations; secondly, they must be as wide as possible; and thirdly, they must be as public as conditions will allow (here, of course, I have only autocratic Russia in mind). On the other hand, the organisations of revolutionists must be comprised first and foremost of people whose profession is that of revolutionists (that is why I speak of organisations of *revolutionists*, meaning revolutionary Social-Democrats). As this is the common feature of the members of such an organisation, *all distinctions as between workers and intellectuals*, and certainly distinctions of trade and profession, must be dropped. Such an organisation must of necessity be not too extensive and as secret as possible. . . .

A small, compact core, consisting of reliable, experienced and hardened workers, with responsible agents in the principal districts and connected by all the rules of strict secrecy with the organisations of revolutionists, can, with the wide support of the masses and without an elaborate set of rules, perform *all* the functions of a trade-union organisation, and perform them, moreover, in the manner Social-Democrats desire. . . .

I assert: 1. That no movement can be durable without a stable organisation of leaders to maintain continuity; 2. that the more widely the masses are drawn into the struggle and form the basis of the movement, the more necessary is it to have such an organisation and the more stable must it be (for it is much easier than for demagogues to side-track the more backward sections of the masses); 3. that the organisation must consist chiefly of persons engaged in revolution as a profession; 4. that in a country with a despotic government, the more we *restrict* the membership of this organisation to persons who are engaged in revolution as a profession and who have been professionally trained in the art of combating the political police, the more difficult will it be to catch the organisation; and 5. the *wider* will be the circle of men and women of the working class or of other classes of society able to join the movement and perform active work in it. . . .

Only a centralised, militant organisation, that consistently carries out a Social-Democratic policy, that satisfies, so to speak, all revolutionary instincts and strivings, can safeguard the movement against making thoughtless attacks and prepare it for attacks that hold out the promise of success. . . .

The only serious organisational principle the active workers of our movement can accept is: Strict secrecy, strict selection of members, and the training of professional revolutionists. If we possessed these qualities, "democracy" and something even more would be guaranteed to us, namely: Complete, comradely, mutual confidence among revolutionists. . . .

A well-organised secret apparatus requires professionally well-trained revolutionists and proper division of labour, but neither of these requirements can be met by separate local organizations, no matter how strong they may be at any given moment. Not only are the general interests of our movement as a whole (consistent training of the workers in Socialist and political principles) better served by non-local newspapers, but even specifically local interests are better served. . . .

. . . the masses will never learn to conduct the political struggle until we help to *train* leaders for this struggle, both from among the intelligent workers and from among the intellectuals; and such leaders can be trained *solely* by systematic and every-day appreciation of *all* aspects of our political life, of *all attempts* at protest and struggle on the part of various classes and on various pretexts. . . . Every one who is at all acquainted with the movement knows perfectly well that the majority of local organisations *never dream* of these things, that many of the prospects of "live political work" *have never* been realised by a single organisation. . . .

. . . a network of agents that would automatically be created in the course of establishing and distributing a common newspaper would not have to "sit around and wait" for the call to rebellion, but would carry on the regular work that would guarantee the highest probability of success in the event of a rebellion. Such work would strengthen our contacts with the broadest strata of the masses of the workers and with all those strata who are discontented with the autocracy and who are so important to have in the event of an uprising. It is precisely such work that would help to cultivate the ability properly to estimate the general political situation and consequently, the ability to select the proper moment for the uprising. It is precisely such work that would train *all* local organisations to respond simultaneously to the same political questions, incidents and events that excite the whole of Russia, to react to these "events" in the most vigorous, uniform and expedient manner possible; for is not rebellion in essence the most vigorous, most uniform and most expedient "reaction" of the whole people to the conduct of the government? And finally, such work would train all revolutionary organisations all over Russia to maintain the most continuous and at the same time the most secret contact with each other, which will create *real* Party unity,—for without such contacts it will be impossible collectively to discuss the plan of rebellion and to take the necessary preparatory measures on the eve of it, which must be kept in the strictest secrecy. . . .

(Extracts from chapters 4 and 5.)

LENIN

The State and Revolution (1917)

The Need for Revolution

The state is the product and the manifestation of the *irreconcilability* of class antagonisms. The state arises when, where, and to the extent that the class antagonisms *cannot* be objectively reconciled. And, conversely, the existence of the state proves that the class antagonisms *are* irreconcilable. . . . According to Marx, the state is an organ of class *domination*, an organ of *oppression* of one class by another; its aim is the creation of "order" which legalises and perpetuates this oppression by moderating the collisions between the classes. . . . if the state is the product of the irreconcilable character of class antagonisms, if it is a force standing *above* society and "increasingly separating itself from it," then it is clear that the liberation of the oppressed class is impossible not only without a violent revolution, *but also without the destruction of* the apparatus of state power, which was created by the ruling class. . . .

. . . the state is a "special repressive force." . . . It follows from this that the "special repressive force" of the bourgeoisie for the suppression of the proletariat, of the millions of workers by a handful of the rich, must be replaced by a "special repressive force" of the proletariat for the suppression of the bourgeoisie (the dictatorship of the proletariat). It is just this that constitutes the destruction of "the state as the state." It is just this that constitutes the "act" of "the seizure of the means of production in the name of society." And it is obvious that such a substitution of one (proletarian) "special represessive force" for another (bourgeois) "special repressive force" can in no way take place in the form of a "withering away." . . .

The replacement of the bourgeois by the proletarian state is impossible without a violent revolution. The abolition of the proletarian state, *i.e.*, of all states, is only possible through "withering away."

The Dictatorship of the Proletariat

The state is a special organisation of force; it is the organisation of violence for the suppression of some class. What class must the proletariat suppress? Naturally, the exploiting class only, *i.e.*, the bourgeoisie. The toilers need the state only to overcome the resistance of the exploiters, and only the proletariat can direct this suppression and bring it to fulfilment, for the proletariat is the only class that is thoroughly revolutionary, the only class that can unite all the toilers and the exploited in the struggle against the bourgeoisie, in completely displacing it.

The exploiting classes need political rule in order to maintain exploitation, *i.e.*, in the selfish interests of an insignificant minority, and against the vast majority of the people. The exploited classes need political rule in order completely to abolish all exploitation, *i.e.*, in the interests of the vasts majority of the people, and against the insignificant minority consisting of the slave-owners of modern times—the landowners and the capitalists. . . .

Only the proletariat—by virtue of its economic rôle in large-scale production—is capable of leading *all* the toiling and exploited masses, who are exploited, oppressed, crushed by the bouregoisie not less, and often more, than the proletariat, but who are incapable of carrying on the struggle for their freedom *independently*.

The doctrine of the class struggle, as applied by Marx to the question of the state and of the Socialist revolution, leads inevitably to the recognition of the *political rule* of the proletariat, of its dictatorship, *i.e.*, of a power shared with none and relying directly upon the armed force of the masses. The overthrow of the bourgeoisie is realisable only by the transformation of the proletariat into the *ruling class*, able to crush the inevitable and desperate resistance of the bourgeoisie, and to organise, for the new economic order, *all* the toiling and exploited masses.

The proletariat needs state power, the centralised organisation of force, the organisation of violence, both for the purpose of crushing the resistance of the exploiters and for the purpose of *guiding* the great mass of the population—the peasantry, the petty-bourgeoisie, the semi-proletarians—in the work of organising Socialist economy.

By educating a workers' party, Marxism educates the vanguard of the proletariat, capable of assuming power and of *leading the whole people* to Socialism, of directing and organising the new order, of being the teacher, guide and leader of all the toiling and exploited in the task of building up their social life without the bourgeoisie and against the bourgeoisie. As against this, the opportunism predominant at present breeds in the workers' party representatives of the better-paid workers, who lose touch with the rank and file, "get along" fairly well under capitalism, and sell their birthright for a mess of pottage, *i.e.*, renounce their rôle of revolutionary leaders of the people against the bourgeoisie.

"The state, *i.e.*, the proletariat organised as the ruling class" —this theory of Marx's is indissolubly connected with all his teaching concerning the revolutionary rôle of the proletariat in history. The culmination of this rôle is proletarian dictatorship, the political rule of the proletariat. . . .

He who recognises *only* the class struggle is not yet a Marxist; he may be found not to have gone beyond the boundaries of bourgeois reasoning and politics. To limit Marxism to the teaching of the class struggle means to curtail Marxism—to distort it, to reduce it to something which is acceptable to the bourgeoisie. A Marxist is one who *extends* the acceptance of class struggle to the acceptance of the *dictatorship of the proletariat*. . . .

Further, the substance of the teachings of Marx about the state is assimilated only by one who understands that the dictatorship of a *single* class is necessary not only for any class society generally, not only for the *proletariat* which has over-thrown the bourgeoisie, but for the entire *historic period* which separates capitalism from "classless society," from Communism. The forms of bourgeois states are exceedingly variegated, but their essence is the same: in one way or another, all these states are in the last analysis inevitably a *dictatorship of the bourgeoisie*. The transition from capitalism to Communism will certainly bring a great variety and abundance of political forms, but the essence will inevitably be only one: *the dictatorship of the proletariat*.

. . . To destroy officialdom immediately, everywhere, completely—this cannot be thought of. That is a Utopia. But to *break up* at once the old bureaucratic machine and to start immediately the construction of a new one which will enable us gradually to reduce all officialdom to naught—this is *no* Utopia, it is the experience of the Commune, it is the direct and urgent task of the revolutionary proletariat.

Capitalism simplifies the functions of "state" administration; it makes it possible to throw off "commanding" methods and to reduce everything to a matter of the organisation of the proletarians (as the ruling class), hiring "workmen and managers" in the name of the whole of society. . . .

But if there be subordination, it must be to the armed vanguard of all the exploited and the labouring—to the proletariat. The specific "commanding" methods of the state officials can and must begin to be replaced—immediately, within twenty-four hours—by the simple functions of "managers" and bookkeepers, functions which are now already within the capacity of the average city dweller and can well be performed for "workingmen's wages."

We organise large-scale production, starting from what capitalism has already created; we workers *ourselves*, relying on our own experience as workers, establishing a strict, an iron discipline, supported by the state power of the armed workers, shall reduce the rôle of the state officials to that of simply carrying out our instructions as responsible, moderately paid "managers" (of course, with technical knowledge of all sorts, types and degrees). This is *our* proletarian task, with this we can and must *begin* when carrying through a proletarian revolution. Such a beginning, on the basis of large-scale production, of itself leads to the gradual "withering away" of all bureaucracy, to the gradual creation of a new order, an order without quotation marks, an order which has nothing to do with wage slavery, an order in which the more and more simplified functions of control and accounting will be performed by each in turn, will then become a habit, and will finally die out as *special* functions of a special stratum of the population. . . .

To organise the *whole* national economy like the postal system, in such a way that the technicians, managers, book-keepers as well as *all* officials, should receive no higher wages than "workingmen's wages," all under the control and leader-ship of the armed proletariat—this is our immediate aim. This is the kind of state and economic basis we need. This is what will produce the destruction of parliamentarism, while retaining representative institutions. This is what will free the labouring classes from the prostitution of these institutions by the bourgeoisie.

. . . democracy is *not* identical with the subordination of the minority to the majority. Democracy is a *state* recognising the subordination of the minority to the majority, *i.e.*, an organisation for the systematic use of *violence* by one class against the other, by one part of the population against an-other.

We set ourselves the ultimate aim of destroying the state, *i.e.*, every organised and systematic violence, every use of violence against man in general. We do not expect the advent of an order of society in which the principle of subordination of minority to majority will not be observed. But, striving for Socialism, we are convinced that it will develop into Com-munism; that, side by side with this, there will vanish all need for force, for the *subjection* of one man to another, and of one part of the population to another, since people will *grow accustomed* to observing the elementary conditions of social existence *without force and without subjection*. . . .

But the dictatorship of the proletariat—*i.e.*, the organisa-tion of the vanguard of the oppressed as the ruling class for the purpose of crushing the oppressors—cannot produce merely an expansion of democracy. *Together* with an im-mese expansion of democracy, which *for the first time* be-comes democracy for the poor, democracy for the people, and not democracy for the rich folk, the dictatorship of the pro-letariat produces a series of restrictions of liberty in the case of the oppressors, the exploiters, the capitalists. We must crush them in order to free humanity from wage-slavery; their resistance must be broken by force; it is clear that where there is suppression there is also violence, there is no liberty, no democracy. . . .

Democracy for the vast majority of the people, and sup-pression by force, *i.e.*, exclusion from democracy, of the exploiters and oppressors of the people—this is the modification of democracy during the *transition* from capitalism to Communism.

Only in Communist society, when the resistance of the capitalists has been completely broken, when the capitalists have disappeared, when there are no classes (*i.e.*, there is no difference between the members of society in their relation to the social means of production), *only then* "the state ceases to exist," and "*it becomes possible to speak of freedom.*" Only then a really full democracy, a democracy without any exceptions, will be possible and will be realised. And only then will democracy itself begin to *wither away.* . . . people will gradually *become accustomed* to the observance of the elementary rules of social life that have been known for centuries and repeated for thousands of years in all school books; they will become accustomed to observing them without force, without compulsion, without subordination, without the *special apparatus* for compulsion which is called the state. . . .

Finally, only Communism renders the state absolutely unnecessary, for there is *no one* to be suppressed—"no one" in the sense of a *class,* in the sense of a systematic struggle with a definite section of the population. We are not Utopians, and we do not in the least deny the possibility and inevitability of excesses on the part of *individual persons,* nor the need to suppress *such* excesses. But, in the first place, no special machinery, no special apparatus of repression is needed for this; this will be done by the armed people itself, as simply and as readily as any crowd of civilised people, even in modern society, parts a pair of combatants or does not allow a woman to be outraged. And, secondly, we know that the fundamental social cause of excesses which consist in violating the rules of social life is the exploitation of the masses, their want and their poverty. With the removal of this chief cause, excesses will inevitably begin to "*wither away.*" We do not know how quickly and in what succession, but we know that they will wither away. With their withering away, the state will also *wither away.* . . .

(Extracts from chapters 1, 2 and 3.)

Communist Society

The first phase of Communism . . . still cannot produce justice and equality; differences, and unjust differences, in wealth will still exist, but the *exploitation* of man by man will have become impossible, because it will be impossible to seize as private property the *means of production,* the factories,

machines, land, and so on. In tearing down Lassalle's petty-
bourgeois, confused phrase about "equality" and "justice" *in
general*, Marx shows the *course of development* of Communist society, which is forced at first to destroy *only* the
"injustice" that consists in the means of production having
been seized by private individuals, and which *is not capable* of
destroying at once the further injustice consisting in the distribution of the articles of consumption "according to work
performed" (and not according to need)....

And so, in the first phase of Communist society (generally
called Socialism) "bourgeois right" is *not* abolished in its
entirety, but only in part, only in proportion to the economic
transformation so far attained, *i.e.*, only in respect of the
means of production. "Bourgeois right" recognises them as
the private property of separate individuals. Socialism converts them into common property. *To that extent,* and to that
extent alone, does "bourgeois right" disappear....

The economic basis for the complete withering away of the
state is that high stage of development of Communism when
the antagonism between mental and physical labour disappears, that is to say, when one of the principal sources of
modern *social* inequality disappears—a source, moreover,
which it is impossible to remove immediately by the mere
conversion of the means of production into public property,
by the mere expropriation of the capitalists....

The state will be able to wither away completely when
society has realised the rule: "From each according to his
ability; to each according to his needs," *i.e.*, when people have
become accustomed to observe the fundamental rules of social
life, and their labour is so productive, that they voluntarily
work *according to their ability*. "The narrow horizon of bourgeois rights," which compels one to calculate, with the hard-
heartedness of a Shylock, whether he has not worked half an
hour more than another, whether he is not getting less pay
than another—this narrow horizon will then be left behind.
There will then be no need for any exact calculation by society of the quantity of products to be distributed to each of its
members; each will take freely "according to his needs." ...

Until the "higher" phase of Communism arrives, the Socialists demand the *strictest* control, *by society and by the state,*
of the quantity of labour and the quantity of consumption;
only this control must *start* with the expropriation of the
capitalists, with the control of the workers over the capitalists,
and must be carried out, not by a state of bureaucrats, but by
a state of *armed workers*.

   ... democracy means only *formal* equality. Immediately

after the attainment of equality for all members of society *in respect of* the ownership of the means of production, that is, of equality of labour and equality of wages, there will inevitably arise before humanity the question of going further from formal equality to real equality, *i.e.*, to realising the rule, "From each according to his ability; to each according to his needs." By what stages, by means of what practical measures humanity will proceed to this higher aim—this we do not and cannot know. . . .

(Extracts from chapter 5.)

TROTSKY

The Revolution Betrayed

Soviet Bureaucracy and Bonapartism

We have defined the Soviet Thermidor as a triumph of the bureaucracy over the masses. . . . The revolutionary Vanguard of the proletariat was in part devoured by the administrative apparatus and gradually demoralized. . . . The tired and disappointed masses were indifferent to what was happening on the summits.

. . . The strength of the compulsion exercised by the masses in a workers' State is directly proportional to the strength of the exploitative tendencies, or the danger of a restoration of capitalism, and inversely proportional to the strength of the social solidarity and the general loyalty to the new régime. Thus the bureaucracy—that is, the 'privileged officials and commanders of a standing army'—represents a special kind of compulsion which the masses cannot or do not wish to exercise, and which . . . is directed against the masses themselves. . . .

The present Soviet society cannot get along without a State, nor even—within limits—without a bureaucracy. But the cause of this is by no means the pitiful remnants of the past, but the mighty forces and tendencies of the present. The justification for the existence of a Soviet State as an apparatus of compulsion lies in the fact that the present transitional structure is still full of social contradictions, which in the sphere of *consumption*—most close and sensitively felt by all—are extremely tense, and forever threaten to break over into the sphere of production. The triumph of socialism cannot be called either final or irrevocable.

The basis of bureaucratic rule is the poverty of society in objects of consumption, with the resulting struggle of each against all. When there is enough goods in a store the purchasers can come whenever they want to. When there is little goods the purchasers are compelled to stand in line. When the lines are very long, it is necessary to appoint a policeman to keep order. Such is the starting-point of the power of the Soviet Bureaucracy. It 'knows' who is to get something and who has to wait.

A raising of the material and cultural level ought, at first glance, to lessen the necessity of privileges, narrow the sphere of application of 'bourgeois law', and thereby undermine the standing ground of its defenders, the bureaucracy. In reality the opposite thing has happened: the growth of the productive forces has been so far accompanied by an extreme development of all forms of inequality, privilege, and advantage, and therewith of bureaucratism. That too is not accidental.

In its first period, the Soviet régime was undoubtedly far more equalitarian and less bureaucratic than now. But that was an equality of general poverty. The resources of the country were so scant that there was no opportunity to separate out from the masses of the population any broad privileged strata. At the same time the 'equalizing' character of wages, destroying personal interestedness, became a brake upon the development of the productive forces. Soviet economy had to lift itself from its poverty to a somewhat higher level before fat deposits of privilege became possible. The present state of production is still far from guaranteeing all necessities to everybody. But it is already adequate to give significant privileges to a minority, and convert inequality into a whip for the spurring on of the majority. That is the first reason why the growth of production has so far strengthened not the socialist, but the bourgeois features of the State.

But that is not the sole reason. Alongside the economic factor dictating capitalistic methods of payment at the present stage there operates a parallel political factor in the person of the bureaucracy itself. In its very essence it is the planter and protector of inequality. It arose in the beginning as the bouregeois organ of a workers' State. In establishing and defending the advantages of a minority, it of course draws off the cream for its own use. Nobody who has wealth to distribute ever omits himself. Thus out of a social necessity there has developed an organ which has far outgrown its socially necessary function, and become an independent factor and therewith the source of great danger for the whole social organism.

The social meaning of the Soviet Thermidor now begins to take form before us. The poverty and cultural backwardness of the masses has again become incarnate in the malignant figure of the ruler with a great club in his hand. The deposed and abused bureaucracy, from being a servant of society, has again become its lord. On this road it has attained such a degree of social and moral alienation from the popular masses, that it cannot now permit any control over either its activities or its income.

In its intermediary and regulating function, its concern to maintain social ranks, and its exploitation of the State apparatus for personal goals, the Soviet bureaucracy is similar to every other bureaucracy, especially the fascist. But it is also in a vast way different. In no other régime has a bureaucracy ever achieved such a degree of independence from the dominating class. In bourgeois society the bureaucracy represents the interests of a possessing and educated class, which has at its disposal innumerable means of everyday control over its administration of affairs. The Soviet bureaucracy has risen above a class which is hardly emerging from destitution and darkness, and has no tradition of dominion or command. . . . It is in the full sense of the word the sole privileged and commanding stratum in the Soviet society.

Another difference is no less important. The Soviet bureaucracy has expropriated the proletariat politically in order by methods of *its own* to defend the social conquests. But the very fact of its appropriation of political power in a country where the principal means of production are in the hands of the State creates a new and hitherto unknown relation between the bureaucracy and the riches of the nation. The means of production belong to the State. But the State, so to speak, 'belongs' to the bureaucracy. If these as yet wholly new relations should solidify, become the norm, and be legalized, whether with or without resistance from the workers, they would, in the long run, lead to a complete liquidation of the social conquests of the proletarian revolution. But to speak of that now is at least premature. The proletariat has not yet said its last word. The bureaucracy has not yet created social supports for its dominion in the form of special types of property. It is compelled to defend State property as the source of its power and its income. In this aspect of its activity it still remains a weapon of proletarian dictatorship.

The attempt to represent the Soviet bureaucracy as a class of 'State capitalists' will obviously not withstand criticism. The bureaucracy has neither stocks nor bonds. It is recruited, supplemented, and renewed in the manner of an administrative hierarchy, independently of any special property relations if its own. The individual bureaucrat cannot transmit to his

heirs his rights in the exploitation of the State apparatus. The
bureaucracy enjoys its privileges under the form of an abuse
of power. It conceals its income; it pretends that as a special
social group it does not even exist. Its appropriation of a vast
share of the national income has the character of social
parasitism. All this makes the position of the commanding
Soviet stratum in the highest degree contradictory, equivocal,
and undignified, notwithstanding the completeness of its
power and the smoke-screen of flattery that conceals it.

To define the Soviet régime as transitional, or intermediate,
means to abandon such finished social categories as *capitalism*
(and therewith 'State capitalism') and also *socialism*. But besides being completely inadequate in itself, such a definition is
capable of producing the mistaken idea that from the present
Soviet régime *only* a transition to socialism is possible. In
reality a backslide to capitalism is wholly possible. A more
complete definition will of necessity be complicated and pon-
derous.

The Soviet Union is a contradictory society half-way between capitalism and socialism, in which: (*a*) the productive
forces are still far from adequate to give the State property a
socialist character; (*b*) the tendency toward primitive accumulation created by want breaks out through innumerable
pores of the planned economy; (*c*) norms of distribution preserving a bourgeois character lie at the basis of a new differentiation of society; (*d*) the economic growth, while slowly
bettering the situation of the toilers, promotes a swift formation of privileged strata; (*e*) exploiting the social antagonisms,
a bureaucracy has converted itself into an uncontrolled caste
alien to socialism; (*f*) the social revolution, betrayed by the
ruling party, still exists in property relations and in the consciousness of the toiling masses; (*g*) a further development of
the accumulating contradictions can as well lead to socialism
as back to capitalism; (*h*) on the road to capitalism the counterrevolution would have to break the resistance of the workers;
(*i*) on the road to socialism the workers would have to overthrow the bureaucracy. In the last analysis, the question will
be decided by a struggle of living social forces, both on the
national and the world arena. . . .

The question we previously raised in the name of the
reader: 'How could the ruling clique, with its innumerable
mistakes, concentrate unlimited power in its hands?'—or, in
other words: 'How explain the contradictions between the
intellectual poverty of the Thermidorians and their material
might?'—now permits a more concrete and categorical answer. The Soviet society is not harmonious. What is a sin for

one class or stratum is a virtue for another. From the point of view of socialist forms of society the policy of the bureaucracy is striking in its contradictions and inconsistencies. But the same policy appears very consistent from the standpoint of strengthening the power of the new commanding stratum.

The State support of the kulak (1923–8) contained a mortal danger for the socialist future. But then, with the help of the petty bourgeoisie the bureaucracy succeeded in binding the proletarian vanguard hand and foot and suppressing the Bolshevik Opposition. This 'mistake' from the point of view of socialism was a pure gain from the point of view of the bureaucracy. When the kulak began directly to threaten the bureacuracy itself it turned its weapons against the kulak. The panic of aggression against the kulak, spreading also to the middle peasant, was no less costly to the economy than a foreign invasion. But the bureaucracy had defended its positions. . . . The more alarmed becomes [their] mood . . . the higher the value they set upon ruthlessness against the least threat to their so justly earned rights. . . .

The progressive role of the Soviet bureaucracy coincides with the period devoted to introducing into the Soviet Union the most important elements of capitalist technique. The rough work of borrowing, imitating, transplanting, and grafting, was accomplished on the bases laid down by the revolution. There was, thus far, no question of any new word in the sphere of technique, science, or art. It is possible to build gigantic factories according to a ready-made Western pattern by bureaucratic command—although, to be sure, at triple the normal cost. But the further you go the more the economy runs into the problem of quality, which slips out of the hands of a bureaucracy like a shadow. The Soviet products are as though branded with the grey label of indifference. Under a nationalized economy *quality* demands a democracy of producers and consumers, freedom of criticism and initiative— conditions incompatible with a totalitarian régime of fear, lies, and flattery.

Behind the question of quality stands a more complicated and grandiose problem which may be comprised in the concept of *independent, technical,* and *cultural creation.* The ancient philosopher said that strife is the father of all things. No new values can be created where a free conflict of ideas is impossible. To be sure, a revolutionary dictatorship means by its very essence strict limitations of freedom. But for that very reason epochs of revolution have never been directly favourable to cultural creation: they have only cleared the arena for it. The dictatorship of the proletariat opens a wider scope to human genius the more it ceases to be a dictatorship. The socialist culture will flourish only in proportion to the dying away of the State. In that simple and unshakeable historic law is contained the death sentence of the present political régime in the Soviet Union. Soviet democracy is not the demand of an abstract policy, still less an abstract moral. It has become a life-and-death need of the country.

If the new State had no other interests than the interests of society, the dying away of the function of compulsion would gradually acquire a painless character. But the State is not pure spirit. Specific functions have created specific organs. The bureaucracy taken as a whole is concerned not so much with its function as with the tribute which this function brings in. The commanding caste tries to strengthen and perpetuate the organs of compulsion. To make sure of its power and income it spares nothing and nobody. The more the course of development goes against it the more ruthless it becomes toward the advanced elements of the population. Like the Catholic Church it has put forward the dogma of infallibility in the period of its decline, but it has raised it to a height of which the Roman pope never dreamed.

The increasingly insistent deification of Stalin is, with all its elements of caricature, a necessary element of the régime. The bureaucracy has need of an inviolable super-arbiter, a first consul if not an emperor, and it raises upon its shoulders him who best responds to its claim for lordship. That 'strength of character' of the leader which so enraptures the literary dilettantes of the West is in reality the sum total of the collective pressure of a caste which will stop at nothing in defence of its position. Each one of them at his post is thinking: *L'État—c'est moi*. In Stalin each one easily finds himself. But Stalin also finds in each one a small part of his own spirit. Stalin is the personification of the bureaucracy. That is the substance of his political personality.

Caesarism, or its bourgeois form, Bonapartism, enters the scene in those moments of history when the sharp struggle of two camps raises the State power, so to speak, above the nation and guarantees it, in appearance, a complete independence of classes—in reality, only the freedom necessary for a defence of the privileged. The Stalin régime, rising above a politically atomized society, resting upon a police and officers' corps, and allowing of no control whatever, is obviously a variation of Bonapartism—a Bonapartism of a new type not before seen in history.

Caesarism arose upon the basis of a slave society shaken by inward strife. Bonapartism is one of the political weapons of the capitalist régime in its critical period. Stalinism is a variety of the same system, but upon the basis of a workers' State torn by the antagonism between an organized and armed Soviet aristocracy and the unarmed toiling masses.

As history testifies, Bonapartism gets along admirably with a universal, and even a secret, ballot. The democratic ritual of Bonapartism is the *plebiscite*. From time to time the question is presented to the citizens: *for* or *against* the leader? And the voter feels the barrel of a revolver between his shoulders. Since the time of Napoleon III, who now seems a provincial dilettante, this technique has received an extraordinary development. The new Soviet constitution which establishes *Bonapartism on a plebiscite basis* is the veritable crown of the system.

In the last analysis, Soviet Bonapartism owes its birth to the belatedness of the world revolution. But in the capitalist countries the same cause gave rise to fascism. We thus arrive at the conclusion, unexpected at first glance, but in reality inevitable, that the crushing of Soviet democracy by an all-powerful bureaucracy and the extermination of bourgois democracy by fascism were produced by one and the same cause: the dilatoriness of the world proletariat in solving the problems set for it by history. Stalinism and fascism, in spite of a deep difference in social foundations, are symmetrical phenomena. In many of their features they show a deadly similarity. A victorious revolutionary movement in Europe would immediately shake not only fascism, but Soviet Bonapartism. In turning its back to the international revolution, the Stalinist bureaucracy was, from its own point of view, right. It was merely obeying the voice of self-preservation.

(Extracts from chapters 5, 9 and 11.)

ANTONIO GRAMSCI
The Prison Notebooks

The State and Hegemony

In reality, the State must be conceived of as an "educator", in as much as it tends precisely to create a new type or level of civilisation. Because one is acting essentially on economic forces, reorganising and developing the apparatus of economic production, creating a new structure, the conclusion must not be drawn that superstructural factors should be left to themselves, to develop spontaneously, to a haphazard and sporadic germination. The State, in this field, too, is an instrument of "rationalisation", of acceleration and of Taylorisation. It operates according to a plan, urges, incites, solicits, and "punishes"; for, once the conditions are created in which a certain way of life is "possible", then "criminal action or omission" must have a punitive sanction, with moral implications, and not merely be judged generically as "dangerous". The Law is the repressive and negative aspect of the entire positive, civilising activity undertaken by the State. The "prize-giving" activities of individuals and groups, etc., must also be incorporated in the conception of the Law; praiseworthy and meritorious activity is rewarded, just as criminal actions are punished (and punished in original ways, bringing in "public opinion" as a form of sanction).

In my opinion, the most reasonable and concrete thing that can be said about the ethical State, the cultural State, is this: every State is ethical in as much as one of its most important functions is to raise the great mass of the population to a particular cultural and moral level, a level (or type) which corresponds to the needs of the productive forces for development, and hence to the interests of the ruling classes. The school as a positive educative function, and the courts as a repressive and negative educative function, are the most important State activities in this sense: but, in reality, a multitude of other so-called private initiatives and activities tend to the same end—initiatives and activities which form the apparatus of the political and cultural hegemony of the ruling classes. Hegel's conception belongs to a period in which the spreading development of the bourgeoisie could seem limitless, so that its ethicity or universality could be asserted: all mankind will be bourgeois. But, in reality, only the social group that poses the end of the State and its own end as the target to be achieved can create an ethical State—i.e. one which tends to put an end to the internal divisions of the ruled, etc., and to create a technically and morally unitary social organism.

Hegel's doctrine of parties and associations as the "private" woof of the State. This derived historically from the political experiences of the French Revolution, and was to serve to give a more concrete character to constitutionalism. Government with the consent of the governed—but with this consent organised, and not generic and vague as it is expressed in the instant of elections. The State does have and request consent, but it also "educates" this consent, by means of the political and syndical associations; these, however, are private organisms, left to the private initiative of the ruling class. Hegel, in

a certain sense, thus already transcended pure constitutionalism and theorised the parliamentary State with its party system. But his conception of association could not help still
being vague and primitive, halfway between the political and
the economic; it was in accordance with the historical experience of the time, which was very limited and offered only one
perfected example of organisation—the "corporative" (a politics grafted directly on to the economy). Marx was not able
to have historical experiences superior (or at least much superior) to those of Hegel; but, as a result of his journalistic
and agitational activities, he had a sense for the masses.
Marx's concept of organisation remains entangled amid the
following elements: craft organisation; Jacobin clubs; secret
conspiracies by small groups; journalistic organisation.

. . . the general notion of State includes elements which
need to be referred back to the notion of civil society (in the
sense that one might say that State = political society + civil
society, in other words hegemony protected by the armour
of coercion). In a doctrine of the State which conceives the
latter as tendentially capable of withering away and of being
subsumed into regulated society, the argument is a fundamental one. It is possible to imagine the coercive element of
the State withering away by degrees, as ever-more conspicuous elements of regulated society (or ethical State or civil
society) make their appearance.

The expressions "ethical State" or "civil society" would thus
mean that this "image" of a State without a State was present
to the greatest political and legal thinkers, in so far as they
placed themselves on the terrain of pure science (pure utopia,
since based on the premise that all men are really equal and
hence equally rational and moral, i.e. capable of accepting the
law spontaneously, freely, and not through coercion, as imposed by another class, as something external to consciousness).

It must be remembered that the expression "nightwatchman" for the liberal State comes from Lassalle, i.e. from a
dogmatic and non-dialectical statalist (look closely at Lassalle's
doctrines on this point and on the State in general, in contrast
with Marxism). In the doctrine of the State as regulated society, one will have to pass from a phase in which "State" will
be equal to "government", and "State" will be identified with
"civil society", to a phase of the State as nightwatchman—i.e.
of a coercive organisation which will safeguard the development of the continually proliferating elements of regulated
society, and which will therefore progressively reduce its own

authoritarian and forcible interventions. Nor can this conjure up the idea of a new "liberalism", even though the beginning of an era of organic liberty be imminent.

If it is true that no type of State can avoid passing through a phase of economic-corporate primitivism, it may be deduced that the content of the political hegemony of the new social group which has founded the new type of State must be predominantly of an economic order: what is involved is the reorganisation of the structure and the real relations between men on the one hand and the world of the economy or of production on the other. The superstructural elements will inevitably be few in number, and have a character of foresight and of struggle, but as yet few "planned" elements. Cultural policy will above all be negative, a critique of the past; it will be aimed at erasing from the memory and at destroying. The lines of construction will as yet be "broad lines", sketches, which might (and should) be changed at all times, so as to be consistent with the new structure as it is formed. This precisely did not happen in the period of the mediaeval communes; for culture, which remained a function of the Church, was precisely anti-economic in character (i.e. against the nascent capitalist economy); it was not directed towards giving hegemony to the new class, but rather to preventing the latter from acquiring it. Hence Humanism and the Renaissance were reactionary, because they signalled the defeat of the new class, the negation of the economic world which was proper to it, etc.

Another element to examine is that of the organic relations between the domestic and foreign policies of a State. Is it domestic policies which determine foreign policy, or vice versa? In this case too, it will be necessary to distinguish: between great powers, with relative international autonomy, and other powers; also, between different forms of government (a government like that of Napoleon III had two policies, apparently—reactionary internally, and liberal abroad).

Conditions in a State before and after a war. It is obvious that, in an alliance, what counts are the conditions in which a State finds itself at the moment of peace. Therefore it may happen that whoever has exercised hegemony during the war ends up by losing it as a result of the enfeeblement suffered in the course of the struggle, and is forced to see a "subordinate" who has been more skilful or "luckier" become hegemonic. This occurs in "world wars" when the geographic situation compels a State to throw all its resources into the crucible: it wins through its alliances, but victory finds it prostrate, etc. This is why in the concept of "great power" it is necessary to take many elements into account, and especially those which are "permanent"—i.e. especially "economic and financial potential" and population.

Organisation of National Societies

I have remarked elsewhere that in any given society nobody is disorganised and without party, provided that one takes organisation and party in a broad and not a formal sense. In this multiplicity of private associations (which are of two kinds: natural, and contractual or voluntary) one or more predominates relatively or absolutely—constituting the hegemonic apparatus of one social group over the rest of the population (or civil society): the basis for the State in the narrow sense of the governmental-coercive apparatus.

It always happens that individuals belong to more than one private association, and often to associations which are objectively in contradiction to one another. A totalitarian policy is aimed precisely: 1. at ensuring that the members of a particular party find in that party all the satisfactions that they formerly found in a multiplicity of organisations, i.e. at breaking all the threads that bind these members to extraneous cultural organisms; 2. at destroying all other organisations or at incorporating them into a system of which the party is the sole regulator. This occurs: 1. when the given party is the bearer of a new culture—then one has a progressive phase; 2. when the given party wishes to prevent another force, bearer of a new culture, from becoming itself "totalitarian"—then one has an objectively regressive and reactionary phase, even if that reaction (as invariably happens) does not avow itself, and seeks itself to appear as the bearer of a new culture.

. . . the concept of the State, which is usually thought of as political society—i.e., a dictatorship or some other coercive apparatus used to control the masses in conformity with a given type of production and economy—and not as a balance between political society and civil society, by which I mean the hegemony of one social group over the entire nation, exercised through so-called private organizations like the Church, trade unions, or schools. For it is above all in civil society that intellectuals exert their influence. Benedetto Croce, for example, is a kind of lay Pope and an extremely efficient instrument of hegemony, even if sometimes he seems to come up against the government in power. I believe that this concept of the function of intellectuals sheds light on the reason, or one of the reasons, for the fall of the medieval

communes. The communes were governed by an economic
class that did not know how to create its own category of
intellectuals, in order to exercise a hegemony beyond dictatorship. Italian intellectuals had a cosmopolitan character mod-
eled on the Church, rather than a popular-national one. This
explains why Leonardo could sell his plans for the Florentine
fortifications to Duke Valentino. The communes formed a
syndicalist State that never succeeded in evolving beyond this
phase into a unified State—as Machiavelli kept pointing out in
vain. Machiavelli had hoped that by increasing and developing military organization, the hegemony of the city over the
countryside could be created, and for this reason can be called
the first Italian Jacobin.

The War of Manoeuvre and the War of Position

In Russia the State was everything, civil society was primor-
dial and gelatinous; in the West, there was a proper relation
between State and civil society, and when the State trembled a
sturdy structure of civil society was at once revealed. The
State was only an outer ditch, behind which there stood a
powerful system of fortresses and earthworks: more or less
numerous from one State to the next, it goes without saying—
but this precisely necessitated an accurate reconnaissance of
each individual country.

. . . This seems to me to be the most important question of
political theory that the post-war period has posed, and the
most difficult to solve correctly. It is related to the problems
raised by Bronstein [Trotsky], who in one way or another
can be considered the political theorist of frontal attack in a
period in which it only leads to defeats. This transition in
political science is only indirectly (mediately) related to that
which took place in the military field, although certainly a
relation exists and an essential one. The war of position demands enormous sacrifices by infinite masses of people. So an
unprecedented concentration of hegemony is necessary, and
hence a more "interventionist" government, which will take
the offensive more openly against the oppositionists and organise permanently the "impossibility" of internal disintegration—with controls of every kind, political, administrative,
etc., reinforcement of the hegemonic "positions" of the dominant group, etc. All this indicates that we have entered a
culminating phase in the political-historical situation, since in
politics the "war of position", once won, is decisive defini-
tively. In politics, in other words, the war of manoeuvre subsists so long as it is a question of winning positions which are

not decisive, so that all the resources of the State's hegemony cannot be mobilised. But when, for one reason or another, these positions have lost their value and only the decisive positions are at stake, then one passes over to siege warfare; this is concentrated, difficult, and requires exceptional qualities of patience and inventiveness. In politics, the siege is a reciprocal one, despite all appearances, and the mere fact that the ruler has to muster all his resources demonstrates how seriously he takes his adversary.

Educative and formative role of the State. Its aim is always that of creating new and higher types of civilisation; of adapting the "civilisation" and the morality of the broadest popular masses to the necessities of the continuous development of the economic apparatus of production; hence of evolving even physically new types of humanity. But how will each single individual succeed in incorporating himself into the collective man, and how will educative pressure be applied to single individuals so as to obtain their consent and their collaboration, turning necessity and coercion into "freedom"? Question of the "Law": this concept will have to be extended to include those activities which are at present classified as "legally neutral", and which belong to the domain of civil society; the latter operates without "sanctions" or compulsory "obligations", but nevertheless exerts a collective pressure and obtains objective results in the form of an evolution of customs, ways of thinking and acting, morality, etc.

Political concept of the so-called "Permanent Revolution", which emerged before 1848 as a scientifically evolved expression of the Jacobin experience from 1789 to Thermidor. The formula belongs to an historical period in which the great mass political parties and the great economic trade unions did not yet exist, and society was still, so to speak, in a state of fluidity from many points of view: greater backwardness of the countryside, and almost complete monopoly of political and State power by a few cities or even by a single one (Paris in the case of France); a relatively rudimentary State apparatus, and greater autonomy of civil society from State activity; a specific system of military forces and of national armed services; greater autonomy of the national economies from the economic relations of the world market, etc. In the period after 1870, with the colonial expansion of Europe, all these elements change: the internal and international organisational relations of the State become more complex and massive, and the Forty-Eightist formula of the "Permanent Revolution" is expanded and transcended in political science by the formula of "civil hegemony". The same thing happens in

the art of politics as happens in military art: war of movement increasingly becomes war of position, and it can be said
that a State will win a war in so far as it prepares for it
minutely and technically in peacetime. The massive structures
of the modern democracies, both as State organisations, and
as complexes of associations in civil society, constitute for the
art of politics as it were the "trenches" and the permanent
fortifications of the front in the war of position: they render
merely "partial" the element of movement which before used
to be "the whole" of war, etc.

Hegemony and Internationalism

. . . it is necessary to study accurately the combination of
national forces which the international class [the proletariat]
will have to lead and develop, in accordance with the international perspective and directives [i.e. those of the Comin-
tern]. The leading class is in fact only such if it accurately
interprets this combination—of which it is itself a component
and precisely as such is able to give the movement a certain
direction, within certain perspectives. It is on this point, in my
opinion, that the fundamental disagreement between Leo
Davidovitch [Trotsky] and Vissarionovitch [Stalin] as interpreter of the majority movement [Bolshevism] really hinges.
The accusations of nationalism are inept if they refer to the
nucleus of the question. If one studies the majoritarians' [Bol-
sheviks'] struggle from 1902 up to 1917, one can see that its
originality consisted in purging internationalism of every
vague and purely ideological (in a pejorative sense) element,
to give it a realistic political content. It is in the concept of
hegemony that those exigencies which are national in character are knotted together; one can well understand how certain
tendencies either do not mention such a concept, or merely
skim over it. A class that is international in character has—in
as much as it guides social strata which are narrowly national
(intellectuals), and indeed frequently even less than national:
particularistic and municipalistic (the peasants)—to "na-
tionalise" itself in a certain sense. Moreover, this sense is not
a very narrow one either, since before the conditions can be
created for an economy that follows a world plan, it is necessary to pass through multiple phases in which the regional
combinations (of groups of nations) may be of various kinds.
Furthermore, it must never be forgotten that historical development follows the laws of necessity until the initiative has
decisively passed over to those forces which tend towards
construction in accordance with a plan of peaceful and soli-

dary division of labour [i.e. to the socialist forces]. That nonnational concepts (i.e. ones that cannot be referred to each individual country) are erroneous can be seen *ab absurdo*: they have led to passivity and inertia in two quite distinct phases: 1. in the first phase, nobody believed that they ought to make a start—that is to say, they believed that by making a start they would find themselves isolated; they waited for everybody to move together, and nobody in the meantime moved or organised the movement; 2. the second phase is perhaps worse, because what is being awaited is an anachronistic and anti-natural form of "Napoleonism" (since not all historical phases repeat themselves in the same form). The theoretical weaknesses of this modern form of the old mechanicism are masked by the general theory of permanent revolution, which is nothing but a generic forecast presented as a dogma, and which demolishes itself by not in fact coming true.

Hegemony of Western Culture over the Whole World Culture

1. Even if one admits that other cultures have had an importance and a significance in the process of "hierarchical" unification of world civilisation (and this should certainly be admitted without question), they have had a universal value only in so far as they have become constituent elements of European culture, which is the only historically and concretely universal culture—in so far, that is, as they have contributed to the process of European thought and been assimilated by it.

2. However, even European culture has undergone a process of unification and, in the historical moment that interests us, this has culminated in Hegel and the critique of Hegelianism.

3. It emerges from these two points that we are dealing with the cultural process that is personified in the intellectuals; one should not talk about popular cultures in this connection, since with regard to these one cannot speak of critical elaboration and process of development.

4. Nor is one speaking here of those cultural processes which culminate in real activity, such as that which took place in France in the eighteenth century: or rather one should speak of them only in connection with the process that culminated in Hegel and in classical German philosophy, using them as a "practical" confirmation . . . of the reciprocal translatability of the two processes; one, the French, political and juridical, the other, German, theoretical and speculative.

5. From the disintegration of Hegelianism derives the beginning of a new cultural process, different in character from its predecessors, a process in which practical movement and theoretical thought are united (or are trying to unite through a struggle that is both theoretical and practical).

6. It is not important that this movement had its origins in mediocre philosophical works, or at best, in works that were not philosophical masterpieces. What matters is that a new way of conceiving the world and man is born and that this conception is no longer reserved to the great intellectuals, to professional philosophers, but tends rather to become a popular, mass phenomenon, with a concretely world-wide character, capable of modifying (even if the result includes hybrid combinations) popular thought and mummified popular culture.

7. One should not be surprised if this beginning arises from the convergence of various elements, apparently heterogenous —Feuerbach, in his role as a critic of Hegel, the Tübingen school as an affirmation of the historical and philosophical critique of religion, etc. Indeed it is worth nothing that such an overthrow could not but have connections with religion.

8. The philosophy of praxis as the result and the crowning point of all previous history. Out of the critique of Hegelianism arose modern idealism and the philosophy of praxis. Hegelian immanentism becomes historicism, but it is absolute historicism only with the philosophy of praxis—absolute historicism or absolute humanism.

Raising Consciousness

The active man-in-the-mass has a practical activity, but has no clear theoretical consciousness of his practical activity, which nonetheless involves understanding the world in so far as it transforms it. His theoretical consciousness can indeed be historically in opposition to his activity. One might almost say that he has two theoretical consciousnesses (or one contradictory consciousness): one which is implicit in his activity and which in reality unites him with all his fellow-workers in the practical transformation of the real world; and one, superficially explicit or verbal, which he has inherited from the past and uncritically absorbed. But this verbal conception is not without consequences. It holds together a specific social group, it influences moral conduct and the direction of will, with varying efficacy but often powerfully enough to produce a situation in which the contradictory state of consciousness does not permit of any action, any decision or any

choice, and produces a condition of moral and political passivity. Critical understanding of self takes place therefore
through a struggle of political "hegemonies" and of opposing
directions, first in the ethical field and then in that of politics
proper, in order to arrive at the working out at a higher level
of one's own conception of reality. Consciousness of being
part of a particular hegemonic force (that is to say, political
consciousness) is the first stage towards a further progressive
self-consciousness in which theory and practice will finally be
one. Thus the unity of theory and practice is not just a matter
of mechanical fact, but a part of the historical process, whose
elementary and primitive phase is to be found in the sense of
being "different" and "apart", in an instinctive feeling of independence, and which progresses to the level of real possession
of a single and coherent conception of the world. This is why
it must be stressed that the political development of the concept of hegemony represents a great philosophical advance as
well as a politico-practical one.

The educational relationship should not be restricted to the
field of the strictly "scholastic" relationships by means of
which the new generation comes into contact with the old and
absorbs its experiences and its historically necessary values
and "matures" and develops a personality of its own which is
historically and culturally superior. This form of relationship
exists throughout society as a whole and for every individual
relative to other individuals. It exists between intellectual and
non-intellectual sections of the population, between the rulers
and the ruled, *élites* and their followers, leaders [*dirigenti*]
and led, the vanguard and the body of the army. Every relationship of "hegemony" is necessarily an educational relationship and occurs not only within a nation, between the various
forces of which the nation is composed, but in the international and world-wide field, between complexes of national
and continental civilisations.

The Role of the Revolutionary Party

The modern prince, the myth-prince, cannot be a real person, a concrete individual. It can only be an organism, a complex element of society in which a collective will, which
has already been recognised and has to some extent asserted
itself in action, begins to take concrete form. History has
already provided this organism, and it is the political party—
the first cell in which there come together germs of a collective will tending to become universal and total. In the modern
world, only those historico-political actions which are imme-

diate and imminent, characterised by the necessity for lightning speed, can be incarnated mythically by a concrete individual. Such speed can only be made necessary by a great and
imminent danger, a great danger which precisely fans passion
and fanaticism suddenly to a white heat, and annihilates the
critical sense and the corrosive irony which are able to destroy
the "charismatic" character of the *condottiere* (as happened
in the Boulanger adventure). But an improvised action of
such a kind, by its very nature, cannot have a long-term and
organic character. It will in almost all cases be appropriate to
restoration and reorganisation, but not to the founding of new
States or new national and social structures (as was at issue in
Machiavelli's *Prince,* in which the theme of restoration was
merely a rhetorical element, linked to the literary concept of
an Italy descended from Rome and destined to restore the
order and the power of Rome).

An important part of *The Modern Prince* will have to be
devoted to the question of intellectual and moral reform, that
is to the question of religion or world-view. In this field too
we find in the existing tradition an absence of Jacobinism and
fear of Jacobinism.

The modern Prince must be and cannot but be the pro-
claimer and organiser of an intellectual and moral reform,
which also means creating the terrain for a subsequent development of the national-popular collective will towards the
realisation of a superior, total form of modern civilisation.

These two basic points—the formation of a national-popular collective will, of which the modern Prince is at one and
the same time the organiser and the active, operative expression; and intellectual and moral reform—should structure the
entire work. The concrete, programmatic points must be incorporated in the first part, that is they should result from the
line of discussion "*dramatically*", and not be a cold and
pedantic exposition of arguments.

Can there be cultural reform, and can the position of the
depressed strata of society be improved culturally, without a
previous economic reform and a change in their position in
the social and economic fields? Intellectual and moral reform
has to be linked with a programme of economic reform—
indeed the programme of economic reform is precisely the
concrete form in which every intellectual and moral reform
presents itself. The modern Prince, as it develops, revolu-
tionises the whole system of intellectual and moral relations,
in that its development means precisely that any given act is
seen as useful or harmful, as virtuous or as wicked, only in so
far as it has as its point of reference the modern Prince itself,

and helps to strengthen or to oppose it. In men's consciences, the Prince takes the place of the divinity or the categorical imperative, and becomes the basis for a modern laicism and for a complete laicisation of all aspects of life and of all customary relationships.

Structure and Superstructure

The proposition contained in the "Preface to a Contribution to the Critique of Political Economy" to the effect that men acquire consciousness of structural conflicts on the level of ideologies should be considered as an affirmation of epistemological and not simply psychological and moral value. From this, it follows that the theoretical-practical principle of hegemony has also epistemological significance, and it is here that Ilich [Lenin]'s greatest theoretical contribution to the philosophy of praxis should be sought. In these terms one could say that Ilich advanced philosophy as philosophy in so far as he advanced political doctrine and practice. The realisation of a hegemonic apparatus, in so far as it creates a new ideological terrain, determines a reform of consciousness and of methods of knowledge: it is a fact of knowledge, a philosophical fact. In Crocean terms: when one succeeds in introducing a new morality in conformity with a new conception of the world, one finishes by introducing the conception as well; in other words, one determines a reform of the whole of philosophy.

Structures and superstructures form an "historical bloc". That is to say the complex, contradictory and discordant *ensemble* of the superstructures is the reflection of the *ensemble* of the social relations of production. From this, one can conclude: that only a totalitarian system of ideologies gives a rational reflection of the contradiction of the structure and represents the existence of the objective conditions for the revolutionising of praxis. If a social group is formed which is one hundred per cent homogeneous on the level of ideology, this means that the premises exist one hundred per cent for this revolutionising: that is that the "rational" is actively and actually real. This reasoning is based on the necessary reciprocity between structure and superstructure, a reciprocity which is nothing other than the real dialectical process.

. . . Meanwhile, in the "relation of forces" various moments or levels must be distinguished, and they are fundamentally the following:

1. A relation of social forces which is closely linked to the structure, objective, independent of human will, and which

can be measured with the systems of the exact or physical sciences. The level of development of the material forces of production provides a basis for the emergence of the various social classes, each one of which represents a function and has a specific position within production itself. This relation is what it is, a refractory reality: nobody can alter the number of firms or their employees, the number of cities or the given urban population, etc. By studying these fundamental data it is possible to discover whether in a particular society there exist the necessary and sufficient conditions for its transformation—in other words, to check the degree of realism and practicability of the various ideologies which have been born on its own terrain, on the terrain of the contradictions which it has engendered during the course of is development.

2. A subsequent moment is the relation of political forces; in other words, an evaluation of the degree of homogeneity, self-awareness, and organisation attained by the various social classes. This moment can in its turn be analysed and differentiated into various levels, corresponding to the various moments of collective political consciousness, as they have manifested themselves in history up till now. The first and most elementary of these is the economic-corporate level: a tradesman feels *obliged* to stand by another tradesman, a manufacturer by another manufacturer, etc., but the tradesman does not yet feel solidarity with the manufacturer: in other words, the members of the professional group are conscious of its unity and homogeneity, and of the need to organise it, but in the case of the wider social group this is not yet so. A second moment is that in which consciousness is reached of the solidarity of interests among all the members of a social class —but still in the purely economic field. Already at this juncture the problem of the State is posed—but only in terms of winning politico-juridical equality with the ruling groups: the right is claimed to participate in legislation and administration, even to reform these—but within the existing fundamental structures. A third moment is that in which one becomes aware that one's own corporate interests, in their present and future development, transcend the corporate limits of the purely economic class, and can and must become the interests of other subordinate groups too. This is the most purely political phase, and marks the decisive passage from the structure to the sphere of the complex superstructures; it is the phase in which previously germinated ideologies become "party", come into confrontation and conflict, until only one of them, or at least a single combination of them, tends to prevail, to gain the upper hand, to propagate itself throughout society—bring-

ing about not only a unison of economic and political aims, but also intellectual and moral unity, posing all the questions around which the struggle rages not on a corporate but on a "universal" plane, and thus creating the hegemony of a fundamental social group over a series of subordinate groups. It is true that the State is seen as the organ of one particular group, destined to create favourable conditions for the latter's maximum expansion. But the development and expansion of the particular group are conceived of, and presented, as being the motor force of a universal expansion, of a development of all the "national" energies. In other words, the dominant group is coordinated concretely with the general interests of the subordinate groups, and the life of the State is conceived of as a continuous process of formation and superseding of unstable equilibria (on the juridical plane) between the interests of the fundamental group and those of the subordinate groups—equilibria in which the interests of the dominant group prevail, but only up to a certain point, i.e. stopping short of narrowly corporate economic interest.

In real history these moments imply each other reciprocally—horizontally and vertically, so to speak—i.e. according to socio-economic activity (horizontally) and to country (vertically), combining and diverging in various ways. Each of these combinations may be represented by its own organised economic and political expression. It is also necessary to take into account the fact that international relations intertwine with these internal relations of nation-states, creating new, unique and historically concrete combinations. A particular ideology, for instance, born in a highly developed country, is disseminated in less developed countries, impinging on the local interplay of combinations. This relation between international forces and national forces is further complicated by the existence within every State of several structurally diverse territorial sectors, with diverse relations of force at all levels.

3. The third moment is that of the relation of military forces, which from time to time is directly decisive. (Historical development oscillates continually between the first and the third moment, with the mediation of the second.) But this too is not undifferentiated, nor is it susceptible to immediate schematic definition. Here too, two levels can be distinguished: the military level in the strict or technical military sense, and the level which may be termed politico-military. In the course of history these two levels have appeared in a great variety of combinations. A typical example, which can serve as a limiting case, is the relation involved in a State's military oppression of a nation seeking to attain its national indepen-

dence. The relation is not purely military, but politico-military; indeed this type of oppression would be inexplicable if it were not for the state of social disintegration of the oppressed people, and the passivity of the majority among them; consequently independence cannot be won with purely military forces, it requires both military and politico-military. If the oppressed nation, in fact, before embarking on its struggle for independence, had to wait until the hegemonic State allowed it to organise its own army in the strict and technical sense of the word, it would have to wait quite a while. (It may happen that the claim to have its own army is conceded by the hegemonic nation, but this only means that a great part of the struggle has already been fought and won on the politico-military terrain.) The oppressed nation will therefore initially oppose the dominant military force with a force which is only "politico-military", that is to say a form of political action which has the virtue of provoking repercussions of a military character in the sense: 1. that it has the capacity to destroy the war potential of the dominant nation from within; 2. that it compels the dominant military force to thin out and disperse itself over a large territory, thus nullifying a great part of its war potential.

(Extracts from *Selections from the Prison Notebooks,* pp. 103, 166, 172, 210, 235, 241, 263, 270, 350.)

SECTION XIII

THEOLOGICAL THOUGHT AND POLITICS

Since Max Weber's challenging book, *The Protestant Ethic and the Spirit of Capitalism* (1904–6), there has been considerable discussion of the interaction between religion and the capitalist economic system. Weber had argued that it was the influence of Calvinism—with its doctrine of a dedicated "calling" and its praise of the qualities of self-discipline, labor and thrift devoted to the glory of God—that stimulated an economic development which called for these very qualities.

Religious thinkers do not concern themselves primarily with political problems or the need for social reform. In the nineteenth century, social Christians, like Lamennais, Lacordaire and Buchez in France, or Maurice and Kingsley in England were peripheral rather than central to Christian thinking. From the latter part of the century and into the twentieth century, the influence of those concerned with social matters has grown stronger and more significant, in the realms both of thought and of politics.

Papal Thought

Throughout history, popes, as supreme teachers of the Church, have issued encyclicals, or circular letters, to the Church hierarchy. For the last seventy years, these letters have been more concerned with economic and social affairs. In 1891, three years after his *Libertas Praestantissimum* (*On Human Liberty*), Leo XIII (1810-1903) issued *Rerum Novarum* (*Of New Things*), which established the attitude of the Catholic Church towards social problems. In it, he steered a middle course, attacking both the Marxists, who were exploiting the poor man's envy of the rich, and irresponsible capitalists, who were covetous and grasping men. For him, the social question was above all a moral question. He dealt with the relations between capital and labor, defending the existence of trade unions and advocating the right of the state to protect workers and intervene in social affairs.

In 1931 Pius XI issued *Quadragesimo Anno* (*Fortieth Anniversary*) to commemorate Pope Leo's encyclical. He indicated the dangers on one hand of economic collectivism, and on the other of economic individualism, as "twin rocks of shipwreck." He argued for more state activity to protect workers.

In recent years, popes have dealt with the problems of fascism and communism. The 1931 encyclical in Italian, *Non Abbiamo Bisogno* (*We Have No Need*), dealt with fascism, the 1937 encyclical in German, *Mit Brennender Sorge* (*With Heavy Heart*) criticized Nazi intolerance, and in the same year *Divini Redemptoris* (*Divine Redeemer*) criticized "atheistic communism."

The 1961 encyclical of Pope John XXIII, *Mater et Magistra* (*Mother and Teacher*), was issued on the seventieth anniversary of *Rerum Novarum*, called by Pope John "the Magna Charta of the economic-social reconstruction of the modern era." He argued in favor of the maintenance of private property and private initiative as safeguards against political tyranny. But he also urged the acceptance of socialization and state welfare programs if "their negative aspects" were removed, and advocated allowing workers to have a greater voice in industrial matters. He denounced all attempts at the creation of a Godless civilization as futile, and warned of the existing world fear. Technological development, and the fear of nuclear warfare showed "the pressing importance of spiritual values." But also, it was essential for the richer nations to give aid to underdeveloped countries without the creation of a "new form of colonialism" or the spread of the "materialistic poison."

Catholic Social Thought

Among contemporary Catholics interested in political problems have been Jacques Maritain (1882–1973) and Emmanuel Mounier. Maritain, one of the most distinguished of modern Thomists and proponents of the immutability of human nature and natural law, believes that the ultimate end, the final end of history, is beyond history. The democratic ideal has its origin in the word of God. Democracy must foresake its connections with atheism; only by becoming Christian can it be entirely human.

Maritain draws a distinction between individualism—the result of the propagation of Luther, Descartes and Rousseau —and the person, who derives from spirit. As an individual, man is treated only as a part, as a person he is treated as a whole. Man seeks the fullness of his personality and autonomy. The body politic exists for man insofar as he is a person. The society of which he is a member must therefore be based on a common good which includes cultural and spiritual as well as material values.

Personalism was also the key concept of Mounier and the group associated with his journal, *Esprit*. The unique status and essential dignity of man also entailed acting on behalf of others; the supreme act was to accept suffering and death in order not to betray human values. Mounier's personalism led to political liberalism, criticism of the capitalist system wrongly organized around the desire for profit, and approval of democracy as a system of autonomous groups based on a decentralization of authority.

Protestant Social Thought

Of the Protestants whose writings have been pertinent to politics, Reinhold Niebuhr (1892–1971), together with his colleague Paul Tillich, has probably been the most influential. Niebuhr is both an ordained minister, pastor in Detroit for thirteen years, and a political reformer, associated with the A.D.A. and the New York Liberal Party. He has constantly denounced the liberal fallacies of optimism and progress, however, and has criticized secular idealism and all attempts to set up universal models, since these mistake both the nature of individual self-interest and the collective egoism of all human societies. His outlook derives from his view of human nature. In the actions of men, there are always elements of good and evil, a mixture of personal ambition with desire to do social good. The idea that man is fundamentally good, can correct the evil in his behavior, and that harmony can be established and social conflicts avoided, is fallacious. If the conservative tends to equate the existing order with the ideal, the liberal and utopian believe they can establish the perfect order. But man's destiny is to attempt an impossible victory and to adjust himself to an inevitable defeat.

Niebuhr suggests the correct role, cautious advance, in the knowledge that our system is imperfect and that there are no ultimate solutions. Utopias are unrealizable, but responsibilities must be borne so that immediate dangers may be avoided and immediate injustices eliminated. Without outlining any systematic theology, Niebuhr holds that Christian principles alone provide the way to salvation by showing that, though man's life can never be perfected, it is not meaningless if based on love of God and neighbor.

POPE LEO XIII

Libertas Praestantissimum (1888)
(On Human Liberty)

Liberty and Law

. . . first of all, it will be well to speak briefly of *natural* liberty; for, though it is distinct and separate from moral liberty, natural freedom is the fountainhead from which liberty of whatsoever kind flows, *sua vi suaque sponte.* The unanimous consent and judgment of men, which is the trusty voice of nature, recognizes this natural liberty in those only who are endowed with intelligence or reason; and it is by his use of this that man is rightly regarded as responsible for his actions. For, while other animate creatures follow their senses, seeking good and avoiding evil only by instinct, man has reason to guide him in each and every act of his life. Reason sees that whatever things that are held to be good upon earth, may exist or may not, and discerning that none of them are of necessity for us, it leaves the will free to choose what it pleases. But man can judge of this *contingency,* as We say, only because he has a soul that is simple, spiritual, and intellectual—a soul, therefore, which is not produced by matter, and does not depend on matter for its existence; but which is created immediately by God, and, far surpassing the condition of things material, has a life and action of its own—so that, knowing the unchangeable and necessary reasons of what is true and good, it sees that no particular kind of good is necessary to us. When, therefore, it is established that man's soul is immortal and endowed with reason and not bound up with things material, the foundation of natural liberty is at once most firmly laid.

As the Catholic Church declares in the strongest terms the simplicity, spirituality, and immortality of the soul, so with unequalled constancy and publicity she ever also asserts its freedom. These truths she has always taught, and has sustained them as a dogma of faith; and whensoever heretics or innovators have attacked the liberty of man, the Church has defended it and protected this noble possession from destruction. . . . At no time, and in no place, has she held true with *fatalism*. Liberty, then, as We have said, belongs only to those who have the gift of reason or intelligence. Considered as to its nature, it is the faculty of choosing means fitted for the end proposed; for he is master of his actions who can choose one thing out of many. . . . The end, or object, both of the rational will and of its liberty is that good only which is in conformity with reason.

Since, however, both these faculties are imperfect, it is possible, as is often seen, that the reason should propose something which is not really good, but which has the appearance of good, and that the will should choose accordingly. For, as the possibility of error, and actual error, are defects of the mind and attests its imperfection, so the pursuit of what has a false appearance of good, though a proof of our freedom, just as a disease is a proof of our vitality, implies defect in human liberty. The will also, simply because of its dependence on the reason, no sooner desires anything contrary thereto, than it abuses its freedom of choice and corrupts its very essence. . . .

Such then being the condition of human liberty, it necessarily stands in need of light and strength to direct its actions to good and to restrain them from evil. Without this the freedom of our will would be our ruin. First of all there must be *law;* that is, a fixed rule of teaching what is to be done and what is to be left undone. This rule cannot affect the lower animals in any true sense, since they act of necessity, following their natural instinct, and cannot of themselves act in any other way. On the other hand, as was said above, he who is free can either act or not act, can do this or do that, as he pleases, because his judgment precedes his choice. And his judgment not only decides what is right or wrong of its own nature, but also what is practically good and therefore to be chosen, and what is practically evil and therefore to be avoided. In other words the reason prescribes to the will what it should seek after or shun, in order to the eventual attainment of man's last end, for the sake of which all his actions ought to be performed. This ordination of *reason* is called law. In man's free will, therefore, or in the moral necessity of our voluntary acts being in accordance with reason, lies the very root of the necessity of law. Nothing more foolish can be uttered or conceived than the notion that because man is free by nature, he is therefore exempt from law. . . .

For law is the guide of man's actions; it turns him towards good by its rewards, and deters him from evil by its punishments.

Foremost in this office comes the *natural law,* which is written and engraved in the mind of every man; and this is nothing but our reason, commanding us to do right and forbidding sin. Nevertheless all prescriptions of human reason can have force of law only inasmuch as they are the voice and the interpreters of some higher power on which our reason and liberty necessarily depend. For, since the force of law consists in the imposing of obligations and the granting of rights, authority is the one and only foundation of all law—the power, that is, of fixing duties and defining rights, as also of assigning the necessary sanctions of reward and chastisement to each and all of its commands. But all this, clearly, cannot be found in man, if, as his own supreme legislator, he is to be the rule of his own actions. It follows therefore that the law of nature is the same thing as the *eternal law,* implanted in rational creatures, and inclining them *to their right action and end;* and can be nothing else but the eternal reason of God, the Creator and Ruler of all the world. To this rule of action and restraint of evil God has vouchsafed to give special and most suitable aids for strengthening and ordering the human will. The first and most excellent of these is the power of His divine *grace,* whereby the mind can be enlightened and the will wholesomely invigorated and moved to the constant pursuit of moral good, so that the use of our inborn liberty becomes at once less difficult and less dangerous. . . .

What has been said of the liberty of individuals is no less applicable to them when considered as bound together in civil society. For, what reason and the natural law do for individuals, that *human law,* promulgated for their good, does for the citizens of States. Of the laws enacted by men, some are concerned with what is good or bad by its very nature; and they command men to follow after what is right and to shun what is wrong, adding at the same time a suitable sanction. But such laws by no means derive their origin from civil society; because just as civil society did not create human nature, so neither can it be said to be the author of the good which befits human nature, or of the evil which is contrary to it. Laws come before men live together in society, and have their origin in the natural, and consequently in the eternal, law. The precepts, therefore, of the natural law, contained bodily in the laws of men, have not merely the force of human law, but they possess that higher and more august sanction which belongs to the law of nature and the eternal law. And within the sphere of this kind of laws, the duty of the civil legislator is, mainly, to keep the community in obedience by the adoption of a common discipline and by putting restrain upon refractory and viciously inclined men, so that, deterred from evil, they may turn to what is good, or at any rate may avoid causing trouble and disturbance to the State. . . . human law, properly so called, consists, binding all citizens to work together for the attainment of the common end proposed to the community, and forbidding them to depart from this end; and in so far as human law is in conformity with the dictates of nature, leading to what is good, and deterring from evil.

From this it is manifest that the eternal law of God is the sole standard and rule of human liberty, not only in each individual man, but also in the community and civil society which men constitute when united. Therefore, the true liberty of human society does not consist in every man doing what he pleases, for this would simply end in turmoil and confusion, and bring on the overthrow of the State; but rather in this, that through the injunctions of the civil law all more easily conform to the prescriptions of the eternal law. . . .

. . . the nature of human liberty, however it be considered, whether in individuals or in society, whether in those who command or in those who obey, supposes the necessity of obedience to some supreme and eternal law, which is no other than the authority of God, commanding good and forbidding evil. And so far from this most just authority of God over men diminishing, or even destroying their liberty, it protects and perfects it, for the real perfection of all creatures is found in the prosecution and attainment of their respective ends; but the supreme end to which human liberty must aspire is God. . . .

Moreover, the highest duty is to respect authority, and obediently to submit to just law; and by this the members of a Community are effectually protected from the wrongdoing of evil men. Lawful power is from God, *and whosoever resisteth authority resisteth the ordinance of God;* wherefore obedience is greatly ennobled when subjected to an authority which is the most just and supreme of all. But where the power to command is wanting, or where a law is enacted contrary to reason, or to the eternal law, or to some ordinance of God, obedience is unlawful, lest, while obeying man, we become disobedient to God. . . .

What *Naturalists* or *Rationalists* aim at in philosophy, that the supporters of *Liberalism,* carrying out the principles laid down by Naturalism, are attempting in the domain of morality and politics. The fundamental doctrine of *Rationalism* is the supremacy of the human reason, which, refusing due submission to the divine and eternal reason, proclaims its own independence, and constitutes itself the supreme principle and source and judge of truth. Hence these followers of Liberalism deny the existence of any divine authority to which obedience is due, and proclaim that every man is the law to himself; from which arises that ethical system which they style *independent* morality, and which, under the guise of liberty, exonerates man from any obedience to the commands of God, and substitutes a boundless license. The end of all this is not difficult to foresee, especially when society is in question. For, when once man is firmly persuaded that he is subject to no one, it follows that the efficient cause of the unity of civil society is not to be sought in any principle external to man, or superior to him, but simply in the free will of individuals; that the authority in the State comes from the people only; and that, just as every man's individual reason is his only rule of life, so the collective reason of the community should be the supreme guide in the management of all public affairs. Hence the doctrine of the supremacy of the greater number, and that all right and all duty reside in the majority. But, from what has been said, it is clear that all this is in contradiction to reason. To refuse any bond of union between man and civil society, on the one hand, and God the Creator and consequently the supreme Law-giver, on the other, is plainly repugnant to the nature, not only of man, but of all created things. . . .

Moreover, besides this, a doctrine of such character is most hurtful both to individuals and to the State. For, once ascribe to human reason the only authority to decide what is true and what is good, and the real distinction between good and evil is destroyed; honor and dishonor differ not in their nature, but in the opinion and judgment of each one; pleasure is the measure of what is lawful; and, given a code of morality which can have little or no power to restrain or quiet the unruly propensities of man, a way is naturally opened to universal corruption. With reference also to public affairs: authority is severed from the true and natural principle whence it derives all its efficacy for the common good; and the law determining what it is right to do and avoid doing is at the mercy of a majority. Now this is simply a road leading straight to tyranny. The empire of God over man and civil society once repudiated, it follows that religion, as a public institution, can have no claim to exist, and that everything that belongs to religion will be treated with complete indifference. Furthermore, with ambitious designs on sovereignty, tumult and sedition will be common amongst the people; and when duty and conscience cease to appeal to them, there will be nothing to hold them back but force, which of itself alone is powerless to keep their covetousness in check. . . .

There are others, somewhat more moderate though not more consistent, who affirm that the morality of individuals is to be guided by the divine law, but not the morality of the State, so that in public affairs the commands of God may be passed over, and may be entirely disregarded in the framing of laws. Hence follows the fatal theory of the need of separation between Church and State. But the absurdity of such a position is manifest. Nature herself proclaims the necessity of the State providing means and opportunities whereby the community may be enabled to live properly, that is to say, according to the laws of God. For since God is the source of all goodness and justice, it is absolutely ridiculous that the State should pay no attention to these laws or render them abortive by contrary enactments. Besides, those who are in authority owe it to the commonwealth not only to provide for its external well-being and the conveniences of life, but still more to consult the welfare of men's souls in the wisdom of their legislation. But, for the increase of such benefits, nothing more suitable can be conceived than the laws which have God for their author; and, therefore, they who in their government of the State take no account of these laws, abuse political power by causing it to deviate from its proper end and from what nature itself prescribes. And, what is still more important, and what We have more than once pointed out, although the civil authority has not the same proximate end as the spiritual, nor proceeds on the same lines, nevertheless in the exercise of their separate powers they must occasionally meet. For their subjects are the same, and not infrequently they deal with the same objects, though in different ways. Whenever this occurs, since a state of conflict is absurd and manifestly repugnant to the most wise ordinance of God, there must necessarily exist some order or mode of procedure to remove the occasions of difference and contention, and to secure harmony in all things. This harmony has been not inaptly compared to that which exists between the body and the soul for the well-being of both one and the other, the separation of which brings irremediable harm to the body, since it extinguishes its very life. . . .

Justice therefore forbids, and reason itself forbids, the State to be godless; or to adopt a line of action which would end in godlessness—namely, to treat the various religions (as they call them) alike, and to bestow upon them promiscuously equal rights and privileges. Since, then, the profession of one religion is necessary in the State, that religion must be professed which alone is true, and which can be recognized without difficulty, especially in Catholic States, because the marks of truth are, as it were, engraven upon it. This religion, therefore, the rulers of the State must preserve and protect, if they would provide—as they should do—with prudence and usefulness for the good of the community. For public authority exists for the welfare of those whom it governs; and although its proximate end is to lead men to the prosperity found in this life, yet, in so doing, it ought not to diminish, but rather to increase, man's capability of attaining to the supreme good in which his everlasting happiness consists: which never can be attained if religion be disregarded. . . .

We must now consider briefly *liberty of speech*, and liberty of the press. It is hardly necessary to say that there can be no such right as this, if it be not used in moderation, and if it pass beyond the bounds and end of all true liberty. . . . Men have a right freely and prudently to propagate throughout the State what things soever are true and honorable, so that as many as possible may possess them; but lying opinions, than which no mental plague is greater, and vices which corrupt the heart and moral life, should be diligently repressed by public authority, lest they insidiously work the ruin of the State. The excesses of an unbridled intellect, which unfailingly end in the oppression of the untutored multitude, are no less rightly controlled by the authority of the law than are the injuries inflicted by violence upon the weak. . . .

From what has been said, it follows that it is quite unlawful to demand, to defend, or to grant unconditional freedom of thought, of speech, of writing, or of worship, as if these were so many rights given by nature to man. For if nature had really granted them, it would be lawful to refuse obedience to God, and there would be no restraint on human liberty. It likewise follows that freedom in these things may be tolerated wherever there is just cause; but only with such moderation as will prevent its degenerating into license and excess. And where such liberties are in use, men should employ them in doing good, and should estimate them as the Church does; for liberty is to be regarded as legitimate in so far only as it affords greater facility for doing good, but no farther.

Whenever there exists, or there is reason to fear, an unjust oppression of the people on the one hand, or a deprivation of the liberty of the Church on the other, it is lawful to seek for such a change of government as will bring about due liberty of action. In such case an excessive and vicious liberty is not sought for, but only some relief, for the common welfare, in order that, while license for evil is allowed by the State, the power of doing good may not be hindered.

Again, it is not of itself wrong to prefer a democratic form of government, if only the Catholic doctrine be maintained as to the origin and exercise of power. Of the various forms of government, the Church does not reject any that are fitted to procure the welfare of the subject; she wishes only—and this nature itself requires—that they should be constituted without involving wrong to any one, and especially without violating the rights of the Church. . . .

POPE JOHN XXIII

Mater et Magistra (1961)
(Mother and Teacher)

Economic Welfare and Socialization

First of all, it should be affirmed that the economic order is the creation of the personal initiative of private citizens themselves working either individually or in association with each other in various ways for the prosecution of common interests.

But . . . the public authorities must not remain inactive, if they are to promote in a proper way the productive development in behalf of social progress for the benefit of all the citizens. . . .

It cannot be denied that today the development of scientific knowledge and productive technology offers the public authorities concrete possibilities of reducing the inequality between the various sectors of production, between the various areas of political communities, and between the various countries themselves on a world-wide scale.

This development also puts it within their capability to control fluctuations in the economy and, with hope of success, to prevent the recurrence of massive unemployment.

Consequently, those in authority, who are responsible for the common good, feel the need not only to exercise in the field of economics a multiform action, at once more vast, more profound, more organic, but also it is required, for this same end, that they give themselves suitable structures, tasks, means and methods.

But the principle must always be reaffirmed that the presence of the state in the economic field, no matter how wide-spread and penetrating, must not be exercised so as to reduce evermore the sphere of freedom of the personal initiative of individual citizens, but rather so as to guarantee in that sphere the greatest possible scope by the effective protection for each and all of the essential personal rights, among which is to be numbered the right that individual persons possess of being always primarily responsible for their own upkeep and that of their own family, which implies that in the economic systems the free development of productive activities should be per-mitted and facilitated.

For the rest, historic evolution itself puts into relief ever more clearly that there cannot be a well-ordered and fruitful society without the support in the economic field both of the individual citizen and of the public authorities, a working together in harmony in the proportions corresponding to the needs of the common good in the changing situations and vicissitudes of human life.

Experience, in fact, shows that where the personal initiative of individuals is lacking, there is political tyranny but there is also stagnation in the economic sectors engaged in the pro-duction, especially of the wide range of consumer goods and of services which pertain, in addition to material needs, to the requirements of the spirit, goods and services which call into play in a special way the creative talents of individuals.

While, where the due services of the state are lacking or defective, there is incurable disorder and exploitation of the weak on the part of the unscrupulous strong who flourish in every land and, at all times, like the cockle among the wheat.

One of the typical aspects which characterize our epoch is socialization, understood as the progressive multiplication of relations in society, with different forms of life and activity, and juridical institutionalization.

This is due to many historical factors, among which must be numbered technical and scientific progress, a greater pro-ductive efficiency and a higher standard of living among citi-zens.

Socialization is, at one and the same time, an effect and a cause of growing intervention of the public authorities in even the most crucial matters, such as those concerning the care of health, and instruction and education of the younger genera-tion, and the controlling of professional careers and the meth-ods of care and rehabilitation of those variously handicapped, but it is also the fruit and expression of a natural tendency, almost irrepressible, in human beings—the tendency to join together to attain objectives which are beyond the capacity and means at the disposal of single individuals.

A tendency of this sort has given life, especially in these last decades, to a wide range of groups, movements, associations and institutions with economic, cultural, social, sporting, recreational, professional and political ends, both within single national communities and on an international level.

It is clear that socialization, so understood, brings many advantages. It makes possible, in fact, the satisfaction of many personal rights, especially those called economic-social, such as, for example, the right to the indispensable means of human maintenance, to health services, to instruction at a higher level, to a more thorough professional formation, to housing, to work, to suitable leisure, to recreation.

In addition, through the ever more perfect organization of the modern means for the diffusion of thought—press, cinema, radio, television—it is made possible for individuals to take part in human events in a world-wide scale.

At the same time, however, socialization multiplies the forms of organization and makes the juridical control of relations between men of every walk of life ever more detailed.

As a consequence, it restricts the range of the individual as regards his liberty of action and uses means, follows methods and creates an atmosphere which make it difficult for each one to think independently of outside influences, to work of his own initiative, to exercise his responsibility, to affirm and enrich his personality.

Ought it to be concluded, then, that socialization, growing in extent and depth, necessarily reduces men to automatons? It is a question which must be answered negatively.

For socialization is not to be considered as a product of natural forces working in a deterministic way. It is, on the contrary, as we have observed, a creation of men, beings conscious, free and intended by nature to work in a responsible way, even if in their so acting they are obliged to recognize and respect the laws of economic development and social progress and cannot escape from all the pressures of their environment.

Hence, we consider that socialization can and ought to be realized in such a way as to draw from it the advantages contained therein and to remove or restrain the negative aspects.

For this purpose, then, it is required that a sane view of the common good be present and operative in men invested with public authority, a view which is formed by all those social conditions which permit and favor for the human race the integral development of their personality.

Moreover, we consider necessary that the intermediary bodies and the numerous social enterprises in which above all socialization tends to find its expression and its activity, enjoy an effective autonomy in regard to the public authorities and pursue their own specific interests in loyal collaboration between themselves, subordinately, however, to the demands of the common good.

Aid to Underdeveloped Nations

Probably the most difficult problem of the modern world concerns the relationship between political communities that are economically advanced and those in the process of development.

The standard of living is high in the former, while in the latter countries poverty, and, in some cases, extreme poverty exists.

The solidarity which binds all men and makes them members of the same family imposes upon political communities enjoying abundance of material goods not to remain indifferent to those political communities whose citizens suffer from poverty, misery, and hunger, and who lack even the elementary rights of the human person.

This is the more so since, given the growing interdependence among the peoples of the earth, it is not possible to preserve lasting peace, if glaring economic and social inequality among them persists.

Mindful of our role of universal father, we feel obliged solemnly to stress what we have in another connection stated: We are all equally responsible for the undernourished peoples.

Therefore, it is necessary to educate one's conscience to the sense of responsibility which weighs upon each and everyone, especially upon those who are more blessed with this world's goods.

It is obvious that the obligation, which the Church has always taught, to help those who find themselves in want and misery, should be felt more strongly by Catholics, who find a most noble motive in the fact that we are all members of Christ's mystical body. . . .

We, therefore, see with satisfaction that those political communities enjoying high economic standards are providing assistance to political communities in the process of economic development in order that they may succeed in raising their standards of living. . . .

However, it is no less necessary and conformable to justice that the riches produced come to be equally distributed among all members of the political community: hence effort should be made that social progress proceed at the same pace as economic development.

This means that it be actuated, as far as possible, gradually and harmoniously in all productive sectors, in those of agriculture, industry, and services.

The political communities on the way towards economic development generally present their own unmistakable individuality, due either to their resources and the specific character of their own natural environment, or due to their traditions frequently abounding in human values, or due to the typical quality of their own members.

The economically developed political communities when lending their help must recognize and respect this individuality . . .

But the bigger temptation with which the economically developed political communities have to struggle is that of profiting from their technical and financial cooperation so as to influence the political situation of the less-developed countries with a view to bringing about plans of world domination.

If this takes place, it must be explicitly declared that it would be a new form of colonialism, which, however cleverly disguised, would not for all that be less blameworthy than that from which many peoples have recently escaped, and which would influence negatively their international relations, constituting a menace and danger to world peace.

And it is, therefore, indispensable and corresponds to the need of justice that the above-mentioned technical and financial aid be given in sincere political disinterestedness, for the purpose of putting those communities on the way to economic development, in a position to realize their own proper economic and social growth. . . .

Scientific and technical progress, economic development, the betterment of living conditions, are certainly positive elements in a civilization. But we must remember that they are not nor can they be considered the supreme values, in comparison with which values they are seen as essentially instrumental in character.

It is with sadness that we point out that in the economically developed countries there are not a few persons in whom the consciousness of the hierarchy of values is weakened, is dead, or confused that is, in whom the spiritual values are neglected, forgotten, denied while the progress of the sciences, of technology, the economic development, the material well-being are often fostered and proposed as the pre-eminent, and even elevated to the unique, reason of life.

This constitutes an insidious poison, and one of the most dangerous, in the work which the economically developed peoples can give to those on the way to development: people in whom ancient tradition has quite often preserved a living and operating consciousness of some of the most important human values.

To undermine this consciousness is essentially immoral. One must respect it and, where possible, clarify and develop it so that it will remain what it is: a foundation for true civilization.

Incomplete and Erroneous Ideologies

After all this scientific and technical progress, and even because of it, there remains the problem that the social relationships be reconstructed in a more human balance both in regard to individual political communities and on a world scale.

In the modern era, different ideologies have been devised and spread abroad with this in mind; some have been dissolved as clouds by the sun; others have undergone or are undergoing substantial changes; others have waned much and are losing still more their attraction on the minds of men.

The reason is that they are ideologies which consider only certain and less profound aspects of man, and this because they do not take into consideration certain inevitable human imperfections, such as sickness and suffering, imperfections which even the most advanced economical-social systems cannot eliminate. Then there is the profound and imperishable religious exigence which constantly expresses itself everywhere, even though trampled down by violence or skillfully smothered.

In fact, the most fundamental modern error is that of considering the religious demands of the human soul as an expression of feeling or of fantasy, or a product of some contingent event, and should be thus eliminated as an anachronism and an obstacle to human progress, whereas by this exigency human beings reveal themselves for what they really are: Beings created by God, and for God, as St. Augustine cries out: "You made us for Thee, o Lord, and our heart is restless until it rests in Thee."

Moreover, whatever the technical and economic progress, there will be neither justice nor peace in this world until men return to a sense of the dignity of creatures and sons of God, the just and final reason of the being of all reality created by him. Man separated from God becomes inhuman to himself and to those of his kind, because the orderly relation of society presupposes the orderly relation of one's conscience with God, fount of truth, of justice and of love.

It is true that the persecution of so many of our dearly beloved brothers and sons, which has been raging for decades in many countries, even those of an ancient Christian civilization, makes ever clearer to us the dignified superiority of the persecuted and the refined barbarity of the persecutors, so that, if it does not give visible signs of repentence, it induces many to think.

But it is always true that the most perniciously typical aspect of the modern era consists in the absurd attempt to reconstruct a solid and fruitful temporal order prescinding from God, the only foundation on which it can endure, and to want to celebrate the greatness of many by drying up the fount from which that greatness springs, and from which it is nourished and hence restraining, and if possible, extinguishing man's sighing for God. . . .

JACQUES MARITAIN
The Rights of Man and Natural Law

Man as a Person

. . . In each of us there dwells a mystery, and that mystery is the human personality. We know that an essential characteristic of any civilization worthy of the name is respect and feeling for the dignity of the human person. . . .

Whenever we say that a man is a person, we mean that he is more than a mere parcel of matter, more than an individual element in nature, such as is an atom, a blade of grass, a fly or an elephant. . . . Man is an animal and an individual, but unlike other animals or individuals. Man is an individual who holds himself in hand by his intelligence and his will. He exists not merely physically; there is in him a richer and nobler existence; he has spiritual superexistence through knowledge and through love. He is thus in some fashion a whole, not merely a part; he is a universe unto himself, a microcosm in which the whole great universe can be encompassed through knowledge; and through love he can give himself freely to beings who are, as it were, other selves to him. For this relationship no equivalent is to be found in the physical world. All this means in philosophical terms, that in the flesh and bones of man there lives a soul which is a spirit and which has a greater value than the whole physical universe. However dependent it may be on the slightest accidents of matter, the human person exists by virtue of the existence of its soul, which dominates time and death. It is the spirit which is the root of personality.

The notion of personality thus involves that of totality and independence; no matter how poor and crushed a person may be, as such he is a whole, and as a person, subsists in an independent manner. To say that a man is a person is to say that in the depth of his being he is more a whole than a part and more independent than servile. It is to this mystery of our nature that religious thought points when it says that the human person is the image of God. The worth of the person, his liberty, his rights, arise from the order of naturally sacred things, which bear upon them the imprint of the Father of Being, and which have in Him the goal of their movement. A person possesses absolute dignity because he is in direct relationship with the absolute, in which alone he can find his complete fulfillment. His spiritual fatherland consists of the entire order of things which have absolute value, and which reflect, in some way, an Absolute superior to the world and which draw our life towards this Absolute. . . .

The person is a whole, but it is not a closed whole, it is an *open* whole. It is not a little god without doors or windows, like Leibnitz's monad, or an idol which sees not, hears not, speaks not. It tends by its very nature to social life and to communion.

This is true not only because of the needs and the indigence of human nature, by reason of which each one of us has need of others for his material, intellectual and moral life, but also because of the radical generosity inscribed within the very being of the person, because of that openness to the communications of intelligence and love which is the nature of the spirit, and which demands an entrance into relationship with other persons. To state it rigorously, the person cannot be alone. . . .

Man is a political animal, which means that the human person craves political life, communal life, not only with regard to the family community, but with regard to the civil community. And the commonwealth, in so far as it deserves the name, is a society of human persons. . . .

The aim of society is its own *common good,* the good of the social body. But if we fail to grasp the fact that this good

of the social body is a common good of *human persons,* as
the social body itself is a whole made up of human persons,
this formula would lead in its turn to other errors, of a col-
lectivist type—or to a type of state despotism. The common
good of society is neither a mere collection of private goods,
nor the good proper to a whole, which . . . draws the parts to
itself alone, and sacrifices these parts to itself. It is the good
human life of the multitude, of a multitude of persons, the
good life of totalities at once carnal and spiritual, and princi-
pally spiritual, although they more often happen to live by the
flesh than by the spirit. The common good of society is their
communion in the good life; it is therefore common *to the
whole and to the parts,* to the parts, which are in themselves
wholes, since the very notion of *person* means totality; it is
common to the whole and to the parts, over which it flows
back and which must all benefit from it. Under pain of being
itself denatured, it implies and demands the recognition of the
fundamental rights of the person (and the rights of the family, in which persons are enmeshed in a more primitive way of
communal living than in political society). It involves, as its
chief value, the highest possible attainment (that is, the highest compatible with the good of the whole) of persons to their
lives as persons, and to their freedom of expansion or autonomy—and to the gifts of goodness which in their turn flow
from it. . . .

A person as such is a whole, open and generous. Indeed if
human society were a society of *pure persons,* the good of
society and the good of each person would be but one and the
same. Yet man is very far from being a pure person; the
human person is a poor, material individual, an animal born
more poverty-stricken than all other animals. Even though the
person, as such, is an independent whole, and that which is
noblest in all nature, the human person is at the lowest level
of personality, stripped and succorless; a person destitute and
full of needs. Because of these deep lacks and in accordance
with all the complements of being which spring from society
and without which the person would remain, as it were, in a
state of latent life, it happens that when a person enters into
the society of his fellows, he becomes a *part* of a whole larger
and better than its parts—a whole which transcends the person
in so far as the latter is a part of that whole—and whose common good is other than the good of each one and other than
the sum of the good of all. Nonetheless, it is by very reason
of *personality* as such, and of the perfections which it carries
with it, as an independent and open whole, that the human
person seeks to enter into society. . . .

Moreover, by reason of his relationship to the absolute, and to the extent that he is called to a life and a destiny superior to time—in other words, in accordance with the highest exigencies of the personality as such—the human person *transcends* all temporal societies and is superior to them. . . .

. . . it is to the perfect fulfillment of the person and of his supra-temporal aspirations that society itself and its common good are indirectly subordinate, as to an end of *another* order, which transcends them. A single human soul is of more worth than the whole universe of bodies and material goods. There is nothing above the human soul except God. In the light of the eternal value and absolute dignity of the soul, society exists for each person and is subordinate thereto. . . .

(Extracts from chapter 1.)

The Free Society

. . . the conception of society which I have outlined may be characterized by the following features: it is *personalist*, because it considers society to be a whole composed of persons whose dignity is anterior to society and who contain within their very being a root of independence and aspire to ever greater degrees of independence until they achieve that perfect spiritual liberty which no human society has within its gift.

This conception is, in the second place, *communal*, because it recognizes the fact that the person tends naturally towards society and communion, in particular towards the political community, and because . . . it considers the common good superior to that of individuals.

In the third place this conception is *pluralist*, because it assumes that the development of the human person normally requires a plurality of autonomous communities which have their own rights, liberties and authority; among these communities there are some of a rank inferior to the political state, which arise either from the fundamental exigencies of nature (as in the case of the family community) or else from the will of persons freely coming together to form diverse groups. Other communities are of a rank superior to the State, as is above all the Church in the mind of Christians, and as would also be, in the temporal Christians, and as would also be, in the temporal realm, that organized international community towards which we aspire today.

Finally the conception of society we are describing is *theist* or *Christian*, not in the sense that it would require every member of society to believe in God and to be Christian, but in the sense that it recognizes that in the reality of things,

God, principle and end of the human person and prime source of natural law, is by the same token the prime source of political society and authority among men; and in the sense that it recognizes that the currents of liberty and fraternity released by the Gospel, the virtues of justice and friendship sanctioned by it, the practical respect for the human person proclaimed by it, the feeling of responsibility before God required by it, as much from him who exercises the authority as from him who is subject to it, are the internal energy which civilization needs to achieve its fulfillment.

. . . Let us sum up those keynotes of a sane political society which we have encountered in the course of the preceding analyses, the common good flowing back over individuals; political authority leading free men towards this common good; intrinsic morality of the common good and of political life. Personalist, communal, and pluralist inspiration of the social organization; organic link between civil society and religion, without religious compulsion or clericalism, in other words, a truly, not decoratively, Christian society. Law and justice, civic friendship and the equality which it implies, as essential principles of the structure, life and peace of society. A common task inspired by the ideal of liberty and fraternity, tending, as its ultimate goal, towards the establishment of a brotherly city wherein the human being will be freed from servitude and misery. . . .

(Extracts from chapter 1.)

REINHOLD NIEBUHR

Moral Man and Immoral Society
and
The Children of Light and the Children of Darkness

Individual and Group Behavior

. . . a sharp distinction must be drawn between the moral and social behavior of individuals and of social groups, national, racial, and economic; and that this distinction justifies and necessitates political policies which a purely individualistic ethic must always find embarrassing. . . . Individual men may be moral in the sense that they are able to consider interests other than their own in determining problems of conduct, and are capable, on occasion, of preferring the advantages of others to their own. They are endowed by nature with a measure of sympathy and consideration for their kind, the breadth of which may be extended by an astute social pedagogy. Their rational faculty prompts them to a sense of justice which educational discipline may refine and purge of egoistic elements until they are able to view a social situation, in which their own interests are involved, with a fair measure of objectivity. But all these achievements are more difficult, if not impossible, for human societies and social groups. In every human group there is less reason to guide and to check impulse, less capacity for self-transcendence, less ability to comprehend the needs of others and therefore more unrestrained egoism than the individuals, who compose the group, reveal in their personal relationships.

The inferiority of the morality of groups to that of individuals is due in part to the difficulty of establishing a rational social force which is powerful enough to cope with the natural impulses by which society achieves its cohesion; but in part it is merely the revelation of a collective egoism, compounded of the egoistic impulses of individuals, which achieve more vivid expression and a more cumulative effect when they are united in a common impulse than when they express themselves separately and discreetly. . . .

The most persistent error of modern educators and moralists is the assumption that our social difficulties are due to the failure of the social sciences to keep pace with the physical sciences which have created our technological civilisation. The invariable implication of this assumption is that, with a little more time, a little more adequate moral and social pedagogy and a generally higher development of human intelligence, our social problems will approach solution. . . .

What is lacking among all these moralists, whether religious or rational, is an understanding of the brutal character of the behavior of all human collectives, and the power of self-interest and collective egoism in all intergroup relations. Failure to recognise the stubborn resistance of group egoism to all moral and inclusive social objectives inevitably involves them in unrealistic and confused political thought. They regard social conflict either as an impossible method of achieving morally approved ends or as a momentary expedient which a more perfect education or a purer religion will make unnecessary. They do not see that the limitations of the human imagination, the easy subservience of reason to prejudice and passion, and the consequent persistence of irrational egoism, particularly in group behavior, make social conflict an inevitability in human history, probably to its very end. . . .

Our contemporary culture fails to realise the power, extent and persistence of group egoism in human relations. It may be possible, though it is never easy, to establish just relations between individuals within a group purely by moral and rational suasion and accommodation. In inter-group relations this is practically an impossibility. The relations between groups must therefore always be predominantly political rather than ethical, that is, they will be determined by the proportion of power which each group possesses at least as much as by any rational and moral appraisal of the comparative needs and claims of each group. . . .

The inevitable hypocrisy, which is associated with all of the collective activities of the human race, springs chiefly from this source: that individuals have a moral code which makes the actions of collective man an outrage to their conscience. They therefore invent romantic and moral interpretations of the real facts, preferring to obscure rather than reveal the true character of their collective behavior. Sometimes they are as anxious to offer moral justifications for the brutalities from which they suffer as for those which they commit. The fact that the hypocrisy of man's group behavior . . . expresses itself not only in terms of self-justification but in terms of moral justification of human behavior in general, symbolises one of the tragedies of the human spirit: its inability to conform its collective life to its individual ideals. As individuals, men believe that they ought to love and serve each other and establish justice between each other. As racial, economic and national groups they take for themselves, whatever their power can command. . . .

Thus society is in a perpetual state of war. Lacking moral and rational resources to organise its life, without resort to coercion, except in the most immediate and intimate social groups, men remain the victims of the individuals, classes and nations by whose force a momentary coerced unity is achieved, and further conflicts are as certainly created. The fact that the coercive factor in society is both necessary and dangerous seriously complicates the whole task of securing both peace and justice. . . . Tolstoian pacifists and other advocates of nonresistance . . . give themselves to the vain illusion that it can be completely eliminated, and society organised upon the basis of anarchistic principles. Their conviction is an illusion, because there are definite limits of moral good will and social intelligence beyond which even the most vital religion and the most astute educational programme will not carry a social group, whatever may be possible for individuals in an intimate society. The problem which society faces is clearly one of reducing force by increasing the factors which make for a moral and rational adjustment of life to life;

of bringing such force as is still necessary under responsibility of the whole of society; of destroying the kind of power which cannot be made socially responsible (the power which resides in economic ownership for instance); and of bringing forces of moral self-restraint to bear upon types of power which can never be brought completely under social control. Every one of these methods has its definite limitations. . . .

(Extracts from *Moral Man and Immoral Society*, Introduction and Chapter 1.)

The Limits of Reason

In analysing the limits of reason in morality it is important to begin by recognising that the force of egoistic impulse is much more powerful than any but the most astute psychological analysts and the most rigorous devotees of introspection realise. If it is defeated on a lower or more obvious level, it will express itself in more subtle forms. If it is defeated by social impulse it insinuates itself into the social impulse, so that a man's devotion to his community always means the expression of a transferred egoism as well as of altruism. Reason may check egoism in order to fit it harmoniously into a total body of social impulse. But the same force of reason is bound to justify the egoism of the individual as a legitimate element in the total body of vital capacities, which society seeks to harmonise. . . . The utilitarian movement of the nineteenth century had the laudable purpose of persuading men to achieve a decent harmony between selfish and social impulse by diverting egoistic impulse to the most inclusive possible social objectives. It was significant that it merely provided the rising middle class with a nice moral justification for following its own interests. . . .

The very forces which lift man above nature give natural impulses a new and a more awful potency in the human world. Man fights his battles with instruments in which mind has sharpened nature's claws; and his ferocities are more sustained than those of the natural world, where they are prompted only by the moods and the necessities of the moment. . . . man's lusts are fed by his imagination, and he will not be satisfied until the universal objectives which the imagination envisages are attained. . . . he is governed more by imagination than by reason and imagination is compounded of mind and impulse.

The rational forces . . . seem weak indeed, when compared with the force arrayed against them. They are all the more inadequate for having no impartial perspective, from which to view, and no transcendent fulcrum, from which to affect human action. They always remain bound to the forces they are intended to discipline. The will-to-power uses reason, as kings use courtiers and chaplains to add grace to their enterprise. Even the most rational men are never quite rational when their own interests are at stake. . . .

This insinuation of the interests of the self into even the most ideal enterprises and most universal objectives . . . makes hypocrisy an inevitable by-product of all virtuous endeavor. It is, in a sense, a tribute to the moral nature of man as well as a proof of his moral limitations; for it is significant that men cannot pursue their own ends with the greatest devotion, if they are unable to attribute universal values to their particular objectives. But men are no more able to eliminate self-interest from their nobler pursuits than they are able to express it fully without hiding it behind and compounding it with honest efforts at or dishonest pretensions of universality. . . .

(Extract from *Moral Man and Immoral Society*, chapter 2.)

The Illusion of Secular Optimism

. . . democracy has a more compelling justification and requires a more realistic vindication than is given it by the liberal culture with which it has been associated in modern history. The excessively optimistic estimates of human nature and of human history with which the democratic credo has been historically associated are a source of peril to democratic society. . . . Man's capacity for justice makes democracy possible; but man's inclination to injustice makes democracy necessary. . . .

Our modern civilization was ushered in on a wave of boundless social optimism. Modern secularism is divided into many schools. But all the various schools agreed in rejecting the Christian doctrine of original sin. . . . the doctrine makes an important contribution to any adequate social and political theory the lack of which has robbed bourgeois theory of real wisdom; for it emphasizes a fact which every page of human history attests . . . [that] . . . there is no level of human moral or social achievement in which there is not some corruption of inordinate self-love.

This sober and true view of the human situation was neatly rejected by modern culture. That is why it conceived so many fatuous and futile plans for resolving the conflict between the self and the community; and between the national and the world community. Whenever modern idealists are confronted with the divisive and corrosive effects of man's self-love, they look for some immediate cause of this perennial tendency, usually in some specific form of social organization. One school holds that men would be good if only political institutions would not corrupt them; another believes that they would be good if the prior evil of a faulty economic organization could be eliminated. Or another school thinks of this evil as no more than ignorance, and therefore waits for a more perfect educational process to redeem man from his partial and particular loyalties. But no school asks how it is that an essentially good man could have produced corrupting and tyrannical political organizations or exploiting economic organizations, or fanatical and superstitious religious organizations.

The result of this persistent blindness to the obvious and tragic facts of man's social history is that democracy has had to maintain itself precariously against the guile and the malice of the children of darkness, while its statesmen and guides conjured up all sorts of abstract and abortive plans for the creation of perfect national and international communities. . . .

The conception of human nature which underlies the social and political attitudes of a liberal democratic culture is that of an essentially harmless individual. The survival impulse, which man shares with the animals, is regarded as the normative form of his egoistic drive. . . . But this survival impulse cannot be neatly disentangled from two forms of its spiritualization. The one form is the desire to fulfill the potentialities of life and not merely to maintain its existence. . . .

On the other hand the will-to-live is also spiritually transmuted into the will-to-power or into the desire for "power and glory." Man, being more than a natural creature, is not interested merely in physical survival but in prestige and social approval. Having the intelligence to anticipate the perils in which he stands in nature and history, he invariably seeks to gain security against these perils by enhancing his power, individually and collectively. Possessing a darkly unconscious sense of his insignificance in the total scheme of things, he seeks to compensate for his insignificance by pretensions of pride. . . .

Since the survival impulse in nature is transmuted into two different and contradictory spiritualized forms, which we may briefly designate as the will-to-live-truly and the will-to-power, man is at variance with himself. The power of the second impulse places him more fundamentally in conflict with his fellowman than democratic liberalism realizes.

. . . it becomes quite apparent that human ambitions, lusts

and desires, are more inevitably inordinate, that both human creativity and human evil reach greater heights, and that conflicts in the community between varying conceptions of the good and between competing expressions of vitality are of more tragic proportions than was anticipated in the basic philosophy which underlies democratic civilization. . . .

Consistent egotists would, of course, wreck any democratic process; for it requires some decent consideration of the needs of others. But some of the greatest perils to democracy arise from the fanaticism of moral idealists who are not conscious of the corruption of self-interest in their professed ideals. Democracy therefore requires something more than a religious devotion to moral ideals. It requires religious humility. Every absolute devotion to relative political ends (and all political ends are relative) is a threat to communal peace. But religious humility is no simple moral or political achievement. It springs only from the depth of a religion which confronts the individual with a more ultimate majesty and purity than all human majesties and values, and persuades him to confess: "Why callest thou me good? there is none good but one, that is, God." . . .

(Extract from *The Children of Light and the Children of Darkness*, Foreword, chapters 1 and 4.)

SECTION XIV

SOCIOLOGY, PSYCHOLOGY AND PLURALISM

Many have decried the absence or exhaustion of political theory in the contemporary word—the result of prosperity and the success of social legislation, the preoccupation with foreign affairs and the influence of logical positivism. Certainly there are notoriously few examples of contemporary systematic political philosophy which attempt to explain the whole of politics through generalizations about man or society. Yet there is a world elsewhere.

Even if Marxism has been the most widely-held ideology in the twentieth century, there has been no deficiency of individual political ideas. They have come from political theorists —Oakeshott's attacks on rationalistic misconceptions in politics, Leo Strauss's insistence on the proper nature of political philosophy and Walter Lippmann's argument for the public philosophy—and from the practitioners of politics, the result of fascism, Nazism and guided democracy. But they have also come from a variety of other fields: from sociology: Mannheim's sociology of knowledge, Mayo's concern with industrial relationships, Riesman's analysis of character and Whyte's organization man; from psychology: the Freudian school— Adler, Jung, Fromm; Lasswell and the behavioral school; from law: Pound's sociological jurisprudence and Kelsen's basic norm; from economics: Keynes' general theory and the neo-liberals—Hayek, Ropke and de Jouvenel; from mathematics: Wiener's cybernetics and Morgenstern's and Von Neumann's game theory; from philosophy: the analyses of the Vienna school, and of existentialism, the exponents of which have identified themselves variously with Nazism, religious liberalism, democratic socialism and neo-Marxism; from anthropology: Malinowski and Fraser; from history: Spengler, the self-styled Copernicus of historiography, and Toynbee; from literature: Proust's kaleidoscopic picture of society, Kafka's unsettling parables, the prophecies of Orwell and Huxley; and from business and public administration.

From this wealth of twentieth century political discussion, five writers have been chosen: Max Weber (1864–1920), Harold Laski (1893–1950), Joseph Schumpeter (1883–1950), Sebastian de Grazia (1917–) and John Rawls (1921–).

Max Weber, the most important sociologist of the twentieth century, was deeply involved in the practice of German politics, but always stressed the need for objectivity in the examination of social problems and for value-free empirical analysis. His lecture, *Politics as a Vocation,* outlined the desirable qualities—passion, responsibility and objectivity—of the man of politics.

In a variety of ways, Weber was concerned with the interrelationship between ideology, social structure and material interests. He showed the affinity between Calvinism and the spirit of capitalism. His studies of religions, Eastern and Western, showed that it was only Judaism, and its offspring, Christianity, that fostered the development of "economic rationality." Rationality was the basis and distinguishing characteristic of modern civilization, illustrated in capitalist economics, the application of science to human affairs and to bureaucracy. Bureaucracy was increasingly the basis of both public and private organization.

Weber's methodological approach was through the typology of institutions. The most desirable way to understand phenomena was through the ideal-type, which was not itself realistic description, but allowed such description to be formulated. He applied this method to the study of political power, and argued that there were three types of authority. Traditional authority was based on hereditary leadership; legal domination on objective law, accepted rules and bureaucracy; and charismatic leadership based on the magnetic personality of the leader and exerted in time of crisis, although it attempted to become routinized because of its instability. Weber was concerned with the analysis of bureaucracy—the inevitable by-product of capitalism and technology—which was based on rational organization of work and supervision. The ten criteria he suggested for the recruitment and functioning of a bureaucracy have had both theoretical and practical value.

Laski was the most articulate and influential British writer of the past generation. Precocious and versatile, a Jew who

had defied his father and renounced his religious upbringing,
he was the embodiment of the rebel, protesting against the
injustices and the evils of the economic and social system. His
complex intellectual inheritance, from individualism and liberalism, neo-idealism, democratic socialism, Marxism and his
Jewish ancestry, help account for the contradictions and
faulty logic in his work.

The young Laski was, with Ernest Barker and A. D. Lindsay, one of the chief exponents of political pluralism which
attacked the idea of sovereignty. The state was neither inevitably superior to other organizations, nor all-powerful. With
Maitland, Gierke and Figgis, he spoke of the personality of
groups, of authority as pluralistic, and of the inability of the
state to coerce if individuals or groups were prepared to resist.
As an individualist, he argued that the state had no claim to
automatic obedience, that individuals might be obliged to disobey if the state offended their conscience and that everyone
had a private section of experience which must be allowed to
become articulated.

Laski could never completely reconcile his socialism, which
became more sympathetic to Marxism after 1931 and the rise
of Hitler in 1933, with his strong individualism and liberalism. His treatment of freedom was ambiguous: at times, he
emphasized the absence of restraint, at other times, practicability of purpose. Sometimes he stressed the common
good; at other times, the value of private experience, the
development of personality and the dignity of man. His view
of the state changed. It became, not simply one association
among others which competed for approval, but the supreme
coercive power. As a socialist, he denounced the capitalist
system, argued that property must be related to duty, and held
that certain conditions—the right to work, reasonable wages,
economic democracy—must exist in any satisfactory society.

Schumpeter, in *Capitalism, Socialism and Democracy*
(1942), discussed the contributions of Marx as prophet, sociologist, economist and teacher. He praised Marx for his
thesis on the decline of capitalism, even though history had
disproved his prophecy of the "increasing misery" of the proletariat. Schumpeter built a model of the economic development of capitalism; like Marx, though for different reasons, he
argued the possibility of its decline.

The reason for capitalist expansion was the innovation of
entrepreneurs. This led to capitalist construction and the establishment of new firms seeking profit and financed by bank

credit. Firms followed the innovator until the initial gains were exhausted. As businesses repaid their bank loans, a process of deflation set in, with consequent readjustment of the economy and slumps. Capitalism was successful in increasing production, raising wages, providing social services and continually bringing new improvements. But it also meant vanishing opportunities for investment and change in industrial control, which shifted from the entrepreneur to the salaried executives, who were less enterprising.

Capitalism might fail for both economc and psychological reasons: partly because of the growing monopoly, lack of investment opportunity and reduction in innovation, but also because it created its own opposition. It even subsidized intellectuals who had no faith in the system—the stock exchange was a poor substitute for the Holy Grail. The very success of capitalism undermined the social institutions which protected it, and "inevitably" created conditions in which it would not be able to live. Socialism, on the other hand, might succeed because it was not handicapped by lack of profit and the profit mechanism. It could maintain its own rational costings and distribution of resources, and might have definite advantages such as the avoidance of the uncertainty of competition.

Schumpeter challenged the reality of the classic theory of democracy. He attempted to redefine democracy to mean, not the formulation by the people of opinions on political issues, but the production of a government responsible for making decisions.

Sebastian de Grazia in *The Political Community* suggests a systematic theory of the state from the psychological perspective. He argues that leadership is dependent on the beliefs of the generality of people not on an elite. Basic political concepts—state, ruler, citizen, law—are defined in terms of beliefs, and the cause and consequences of beliefs are related to their psychological function.

The psychological approach to politics, emerging from writers like Wallas, Lippmann and Lasswell, with antecedents in Bentham and Bagehot, has been deepened by advances in new branches of psychology such as psychiatry and psychoanalysis. It has been stimulated by a disenchantment by some over the preoccupation of traditional political philosophy with formal institutions of government and law and with moralizing about rights, duties and freedom.

The Political Community draws on anthropology, theology and sociology to try to bridge the gap between traditional political philosophy and the newer social science empiricism. It has influenced contemporary ideas of authority, alienation and identity, political psychology, socialization, and ideological factors in mental disorder and mass movements.

The argument that political philosophy was dead was dispelled by the appearance in 1971 of John Rawls' *A Theory of Justice*, an attempt at grand theory with its comprehensive discussion of the normative standards applicable to the idea of justice.

Arguing against the utilitarian position in which justice is the outcome of utility as well as against a purely intuitive view of ethics by which people have some source of knowledge or intuition that explains our moral judgments and the right way of life, Rawls bases his theory of justice on a social contract. Created from a hypothetical state of nature, the social contract is one in which people choose the principles without knowing their own natural abilities or positions in the social order.

The first requirement of a society that is rationally acceptable to its members is justice. The core of justice is fairness, and a theory of justice should provide an acceptable standard for a just distribution of social primary goods such as liberty, income, wealth and opportunity. Inequality in the distribution is permissable only if it improved the position of the worst-off social group, and liberty would be restricted only for the sake of greater liberty.

Rawls' work and his tight analysis of the principles governing a just social order has given rise to considerable discussion in the 1970s.

MAX WEBER

Politics as a Vocation
(from Wirtschaft und Gesellschaft)

The Types of Political Authority

When a question is said to be a 'political' question, when a cabinet minister or an official is said to be a 'political' official, or when a decision is said to be 'politically' determined, what is always meant is that interests in the distribution, maintenance, or transfer of power are decisive for answering the questions and determining the decision or the official's sphere of activity. He who is active in politics strives for power either as a means in serving other aims, ideal or egoistic, or as 'power for power's sake,' that is, in order to enjoy the prestige-feeling that power gives.

Like the political institutions historically preceding it, the state is a relation of men dominating men, a relation supported by means of legitimate (i.e. considered to be legitimate) violence. If the state is to exist, the dominated must obey the authority claimed by the powers that be. When and why do men obey? Upon what inner justifications and upon what external means does this domination rest?

To begin with, in principle, there are three inner justifications, hence basic *legitimations* of domination.

First, the authority of the 'eternal yesterday,' i.e. of the mores sanctified through the unimaginably ancient recognition and habitual orientation to conform. This is 'traditional' domination exercised by the patriarch and the patrimonial prince of yore.

There is the authority of the extraordinary and personal *gift of grace* (charisma), the absolutely personal devotion and personal confidence in revelation, heroism, or other qualities of individual leadership. This is 'charismatic' domination, as exercised by the prophet or—in the field of politics—by the elected war lord, the plebiscitarian ruler, the great demagogue, or the political party leader.

Finally, there is domination by virtue of 'legality,' by virtue of the belief in the validity of legal statute and functional 'competence' based on rationally created *rules*. In this case, obedience is expected in discharging statutory obligation. This is domination as exercised by the modern 'servant of the state' and by all those bearers of power who in this respect resemble him. . . .

. . . in asking for the 'legitimations' of obedience, one meets with these three 'pure' types: 'traditional,' 'charismatic,' and 'legal.' . . .

Here we are interested above all in the second of these types: domination by virtue of the devotion of those who obey the purely personal 'charisma' of the 'leader.' For this is the root of the idea of a *calling* in its highest expression.

Devotion to the charisma of the prophet, or the leader in war, or to the great demagogue in the *ecclesia* or in parliament, means that the leader is personally recognized as the innerly 'called' leader of men. Men do not obey him by virtue of tradition or statute, but because they believe in him. If he is more than a narrow and vain upstart of the moment, the leader lives for his cause and 'strives for his work.' The devotion of his disciples, his followers, his personal party friends is oriented to his person and to its qualities.

Charismatic leadership has emerged in all places and in all historical epochs. Most importantly in the past, it has emerged in the two figures of the magician and the prophet on the one hand, and in the elected war lord, the gang leader and *condottierre* on the other hand. *Political* leadership in the form of the free 'demagogue' who grew from the soil of the city state is of greater concern to us; like the city state, the demagogue is peculiar to the Occident and especially to Mediterranean culture. Furthermore, political leadership in the form of the parliamentary 'party leader' has grown on the soil of the constitutional state, which is also indigenous only to the Occident.

These politicians by virtue of a 'calling' . . . are of course nowhere the only decisive figures in the cross-currents of the political struggle for power. The sort of auxiliary means that are at their disposal is also highly decisive. . . .

The administrative staff, which externally represents the organization of political domination, is, of course, like any other organization, bound by obedience to the power-holder and not alone by the concept of legitimacy. . . . There are two other means, both of which appeal to personal interests: material reward and social honor. The fiefs of vassals, the prebends of patrimonial officials, the salaries of modern civil servants, the honor of knights, the privileges of estates, and the honor of the civil servant comprise their respective wages. The fear of losing them is the final and decisive basis for solidarity between the executive staff and the power-holder. . . .

Either politics can be conducted 'honorifically' by 'independent,' that is, by wealthy, men, and especially by rentiers. Or, political leadership is made accessible to propertyless men who must then be rewarded. The professional politician who lives 'off' politics may be a pure 'prebendary' or a salaried 'official.' Then the politician receives either income from fees and perquisites for specific services—tips and bribes are only an irregular and formally illegal variant of this category of income —or a fixed income in kind, a money salary, or both. He may assume the character of an 'entrepreneur,' like the *condottiere* or the holder of a farmed-out or purchased office, or like the American boss who considers his costs a capital investment which he brings to fruition through exploitation of his influence. Again, he may receive a fixed wage, like a journalist, a party secretary, a modern cabinet minister, or a political official. . . . For loyal services today, party leaders give offices of all sorts—in parties, newspapers, co-operative societies, health insurance, municipalities, as well as in the state. *All* party struggles are struggles for the patronage of office, as well as struggles for objective goals. . . .

Politics and Ethics

. . . the career of politics grants a feeling of power. The knowledged of influencing men, of participating in power over them, and above all, the feeling of holding in one's hands a nerve fiber of historically important events can elevate the professional politician above everyday routine even when he is placed in formally modest positions. . . .

One can say that three pre-eminent qualities are decisive for the politician: passion, a feeling of responsibility, and a sense of proportion.

This means passion in the sense of *matter-of-factness,* of passionate devotion to a 'cause,' to the god or demon who is its overlord. It is not passion in the sense of that inner bearing which . . . Georg Simmel used to designate as 'sterile excitation.' . . .

To be sure, mere passion, however genuinely felt, is not enough. It does not make a politician, unless passion as devotion to a 'cause' also makes responsibility to this cause the guiding star of action. And for this, a sense of proportion is needed. This is the decisive psychological quality of the politician: his ability to let realities work upon him with inner concentration and calmness. Hence his *distance* to things and men. 'Lack of distance' *per se* is one of the deadly sins of every politician. . . . For the problem is simply how can warm passion and a cool sense of proportion be forged together in one and the same soul? Politics is made with the head, not with other parts of the body or soul. And yet devotion to politics, if it is not to be frivolous intellectual play but rather genuinely human conduct, can be born and nourished from passion alone. However, that firm taming of the soul, which distinguishes the passionate politician and differentiates him from the 'sterilely excited' and mere political dilettante, is possible only through habituation to detachment in every sense of the word. The 'strength' of a political 'personality' means, in the first place, the possession of these qualities of passion, responsibility, and proportion.

Therefore, daily and hourly, the politician inwardly has to overcome a quite trivial and all-too-human enemy: a quite vulgar vanity, the deadly enemy of all matter-of-fact devotion to a cause, and of all distance, in this case, of distance towards one's self. . . .

The sin against the lofty spirit of his vocation, however, begins where this striving for power ceases to be *objective* and becomes purely personal self-intoxication, instead of exclusively entering the service of 'the cause.' For ultimately there are only two kinds of deadly sins in the field of politics: lack of objectivity and—often but not always identical with it—irresponsibility. . . . [The politician's] lack of objectivity tempts him to strive for the glamorous semblance of power rather than for actual power. His irresponsibility, however, suggests that he enjoy power merely for power's sake without a substantive purpose. . . . The mere 'power politician' may get strong effects, but actually his work leads nowhere and is senseless. . . . It is a product of a shoddy and superficially blasé attitude towards the meaning of human conduct; and it has no relation whatsoever to the knowledge of tragedy with which all action, but especially political action, is truly interwoven.

The final result of political action often, no, even regularly, stands in completely inadequate and often even paradoxical relation to its original meaning. . . . But because of this fact, the serving of a cause must not be absent if action is to have inner strength. . . . The politician may serve national, humanitarian, social, ethical, cultural, worldly, or religious ends. . . . He may claim to stand in the service of an 'idea' or, rejecting this in principle, he may want to serve external ends of everyday life. However, some kind of faith must always exist. Otherwise, it is absolutely true that the curse of the creature's worthlessness overshadows even the externally strongest political successes. . . .

. . . what relations do ethics and politics actually have? Have the two nothing whatever to do with one another? Or, is the reverse true: that the ethic of political conduct is identical with that of any other conduct? Occasionally an exclusive choice has been believed to exist between the two propositions —either the one or the other proposition must be correct. But is it true that any ethic of the world could establish commandments of identical content for erotic, business, familial, and official relations; for the relations to one's wife, to the green-grocer, the son, the competitor, the friend, the defendant? Should it really matter so little for the ethical demands on politics that politics operates with very special means, namely, power backed up by *violence?* Do we not see that the Bolshevik and the Spartacist ideologists bring about exactly the same results as any militaristic dictator just because they use this political means? . . . the adversaries, in complete subjective sincerity, claim, in the very same way, that their ultimate intentions are of lofty character. . . .

. . . all ethically oriented conduct may be guided by one of two fundamentally differing and irreconcilably opposed maxims: conduct can be oriented to an 'ethic of ultimate ends' or to an 'ethic of responsibility.' This is not to say that an ethic of ultimate ends is identical with irresponsibility, or that an ethic of responsibility is identical with unprincipled opportunism. . . . However, there is an abysmal contrast between conduct that follows the maxim of an ethic of ultimate ends—that is, in religious terms, 'The Christian does rightly and leaves the results with the Lord'—and conduct that follows the maxim of an ethic of responsibility, in which case one has to give an account of the foreseeable results of one's action.

You may demonstrate to a convinced syndicalist, believing in an ethic of ultimate ends, that his action will result in increasing the opportunities of reaction, in increasing the oppression of his class, and obstructing its ascent—and you will not make the slightest impression upon him. If an action of good intent leads to bad results, then, in the actor's eyes, not he but the world, or the stupidity of other men, or God's will who made them thus, is responsible for the evil. However a man who believes in an ethic of responsibility takes account of precisely the average deficiencies of people . . . he will say: these results are ascribed to my action. The believer in an ethic of ultimate ends feels 'responsible' only for seeing to it that the flame of pure intentions is not quelched: for example, the flame of protesting against the injustice of the social order. To rekindle the flame ever anew is the purpose of his quite irrational deeds, judged in view of their possible success. . . .

No ethics in the world can dodge the fact that in numerous instances the attainment of 'good' ends is bound to the fact that one must be willing to pay the price of using morally dubious means or at least dangerous ones—and facing the possibility or even the probability of evil ramifications. From no ethics in the world can it be concluded when and to what extent the ethically good purpose 'justifies' the ethically dangerous means and ramifications. The decisive means for politics is violence. . . .

The ethic of ultimate ends apparently must go to pieces on the problem of the justification of means by ends. . . . logically it has only the possibility of rejecting all action that employs morally dangerous means—in theory! In the world of realities, as a rule, we encounter the ever-renewed experience that the adherent of an ethic of ultimate ends suddenly turns into a chiliastic prophet. Those, for example, who have just preached 'love against violence' now call for the use of force for the *last* violent deed, which would then lead to a state of affairs in which *all* violence is annihilated. . . . The proponent of an ethic of absolute ends cannot stand up under the ethical irrationality of the world. He is a cosmic-ethical 'rationalist.' . . .

Whoever wants to engage in politics at all, and especially in politics as a vocation, has to realize these ethical paradoxes. He must know that he is responsible for what may become of himself under the impact of these paradoxes. . . . He lets himself in for the diabolic forces lurking in all violence. The great *virtuosi* of acosmic love of humanity and goodness, whether stemming from Nazareth or Assisi or from Indian royal castles, have not operated with the political means of violence. Their kingdom was 'not of this world' and yet they worked and still work in this world. . . . He who seeks the salvation of the soul, of his own and of others, should not seek it along the avenue of politics, for the quite different tasks of politics can only be solved by violence. The genius or demon of politics lives in an inner tension with the god of love, as well as with the Christian God as expressed by the church. This tension can at any time lead to an irreconcilable conflict. . . .

Everything that is striven for through political action operating with violent means and following an ethic of responsibility endangers the 'salvation of the soul.' If, however, one chases after the ultimate good in a war of beliefs, following a pure ethic of absolute ends, then the goals may be damaged and discredited for generations, because responsibility for *consequences* is lacking. . . .

Surely, politics is made with the head, but it is certainly not made with the head alone. In this the proponents of an ethic of ultimate ends are right. One cannot prescribe to anyone whether he should follow an ethic of absolute ends or an ethic of responsibility, or when the one and when the other. . . . it is immensely moving when a *mature* man—no matter whether old or young in years—is aware of a responsibility for the consequences of his conduct and really feels such responsibility with heart and soul. He then acts by following an ethic of responsibility and somewhere he reaches the point where he says: 'Here I stand; I can do no other.' That is something genuinely human and moving. And every one of us who is not spiritually dead must realize the possibility of finding himself at some time in that position. In so far as this is true, an ethic of ultimate ends and an ethic of responsibility are not absolute contrasts but rather supplements, which only in unison constitute a genuine man—a man who *can* have the 'calling for politics.' . . .

Politics is a strong and slow boring of hard boards. It takes both passion and perspective. Certainly all historical experience confirms the truth—that man would not have attained the possible unless time and again he had reached out for the impossible. But to do that a man must be a leader, and not only a leader but a hero as well, in a very sober sense of the word. And even those who are neither leaders nor heroes must arm themselves with that steadfastness of heart which can brave even the crumbling of all hopes. This is necessary right now, or else men will not be able to attain even that which is possible today. Only he has the calling for politics who is sure that he shall not crumble when the world from his point of view is too stupid or too base for what he wants to offer. Only he who in the face of all this can say 'In spite of all!' has the calling for politics. . . .

Charismatic Authority

The provisioning of all demands that go beyond those of everyday routine has had, in principle, an entirely heterogeneous, namely, a *charismatic*, foundation; the further back we look in history, the more we find this to be the case. This means that the 'natural' leaders—in times of psychic, physical, economic, ethical, religious, political distress—have been neither officeholders nor incumbents of an 'occupation' in the present sense of the word, that is, men who have acquired expert knowledge and who serve for remuneration. The natural leaders in distress have been holders of specific gifts of the body and spirit; and these gifts have been believed to be supernatural, not accessible to everybody. The concept of 'charisma' is here used in a completely 'value-neutral' sense. . . .

In contrast to any kind of bureaucratic organization of offices, the charismatic structure knows nothing of a form or of an ordered procedure of appointment or dismissal. It knows no regulated 'career,' 'advancement,' 'salary,' or regulated and expert training of the holder of charisma or of his aids. It knows no agency of control or appeal, no local bailiwicks or exclusive functional jurisdictions; nor does it embrace permanent institutions like our bureaucratic 'departments,' which are independent of persons and of purely personal charisma.

Charisma knows only inner determination and inner restraint. The holder of charisma seizes the task that is adequate for him and demands obedience and a following by virtue of his mission. His success determines whether he finds them. His charismatic claim breaks down if his mission is not recognized by those to whom he feels he has been sent. If they recognize him, he is their master—so long as he knows how to maintain recognition through 'proving' himself. But he does not derive his 'right' from their will, in the manner of an election. Rather, the reverse holds: it is the *duty* of those to whom he addresses his mission to recognize him as their charismatically qualified leader. . . .

Charisma can be, and of course regularly is, qualitatively particularized. This is an internal rather than an external affair, and results in the qualitative barrier of the charisma holder's mission and power. In meaning and in content the mission may be addressed to a group of men who are delimited locally, ethnically, socially, politically, occupationally, or in some other way. If the mission is thus addressed to a limited group of men, as is the rule, it finds its limits within their circle.

In its economic sub-structure, as in everything else, charismatic domination is the very opposite of bureaucratic domination. . . . Charismatic political heroes seek booty and, above all, gold. But charisma, and this is decisive, always rejects as undignified any pecuniary gain that is methodical and rational. In general, charisma rejects all rational economic conduct.

The sharp contrast between charisma and any 'patriarchal' structure that rests upon the ordered base of the 'household' lies in this rejection of rational economic conduct. . . . It is the opposite of all ordered economy. It is the very force that disregards economy. This also holds, indeed precisely, where the charismatic leader is after the acquisition of goods, as is the case with the charismatic warrior hero. Charisma can do this because by its very nature it is not an 'institutional' and permanent structure, but rather, where its 'pure' type is at work, it is the very opposite of the institutionally permanent.

In order to do justice to their mission, the holders of charisma, the master as well as his disciples and followers, must stand outside the ties of this world, outside of routine occupations, as well as outside the routine obligations of family life. . . .

By its very nature, the existence of charismatic authority is specifically unstable. The holder may forego his charisma; he may feel 'forsaken by his God,' as Jesus did on the cross; he may prove to his followers that 'virtue is gone out of him.' It is then that his mission is extinguished, and hope waits and searches for a new holder of charisma. The charismatic holder is deserted by his following, however, (only) because pure charisma does not know any 'legitimacy' other than that flowing from personal strength, that is, one which is constantly being proved. The charismatic hero does not deduce his authority from codes and statutes, as is the case with the jurisdiction of office; nor does he deduce his authority from traditional custom or feudal vows of faith, as is the case with patrimonial power.

The charismatic leader gains and maintains authority solely by proving his strength in life. If he wants to be a prophet, he must perform miracles; if he wants to be a war lord, he must perform heroic deeds. Above all, however, his divine mission must 'prove' itself in that those who faithfully surrender to him must fare well. If they do not fare well, he is obviously not the master sent by the gods.

This very serious meaning of genuine charisma evidently stands in radical contrast to the convenient pretensions of present rulers to a 'divine right of kings,' with its reference to the 'inscrutable' will of the Lord, 'to whom alone the monarch is responsible.' The genuinely charismatic ruler is responsible precisely to those whom he rules. He is responsible for but one thing, that he personally and actually be the God-willed master. . . .

The subjects may extend a more active or passive 'recognition' to the personal mission of the charismatic master. His power rests upon this purely factual recognition and springs from faithful devotion. It is devotion to the extraordinary and unheard-of, to what is strange to all rule and tradition and which therefore is viewed as divine. It is a devotion born of distress and enthusiasm.

Genuine charismatic domination therefore knows of no abstract legal codes anl statutes and of no 'formal' way of adjudication. Its 'objective' law emanates concretely from the highly personal experience of heavenly grace and from the god-like strength of the hero. Charismatic domination means a rejection of all ties to any external order in favor of the exclusive glorification of the genuine mentality of the prophet and hero. Hence, its attitude is revolutionary and transvalues everything; it makes a sovereign break with all traditional or rational norms: 'It is written, but I say unto you.'

The specifically charismatic form of settling disputes is by way of the prophet's revelation, by way of the oracle, or by way of 'Solomonic' arbitration by a charismatically qualified sage. This arbitration is determined by means of strictly concrete and individual evaluations, which, however, claim absolute validity. . . .

Genuinely charismatic justice always acts in this manner. In its pure form it is the polar opposite of formal and traditional bonds, and it is just as free in the face of the sanctity of

tradition as it is in the face of any rationalist deductions from
abstract concepts. . . .

(Extract from *Wirtschaft und Gesellschaft,* Part III, chapter 9.)

LASKI

The Foundations of Sovereignty (1921)
and
Studies in the Problem of Sovereignty (1917)

The Illusion of Sovereignty

It is our fashion to make of political theory the search for
that ultimate unity of interest which the ideal purpose of the
state suggests may one day be found. It is at least permissible
to doubt whether the unity so postulated is more, at least thus
far in history, than a fantastic dream. The idealist philosophy
may tell us that the "pure" instance only is important. The
difficulty yet is that the variations with which practice must
reckon make the "pure" instance at best of doubtful application. . . . For the fact surely is that those who possess the
engines of power will, for the most part, tend to regard their
private good as identical with the general good. That is, in
fact, contrary to much of the evidence we possess. At the best,
it equates the intention to do good with the achievement of
good itself. It is yet not enough, as Plato again and again
insisted, to will what is right; it is also necessary to know what
it is right to will. Whatever theory may say, an analysis of the
modern state reveals it as a complex of interests between
which there is no necessary or even predominant harmony. . . .
The social interests which are translated into legal rights are
almost always the rights of a limited group of men.

This, indeed, does no more than indicate the general nature
of the problem. Perhaps, also, it suggests a method of approach to social questions which, if less metaphysically exact
than such analyses as those of Green and Bosanquet, would,
if rightly used, lead to results of more practical character. In
the analysis of political problems the starting-point of inquiry
is the relation between the government of a state and its
subjects. For the lawyer, all that is immediately necessary is a
knowledge of the authorities that are legally competent to deal
with the problems that arise. For him, then, the idea of sovereignty has a particular and definite meaning. It does not
matter that an act is socially harmful or unpopular or morally
wrong; if it issues from the authority competent to act, and is

issued in due form, he has, from the legal stand-point, no further problems.

For political philosophy, on the other hand, legal competence is no more than a contingent index to the facts it needs. The political philosopher is concerned with the discovery of motives, the measure of wills, the balance of interests. It is important for him that an act, in theory the will of Parliament, is in fact the will of a subordinate official in the Colonial office. He cannot neglect the implications of the perversion of a legislature to selfish ends by a criminal adventurer like Tweed. The sovereignty of Parliament will interest him as a legal instrument, but its workings he will have to view in the light of the numerous defeats it has suffered.

He will, in fact, be driven to the perception that, politically, there is no such thing as sovereignty at all. He will find himself, rather, in the presence of different wills, some of which, from their strength, have more importance than others. He will ascribe to none a moral pre-eminence by the mere reason that it claims political priority. He will be satisfied simply with the ascription to these wills of a power which is never constant and rarely capable of prophetic announcement.

. . . the legal theory of sovereignty can never offer a basis for a working philosophy of the state. For a legal theory of sovereignty takes its stand upon the beatification of order; and it does not inquire—it is not its business to inquire—into the purposes for which order is maintained. The foundations of sovereignty must strike deeper roots if they are to give us a true philosophy. Above all we shall need inquiry into the psychological impulses it is the business of social organization to satisfy. The instruments with which we work bear upon their face the marks of a crisis in which men sought at all costs release from the misery of religious difference. They do not suit a temper in which the development of initiative in the humble man is the main effort of the time. The liberty they gained was specialized to the epoch in which the recognition of difference was possible without material consequence to individual personality. Since at least the Industrial Revolution that day has passed. The main effort is in a direction which challenges the legal rights established by prescription in the name of an equality for which our institutions are unsuited. The implied corollary of our purpose is the widespread distribution of power. It will need a new philosophy of the state to satisfy the institutions that purpose will demand.

(Extracts from *The Foundations of Sovereignty*, chapter 1.)

The Pluralistic State

The pluralistic theory of the State . . . is what Dewey calls 'consistently experimentalist,' in form and content. It denies the rightness of force. It dissolves . . . the inherent claim of the State to obedience. . . . It sets group competing against group in a ceaseless striving of progressive expansion. . . . It makes claim of the member of the State that he undertake ceaseless examination of its moral foundations. . . . It predicates no certainty, because history . . . does not repeat itself. It recognizes the validity of all wills to exist and argues no more than that in their conflict men should give their allegiance to that which is possessed of superior moral purpose. It is in fact an individualistic theory of the State—no pluralistic attitude can avoid that. But it is individualistic only in so far as it asks of man that he should be a social being . . . at all. His personality, for him the most real of all things, is sacrificed to an idol which the merest knowledge of history would prove to have feet of clay.

I am well enough aware that in any such voluntarism as this, room is left for a hint of anarchy. To discredit the State seems like enough to dethroning it. And when the voice of the State is viewed as the deliberate expression of public opinion it seems like the destruction of the one uniquely democratic basis we have. . . . But this objection . . . assumes the homogeneity of public opinion. . . . Nor is the absence of such homogeneity a defect. On the contrary, it seems to me that it is essentially a sign that real thought is present. . . . This is to postulate a State far from uniquely sovereign, since on occasion it will not prevail as on occasion it may not be right.

I imagine the absolute Hobbes, who has seen internal dissension tear a great kingdom in pieces, hold up hands of horror at such division of power. Maybe I who write in a time when the State enjoys its beatification can sympathise but too little with that prince of monistic thinkers. And the reason is simple enough. It is from the selection of variations, not from the preservation of uniformities, that progress is born. We do not want to make our State a cattle-yard in which only the shepherd shall know one beast from another. Rather we may hope to bring from the souls of men and women their richest fruition. If they have intelligence we shall ask its application to our problems. If they have courage we shall ask the aid of its compelling will. We shall make the basis of our State consent to disagreement. Therein shall we ensure its deepest harmony.

(Extract from *Studies in the Problem of Sovereignty,* chapter 1.)

The False Claim to Unlimited Authority

. . . That government is the most important of institutions few, except theocrats, could be found to deny; but that its importance warrants the monistic assumption herein implied raises far wider questions. The test, I would urge, is not an *a priori* statement of claim. Nothing has led us farther on the wrong path than the simple teleological terms in which Aristotle stated his conclusions. For when we say that political institutions aim at the good life, we need to know not only the meaning of good, but also those who are to achieve it, and the methods by which it is to be attained. What, in fact, we have to do is to study the way in which this monistic theory has worked; for our judgment upon it must depend upon consequences to the mass of men and women. . . . It is worth while to bear in mind that this worship of state-unity is almost entirely the offspring of the Reformation and therein, most largely, an adaptation of the practice of the medieval church. The fear of variety was not, in its early days, an altogether unnatural thing. Challenged from within and from without, uniformity seemed the key to self-preservation. But when the internal history of the state is examined, its supposed unity of purpose and of effort sinks, with acquaintance, into nothingness. What in fact confronts us is a complex of interests; and between not few of them ultimate reconciliation is impossible. . . . Historically, we always find that any system of government is dominated by those who at the time wield economic power; and what they mean by "good" is, for the most part, the preservation of their own interests. . . .

It thus seems that we have a twofold problem. The monistic state is an hierarchical structure in which power is, for ultimate purposes, collected at a single centre. The advocates of pluralism are convinced that this is both administratively incomplete and ethically inadequate. You will observe that I have made no reference here to the lawyer's problem. Nor do I deem it necessary; for when we are dealing, as the lawyer deals, with sources of ultimate reference, the questions are no more difficult, perhaps I should also add, no easier, than those arising under the conflict of jurisdictions in a federal state. . . .

I have spoken of the desire for genuine responsibility and the direction in which it may be found for administrative purposes. To this aspect the ethical side of political pluralism stands in the closest relation. Fundamentally, it is a denial that a law can be explained merely as a command of the sovereign for the simple reason that it denies, ultimately, the sovereignty of anything save right conduct. The philosophers since, particularly, the time of T. H. Green, have told us insistently that the state is based upon will; though they have too little examined the problem of what will is most likely to receive obedience. With history behind us, we are compelled to conclude that no such will can by definition be a good will; and the individual must therefore, whether by himself or in concert with others, pass judgment upon its validity by examining its substance. That, it is clear enough, makes an end of the sovereignty of the state in its classical conception. It puts the state's acts—practically, as I have pointed out, the acts of its primary organ, government—on a moral parity with the acts of any other association. . . . It therefore becomes a moral duty on our part to examine the foundations of state-action. The last sin in politics is unthinking acquiescence in important decisions. . . .

(Extract from *The Foundations of Sovereignty*, chapter 7.)

SCHUMPETER

Capitalism, Socialism and Democracy

Competition for Political Leadership

. . . our chief troubles about the classical theory centered in the proposition that "the people" hold a definite and rational opinion about every individual question and that they give effect to this opinion—in a democracy—by choosing "representatives" who will see to it that that opinion is carried out. Thus the selection of the representatives is made secondary to the primary purpose of the democratic arrangement which is to vest the power of deciding political issues in the electorate. Suppose we reverse the roles of these two elements and make the deciding of issues by the electorate secondary to the election of the men who are to do the deciding. To put it differently, we now take the view that the role of the people is to produce a government, or else an intermediate body which in turn will produce a national executive or government. And we define: the democratic method is that institutional arrangement for arriving at political decisions in which individuals acquire the power to decide by means of a competitive struggle for the people's vote.

Defense and explanation of this idea will speedily show that, as to both plausibility of assumptions and tenability of propositions, it greatly improves the theory of the democratic process.

First of all, we are provided with a reasonably efficient criterion by which to distinguish democratic governments from others. . . . the classical theory meets with difficulties on that score because both the will and the good of the people may be, and in many historical instances have been, served just as well or better by governments that cannot be described as democratic according to any accepted usage of the term. Now we are in a somewhat better position partly because we are resolved to stress a *modus procedendi* the presence or absence of which it is in most cases easy to verify.

For instance, a parliamentary monarchy like the English one fulfills the requirements of the democratic method because the monarch is practically constrained to appoint to cabinet office the same people as parliament would elect. A "constitutional" monarchy does not qualify to be called democratic because electorates and parliaments, while having all the other rights that electorates and parliaments have in parliamentary monarchies, lack the power to impose their choice as to the governing committee: the cabinet ministers are in this case servants of the monarch, in substance as well as in name, and can in principle be dismissed as well as appointed by him. Such an arrangement may satisfy the people. The electorate may reaffirm this fact by voting against any proposal for change. The monarch may be so popular as to be able to defeat any competition for the supreme office. But since no machinery is provided for making this competition effective the case does not come within our definition.

Second, the theory embodied in this definition leaves all the room we may wish to have for a proper recognition of the vital fact of leadership. The classical theory did not do this but . . . attributed to the electorate an altogether unrealistic degree of initiative which practically amounted to ignoring leadership. But collectives act almost exclusively by accepting leadership—this is the dominant mechanism of practically any collective action which is more than a reflex. Propositions about the working and the results of the democratic method that take account of this are bound to be infinitely more realistic than propositions which do not. They will not stop at the execution of a *volonté générale* but will go some way toward showing how it emerges or how it is substituted or faked. What we have termed Manufactured Will is no longer outside the theory, an aberration for the absence of which we piously pray; it enters on the ground floor as it should.

Third, however, so far as there are genuine group-wise volitions at all—for instance the will of the unemployed to receive unemployment benefit or the will of other groups to help—our theory does not neglect them. On the contrary we are now able to insert them in exactly the role they actually play. Such volitions do not as a rule assert themselves directly. Even if strong and definite they remain latent, often for decades, until they are called to life by some political leader who turns them into political factors. This he does, or else his agents do it for him, by organizing these volitions, by working them up and by including eventually appropriate items in his competitive offering. The interaction between sectional interests and public opinion and the way in which they produce the pattern we call the political situation appear from this angle in a new and much clearer light.

Fourth, our theory is of course no more definite than is the concept of competition for leadership. This concept presents similar difficulties as the concept of competition in the economic sphere, with which it may be usefully compared. In economic life competition is never completely lacking, but hardly ever is it perfect. Similarly, in political life there is always some competition, though perhaps only a potential one, for the allegiance of the people. To simplify matters we have restricted the kind of competition for leadership which is to define democracy, to free competition for a free vote. The justification for this is that democracy seems to imply a recognized method by which to conduct the competitive struggle, and that the electoral method is practically the only one available for communities of any size. But though this excludes many ways of securing leadership which should be excluded, such as competition by military insurrection, it does not exclude the cases that are strikingly analogous to the economic phenomena we label "unfair" or "fraudulent" competition or restraint of competition. And we cannot exclude them because if we did we should be left with a completely unrealistic ideal. Between this ideal case which does not exist and the cases in which all competition with the established leader is prevented by force, there is a continuous range of variation within which the democratic method of government shades off into the autocratic one by imperceptible steps. But if we wish to understand and not to philosophize, this is as it should be. The value of our criterion is not seriously impaired thereby.

Fifth, our theory seems to clarify the relation that subsists between democracy and individual freedom. If by the latter we mean the existence of a sphere of individual self-government the boundaries of which are historically variable—*no* society tolerates absolute freedom even of conscience and of speech, *no* society reduces that sphere to zero—the question clearly becomes a matter of degree. We have seen that the democratic method does not necessarily guarantee a greater amount of individual freedom than another political method would permit in similar circumstances. It may well be the other way round. But there is still a relation between the two. If, on principle at least, everyone is free to compete for political leadership by presenting himself to the electorate, this will in most cases though not in all mean a considerable amount of freedom of discussion *for all*. In particular it will normally mean a considerable amount of freedom of the press. This relation between democracy and freedom is not absolutely stringent and can be tampered with. But, from the standpoint of the intellectual, it is nevertheless very important. At the same time, it is all there is to that relation.

Sixth, it should be observed that in making it the primary function of the electorate to produce a government (directly or through an intermediate body) I intended to include in this phrase also the function of evicting it. The one means simply the acceptance of a leader or a group of leaders, the other means simply the withdrawal of this acceptance. This takes care of an element the reader may have missed. He may have thought that the electorate controls as well as installs. But since electorates normally do not control their political leaders in any way except by refusing to re-elect thm or the parliamentary majorities that support them, it seems well to reduce our ideas about this control in the way indicated by our definition. Occasionally, spontaneous revulsions occur which upset a government or an individual minister directly or else enforce a certain course of action. But they are not only exceptional, they are, as we shall see, contrary to the spirit of the democratic method.

Seventh, our theory sheds much-needed light on an old controversy. Whoever accepts the classical doctrine of democracy and in consequence believes that the democratic method is to guarantee that issues be decided and policies framed according to the will of the people must be struck by the fact that, even if that will were undeniably real and definite, decision by simple majorities would in many cases distort it rather than give effect to it. Evidently the will of the majority is the will of the majority and not the will of "the people." The latter is a mosaic that the former completely fails to "represent." To equate both by definition is not to solve the problem. Attempts at real solutions have however been made by the authors of the various plans for Proportional Representation.

These plans have met with adverse criticism on practical grounds. It is in fact obvious not only that proportional representation will offer opportunities for all sorts of idiosyncrasies to assert themselves but also that it may prevent democracy from producing efficient governments and thus prove a danger in times of stress. But before concluding that democracy becomes unworkable if its principle is carried out consistently, it is just as well to ask ourselves whether this principle really implies proportional representation. As a matter of fact it does not. If acceptance of leadership is the true function of the electorate's vote, the case for proportional representation collapses because its premises are no longer binding. The principle of democracy then merely means that the reins of government should be handed to those who command more support than do any of the competing individuals or teams. And this in turn seems to assure the standing of the majority system within the logic of the democratic method, although we might still condemn it on grounds that lie outside of that logic.

(Extract from chapter 22.)

SEBASTIAN DE GRAZIA
The Political Community

The Community and Belief Systems

The Great Community, as the ancient Greeks understood well, the community which embraces all other communities, is the political community. Holding it together are systems of beliefs, flexible bands weaving through and around each member of the community, compacting it, allowing some stretch at times, coiling like a steel spring at others. The basic denominator of citizens is these belief-systems which express their ideas concerning their relationship to one another and to their rulers. Without them, without this fundament of commonness, no political community can be said to exist. The study of anomie is the study of the ideological factors that weaken or destroy the bonds of allegiance which make the political community. The rupture or twisting of these bonds affects the ties of all the lesser associations within the community in a graver manner than has been suspected.

. . . What is it that makes a group of people a community? The answer is—their religious and political beliefs. And these beliefs fulfil a need common to man everywhere. Never mind their variety. There are many lands and diverse customs, but it is the same need in all men that brings them together. What this need is, is the problem that makes the pages of this book akin from cover to cover.

Today the great nations of the West neither bask in the sunlight of community nor shiver in the darkness of anarchy. They wander somewhere in the dusk of a "society." The fabric of their political and religious beliefs is pierced and rent by the intrusion of ideologies which are not fundamental, which are not universal, which need not stay to wreak confusion and play hob with men's souls. A collection of individual consumers men will never be. They could not if they wanted to. It goes against the grain. But neither are they Citizens or Believers. Instead, men stand today in this twilight zone of a "society," uneasy, distressed, feeling joined to their fellows only in war or crisis; and behind the inner doors of their mind they welcome war or crisis for the feeling of community it gives them.

Modern political science, too, has had a tendency—here more largely due no doubt to the influence of Marxian theory —to consider beliefs only on a superficial plane. In part, also, this surface consideration is due to the fact that in restful epochs systems of beliefs behave like the blood's circulation— they run quiet and deep. But if a threat disrupts an ideological system (if a wound, for that matter, breaks the skin), the vital psychological function of beliefs stands out in scarlet vividness. Out of disturbances in the reigning belief-systems anomie arises, a mental tension which in its moderate type reveals an intermittent apprehension in the adult of a danger before which he is helpless and which in its severe type mounts to an anxiety fraught with terrifying images of a menacing world.

In the social sciences problems have a way of spilling over one discipline onto another. The field would be awash were it not for the resistant dams that exist in the form of different terms for similar things in the political, sociological, and psychological areas. The concept of anomie which is introduced here is a good example of an idea that from the beginning has had difficulties in remaining within the confines of its birth. Its first important appearance occurred in 1893 in a book by Émile Durkheim entitled *De la division du travail social*. The division of labor was an idea developed by Adam Smith, the classical economist. But Émile Durkheim, who in his book associated the idea of anomie with the idea of the division of labor, was a great French sociologist.

. . . To be satisfied desires must have upper and lower limits imposed and met by the community. When no body of common values and sentiments exists, a person feels isolated or lost, without standards. He is sure of neither his place in the community nor what action he should perform; he cannot discover what his fellow-men value since they, too, are confused. In depression expectations are so frustrated and in unusual prosperity so satiated that in both cases a sense of confusion results, a loss of orientation, a sense of getting nowhere fast. This is anomie. It stands in contrast to *solidarité*, the expression Durkheim used to designate the perfect integration of a society with clear-cut values that define the status of each member of the community.

The theory of the political community could not have been significantly furthered were it not for recent advances in the social sciences. Psychology and its closely related branches of psychiatry and psychoanalysis in particular have made far-reaching additions to knowledge in the last fifty years. The swiftly expanding body of facts and propositions in modern psychology proved to be the most useful lieutenant in this attack on the problem of anomie and the political community. "Politics uses the rest of the sciences," said Aristotle.

This is not the place to discuss the many implications which emerge from this study of the political community, but some of the distinctive features of the approach may be touched upon: (1) It demonstrates the close psychological connection and mutual support of religious and political ideologies and thus asks for a reopening of their joint study by political scientists. (2) It shifts the concentration of political theory away from economic classes and their antagonistic interests to the genuine political groupings of ruler and ruled. (3) Of these political groups, it studies primarily the ruled population, the people; and in its stress on their common need of a ruler, it lays aside the emphasis placed by modern élite theory on the methods by which a ruling class preserves its ascendancy, an emphasis which often seems to deny the possibility of a genuine need for leadership among the people.

. . . As far as this investigation is concerned, no social organization is comprehensible apart from a political organization. The reasons for this will become apparent later in the book. It may help, however, to state preliminarily that, although the collection of people under question be composed only of groups of families, so long as there is any degree of communication, enterprise, or distribution among the families, political organization in the sense here intended must be present. Existing family contacts would break, members of different families would treat each other unmorally, agreements would evaporate, perhaps in the flare of violence, unless the rules of interfamily communication were made moral rules, that is, rules of good and evil. And the only way that they can become morals is by being made a matter of conscience in children. Once they are thus implanted, a community exists, for the ethicizing process requires (again, as will be later made clear) that conformity to the rules of interfamily behavior be demanded of children in the name of a person or anthropomorphism which can be only a personalized religious or political entity. Thus for the purposes of this study it is only necessary that the groups under consideration have a name to refer to their collective selves and common history; they will then have interfamily morals plus a pattern of subordination to persons, real or symbolic. In short, they will have a state. Henceforth, the italicized word, *ruler*, will be used to denote the entity, tangible or intangible, which members of a community believe able to control those aspects of the environment most necessary for the commonweal.

The term *ruler* was chosen for its several advantages. It can convey the idea of ruling over subjects, as well as the hitherto neglected idea of ruling or regulating aspects of the material environment. It connotes the political realm which is the sense most necessary here, and yet, when italicized, it can remind the reader of its difference from common usage in also embracing religious and economic figures and intangible entities. In ordinary parlance the word may have an authoritarian connotation, but here it has none; for a person is not a *ruler*, no matter how powerful the forces at his command, unless the members of the community believe in his capacity and willingness to guide and provide for them. Nor has the word any relation to the manner of the *ruler*'s selection. His may be a hereditary or an elected succession; he may be, as will be seen, a feudal lord, a president, a prime minister, a god, or the personification of a nation. In every case, he is dependent on popular belief. Once that is gone, he too is gone. He lives or dies in the minds of his subjects.

The term "directives," like the term *ruler*, refers to people's beliefs. They are ways people believe they must act to avoid trouble, fear, and anxiety. From the positive side they are formulas for salvation or for success or for the good life. The human being almost from its beginnings is showered with prohibitions, directions, and threats. Conformity to these "thou shalt's" and "thou shalt not's" becomes virtue and brings happiness, whereas disobedience becomes evil and brings grief. Thus these directives embody the community's ideas of good and bad.

Anxiety and Belief

Intentionally or not adults begin to describe their belief-systems to the child shortly after he acquires speech. It appears, however, that a system of beliefs acquires major psychological function for the child only after he experiences certain shocks. In the history of the human organism it is possible to make out a series of such critical experiences. All originate in the inability of the human organism from infancy to adolescence to provide alone for its recurring biological needs.

One type of anxiety serves as the prototype for the ensuing shocks. It occurs shortly after the infant links the gratification of his needs with the presence of discernible attendants. Then, given the inevitable absence of attendants and the equally inevitable onset of the needs of hunger and thirst and the like, the organism shows signs of extreme uneasiness, such as panicky screaming fits, which disappear only at the ministering presence of the returned attendants. Some of the physiological and psychological effects of this experience recur with every subsequent similar situation, for a salient characteristic of anxiety is its renewal properties. The anxieties of adulthood repeat the symptoms that appeared in adolescence, and the anxieties of adolescence in turn reactivate the pattern of anxiety of approximately the first three years of life.

. . . Anxiety usually reveals itself in both physiological and psychological conditions. There may be disturbances of gastrointestinal activity (such as diarrhea, an urge to defecate, constipation, or sinking feelings in the pit of the stomach), vasomotor phenomena (for example, flushed or cold skin or cold sweat), and cardiac or respiratory irregularities (pounding heart, choking or gasping breath). Psychologically, there is a deep fear or terror without definite sense of cause, a mental anguish so intense as to be avoided at all costs.

. . . When supplemented by psychological and anthropological research, the clues to anomie left by Durkheim sufficed to call attention to four important situations of anxiety in the early history of the human organism: absence of attendants, withdrawal of affection by attendants, discovery of the limitations of attendants, and, lastly, partial abandonment by attendants. Because of the protracted inability of the newborn of the species to provide for its basic needs, all human beings can be said to have passed through these critical situations. In facing each of them the child reacts similarly because each revives separation-anxiety—the initial terror of helplessness felt in periods of isolation from the only sources of support. The relationship of anomie to separation-anxiety was further clarified by the realization that each of these crises commences with the deterioration of the child's system of beliefs about the world and terminates with the acquisition of a new or revised set of beliefs. Although the child is presented early in life with the ideational content of political and religious beliefs, he accepts them only after being confronted with the possibility of the loss of loving care and an orderly, gratifying world. Beliefs can perform their psychological function because they define the proper ways of obtaining protective assurance and they designate the beings of superior power, the environmental regulators, who alone can provide that assurance. The need for a body of moral beliefs can now be seen more fundamentally as a need for assurance that critical situations of certain helplessness will not recur. Thus, belief-systems serve as protection against the anxiety of separation provoked by such situations.

The Genesis of Political Belief Systems

For good or for evil, anthropomorphic beliefs cannot be stifled in the child. Outside the home, parental information finds support in the schools.

. . . Not only in books but in many other phases of the early life of the modern child religious and political beliefs coexist. In the world of nation-states, the religious symbolism imparted by home and school is joined at almost every step by the personalized symbols of nationalism. The kings, the presidents, the nations, the heroes, and the fathers of countries cannot avoid mention in the modern household. Policemen, too, become extremely important, for parents frequently refer to them as the ones who punish by "arrest" those who break the law. "What is the law?" asks the child. The law, he may then be told, is something everyone must obey. Like the highly wrought and metaphysical notions of God, the idea that people make the laws through their representatives is something the child would find hard to digest, especially since those who make the laws must themselves obey them. He is like the seventeenth-century good citizen of Paris who, having heard it said that there was no king in Venice, was astounded and nearly died from laughter at the mere mention of so ridiculous an idea. It is much more understandable to the child that the king or Congress or the president makes the law; and if people are not good in thought and deed, they are punished.

. . . The political world of the child under five years of age

is peopled with awe-inspiring chief executives, fantastic policemen, soldiers, firemen (for firemen control fires and save
people), together with good people (law-abiding citizens),
who are happy and content, and bad (law-breaking persons),
who are jailed or hanged.

Once in the elementary public schools, the attitudes of awe
toward political concepts are reinforced with conduct. The
pledge of allegiance to the flag is required in most public
schools. The assembled singing of patriotic songs is rarely
omitted from the curriculum. The content of textbooks, which
pupils are often made to recite aloud to develop their reading
and speaking faculties, also requires little elaboration. Still it
is worth while to stress that the deeds of the presidents of the
United States are eulogized in elementary-school books, while
the virtues therein held up for the child to acquire are those of
the citizen who renders political service to his country by
defending it in war or advancing it in peace.

The nation thus becomes an expanded home. Conversely,
Rousseau sometimes described the home as "that miniature
fatherland." The parental superbeings instead are the chief
executives, past and present, the founding fathers, and other
national heroes. The methods for retaining their protection
are embodied in the words "law" and "duty." The law makes
known what conduct to avoid in order to keep the environment in harmony. The child is seeking a kind attendant behind phenomena. He finds it in the chief executive. For this
reason, the discovery of the existence of law, clear and fixed,
is a happy one. By obeying its rules, the child can retain the
friendship of the political *rulers* and the ensuing enjoyment of
a governed universe. "Duty" is made up of the deeds one
should perform for one's country out of love. Failure to follow law or duty invokes catastrophe—death or disgrace, the
exile of a Benedict Arnold or the lonely misery of a man
without a country.

The religious and political ideologies of the modern child
do not change appreciably until adolescence. The cosmos is so
well ordered by the protection of the home with its religious
and political ceiling, that the child gives small heed to systems
of belief. Questions and other attempts to verify his notions
greatly decline. It is not until adolescence, when a new crisis
approaches, that the youth's ideologies meet an ordeal.

The Political Void in Adolescence

From the record of ancient and primitive societies it might
be expected that at this time the secular and sacredotal figures

would take the leading role in ushering the youth into a new status. Certainly it is true that at the approximate age of puberty the major religions, Catholic, Jewish, and Protestant, use their ceremonies of confirmation to mark a new status in the religious community. But in the political orbit the rites of passage are conspicuously absent.

Perhaps the age of maturity—twenty-one years—the age of voting, brings the equivalence of the status-giving customs of the simpler societies. The possession of the vote does give the youth some additional influence, but there is no real ceremony. In states with permanent registration laws there is the necessity of affixing one's signature to governmental forms; other than this, there are no observances. The disuse in which a good share of youth lets its franchise fall wherever in the world it has it is well known.

The closest approximation appears to be the ritual of graduation from secondary school. Yet, only about one-fourth of the adolescent group emerges fully graduated from public secondary school. Even so, can the principal of a high school be conceived of as a political chief, or the paper diploma as the bow and spear or *toga virilis?* Where are the reaffirmations of allegiance to the political ideology? Wherein lies the individual's new status as a full member of the body politic? He finds himself instead in what has been feelingly called the "the floundering period." Apparently, then, graduation is solely what the word denotes: a graded step has been taken. The youth is now stamped with the label, "mentally and physically able," but in a society with freedom of occupational choice, the answer to "able for what and for whom?" is not quickly forthcoming.

No matter how few the persons who wander through modern life without ever obtaining a permanent position in the economy, their number is in sharp contrast to that of primitive communities where no one fails his adolescent tests and finds himself without a niche in communal life. The rebuffs the youth gets from trying to "land a job" reinforce the threat of isolation which he feels at the thought of leaving the home. . . . Thus the revived conception of a hostile environment begins to affect adolescents. Their anxiety makes them extremists. They seek for solutions and their desperate single-mindedness borders on radicalism. The adolescent attraction toward political extremisms and the poles of fundamentalism and atheism is a familiar observation. In crime, as in conversion, adolescence is a crucial period. The peak of the age curve of crime fluctuates around late adolescence, and writings on juvenile delinquency, popular and scientific, are legion.

The life of crime, however, is a career adopted by relatively few. Eventually most adolescents get jobs. The fever of the prolonged period of dangling between school and vocation is drowned in a wave of relief. Who or what has given the young man surcease? In the preliterate societies and at times even in Athens and Rome the answer was the political *rulers* who either personally or symbolically participated in presenting him with his new status. But, as just noted, in the modern Western world this does not happen. The youth does not feel he owes his new job to the government but to an entity he may never see, the businessman.

But when the matter of "After school, what?" approaches, when news columns of the newspapers are scanned incidentally to the "Help Wanted" advertisements, then knowledge of the source of jobs becomes vital, then the promptings of vague memory or of press editorials teach that the economic system of the United States is free enterprise, that it regulates itself by a law of supply and demand, that it had therefore better not be interfered with, that some persons of foresight, enterprise, and stick-to-itiveness—called businessmen—are the ones who provide employment for the millions of Americans. And suddenly the young man has a new conception of the world. In the account given of the crisis of modern adolescence it was stated that the job is the distinctive mark of status. The job, and the businessman too, however, are not entities of political or religious ideologies but of the economic process. For the first time, then, in this tracing of the roots of anomie, a way of life is encountered which presents a new ideology at adolescence, instead of reinforcing the existing political and religious traditions already long in existence.

Anomie and Obligation

Because of clear differences in precipitating conditions and in consequences, the forms of anomie fall into two types: a moderate form called simple anomie and a severe form called acute anomie. Simple anomie, the less dramatic order, should not be slighted. Its influence is pervasive; insidious, one might say. It affords a clear example of the interconnection of all aspects of the life of man as a political animal. Thus, scarcely an hour of the leisure time spent by the average person today would measure up to the standards of self-development and political education set by the most renowned philosopher of democracy, John Stuart Mill. Responsibility for this fact rests in no small part on the disorder of simple anomie. Even the milder form of anomie, then, can adversely affect the individual's chances for the growth of his potentialities, his use of the freedom offered by a democracy in that sphere which the French call *la vie privée*.

In a country where an essential part of the *ruler*'s obligations is military victory the rout of his armies in the field frequently leads to his overthrow at home. The populace has firsthand evidence that in this matter so vital for them the *ruler* is impotent. Chiefly for this reason defeats in war are often followed by revolutions. In capitalist countries prosperity is the primary obligation of the businessman. Prosperity means the provision of jobs to all who follow the directives of the economic ideology. Possession of a job insures the holder of his status in the community; he has the income and respect which fend off separation-anxiety. Periods of deep unemployment, therefore, ought to contribute much to the existing stock of observations, for if the jobholder loses the job, he should be gripped by acute anomie.

All students of the psychological effects of unemployment seem to agree that a definite sequence appears in persons who have lost their jobs: First, there is shock or great fear, followed (after an attempt to calm down) by an intensive hunt for work. If all efforts fail, the person becomes anxious, suffering active distress. This, say the writers, is the most critical stage, with attacks of fear and thoughts or attempts at suicide. And, third, the individual becomes fatalistic or resigned, his behavior marked by sober acquiescence or dumb apathy. Both the first shock and the anxiety of the second period are attacks of acute anomie. The unemployed frequently resemble patients suffering from anxiety neurosis. As one study observed, "Fear seems to be taken into account far too little when considering the experiences of the unemployed. However, it seems that fear of the cruel tomorrow, the feeling of being hunted to earth, of being hemmed in, and absolute helplessness, are very typical."

This is a lucid statement of the image of a hostile environment which characterizes the anxiety of acute anomie. The "hemmed in" and "trapped" feeling has etymological connections with the Latin *angustiae*, the French *angoisse*, and the German *Angst*, which all stem from a root meaning "pressure," "constriction," or "narrowness." Variations in the image will appear, for in each case different individual factors will have contributed to the person's conception of the environment. But in almost every instance the feeling of a hostile world is present. One author states that the unemployed feel that "life has forgotten them." The members of one family feel "as if the end of the world had come and they almost lost their desire to live." Others say that there are many times when "we feel the water closing over our heads." While yet another person asserts that "for a time, awakening in the morning is unbearable. The world becomes ever gloomier and viler. One sees in it neither pity nor friendship." These statements should not be accepted as mere figures of speech. To regard them as such is to follow the example of the man who said, "I don't believe in ghosts, but I've been afraid of them all my life." People actually feel themselves in the fell clutch of sinister circumstance. At the moment the blow falls —"Your services are no longer required"—the world turns darker and chillier. Later, in a period prolonged by anxiety, it has grown cold, bleak, and hostile.

. . . The impact of the environment's depriving nature comes from its utter disorderliness, its unpredictability, its rulelessness. There seem to be no directives for securing assurance against anxiety. The key the person holds in his hand no longer opens the gate. Yet it is the same key that smoothly tumbled the lock before. The confusion of jobless men in a depression is that they can see no responsibility of their own, no evil action on their part, with which to rationalize their loss of status. "If I only knew," cries the man out of work, "if I only knew what handsprings these chaps want me to turn for them, I'd turn them; but I just can't find out." Despite the hopelessness of continued attempts, the unemployed often will go back again and again to their last place of work. The sense of futility of all efforts is a regular finding in unemployment researches. . . .

Mass Movements

When men find their present and future painful to behold, they search for new ideologies, and oftentimes, like the man with a toothache who believed the time when he had no toothache his happiest, they glance backward toward a golden age. Some writers delight in applying the psychological term "regression" to this tendency. This is an inexcusable usage, which seeks with mammoth subtlety to condemn the retrospection as infantile. Unless one is prepared to call "regressive" all learning which makes use of past knowledge or experience, one should simply state that these systems of belief are built around the history or traditions available to their adherents, for all mass movements contain archaic elements. An ideological movement will not grow unless a thorough disruption of existing belief-systems takes place. In the United States today many small sects exist. Relative to the urban standard of living they are extremely poor. They adopt devices to stir the emotions to high pitch. They are intolerant, allowing no deviations from their way of life. All persons must think alike on sectarian matters, and departures even in minutiae cause lasting schisms. Nearly all hark back to the first century and believe it their holy duty to reconstruct the primitive Christian church. The larger number of them trace their ancestry back to Christ and the Apostles. Toward modern scholarship, which they call "Modernism," they have nothing but hatred, a hatred balanced only by their worship of the remote past. The present world is evil and untrustworthy. Their one forward glance is toward the millennium.

. . . In the belief-systems of these religious and political sects the negative elements are the protests against an inimical world, the absence of brotherly ties, and the lack of faith. Their positive features include the re-establishment of an old homeland and the banishing of a modern hostile world for one of a blood brotherhood with faith and love for a common ancestor who will actively intervene to effectuate all the necessary changes. By turning now to whole communities which have suffered a complete disruption of belief-systems, one will be able to see both the details and the diffusion of embryonic ideologies.

Let is be once more noted that belief-systems deteriorate when members are convinced of one or the other of two things—that their *ruler* is either unable or unwilling to provide for them in the manner prescribed in the ideology. To choose an example, the difficulties of the American Plains Indians affected the former conviction, the one concerning the power rather than the unwillingness of their *ruler*. The white man came in, killed off the buffalo, expropriated Indian lands, segregated tribes on reservations—and then tried to force on them new systems of religious and political beliefs. But the new gods could not provide them with the patterns of satisfaction and nutrition that had been built about their buffalo-hunting life. Therefore the new gods were weak, not gods at all, tin gods. As it happens, twenty Indian messianic movements are recorded in the United States prior to 1890 alone.

Messianic movements are genuine mass movements: they include the whole community. Their doctrines assert that in the immediate future a hero will appear and lead the people to a terrestrial paradise.

Through the intervention of the Great Spirit or of his emissary, the earth will shortly be transformed into a paradise,

*enjoyed by both the living and the resurrected dead. In antici-
pation of the happy return to the golden age, believers must
immediately return to the aboriginal mode of life. Traits and
customs which are symbolic of foreign influence must be put
aside. All members of the community—men, women, and
children—must participate. . . . The exclusion of the whites
from the golden age is not so much a reflection of hostility
toward them as a symbolization of the fulfilment of the
former way of life. The millennium is to be established
through divine agency; believers need only watch and pray.*
Prophets in their visions depict the old regime. They see an
old-fashioned buffalo hunt or they promise the restoration of
original tribal lands or they describe a new order which, like
the golden age, will give the unconflicting directives that make
a warrior's life meaningful. Today, the anthropologist finds
the Plains Indian without a messianic movement, spending his
days in vivid fantasy. "Hunting and warfare, living in tepees,
wearing the old Indian dress, and dancing the old dances are
presented as things that, it is hoped, will come again. They are
not recounted as past glories but as satisfactions that may
return to make up for the hardships and fears of the present."

Once the vast mass of people feel that the *ruler* cannot carry
out his obligations, a belief-system that offers a new order, yet
one in which the old will be revived, spreads like fire through
dry brush. Such was the history of the Ghost Dance revival
among the American Indians. Those tribes whose previous
modes of life had been most disturbed participated with fervor; those whose life resembled the stage before the white
occupation were little affected. Among the whites themselves,
messianic and adventist movements surged up after the American Revolution, the Civil War, and World War I.

It is a recurring thing, this acute anomie. A few concluding
words might be appended concerning its wider significance. In
modern times its greater frequency is due to the widespread
loss of status during economic contractions. On the basis of
past experience, an authoritative statement declares, the
American citizen may expect to spend one quarter of his life
in periods of economic stagnation.

To sum up, if more than a majority of the adult population
in a political community loses primary secular status, faith in
the ruling entity will dissolve and the entire political belief-
system will disintegrate. In consequence the incidence of
acute anomie will be high. Under pressure of anxiety people
will attempt a solution which sets up the family pattern of
political relationships. They will seek succor in one person
who claims to be able to control the environment so that they

will regain status, one person who directs them to love one another as brothers, one person who demands of them unquestioning faith and obedience. The identity of feeling among those with acute anomie will cluster them about such persons. This way of solving the problem is necessarily chosen; it involves the same attitudes and behavior patterns that the individual successfully maintained in earlier attempts to free himself from separation-anxiety. In time a mass movement starts, one person emerges clear, and the march toward a new ideology for the whole political community begins. The recency of popular anxiety colors the movement with a strong interrelatedness which invariably brings the blood brotherhood and the physical and moral authority of the *ruler* to the foreground. Conduct takes on the appearance of a strain to convert communal ties into the stereotypes of family bonds. The beliefs behind this action are extreme when compared to those that characterize the political and religious ideologies in periods without a disintegrating threat. The exaggeration can be likened to the growth of protective bony cells around the healing area of a fracture. Freshly recovered from panic, the mind takes extraordinary precautions to prevent a relapse. Had there been no breakdown of the system of beliefs, the political ideology would have performed its primary protective function in customary quietness. Once the psyche is long removed from the terror of acute anomie, it proves itself more adaptable than the soma. It sloughs off the extra growth.

(Extracts from *The Political Community*, chapters 1, 2, 7, and 10.)

JOHN RAWLS
A Theory of Justice

Justice as Fairness

My aim is to present a conception of justice which generalizes and carries to a higher level of abstraction the familiar theory of the social contract as found, say, in Locke, Rousseau, and Kant. In order to do this we are not to think of the original contract as one to enter a particular society or to set up a particular form of government. Rather, the guiding idea is that the principles of justice for the basic structure of society are the object of the original agreement. They are the principles that free and rational persons concerned to further their own interests would accept in an initial position of equality as defining the fundamental terms of their association. These principles are to regulate all further agreements;

they specify the kinds of social cooperation that can be entered into the forms of government that can be established. This way of regarding the principles of justice I shall call justice as fairness.

Thus we are to imagine that those who engage in social cooperation choose together, in one joint act, the principles which are to assign basic rights and duties and to determine the division of social benefits. Men are to decide in advance how they are to regulate their claims against one another and what is to be the foundation charter of their society. Just as each person must decide by rational reflection what constitutes his good, that is, the system of ends which it is rational for him to pursue, so a group of persons must decide once and for all what is to count among them as just and unjust. The choice which rational men would make in this hypothetical situation of equal liberty, assuming for the present that this choice problem has a solution, determines the principles of justice.

In justice as fairness the original position of equality corresponds to the state of nature in the traditional theory of the social contract. This original position is not, of course, thought of as an actual historical state of affairs, much less as a primitive condition of culture. It is understood as a purely hypothetical situation characterized so as to lead to a certain conception of justice. Among the essential features of this situation is that no one knows his place in society, his class position or social status, nor does any one know his fortune in the distribution of natural assets and abilities, his intelligence, strength, and the like. I shall even assume that the parties do not know their conceptions of the good or their special psychological propensities. The principles of justice are chosen behind a veil of ignorance. This ensures that no one is advantaged or disadvantaged in the choice of principles by the outcome of natural chance or the contingency of social circumstances. Since all are similarly situated and no one is able to design principles to favor his particular condition, the principles of justice are the result of a fair agreement or bargain. For given the circumstances of the original position, the symmetry of everyone's relations to each other, this initial situation is fair between individuals as moral persons, that is, as rational beings with their own ends and capable, I shall assume, of a sense of justice. The original position is, one might say, the appropriate initial status quo, and thus the fundamental agreements reached in it are fair. This explains the propriety of the name "justice as fairness": it conveys the idea that the principles of justice are agreed to in an initial situation that is fair. The name does not mean that the concepts of justice and fairness are the same, any more than the phrase "poetry as metaphor" means that the concepts of poetry and metaphor are the same.

Justice as fairness begins, as I have said, with one of the most general of all choices which persons might make together, namely, with the choice of the first principles of a conception of justice which is to regulate all subsequent criticism and reform of institutions. Then, having chosen a conception of justice, we can suppose that they are to choose a constitution and a legislature to enact laws, and so on, all in accordance with the principles of justice initially agreed upon. Our social situation is just as if it is such that by this sequence of hypothetical agreements we would have contracted into the general system of rules which defines it. Moreover, assuming that the original position does determine a set of principles (that is, that a particular conception of justice would be chosen), it will then be true that whenever social institutions satisfy these principles those engaged in them can say to one another that they are cooperating on terms to which they would agree if they were free and equal persons whose relations with respect to one another were fair. They could all view their arrangements as meeting the stipulations which they would acknowledge in an initial situation that embodies widely accepted and reasonable constraints on the choice of principles. The general recognition of this fact would provide the basis for a public acceptance of the corresponding principles of justice. No society can, of course, be a scheme of cooperation which men enter voluntarily in a literal sense; each person finds himself placed at birth in some particular position in some particular society, and the nature of this position materially affects his life prospects. Yet a society satisfying the principles of justice as fairness comes as close as a society can to being a voluntary scheme, for it meets the principles which free and equal persons would assent to under circumstances that are fair. In this sense its members are autonomous and the obligations they recognize self-imposed.

One feature of justice as fairness is to think of the parties in the initial situation as rational and mutually disinterested. This does not mean that the parties are egoists, that is, individuals with only certain kinds of interests, say in wealth, prestige, and domination. But they are conceived as not taking an interest in one another's interests. They are to presume that even their spiritual aims may be opposed, in the way that the aims of those of different religions may be opposed. Moreover, the concept of rationality must be interpreted as far as possible in the narrow sense, standard in economic theory, of taking the most effective means to given ends.

It may be observed that once the principles of justice are thought of as arising from an original agreement in a situation of equality, it is an open question whether the principle of utility would be acknowledged. Offhand it hardly seems likely that persons who view themselves as equals, entitled to press their claims upon one another, would agree to a principle which may require lesser life prospects for some simply for the sake of a greater sum of advantages enjoyed by others. Since each desires to protect his interests, his capacity to advance his conception of the good, no one has a reason to acquiesce in an enduring loss for himself in order to bring about a greater net balance of satisfaction. In the absence of strong and lasting benevolent impulses, a rational man would not accept a basic structure merely because it maximized the algebraic sum of advantages irrespective of its permanent effects on his own basic rights and interests. Thus it seems that the principle of utility is incompatible with the conception of social cooperation among equals for mutual advantage. It appears to be inconsistent with the idea of reciprocity implicit in the notion of a well-ordered society. Or, at any rate, so I shall argue.

I shall maintain instead that the persons in the initial situation would choose two rather different principles: the first requires equality in the assignment of basic rights and duties, while the second holds that social and economic inequalities, for example inequalities of wealth and authority, are just only if they result in compensating benefits for everyone, and in particular for the least advantaged members of society. These principles rule out justifying institutions on the grounds that the hardships of some are offset by a greater good in the aggregate. It may be expedient but it is not just that some should have less in order that others may prosper. But there is no injustice in the greater benefits earned by a few provided that the situation of persons not so fortunate is thereby improved. The intuitive idea is that since everyone's well-being depends upon a scheme of cooperation without which no one could have a satisfactory life, the division of advantages should be such as to draw forth the willing cooperation of everyone taking part in it, including those less well situated. Yet this can be expected only if reasonable terms are proposed. The two principles mentioned seem to be a fair agreement on the basis of which those better endowed, or more fortunate in their social position, neither of which we can be said to deserve, could expect the willing cooperation of others when some workable scheme is a necessary condition of the welfare of all. Once we decide to look for a conception of justice that nullifies the accidents of natural endowment and the contingencies of social circumstance as counters in quest for political and economic advantage, we are led to these principles. They express the result of leaving aside those aspects of the social world that seem arbitrary from a moral point of view.

The problem of the choice of principles, however, is extremely difficult. I do not expect the answer I shall suggest to be convincing to everyone. It is, therefore, worth noting from the outset that justice as fairness, like other contract views, consists of two parts: (1) an interpretation of the initial situation and of the problem of choice posed there, and (2) a set of principles which, it is argued, would be agreed to. One may accept the first part of the theory (or some variant thereof), but not the other, and conversely. The concept of the initial contractual situation may seem reasonable although the particular principles proposed are rejected. To be sure, I want to maintain that the most appropriate conception of this situation does lead to principles of justice contrary to utilitarianism and perfectionism, and therefore that the contract doctrine provides an alternative to these views. Still, one may dispute this contention even though one grants that the contractarian method is a useful way of studying ethical theories and of setting forth their underlying assumptions.

Justice as fairness is an example of what I have called a contract theory. Now there may be an objection to the term "contract" and related expressions, but I think it will serve reasonably well. Many words have misleading connotations which at first are likely to confuse. The terms "utility" and "utilitarianism" are surely no exception. They too have unfortunate suggestions which hostile critics have been willing to exploit; yet they are clear enough for those prepared to study utilitarian doctrine. The same should be true of the term "contract" applied to moral theories. As I have mentioned, to understand it one has to keep in mind that it implies a certain level of abstraction. In particular, the content of the relevant agreement is not to enter a given society or to adopt a given form of government, but to accept certain moral principles. Moreover, the undertakings referred to are purely hypothetical: a contract view holds that certain principles would be accepted in a well-defined initial situation.

The merit of the contract terminology is that it conveys the idea that principles of justice may be conceived as principles that would be chosen by rational persons, and that in this way conceptions of justice may be explained and justified. The theory of justice is a part, perhaps the most significant part, of the theory of rational choice. Furthermore, principles of justice deal with conflicting claims upon the advantages won by social cooperation; they apply to the relations among several persons or groups. The word "contract" suggests this plurality as well as the condition that the appropriate division of advantages must be in accordance with principles acceptable to all parties. The condition of publicity for principles of justice is also connoted by the contract phraseology. Thus, if these principles are the outcome of an agreement, citizens have a knowledge of the principles that others follow. It is characteristic of contract theories to stress the public nature of political principles. Finally there is the long tradition of the contract doctrine. Expressing the tie with this line of thought helps to define ideas and accords with natural piety. There are then several advantages in the use of the term "contract." With due precautions taken, it should not be misleading.

A final remark. Justice as fairness is not a complete contract theory. For it is clear that the contractarian idea can be extended to the choice of more or less an entire ethical system, that is, to a system including principles for all the virtues and not only for justice. Now for the most part I shall consider only principles of justice and others closely related to them; I make no attempt to discuss the virtues in a systematic way. Obviously if justice as fairness succeeds reasonably well, a next step would be to study the more general view suggested by the name "rightness as fairness." But even this wider theory fails to embrace all moral relationships, since it would seem to include only our relations with other persons and to leave out of account how we are to conduct ourselves toward animals and the rest of nature. I do not contend that the contract notion offers a way to approach these questions which are certainly of the first importance; and I shall have to put them aside. We must recognize the limited scope of justice as fairness and of the general type of view that it exemplifies. How far its conclusions must be revised once these other matters are understood cannot be decided in advance.

Principles of Justice

I shall now state in a provisional form the two principles of justice that I believe would be chosen in the original position. In this section I wish to make only the most general comments, and therefore the first formulation of these principles is tentative. As we go on I shall run through several formula-

ons and approximate step by step the final statement to be
iven much later. I believe that doing this allows the exposi-
on to proceed in a natural way.

The first statement of the two principles reads as follows.

First: each person is to have an equal right to the most
extensive basic liberty compatible with a similar liberty for
others.

Second: social and economic inequalities are to be arranged so that they are both (a) reasonably expected to be
to everyone's advantage, and (b) attached to positions and
offices open to all.

By way of general comment, these principles primarily
pply, as I have said, to the basic structure of society. They
re to govern the assignment of rights and duties and to
:gulate the distribution of social and economic advantages.
.s their formulation suggests, these principles presuppose that
1e social structure can be divided into two more or less
istinct parts, the first principle applying to the one, the sec-
nd to the other. They distinguish between those aspects of
1e social system that define and secure the equal liberties of
itizenship and those that specify and establish social and
:onomic inequalities. The basic liberties of citizens are,
)ughly speaking, political liberty (the right to vote and to be
ligible for public office) together with freedom of speech and
ssembly; liberty of conscience and freedom of thought; free-
om of the person along with the right to hold (personal)
roperty; and freedom from arbitrary arrest and seizure as
efined by the concept of the rule of law. These liberties are
ll required to be equal by the first principle, since citizens of
just society are to have the same basic rights.

The second principle applies, in the first approximation, to
1e distribution of income and wealth and to the design of
rganizations that make use of differences in authority and
:sponsibility, or chains of command. While the distribution
f wealth and income need not be equal, it must be to every-
ne's advantage, and at the same time, positions of authority
nd offices of command must be accessible to all. One applies
1e second principle by holding positions open, and then,
ıbject to this constraint, arranges social and economic in-
qualities so that everyone benefits.

These principles are to be arranged in a serial order with
1e first principle prior to the second. This ordering means
1at a departure from the institutions of equal liberty required
y the first principle cannot be justified by, or compensated
)r, by greater social and economic advantages. The distribu-
on of wealth and income, and the hierarchies of authority,

must be consistent with both the liberties of equal citizenship and equality of opportunity.

A theory of justice depends upon a theory of society. . . . It should be observed that the two principles (and this holds for all formulations) are a special case of a more general conception of justice that can be expressed as follows.

All social values—liberty and opportunity, income and wealth, and the bases of self-respect—are to be distributed equally unless an unequal distribution of any, or all, of these values is to everyone's advantage.

Injustice, then, is simply inequalities that are not to the benefit of all. Of course, this conception is extremely vague and requires interpretation.

As a first step, suppose that the basic structure of society distributes certain primary goods, that is, things that every rational man is presumed to want. These goods normally have a use whatever a person's rational plan of life. For simplicity, assume that the chief primary goods at the disposition of society are rights and liberties, powers and opportunities, income and wealth. These are the social primary goods. Other primary goods such as health and vigor, intelligence and imagination, are natural goods; although their possession is influenced by the basic structure, they are not so directly under its control. Imagine, then, a hypothetical initial arrangement in which all the social primary goods are equally distributed: everyone has similar rights and duties, and income and wealth are evenly shared. This state of affairs provides a benchmark for judging improvements. If certain inequalities of wealth and organizational powers would make everyone better off than in this hypothetical starting situation, then they accord with the general conception.

Now it is possible, at least theoretically, that by giving up some of their fundamental liberties men are sufficiently compensated by the resulting social and economic gains. The general conception of justice imposes no restrictions on what sort of inequalities are permissible; it only requires that everyone's position be improved. We need not suppose anything so drastic as consenting to a condition of slavery. Imagine instead that men forego certain political rights when the economic returns are significant and their capacity to influence the course of policy by the exercise of these rights would be marginal in any case. It is this kind of exchange which the two principles as stated rule out; being arranged in serial order they do not permit exchanges between basic liberties and economic and social gains. The serial ordering of principles expresses an underlying preference among primary social goods. When this preference is rational so likewise is the choice of these principles in this order.

In developing justice as fairness I shall, for the most part, leave aside the general conception of justice and examine instead the special case of the two principles in serial order. The advantage of this procedure is that from the first the matter of priorities is recognized and an effort made to find principles to deal with it. One is led to attend throughout to the conditions under which the acknowledgment of the absolute weight of liberty with respect to social and economic advantages, as defined by the lexical order of the two principles, would be reasonable. Offhand, this ranking appears extreme and too special a case to be of much interest; but there is more justification for it than would appear at first sight. Furthermore, the distinction between fundamental rights and liberties and economic and social benefits marks a difference among primary social goods that one should try to exploit. It suggests an important division in the social system. Of course, the distinctions drawn and the ordering proposed are bound to be at best only approximations. There are surely circumstances in which they fail. But it is essential to depict clearly the main lines of a reasonable conception of justice; and under many conditions anyway, the two principles in serial order may serve well enough. When necessary we can fall back on the more general conception.

The fact that the two principles apply to institutions has certain consequences. Several points illustrate this. First of all, the rights and liberties referred to by these principles are those which are defined by the public rules of the basic structure. Whether men are free is determined by the rights and duties established by the major institutions of society. Liberty is a certain pattern of social forms. The first principle simply requires that certain sorts of rules, those defining basic liberties, apply to everyone equally and that they allow the most extensive liberty compatible with a like liberty for all. The only reason for circumscribing the rights defining liberty and making men's freedom less extensive than it might otherwise be is that these equal rights as institutionally defined would interfere with one another.

Another thing to bear in mind is that when principles mention persons, or require that everyone gain from an inequality, the reference is to representative persons holding the various social positions, or offices, or whatever, established by the basic structure. Thus in applying the second principle I assume that it is possible to assign an expectation of well-being to representative individuals holding these positions. This expectation indicates their life prospects as viewed from their social station. In general, the expectations of representative persons depend upon the distribution of rights and duties throughout the basic structure. When this changes, expectations change. I assume, then, that expectations are connected: by raising the prospects of the representative man in one position we presumably increase or decrease the prospects of representative men in other positions. Since it applies to institutional forms, the second principle (or rather the first part of it) refers to the expectations of representative individuals. Neither principle applies to distribution of particular goods to particular individuals who may be identified by their proper names. The situation where someone is considering how to allocate certain commodities to needy persons who are known to him is not within the scope of the principles. They are meant to regulate basic institutional arrangements. We must not assume that there is much similarity from the standpoint of justice between an administrative allotment of goods to specific persons and the appropriate design of society. Our common sense intuitions for the former may be a poor guide to the latter.

Now the second principle insists that each person benefit from permissible inequalities in the basic structure. This means that it must be reasonable for each relevant representative man defined by this structure, when he views it as a going concern, to prefer his prospects with the inequality to his prospects without it. One is not allowed to justify differences in income or organizational powers on the ground that the disadvantages of those in one position are outweighed by the greater advantages of those in another. Much less can infringements of liberty be counterbalanced in this way. Applied to the basic structure, the principle of utility would have us maximize the sum of expectations of representative men (weighted by the number of persons they represent, on the classical view); and this would permit us to compensate for the losses of some by the gains of others. Instead, the two principles require that everyone benefit from economic and social inequalities.

I now wish to give the final statement of the two principles of justice for institutions. For the sake of completeness, I shall give a full statement including earlier formulations.

First Principle

Each person is to have an equal right to the most extensive total system of equal basic liberties compatible with a similar system of liberty for all.

Second Principle
Social and economic inequalities are to be arranged so that they are both:
  (a) to the greatest benefit of the least advantaged, consistent with the just saving principle, and
  (b) attached to offices and positions open to all under conditions of fair equality of opportunity.

First Priority Rule (The Priority of Liberty)
The principles of justice are to be ranked in lexical order and therefore liberty can be restricted only for the sake of liberty. There are two cases:
  (a) a less extensive liberty must strengthen the total system of liberty shared by all;
  (b) a less than equal liberty must be acceptable to those with the lesser liberty.

Second Priority Rule (The Priority of Justice over Efficiency and Welfare)
The second principle of justice is lexically prior to the principle of efficiency and to that of maximizing the sum of advantages; and fair opportunity is prior to the difference principle. There are two cases:
  (a) an inequality of opportunity must enhance the opportunities of those with the lesser opportunity;
  (b) an excessive rate of saving must on balance mitigate the burden of those bearing this hardship.

General Conception
All social primary goods—liberty and opportunity, income and wealth, and the bases of self-respect—are to be distributed equally unless an unequal distribution of any or all of these goods is to the advantage of the least favored.

(Extracts from *A Theory of Justice*, chapters 1, 2, 3, 4, 5 and 9.)

SELECTED BIBLIOGRAPHY

I. *Rousseau, Condorcet and Kant*

M. Berman, *The Politics of Authenticity* (New York, 1970).

A. E. Burlingame, *Condorcet, the Torch Bearer of the French Revolution* (New York, 1930).

E. Cassirer, *Rousseau, Kant, Goethe* (Princeton, 1945).

————, *The Question of Jean-Jacques Rousseau* (New York, 1954).

J. W. Chapman, *Rousseau—Totalitarian or Liberal?* (New York, 1956).

J. Charvet, *The Social Problem in the Philosophy of Rousseau* (New York, 1974).

A. Cobban, *Rousseau and the Modern State* (London, 1934).

R. Derathé, *Le rationalisme de J. J. Rousseau* (Paris, 1948).

————, *Jean-Jacques Rousseau et la science politique de son temps* (Paris, 1950).

E. Durkheim, *Montesquieu and Rousseau* (Ann Arbor, Michigan, 1960).

S. Ellenburg, *Rousseau's Political Philosophy* (Ithaca, 1976).

F. C. Green, *Jean-Jacques Rousseau* (London, 1955).

P. Hazard, *European Political Thought in the 18th Century* (London, 1954).

C. W. Hendel, *Jean-Jacques Rousseau, Moralist* (London, 1934).

————, *The Philosophy of Kant and Our Modern World* (New York, 1957).

H. Höffding, *Jean-Jacques Rousseau and His Philosophy* (New Haven, 1930).

A. D. Lindsay, *Kant* (London, 1934).

R. Masters, *The Political Philosophy of Rousseau* (Princeton, 1968).

A. M. Osborn, *Rousseau and Burke* (London, 1940).

H. J. Paton, *The Categorical Imperative* (Chicago, 1948).

W. D. Ross, *Kant's Ethical Theory* (Oxford, 1954).

H. Sauer, *Kant's Political Thought* (Chicago, 1967).

J. S. Schapiro, *Condorcet and the Rise of Liberalism* (New York, 1934).

A. Schinz, *La Pensée de Jean-Jacques Rousseau* (Paris, 1929).

J. N. Shklar, *Men and Citizens: A Study of Rousseau's Social Theory* (Cambridge, 1969).

J. Talmon, *The Rise of Totalitarian Democracy* (Boston, 1952).

E. H. Wright, *The Meaning of Rousseau* (London, 1929).

II.   *Revolution and Counterrevolution*

E. Barker, *Essays on Government* (Oxford, 1945).

I. Berlin, *The Hedgehog and the Fox* (London, 1953).

F. P. Canavan, *The Political Reason of Edmund Burke* (Durham, NC, 1960).

A. Cobban, *Edmund Burke and the Revolt Against the 18th Century* (London, 1929).

C. B. Cone, *Burke and the Nature of Politics* (Lexington, Kentucky, 1957).

T. W. Copeland, *Our Eminent Friend Edmund Burke* (New Haven, 1949).

E. Faguet, *Politiques et moralistes du dix-neuvième Siècle* (Paris, 1890).

S. R. Graubard, *Burke, Disraeli and Churchill: The Politics of Perseverance* (Cambridge, 1961).

F. Holdsworth, *Joseph de Maistre et l'Angleterre* (Paris, 1935).

R. Kirk, *The Conservative Mind* (Chicago, 1953).

H. J. Laski, *Studies in the Problem of Sovereignty* (New Haven, 1917).

J. MacCunn, *The Political Philosophy of Burke* (New York, 1913).

K. Mannheim, *Essays on Sociology and Social Psychology* (London, 1953).

J. Morley, *Edmund Burke* (London, 1867).

F. Smith, *Thomas Paine, Liberator* (New York, 1938).

R. H. Soltau, *French Political Thought in the 19th Century* (London, 1931).

P. J. Stanlis, *Edmund Burke and the Natural Law* (Ann Arbor, 1958).

III. Romanticism and Idealism

R. Aris, *History of Political Thought in Germany from 1787–1815* (London, 1936).

S. Avineri, *Hegel's Theory of the Modern State* (Cambridge, 1972).

F. M. Barnard, *Herder's Social and Political Thought* (Oxford, 1965).

E. R. Bentley, *A Century of Hero-Worship* (New York, 1944).

E. F. Carritt, *Morals and Politics* (London, 1955).

E. Cassirer, *The Myth of the State* (New Haven, 1946).

J. Dewey, *German Philosophy and Politics* (New York, 1915).

H. C. Engelbrecht, *Fichte, a Study of His Political Writings* (New York, 1933).

H. C. Grierson, *Carlyle and Hitler* (Cambridge, 1933).

C. F. Harrold, *Carlyle and German Thought: 1819–34* (New Haven, 1934).

J. Hyppolite, *Etudes sur Marx et Hegel* (Paris, 1955).

W. Kaufmann, ed., *Hegel's Political Philosophy* (New York, 1970).

G. A. Kelly, *Idealism, Politics and History: Sources of Hegelian Thought* (Cambridge, 1969).

P. Lasserre, *Le Romanticisme français* (Paris, 1907).

B. E. Lippincott, *Victorian Critics of Democracy* (London, 1938).

A. O. Lovejoy, *Essays in the History of Ideas* (Baltimore, 1948).

H. Marcuse, *Reason and Revolution* (New York, 1941).

Z. A. Pelczynski, ed., *Hegel's Political Philosophy* (Cambridge, 1971).

R. Plant, *Hegel* (London, 1973).

F. Rosenzweig, *Hegel und der Staat* (Berlin, 1920).

H. Shine, *Carlyle and the Saint-Simonians* (Baltimore, 1941).

W. T. Stace, *The Philosophy of Hegel* (London, 1924).

C. Taylor, *Hegel* (Cambridge, 1975).

E. Weil, *Hegel et l'etat* (Paris, 1950).

T. D. Weldon, *States and Morals* (London, 1946).

IV. *Utilitarianism*

E. Albee, *A History of English Utilitarianism* (New York, 1902).

D. Baumgardt, *Bentham and the Ethics of Today* (Princeton, 1952).

I. Berlin, *Two Concepts of Liberty* (Oxford, 1959).

C. Brinton, *English Political Thought in the 19th Century* (London, 1933).

J. Cropsey, *Polity and Economy* (The Hague, 1957).

W. L. Davidson, *Political Thought in England from Bentham to J. S. Mill* (New York, 1916).

E. Halevy, *The Growth of Philosophic Radicalism* (Boston, 1955).

G. W. Keeton and G. Schwarzenberger, *Jeremy Bentham and the Law: A Symposium* (London, 1948).

H. J. Laski, *Political Thought from Locke to Bentham* (London, 1920).

D. Lyons, *In the Interest of the Governed: A Study in Bentham's Philosophy of Law* (Oxford, 1973).

J. MacCunn, *Six Radical Thinkers* (London, 1907).

M. P. Mack, *Jeremy Bentham: An Odyssey of Ideas 1748–92* (London, 1962).

J. S. Mill, *Dissertations and Discussions* (Boston, 1865).

M. St. J. Packe, *The Life of J. S. Mill* (London, 1954).

J. Plamenatz, *The English Utilitarians* (Oxford, 1949).

L. Robbins, *The Theory of Economic Policy in English Classical Political Economy* (London, 1952).

L. Stephens, *The English Utilitarians* (London, 1900).

E. Stokes, *The English Utilitarians and India* (Oxford, 1959).

O. H. Taylor, *The Classical Liberalism, Marxism and the 20th Century* (Cambridge, 1960).

B. Willey, *Nineteenth Century Studies* (London, 1949).

S. Wolin, *Politics and Vision* (Boston, 1960).

T. Woods, *Poetry and Philosophy: A Study of the Thought of J. S. Mill* (London, 1961).

V. *Early Socialism and Positivism*

H. L. Beales, *The Early English Socialists* (London, 1933).

I. Berlin, *Historical Inevitability* (London, 1954).

H. N. Brailsford, *Shelley, Godwin and Their Circle* (New York, 1913).

M. Buber, *Paths in Utopia* (London, 1949).

E. H. Carr, *Studies in Revolution* (London, 1950).

G. D. H. Cole, *Socialist Thought—The Forerunners* (New York, 1953).

M. M. Dondo, *The French Faust, Henri de Saint-Simon* (New York, 1955).

E. Durkheim, *Le Socialisme* (Paris, 1928).

A. Gray, *The Socialist Tradition* (London, 1946).

F. A. Hayek, *The Counter-Revolution in Science* (Glencoe, 1952).

J. O. Hertzler, *The History of Utopian Thought* (New York, 1923).

G. Iggers, *The Cult of Authority* (The Hague, 1958).

J. H. Jackson, *Marx, Proudhon and European Socialism* (London, 1957).

G. Lichtheim, *The Origins of Socialism* (New York, 1969).

S. Y. Lu, *The Political Theories of Proudhon* (New York, 1922).

F. E. Manuel, *The New World of Henri Saint-Simon* (Cambridge, 1956).

————, ed., *Utopias and Utopian Thought* (Boston, 1966).

F. E. and F. P. Manuel, *Utopian Thought in the Western World* (New York, 1979).

G. Pirou, *Proudhonisme et syndicalisme revolutionnaire* (Paris, 1910).

A. Salomon, *The Tyranny of Progress* (New York, 1955).

R. H. Soltau, *French Political Thought in the 19th Century* (New Haven 1931).

J. L. Talmon, *Political Messianism* (New York, 1960).

G. Woodcock, *Pierre-Joseph Proudhon* (London, 1956).

VI. *Marxism*

H. B. Acton, *The Illusion of an Epoch* (Boston, 1957).

S. Avineri, *The Social and Political Thought of Karl Marx* (Cambridge, 1970).

I. Berlin, *Karl Marx* (London, 1948).

S. Bloom, *The World of Nations* (New York, 1941).

M. M. Bober, *Karl Marx's Interpretation of History* (Cambridge, 1927).

S. H. Chang, *The Marxian Theory of the State* (Philadelphia, 1931).

G. D. H. Cole, *The Meaning of Marxism* (London, 1948).

————, *The History of Socialist Thought: Marxism and Anarchism* (London, 1954).

A. Cornu, *The Origins of Marxian Thought* (Springfield, 1957).

B. Croce, *Historical Materialism and the Economics of Karl Marx* (New York, 1914).

M. Eastman, *Marxism, Is It Science?* (New York, 1940).

K. Federn, *The Materialist Conception of History* (London, 1939).

F. Gottheil, *Marx's Economic Predictions* (Evanston, 1966).

S. Hook, *Towards the Understanding of Karl Marx* (New York, 1933).

————, *From Hegel to Marx* (New York, 1936).

R. N. Hunt, *The Political Ideas of Marx and Engels* (London, 1975).

H. J. Laski, *Karl Marx: An Essay* (London, 1922).

G. Lichtheim, *Marxism, An Historical and Critical Study* (2nd ed., London, 1964).

G. Lukacs, *Existentialisme ou Marxisme* (Paris, 1950).

D. McLellan, *Karl Marx, His Life and Thought* (New York, 1974).

G. V. Plekhanov, *Fundamental Problems of Marxism* (New York, 1929).

K. Popper, *The Open Society and Its Enemies* (London, 1945).

M. M. Rader, *Marx's Interpretation of History* (New York, 1979).

M. Rubel, *Marx without Myth* (Oxford, 1975).

R. C. Tucker, *Philosophy and Myth in Karl Marx* (New York, 1961).

A. Walker, *Marx, His Theory and Its Context* (New York, 1978).

G. A. Wetter, *Dialectical Materialism* (New York, 1958).

VII.   *Liberalism and Aristocratic Conservatism*

B. Adams, *The Law of Civilisation and Decay* (New York, 1896).

M. Arnold, *Culture and Anarchy* (New York, 1895).

I. Babbitt, *Democracy and Leadership* (Boston, 1924).

I. Berlin, *Four Essays on Liberty* (London, 1969).

A. Bullock and M. Shock, eds., *The Liberal Tradition: From Fox to Keynes* (New York, 1967).

Lord H. Cecil, *Conservatism* (London, 1912).

F. A. Hayek, *Individualism and Economic Order* (Chicago, 1948).

————, *The Constitution of Liberty* (Chicago, 1960).

G. Himmelfarb, *On Liberty and Liberalism: The Case of J. S. Mill* (New York, 1974).

W. Kendall, *The Conservative Affirmation* (Chicago, 1963).

J. C. Levenson, *The Mind and the Art of Henry Adams* (Boston, 1957).

J. Lively, *The Social and Political Thought of Alexis de Tocqueville* (Oxford, 1962).

K. Löwith, *Jacob Burckhardt* (Lucerne, 1936).

H. Maine, *Popular Government* (New York, 1886).

A. W. O. Martin, *Nietzsche und Burckhardt* (Basel, 1945).

J. P. Mayer, *Alexis de Tocqueville, Prophet of the Mass Age* (London, 1939).

H. L. Mencken, *Notes on Democracy* (New York, 1926).

W. Röpke, *The Social Crisis of Our Time* (Chicago, 1950).

G. Ruggiero, *The History of English Liberalism* (London, 1927).

A. Ryan, *The Philosophy of John Stuart Mill* (London, 1970).

J. F. Stephen, *Liberty, Equality, Fraternity* (New York, 1873).

D. F. Thompson, *John Stuart Mill and Representative Government* (Princeton, 1976).

P. Viereck, *Conservatism from J. Adams to Churchill* (New York, 1956).

——, *Conservatism Revisited* (New York, 1949).

Y. Winters, *In Defense of Reason* (New York, 1947).

A. B. Wolfe, *Conservatism, Radicalism and Scientific Method* (New York, 1923).

VIII. *Nationalism*

H. Arendt, *The Origins of Totalitarianism* (New York, 1951).

S. W. Baron, *Modern Nationalism and Religion* (New York, 1947).

J. Benda, *The Treason of the Intellectuals* (New York, 1928).

K. D. Bracher, *The German Dictatorship* (New York, 1970).

W. C. Buthman, *The Rise of Integral Nationalism in France* (New York, 1939).

H. M. Chadwick, *The Nationalities of Europe and the Growth of National Ideologies* (Cambridge, 1945).

M. Curtis, *Totalitarianism* (New Brunswick, 1979).

A. Dorpalen, *Treitschke* (New Haven, 1957).

R. Emerson, *From Empire to Nation* (Cambridge, 1960).

W. Friedmann, *The Crisis of the National State* (London, 1943).

J. Gobineau, *The Inequality of Human Races* (London, 1915).

G. Guy-Grand, *La Philosophie nationaliste* (Paris, 1911).

C. J. H. Hayes, *Essays on Nationalism* (New York, 1926).

————, *Nationalism: A Religion* (New York, 1960).

E. Jäckel, *Hitler's Weltanschauung* (Middletown, 1972).

E. Kamenka, ed., *Nationalism: The Nature and Evolution of an Idea* (Canberra, 1973).

E. Kedourie, *Nationalism* (London, 1960).

H. Kohn, *The Idea of Nationalism* (New York, 1944).

————, *Prophets and Peoples* (New York, 1946).

W. Lacqueur, *Fascism: A Reader's Guide* (Berkeley, 1976).

J. Madaule, *Le Nationalisme de Maurice Barrès* (Marseilles, 1943).

F. Meinecke, *Machiavellism* (London, 1957).

G. Mosse, *The Crisis of German Ideology* (New York, 1964).

K. S. Pinson, *Nationalism in the Western World* (Washington, 1959).

B. Shafer, *Nationalism: Myth and Reality* (New York, 1955).

L. L. Snyder, *The Meaning of Nationalism* (New Brunswick, 1954).

E. Weber, *Varieties of Fascism* (Princeton, 1964).

S. J. Woolf, ed., *European Fascism* (New York, 1968).

IX. Social Darwinism, History and Neo-idealism

J. Barzun, *Darwin, Marx, Wagner* (Boston, 1941).

B. Bosanquet, *The Philosophic Theory of the State* (London, 1920).

F. H. Bradley, *Ethical Studies* (Oxford, 1876).

A. Buchan, *The Spare Chancellor* (London, 1959).

R. C. Collingwood, *The Idea of History* (Oxford, 1946).

J. Dewey, *The Influence of Darwin on Philosophy* (New York, 1910).

M. P. Follett, *The New State* (New York, 1918).

F. P. Harris, *The Neo-Idealist Political Theory* (New York, 1944).

G. Himmelfarb, *Darwin and the Darwinian Revolution* (New York, 1959).

T. H. Huxley, *Evolution and Ethics* (London, 1893).

R. Hofstadter, *Social Darwinism in American Thought* (Boston, 1944).

L. T. Hobhouse, *The Metaphysical Theory of the State* (London, 1918).

W. Irvine, *Apes, Angels and Victorians* (New York, 1955).

J. G. Kennedy, *Herbert Spencer* (Boston, 1978).

W. D. Lamont, *Introduction to Green's Moral Philosophy* (London, 1934).

J. D. Y. Peel, *Herbert Spencer: The Evolution of a Sociologist* (New York, 1971).

D. G. Ritchie, *Darwinism and Politics* (London, 1889).

N. St. John Stevas, *Walter Bagehot* (London, 1959).

L. Tiger and R. Fox, *The Imperial Animal* (New York, 1971).

P. L. van den Berghe, *Race and Racism* (New York, 1967).

M. White, *Social Thought in America* (Boston, 1957).

X. *Irrationalism and Psychology*

T. W. Adorno, *et al.*, *The Authoritarian Personality* (New York, 1950).

G. W. Allport, *The Nature of Prejudice* (Cambridge, 1954).

P. Andreu, *Notre Maître, M. Sorel* (Paris, 1953).

M. Curtis, *Three Against the Third Republic* (Princeton, 1959).

W. Y. Elliott, *The Pragmatic Revolt in Politics* (New York, 1928).

H. J. Eysenck, *The Psychology of Politics* (New York, 1954).

E. Fromm, *Escape from Freedom* (New York, 1941).

P. Gay, *Freud, Jews and Other Germans* (New York, 1978).

D. Halevy, *Nietzsche* (Paris, 1945).

E. Heller, *The Disinherited Mind* (Philadelphia, 1952).

K. Horney, *The Neurotic Personality of Our Time* (New York, 1937).

I. L. Horowitz, *Radicalism and the Revolt against Reason* (London, 1961).

T. E. Hulme, *Speculations* (London, 1924).

R. Humphrey, *Georges Sorel: Prophet without Honor* (Cambridge, 1951).

W. Kaufmann, *Nietzsche: Philosopher, Psychologist, Anti-Christ* (Princeton, 1950).

H. D. Lasswell, *Psychopathology and Politics* (Chicago, 1930).

G. Le Bon, *The Crowd* (London, 1917).

K. Mannheim, *Ideology and Utopia* (New York, 1936).

H. Marcuse, *Eros and Civilization* (Boston, 1955).

E. Mayo, *The Human Problems of an Industrial Civilization* (New York, 1933).

J. H. Meisel, *The Genesis of Georges Sorel* (Ann Arbor, 1951).

P. Ricoeur, *Freud and Philosophy* (New Haven, 1970).

P. Rieff, *Freud: The Mind of the Moralist* (New York, 1959).

P. Roazen, *Freud: Political and Social Thought* (New York, 1968).

J. P. Stern, *Nietzsche* (London, 1978).

L. Trilling, *Freud and the Crisis of Our Culture* (Boston, 1955).

XI. *The Elitists*

T. Arnold, *The Symbols of Government* (New Haven, 1935).

J. Burnham, *The Machiavellians* (New York, 1943).

G. E. C. Catlin, *A Study of the Principles of Politics* (New York, 1930).

J. Dewey, *The Public and Its Problems* (New York, 1927).

D. Easton, *The Political System* (New York, 1953).

C. Forcey, *The Crossroads of Liberalism* (New York, 1961).

C. Friedrich, *The New Belief in the Common Man* (Boston, 1945).

Ortega y Gasset, *The Revolt of the Masses* (New York, 1932).

G. C. Homans, *An Introduction to Pareto* (New York, 1934).

B. de Jouvenel, *Sovereignty* (Chicago, 1957).

H. D. Lasswell and A. Kaplan, *Power and Society* (New Haven, 1950).

H. D. Lasswell, *Politics: Who Gets What, When, How* (New York, 1936).

E. Lederer, *The State of the Masses* (New York, 1940).

K. Mannheim, *Freedom, Power and Democratic Planning* (London, 1951).

J. H. Meisel, *The Myth of the Ruling Class* (Ann Arbor, 1958).

R. K. Merton, *Social Theory and Social Structure* (Glencoe, 1957).

R. Michels, *First Lectures in Political Sociology* (Minneapolis, 1949).

C. W. Mills, *The Power Elite* (New York, 1959).

H. J. Morgenthau, *Scientific Man v. Power Politics* (Chicago, 1946).

T. Parsons, *Essays in Sociological Theory* (Glencoe, 1949).

D. Spitz, *Patterns of Anti-Democratic Thought* (New York, 1949).

XII. *Anarchism and Democratic Socialism*

R. Aron, *The Opium of the Intellectuals* (New York, 1957).

E. H. Carr, *Michael Bakunin* (London, 1937).

A. Carter, *The Political Theory of Anarchism* (New York, 1971).

M. Clark, *Antonio Gramsci and the Revolution that Failed* (New Haven, 1977).

M. Cole, *The Story of Fabian Socialism* (London, 1961).

C. A. R. Crosland, *The Future of Socialism* (London, 1956).

R. H. S. Crossman, ed., *The God that Failed* (London, 1952).

————, *The Politics of Socialism* (New York, 1965).

M. Djilas, *The New Class* (New York, 1958).

M. M. Drachkovitch, *De Karl Marx à Leon Blum* (Geneva, 1955).

W. Gurian, *Bolshevism: An Introduction to Soviet Communism* (Indiana, 1952).

M. Harrington, *Socialism* (New York, 1972).

L. T. Hobhouse, *Elements of Social Justice* (New York, 1922).

R. H. Carew Hunt, *The Theory and Practice of Communism* (New York, 1950).

D. N. Jacobs, *The New Communists* (New York, 1969).

L. Kolakowski and S. Hampshire, eds., *The Socialist Idea: A Reappraisal* (New York, 1974).

G. Lichtheim, *Marxism: An Historical and Critical Study* (New York, 1961).

H. M. Magid, *English Political Pluralism* (New York, 1941).

H. Marcuse, *Soviet Marxism* (New York, 1958).

G. P. Maximoff, *The Political Philosophy of Bakunin* (Glencoe, 1953).

F. Neal, *Titoism in Action* (Berkeley, 1958).

J. F. Revel, *Without Marx or Jesus* (New York, 1971).

J. P. Plamenatz, *German Marxism and Russian Communism* (New York, 1954).

C. Tsuzuki, *Hyndman and British Socialism* (London, 1961).

R. C. Tucker, *The Soviet Political Mind* (New York, 1971).

A. B. Ulam, *The Philosophic Foundations of English Socialism* (Cambridge, 1951).

E. Wilson, *To the Finland Station* (New York, 1940).

G. Woodcock and I. Avakumovic, *The Anarchist Prince: Kropotkin* (London, 1950).

XIII. *Theological Thought and Politics*

K. Barth, *Church and State* (London, 1939).

N. Berdyaev, *The Meaning of the Creative Act* (New York, 1955).

H. Bergson, *The Two Sources of Morality and Religion* (New York, 1935).

H. E. Brunner, *The Philosophy of Religion from the Standpoint of Protestant Theology* (New York, 1937).

R. Bultmann, *The Presence of Eternity* (New York, 1957).

M. C. D'Arcy, *The Meaning and Matter of History* (New York, 1959).

C. Dawson, *Progress and Religion* (London, 1934).

M. Eliade, *Cosmos and History* (New York, 1959).

E. Fromm, *Psychoanalysis and Religion* (New Haven, 1950).

E. Gilson, *God and Philosophy* (New Haven, 1941).

E. E. Y. Hales, *The Catholic Church in the Modern World* (New York, 1958).

W. Herberg, *Protestant, Catholic, Jew* (New York, 1955).

S. Kierkegaard, *The Present Age* (New York, 1949).

G. Marcel, *Man Against Mass Society* (Chicago, 1952).

H. J. Paton, *The Modern Predicament: A Study in the Philosophy of Religion* (London, 1955).

B. W. Smith, *Jacques Maritain, Antimodern or Ultramodern?* (New York, 1976).

W. T. Stace, *Religion and the Modern Mind* (Philadelphia, 1952).

W. Temple, *Christianity and the Social Order* (London, 1942).

P. Tillich, *Love, Power and Justice* (New York, 1954).

E. Troeltsch, *Protestantism and Progress* (New York, 1912).

R. K. Ullman, *Between God and History* (London, 1960).

M. de Unamuno, *The Tragic Sense of Life* (London, 1921).

S. Weil, *The Need for Roots* (New York, 1952).

XIV. *Sociology, Psychology and Pluralism*

D. Beetham, *Max Weber and the Theory of Modern Politics* (London, 1974).

D. Bell, *The End of Ideology* (Glencoe, 1960).

————, *The Coming of Post-Industrial Society* (New York, 1973).

R. Bendix, *Max Weber: An Intellectual Portrait* (New York, 1960).

A. Brecht, *Political Thought* (Princeton, 1959).

E. Cassirer, *An Essay on Man* (New Haven, 1944).

H. A. Deane, *The Political Ideas of Harold Laski* (New York, 1955).

L. Feuer, *The Conflict of Generations* (New York, 1969).

C. Frankel, *The Case for Modern Man* (New York, 1956).

W. Friedmann, *Legal Theory* (London, 1951).

J. K. Galbraith, *The New Industrial State* (3rd ed., Boston, 1978).

S. Hampshire, *Thought and Action* (London, 1959).

E. Hoffer, *The True Believer* (New York, 1951).

H. S. Hughes, *Consciousness and Society* (New York, 1958).

————, *The Obstructed Path* (New York, 1966).

P. Laslett, ed., *Philosophy, Politics and Society* (Oxford, 1956).

H. D. Lasswell, and A. Kaplan, *Power and Society* (New Haven, 1950).

P. F. Lazarsfeld, ed., *The Language of Social Research* (Glencoe, 1955).

W. Lippmann, *The Public Philosophy* (Boston, 1955).

R. M. MacIver, *The Web of Government* (New York, 1947).

F. Neumann, *The Democratic and the Authoritarian State* (Glencoe, 1957).

R. Nozick, *Anarchy, State and Utopia* (New York, 1974).

J. R. Pennock, *Liberal Democracy* (New York, 1950).

J. P. Sartre, *Critique de la raison dialectique* (Paris, 1960).

J. N. Shklar, *After Utopia* (Princeton, 1957).

H. J. Storing, ed., *Essays on the Scientific Study of Politics* (New York, 1962).

L. Strauss, *Natural Right and History* (Chicago, 1953).

————, *Liberalism: Ancient and Modern* (New York, 1968).

J. Wild, *The Challenge of Existentialism* (Bloomington, 1955).

INDEX

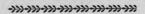

INDEX

➤➤➤-➤➤➤-➤➤➤-➤➤➤-➤➤➤-➤➤➤-➤➤➤-➤➤➤

Adams, Henry, 183, 185–86, 194–99; Marx, 195
Addresses to the German Nation, 79
Adler, Alfred, 287
Adolescence: political void in, 450–52
Age of Constantine, The, 184–85
Alienation, 18–19
Anarchism: 348–79; Kropotkin, 357–58
Ancient Law, 256, 272–77
Anomie, 444–57
Anti-Semitism, 244, 245, 246, 247–48
Austin, John, 106
Authority: Bakunin, 352–57; Herzen, 200–204
Autobiography (J. S. Mill), 107

Babbitt, Irving, 76
Bagehot, Walter, 254–56, 267–72, 425
Bakunin, Mikhail, 131, 348, 352–57
Barrès, Maurice, 236
Bebel, August, 349
Belief systems: and mass movements, 454–57; political 448–50
Bentham, Jeremy, 105, 106, 107, 108, 425; pleasure and pain, 119–20; utility, 117–19
Bergson, Henri, 285, 286
Bernstein, Eduard, 349–50,

358–62; *Communist Manifesto*, 359, 360, 361
Beyond Good and Evil, 288–92
Bismarck, Otto von, 254
Bonapartism, 378–79
Bourgeoisie, 159–62. *See also* Marxism
Brahmins, 76
Browning, Robert, 256
Burckhardt, Jacob, 183, 184–85, 285, 222–28; Carlyle, 223; church, 227; Germany, 227; Italy, 227
Burke, Edmund, 48–49, 50, 51; aristocratic rule, 55–57; Carlyle, 86; constitution, 53; Paine, 65; rights of man, 57–58
Bury, J. B., 17

Cabet, 130
Caesarism. *See* Bonapartism
Capital, 155, 177–78
Capitalism: 130, 349; Schumpeter, 424–25. *See also* Marxism
Capitalism, Socialism and Democracy, 424, 440–44
Carlyle, Thomas, 77–78; Burckhardt, 223; Burke, 86; heroes, 80–85; modern hero, 86–88
Categorical imperative, 18, 42–45
Cavour, Camillo di, 235
Chateaubriand, François de, 76

Chamberlain, H. S., 237
Chamberlain, Joseph, 254, 348
Children of Light and the Children of Darkness, The, 415, 419–21
Citizens, 19
City, 19
Civilization of the Renaissance in Italy, The, 184–85
Class struggle, 158–69
Cole, G. D. H., 349
Coleridge, Samuel, 76, 77, 256
Common Sense, 50
Communism: anarchist, 357–358; popes and, 395–96
Communist Manifesto, The, 155, 158–74; Bernstein, 359–61
Community, political, 444–57
Comte, Auguste, 51, 80, 132–33, 147
Condorcet, Antoine Nicholas de, 17, 35
Consciousness, 388–89
Considerations on the Government of Poland, 14
Considérations sur la France, 68–70
Course of Positive Philosophy, 133
Counterrevolution, 48–75
Country: Mazzini, 237–42
Critique of Political Economy, 173–75
Croce, Benedetto, 285, 383
Cultural reform, 390–91
Culture: hegemony of Western, 387–88
Custom, despotism of, 182, 198–200

Darwin, Charles, 158, 254, 256

Darwinism: social, 254–84, Spencer, 262–65
Democracy in America, 183–84, 214–22
Democracy: de Maistre, 70–71; de Tocqueville, 215–16
Diderot, Denis, 15
Dignity of Man, The, 91–94
"Dinner Bell," 48
Discourse on Inequality, 15
Djilas, Milovan, 351
Dreyfus Affair, 236
Du Pape, 72–73
Durkheim, Emile, 349, 445–46
Duties of Man, The, 237–42

Education of Henry Adams, The, 185–86, 228–33
Ego: Fichte, 88–94; Herzen, 212–13
Elite: Pareto, 323–27
Elitists, 320–47. *See also* Pareto, Mosca, Michels
Emile, 15, 16
Engels, Friedrich, 132, 155, 156, 158, 359, 360, 361
English Constitution, The, 255
Essai sur la Vie de Sénèque le Philosophe, 15
Etude sur la Souveraineté, 70–72
Evolutionary Socialism, 358–62

Family, 95, 446–47
Feuerbach, 157
Fichte, Johann Gottlieb, 77, 83, 88, 236
First International, 131
Foundations of Sovereignty, 436–37, 439–40
Fourier, François, 130, 344–45
Freedom: Herzen on, 206–10; Mill on, 182

Freud, Sigmund, 285, 287–88

From the Far Shore, 182–83, 204–14

Fundamental Principles of the Metaphysics of Morals, 40–47

Garibaldi, Giuseppe, 235

Gaulle, Charles de, 16

General Idea of the Revolution in the Nineteenth Century, The, 133, 135–40

General View of Positivism, A, 147–54

German Ideology, The, 175–76

Ghost Dance revival, 456

Gibbon, Edward, 231

Ginzberg, Asher, 237

Gobineau, 237

God and the State, 352–57

Godwin, William, 348

Goethe, Johann Wolfgang von, 76, 83

Government: liberty and, 186–204; Paine, 67–68; utilitarianism, 106; end of, 120–23. *See also* Society

Gramsci, Antonio: cultural reform, 390–91; French Revolution, 380–81, 385; Hegel, 387–88; internationalism, 386–87; Marxism, 251–52, 381; military force, 393–94; nationalism, 383–94; Permanent Revolution, 385–86; revolutionary party, 387–91; Russian Revolution, 386–87; State, 379–94; superstructure, 391; Western culture, 387–88

Grazia, Sebastian de, 423, 425–26, 444–57; anxiety and belief, 448–49; community and belief systems, 444–47; mass movements, 454–57; political belief systems, 449–50

Green, T. H., 256–57, 277–84; Rousseau, 279, 280

Gumplowicz, 254

Ha'am, Ahad. *See* Asher Ginzberg

Hardenberg, Friedrich von (Novalis), 76

Hayek, 132

Hedonism, 105, 107–108

Hegel, Georg Wilhelm Friedrich, 78, 79, 80, 94–104; freedom, 94–95; state, 95–96, 387–88

Herder, J. G., 77, 236

Heroes, Hero-worship and the Heroic in History, On, 80–88

Herzen, Alexander, 182–83, 204–14; on Egoists, 212–13; free choice, 210–12; free will, 209; individual liberty, 204–14; morality, 212–14; Nature and freedom, 206–10

Herzl, Theodor, 236, 237, 242–48

Hess, Rudolf, 237

Hitler, Adolf, 237, 248–53

Hobbes, Thomas, 106

Hulme, T. E., 76

Human Nature in Politics, 287, 314–19

Humboldt, Friedrich Heinrich von, 183

Idealism: 75–104, 285; British, 256–57; German, 78; Gramsci, 388; Herzen, 183

Individual: liberty, 204–14; society and, 182, 201–204

Infallibility, assumption of, 190–91, 196

Intellectualism, 286

Internationalism: Gramschi, 386–87

Introduction to the Principles of Morals and Legislation, An, 105, 117–20

Irrationalism, 285–319

Jacobinism, 183

James, William, 286

Jaurès, Jean. 349

Jewish Company, 246–47

Jewish State, The, 236, 242–48; need for, 242; anti-Semitism, 244; plan, 246

Jung, C. G., 287

Justice: Rawls, 457–67

Kant, Immanuel, 17–18, 40, 214

Kardelj, Edward, 351

Kautsky, Karl Johann, 349

Keynes, John Maynard, 131, 181

King. *See* Monarch

Kingsley, Charles, 130

Kropotkin, Prince Pëtr, 348, 357; anarchy, 319–20; Spencer, 358

Labor, division of, 108–10

Laski, Harold, 349, 423–24, 436

Lebensraum, 237

Le Bon, 285

Lectures on the Principles of Political Obligation, 256–57, 277–84; morality, 279–80; power, 283–84

Legislation: Rousseau, 27–30

Lenin, Nikolai, 350–51, 362–73, 391; proletariat, dictatorship of, 366–71; revolution, 366–67: socialism, 362–63

Letters from the Mountain, 15

Libertas Praestantissimum, 395, 398–405; natural law, 400–401

Liberty: of action, 196–99; Mill, 182–204; Herzen, 204–14; Rawls, 426, 463–67; of thought, 190–96. *See also* Negative liberty

Liberty, On, 182, 186–204

Lippmann, Walter, 285, 425

Lombard Street, 255

Luddites, 130

Lycurgus, 23

Maine, Sir Henry, 256, 272–77; law, 272–73

Maistre, de, 50–51, 68–75; French revolution, 68–70; power, absolute, 70–71; papal, 72–73

Marat, Jean Paul, 16

Marie Antoinette, 16

Maritain, Jacques, 396, 411–15; society, 414–15

Martineau, 256

Marx, Karl, 107, 130, 131, 155–180; Adams, 228; *Communist Manifesto*, 158–73

Marxism: 79, 155–80, 348–79; bourgeoisie, 159–62; fundamental propositions of, 158; Gramsci, 251–52; *Mein Kampf*, 251–52; proletariat, 179–80; revisionist socialism, 349–50; Russian, 350–51, 445

Mass movements, 454–57

Mater et Magistra, 396, 405–11; socialization, 405–408

Maurice, 256

Maurras, Charles, 236

Mazzini, Giuseppe, 235, 237; country, 237–42

Mein Kampf, 237, 248–53; Marxism, 251–52

Messianic movements, 455–56

Michels, Roberto, 320, 321, 322, 341–47; power, 341–43

Middle Ages, 76

Military force, 393–94

Mill, James, 105, 120–25. *See also* Bentham

Mill, John Stuart, 105, 107–108, 182, 184, 452; authority, limits to, 200–204; despotism of custom, 198–200; liberty of action, 196–99; liberty of thought, 190–96; negative liberty, 186–90; power, 186–90

Mind and Society, The, 322–32

Monarch: Hegel, 100–101

Monarchy: Paine, 49–50; de Maistre, 70–71

Montesquieu, Charles, 256

Moral Man and Immoral Society, 415–19

Morality, 182–83, 212–14

Mosca, Gaetano, 320, 321, 322, 332–41; minority, rule by, 332–35; political formula, 335–37

Mounier, Emmanuel, 396–97

Muller, Adam, 76

Myths, 306–14

National Socialism. *See Mein Kampf*

Nationalism: 77, 234–53, Gramsci, 383–94; Jewish state, 242–48; military force and, 393–94; racist, 237; right-wing, 235–36

Natural rights, 66–67

Negative liberty, 181–82

Neo-Idealism, 254–84

New Christianity, The, 140, 143–58

New Jerusalem, 171

Niebuhr, Reinhold, 397–98, 415–21; utilitarianism, 418

Nietzsche, Friedrich, 285–86; 288–304; self-mastery, 294–96; values, transvaluation of, 292–94; will to power, 288–92

Novalis. *See* Friedrich von Hardenberg

Numa, 23

Organizer, The, 140–42

Origin of the Family, Private Property and the State, The, 178–80

Origin of Species, 256

Orwell, George, 351

Owen, Robert, 130

Paine, Thomas, 49–50, 61; Burke, 65; monarchy, 50; natural rights, 66–67; society, 67–68

Panopticon, 106

Pareto, Vilfreda, 285, 320–21, 322, 322–332; *élite*, 322–27; index, 322–23

Paris Commune, 131, 360

Péguy, Charles, 286

Permanent Revolution: Gramsci, 385–86

Phalanstères, 171

Philosophes, 15, 107

Philosophy, of history, 80

Philosophy of Right, The, 94–104

Physics and Politics, 255, 267–272

Political Community, The, 423, 425–26, 444–57

Political Parties, 321, 341–47

Politics as a Vocation, 426–36

Pope John XXIII, 396, 405–11; ideologies, erroneous, 410–11; socialization, 405–408

Pope Leo XIII, 395, 398–405; natural law, 400–401

Positivism, 130–54, 236, 285

Power: de Maistre, 70–71, 72–73; Green, 283; of leaders, 341–43; of majority, 217–22; Mill, 186–90; will to, 288–92

Praxis, philosophy of, 388, 391

Prison Notebooks, The, 379–94

Project of a Constitution for Corsica, 16

Prolegomena to Ethics, 256–57

Proletariat, 179, 180; dictatorship of, 367–71. *See also* Marxism

Proudhon, Pierre Joseph, 130, 131–40, 287, 348

Psychology, 285–319, 446–57; politics and, 425–26

Rawls: justice as fairness, 457–62; principles of justice, 462–67

Reflections on the Revolution in France, 49, 51–64

Reflections on Violence, 305–14

Religion: Burke, 60–61; Rousseau, 33–34; *See also* Niebuhr, Pope John, Pope Leo

Renan, Ernest, 234

Republic, 19

Rerum Novarum, 395

Revisionist socialism, 349–50

Revolution: 48–75; Gramsci, 380–81, 385, 386–87; de Maistre, 68–70; de Tocqueville, 214–17; Lenin, 366–67. *See also* Permanent Revolution theory

Revolution Betrayed, The, 351, 373–79

Revolutionary party, role of, 387–91

Rights of Man, The, 50, 64–68

Rights of Man and Natural Law, The, 411–15

Robespierre, Maximilien de, 16

Romanticism, 76–104

Roosevelt, Theodore, 254

Rousseau, Jean-Jacques, 15–17, 76, 212, 234; general will, 19, 21–23; Green, 279, 280; Mosca, 334; religion, 33–34; state, 19

Ruling Class, The, 320, 332–41

Ruskin, John, 130, 231

Russian Maxism, 350–52

Saint-Gaudens, Augustus, 231–32

Saint-Simon, Claude Henri de, 80, 130, 132, 133, 140–47; society, 140–42

Savigny, 256

Schlegel, August Wilhelm von, 76

Schlegel, Friedrich von, 76

Schumpeter, Joseph, 423, 424–25, 440–44; socialism, 425

Science of Knowledge, The, 88–94

Sects, 454–55

Self-determination, 18

Self-mastery, 294–96

Sentiment des Citoyens, Le, 15

Servius, 23

Shaftesbury, Anthony Ashley, 130

Sketch for a Historical Picture of the Progress of the Human Mind, 17, 35–40

Smith, Adam, 107, 108–17; labor, division of, 108–10

Social Contract, The, 16, 18–34; general will, 19, 21–23; justice and, 426, 457–67

Social Darwinism, 262–67

Social Organization, On, 140, 142–43

Social Statics, 257, 265–67

Socialism: 130–54; democratic, 348–94; Lenin, 362–63; national, *See Mein Kampf;* revisionist, 349–50; scientific, 155; Schumpeter, 424–25

Socialism: Utopian and Scientific, 174, 180

Socialists, Utopian, 130

Socialization, 406–408

Society: civil, 95–96; Communist, 371–73; community and, 444–57; individual and, 182, 201–204, 212–14; Jews, 246–47; Maritain, 414–15; Mill, 186–204; Paine, 67–68; Saint-Simon, 140–42; structure and superstructure, 391. *See also* Government

Soirées de Saint-Petersbourg, Les, 73–75

Solon, 23

Sorel, Georges, 285, 286–87, 305–14; myths, 306–14

Southey, Robert, 76

Sovereignty: Paine, 50; de Maistre, 70–71

Soviet Union, 373–79

Spencer, Herbert, 254–55, 257–67; Social Darwinism, 262–67

Stalin, Joseph, 378, 386

State: Fichte, 79; Gramsci, 379–94; Green, 277–84; growth of power, 222–24; Hegel, 95–100; Laski, 438–39; Lenin, 366–70; preservation of, 30–33; Rousseau, 19; Trotsky, 378; withering of, 178–80

State and Revolution, The, 365–73

Stirner, Max, 348

Studies in the Problem of Sovereignty, 438–39

Study of Sociology, The, 257–62

Superstructure, 391

System of Positive Polity, The, 133

Taine, Hippolyte, 236

Tawney, R. H., 349

Theory of Justice, A, 457–67

Thus Spake Zarathustra, 292–304; self-mastery, 292–96; values, transvaluation of, 292–94

Tillich, Paul, 397

Tocqueville, Alexis de, 183–84, 185, 214–22; majority, 217–22; revolution, 214–17

Treitschke, 236

Trotsky, Leon, 350–51, 373–

Trotsky, Leon (*continued*) 79, 384, 386; Bonapartism, 378–79; Stalin, 378; state, 378

Uniqueness, 76
Utilitarianism, 105–29; Niebuhr, 418. *See also* Bentham, Mill, James
Utopians, 130–31

Vates, 83–84

Wallas, Graham, 285, 287, 314–19

War, Hegel, 101–103
Wealth of Nations, The, 107, 108–117; labor, division of, 108–10
Weber, Max, 395, 423, 426–36
What Is Property? 133–35
What Is to be Done? 362–66
Will, general, 19, 21–23; to power, 288–92
Wordsworth, William, 76, 107, 256

Zionism, 236–37